CHOCTAW BY BLOOD ENROLLMENT CARDS 1898-1914

VOLUME I

TRANSCRIBED BY

JEFF BOWEN

NATIVE STUDY
Gallipolis, Ohio
USA

Originally published:
Baltimore, Maryland
2015

Reprinted by:

Native Study LLC
Gallipolis, OH
www.nativestudy.com

Library of Congress Control Number: 2020911767

ISBN: 978-1-64968-001-3

Made in the United States of America.

This series is dedicated to
Mike Marchi,
who keeps my spirits up.

CREEK CENSUS.

SECOND NOTICE.

Members of the Dawes Commission will be present at the following times and places for the purpose of enrolling Creek citizens, as required by Act of Congress of June 10, 1896:

At Muskogee, Nov. 8 to 30, 1897, inclusive.
At Wagoner, Nov. 8 to 13, " inclusive.
At Eufaula, Nov. 8 to 13, " inclusive.
At Sapulpa, Nov. 15 to 20, " inclusive.
At Wetumpka, Nov. 15 to 20, " inclusive.
At Okmulgee, Nov. 22 to 30, " inclusive.

All persons who have not heretofore enrolled before the Dawes Commission should appear and enroll. Parents and guardians can enroll their families and wards.

TAMS BIXBY,
FRANK C. ARMSTRONG,
A. S. McKENNON,
THOS. B. NEEDLES,
Commissioners.

The above illustration is similar in nature to what was found throughout Indian Territory for different tribes as far as postings on bulletin boards, public centers, or wherever they could be read so people would be notified of where and when they needed to be for enrollment with the Dawes Commission.

This is a picture of the Dawes Commission at Camp Jones in Stonewall, Indian Territory on September 8, 1898.

The images below are of two of the original cards given on the microfilm. The cards given in this book have been formatted to fit on one page and still give all the information found on the original cards.

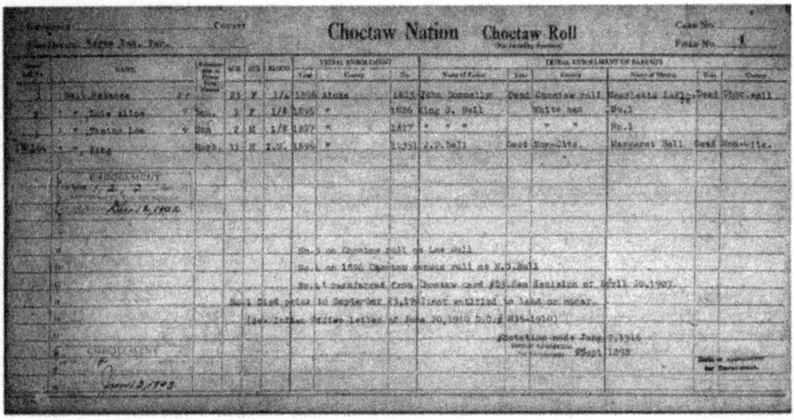
Choctaw Nation Choctaw Roll

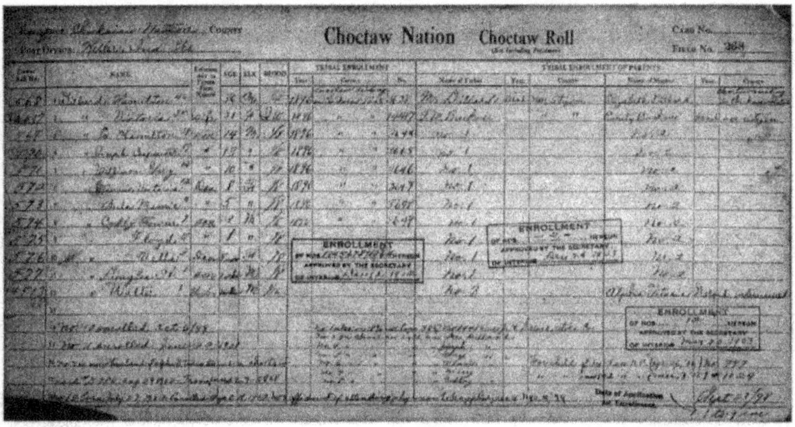
Choctaw Nation Choctaw Roll

Introduction

This series of Choctaw Enrollment Cards for the Five Civilized Tribes 1898-1914 has been transcribed from National Archive Film M-1186 Rolls 39-46.

The series contains more than 6100 Choctaw enrollment cards. All of the cards list age, sex and degree of blood, the parties' Dawes Roll Numbers, and date of enrollment by the Secretary of Interior for each person. The contents also give the enrollee's parents' names as well as miscellaneous notes pertaining to the enrollee's circumstances, when needed. Most entries indicate whether or not a spouse is an Intermarried White, with the initials I.W.

Enrollment wasn't as simple a process as most would think just by going through these pages. The relationships between the Five Tribes and the Dawes Commission were weak at best. There were political battles going on between the tribes and the U.S. Government as it was, but the struggles didn't stop there. Each tribe had its own political factions pulling it from every direction. On top of everything else, people from every corner of the United States were trying to figure how to get in on the spoils (Money and Land Allotment) by means of political favor. Kent Carter, author of *The Dawes Commission*, describes the continuous effort required to enroll the different tribes and the pressure the Commission incurred from people all over the country who tried to insinuate themselves into the equation:

"In May 1896 the Dawes Commission Returned To Indian Territory for its third visit, establishing its headquarters at Vinita in the Cherokee Nation. It now had to process applications for citizenship in addition to negotiating allotment agreements; these circumstances make the narrative of events more confusing because the commission attempted the two tasks concurrently. The commissioners resumed making their usual speeches to tribal officials and public gatherings to promote negotiations, but now they inevitably had to respond to questions about how the application process for citizenship would work. They also began receiving letters from people all over the United States asking how they could 'get on the rolls' so they could 'get Indian land'."[1]

For the actual process of Choctaw enrollment, "A commission was appointed in each county of the Choctaw Nation under an act of September 18 to make separate rolls of citizens by blood, by intermarriage, and freedmen; it was to deliver them to recently elected Chief Green McCurtain by October 20, but he rejected them even before they were completed because of charges that people were being left off for political reasons. On October 30, the National Council authorized establishment of a five-member

---

[1] *The Dawes Commission* by Kent Carter, page 15, para. 1

commission to revise the rolls within ten days and then directed McCurtain to turn them over to the Dawes Commission on November 11, 1896. The Choctaws hired the law firm of Stuart, Gordon, and Hailey, of South M^c^Alester to represent the tribe at all proceedings held by the Dawes Commission,"[2] another indication that throughout the Commission's efforts there was always controversy between the tribes and the negotiators.

When completed, this multi-volume series will contain thousands of names, all of them accounted for in the indexes carefully prepared by the author. Hopefully this work will help many researchers find their ancestors and satisfy the questions that so many have had about their Native American heritage.

Jeff Bowen
Gallipolis, Ohio
NativeStudy.com

---

[2] *The Dawes Commission* by Kent Carter, page 16, para. 5

Choctaw By Blood Enrollment Cards 1898-1914

RESIDENCE: COUNTY. **Choctaw Nation** **Choctaw Roll** *(Not Including Freedmen)* CARD NO.
POST OFFICE: Wayne Ind. Ter. FIELD NO. 1

Dawes' Roll No.	NAME	Relationship to Person First Named	AGE	SEX	BLOOD	TRIBAL ENROLLMENT Year	County	No.
1	1 Bell, Rebecca 29	First Named	25	F	1/4	1896	Atoka	1825
2	2 " , Zola Alice 7	Dau.	3	F	1/8	1896	"	1826
3	3 " , Thetas Lee 6	Son	2	M	1/8	1827	"	1827
IW164	4 " , King	Husb.	35	M	I.W.	1896	"	14351

ENROLLMENT OF NOS. 1, 2, 3 HEREON APPROVED BY THE SECRETARY OF INTERIOR Dec. 12, 1902

ENROLLMENT OF NOS. 4 HEREON APPROVED BY THE SECRETARY OF INTERIOR June 13, 1903

TRIBAL ENROLLMENT OF PARENTS

Name of Father	Year	County	Name of Mother	Year	County
1 John Donnelly	Dead	Choctaw roll	Henrietta LaFlore	Dead	Choc. roll
2 King G. Bell		White man	No.1		
3 " " "		" "	No.1		
4 J.P. Bell	Dead	Non-Citz.	Margaret Bell	Dead	Non-Citz.

No.3 on Choctaw roll as Lee Bell
No.4 on 1896 Choctaw census roll as K.G. Bell
No.4 transferred from Choctaw card #D3. See decision of April 20, 1903.

No.1 Died prior to September 25, 1902; not entitled to land or money.
(See Indian Office letter of June 20. 1910 D.C. #836-1910)

#Notation made Janv. 7. 1916
Date of Application for Enrollment. #Sept. 1898

Date of Application for Enrollment.

RESIDENCE: Chickasaw Nation ~~COUNTY~~.
POST OFFICE: Newton, Ind. Ter.

Choctaw Nation

Choctaw Roll (Not Including Freedmen)

CARD NO.
FIELD NO. 2

Dawes' Roll No.	NAME	Relationship to Person First Named	AGE	SEX	BLOOD	TRIBAL ENROLLMENT Year	County	No.
4	1 Oliver, Marietta E 24	First Named	20	F	1/2	1896	Blue	3529
5	2 Dennis, Josie Juanita 7	Dau	3	"	1/4	1896	"	3530
6	3 " Harriet 5	"	1	"	1/4	1896	"	3531
7	4 Oliver, Thomas J 41	Son	8mo	M	1/4			
8	5 " Reita Maud 2	Dau.	1mo	F	1/4			
9	6 " William Roosevelt 1	Son	2wks	M	1/4			
IW805	7 " Leonard C. (47)	Hus.	47	M	I.W.			
	8							
	9							
	10							
	11							
	12							
	13							
	14							
	15							
	16							
	17							

ENROLLMENT OF NOS. 1,2,3,4,5 and 6 HEREON APPROVED BY THE SECRETARY OF INTERIOR Dec. 12 1902

Agnes Blanch[sic]

ENROLLMENT OF NOS. 7 HEREON APPROVED BY THE SECRETARY OF INTERIOR May 21, 1904

TRIBAL ENROLLMENT OF PARENTS

	Name of Father	Year	County	Name of Mother	Year	County
1	Jeff Latta	Dead	Cherokee City	Harriet Robinson		Blue
2	Frank Dennis (IW)	"	Blue	No.1		
3	" "		"	No.1		
4	Leonard Oliver			No.1		
5	" "			No.1		
6	" "			No.1		
7	Jas H Oliver	Dead	non Citizen	Harriet C. Oliver		non Citizen

~~No.1 on Choctaw roll as Marietta Dennis~~
No.2 " " " " Juanita "
No.1 is the wife of Leonard C Oliver on Choctaw Card ~~#D-294~~
~~No.5 Enrolled May 24, 1900.~~
No.6 Born may 20, 1902: enrolled May 31, 1902.
No.7 transferred from Choctaw Card D-294 April 15, 1904.
See decision of March 15, 1904 No.4 Enrolled Nov 1/99
~~For child of No[s] 1 & 7 see N.B. (Apr 26, 1906) Card No.110~~
" " " " " " (Mar 3-1905) " " 33
P.O. Frances, I.T.

#1 to 4 inc
~~Date of Application~~ for Enrollment.
Sept 1898

RESIDENCE: Chickasaw Nation ~~COUNTY~~.
POST OFFICE: Center, Ind. Ter.

Choctaw Nation — **Choctaw Roll** (Not Including Freedmen)

CARD NO.
FIELD NO. 3

Dawes' Roll No.		NAME		Relationship to Person First Named	AGE	SEX	BLOOD	TRIBAL ENROLLMENT Year	County	No.
10	1	Goodson, John J	28	First Named	24	M	1/8	1896	Chickasaw Dist	CCR #2 215
11	2	" , John J Jr	7	Son	3	"	1/16	1896	" "	CCR #2 215

ENROLLMENT OF NOS. 1 and 2 HEREON APPROVED BY THE SECRETARY OF INTERIOR Dec. 12 1902

No 1 1896 Chickasaw Dist 5038 as J.J. Goodson
~~No 2 1896 " " 5039 " Jno J. "~~
No 1 is confined in Leavenworth Penitentiary under a sentence of five years from March 1 1900

TRIBAL ENROLLMENT OF PARENTS

	Name of Father	Year	County	Name of Mother	Year	County
1	Benj Goodson	Dead	non citizen	Esther E Goodson	Dead	Choctaw roll
2	No.1			Nettie Goodson		non citizen

~~Nettie Goodson divorced from John J Goodson and now married to one Steel.~~
No 1 is the husband of Mattie Goodson on Choctaw Card #275
No 1 admitted by U.S. Indian Agent Oct. 12, 1889 in case of Nancy Stewart

~~For child of No 1 see N.B. (Mar 3-1905) Card #56~~

Date of Application for Enrollment. Sept. 1898

PO Bebee I.T. 3/20/05

RESIDENCE: Chickasaw Nation ~~COUNTY~~.
POST OFFICE: Center, Ind. Ter.

Choctaw Nation

Choctaw Roll (Not Including Freedmen)
CARD NO.
FIELD NO. 4

Dawes' Roll No.		NAME	Relationship to Person First Named	AGE	SEX	BLOOD	TRIBAL ENROLLMENT Year	County	No.
12	1	Williams, America 18	First Named	14	F	1/2		Atoka	CCR #2 483
	2						1896	Atoka	13930
	3								
	4								
	5								
	6								
	7								
	8								
	9								
	10								
	11								
	12								
	13								
	14								
	15								
	16								
	17								

ENROLLMENT
OF NOS. 1 HEREON
APPROVED BY THE SECRETARY
OF INTERIOR Dec. 12 1902

Robert C. Sullivan is guardian of above girl, appointed by U.S. Court at Pauls Valley.

TRIBAL ENROLLMENT OF PARENTS

	Name of Father	Year	County	Name of Mother	Year	County
1	Reuben Williams	Dead	Chickasaw Citz	Susanna Lowery	Dead	Choctaw Roll
2				No 1	Born	July 18, 1905
3						
4						
5						
6						
7						
8						
9						
10						
11						
12						
13						
14						
15						
16						
17						

For child of No.1 see N.B. (Apr. 26, 1906) Card No 238.

Date of Application for Enrollment.
Sept. 1 1898.

RESIDENCE: Chickasaw Nation ~~COUNTY~~.
POST OFFICE: Center Ind. Ter.

Choctaw Nation

Choctaw Roll *(Not Including Freedmen)* CARD NO. FIELD NO. 5

Dawes' Roll No.	NAME	Relationship to Person First Named	AGE	SEX	BLOOD	TRIBAL ENROLLMENT Year	County	No.
IW206	1 Sturdivant, Chame [42]	First Named	36	M	I.W.			
13	2 " Sallie [28]	wife	24	F	1/2		Atoka	CCR #2 432
14	3 " Claud Osa [5]	Son	1	M	1/4		"	CCR #2 432

ENROLLMENT OF NOS. **2 and 3** HEREON APPROVED BY THE SECRETARY OF INTERIOR **Dec. 12 1902**

ENROLLMENT OF NOS. 1 HEREON APPROVED BY THE SECRETARY OF INTERIOR Sep 12 1903

No 2 1896 Atoka 11687 as Sallie Stureivan

~~No.1 admitted as an intermarried citizen by Dawes Commission Choctaw Case #807; no appeal.~~

Evidence of birth of No.3 received and filed Feby 8th 1902

No 2 admitted by U.S. Indian Agent Oct 12 1889

TRIBAL ENROLLMENT OF PARENTS

Name of Father	Year	County	Name of Mother	Year	County
1 Raney Sturdivant	Dead	non citizen	Martha Sturdivant	Dead	non citizen
2 John Stewart (I.W.)		White man	Nancy J Stewart	Dead	Choctaw roll
3 No.1			No.2		

Date of Application for Enrollment. Sept 1 1898

P.O Address Lehigh I.T. 8/3/03

RESIDENCE: Chickasaw Nation ~~COUNTY~~.
POST OFFICE: Wayne, Ind. Ter.

Choctaw Nation

Choctaw Roll (*Not Including Freedmen*) CARD NO. FIELD NO. 6

Dawes' Roll No.	NAME		Relationship to Person First Named	AGE	SEX	BLOOD	TRIBAL ENROLLMENT Year	County	No.
IW 58	1 Fox, William R	48	First Named	44	M	I.W.	1896	Chickasaw Dist	14552
15	2 " Angie	41	wife	37	F	1/8		" "	CCR #2 195
16	3 " Clarence	18	son	14	M	1/16		" "	CCR #2 195
17	4 " Edith	16	dau	12	F	1/16		" "	CCR #2 195
18	5 " Vera	13	"	9	F	1/16		" "	CCR #2 195
19	6 " Ethel	12	"	8	F	1/16		" "	CCR #2 195
20	7 " William A	3	son	4mo	M	1/16			
	17 P.O. Purcell I.T.								

ENROLLMENT
OF NOS. 2,3,4,5,6 and 7 HEREON
APPROVED BY THE SECRETARY
OF INTERIOR Dec. 12 1902

ENROLLMENT
OF NOS. 1 HEREON
APPROVED BY THE SECRETARY
OF INTERIOR Jun 13 1903

TRIBAL ENROLLMENT OF PARENTS

Name of Father	Year	County	Name of Mother	Year	County
1 John Fox	Dead	non-citizen	Elizabeth Fox	Dead	non citizen
2 Thos Manning (I.W.)	"	" "	Matilda Manning	1896	Blue
3 No.1			No.2		
4 No.1			No.2		
5 No.1			No.2		
6 No.1			No.2		
7 No.1			No.2		

~~No 2 1896 Chickasaw Dist 4583~~
~~No 3 1896 " " 4584 as Clammie Fox~~
~~No 4 1896 " " 4585~~
~~No 5 1896 " " 4586 as Vara Fox~~
~~No 6 1896 " " 4587~~
~~No 1 1896 " " 14552 as Wm A Fox~~

1 to 6 inc.
Date of Application for Enrollment. Sept 1 1898

No 7 admitted by Dawes Commission in 1896 as an ~~intermarried citizen Choctaw Case #434. No appeal~~

Testimony as to his status as an intermarried citizen given by No 7 at Pauls Valley Oct 21 1902

No 7 Enrolled Oct. 6/99

RESIDENCE: Chickasaw Nation ~~COUNTY~~.
POST OFFICE: Center Ind. Ter.

Choctaw Nation

Choctaw Roll *(Not Including Freedmen)*
CARD NO.
FIELD NO. 7

Dawes' Roll No.		NAME	Relationship to Person First Named	AGE	SEX	BLOOD	TRIBAL ENROLLMENT Year	County	No.
IW486	1	Johnson, James C 55		51	M	I.W.	1896	Chick Dist	14713
14471	2	" Malvina 52	wife	49	F	Full		Chickasaw Dist	CCR #2 310
14472	3	" Robert 12	son	9	M	1/2		" "	CCR #2 310
	4	ENROLLMENT OF NOS. 2 & 3 HEREON							
	5	APPROVED BY THE SECRETARY							
	6	OF INTERIOR May 20 1903							
	7	ENROLLMENT							
	8	OF NOS. 1 HEREON							
	9	APPROVED BY THE SECRETARY OF INTERIOR Dec. 24 1903							
	10								
	11								
	12								
	13								
	14								
	15								
	16								
	17								

TRIBAL ENROLLMENT OF PARENTS

	Name of Father	Year	County	Name of Mother	Year	County
1	James Johnson	Dead	non citizen	Elizabeth Johnson	Dead	non citizen
2	Robert James	"	Choctaw roll	Christine James	Dead	Choctaw roll
3	No 1			No 2		

~~No 2 1896 Chickasaw Dist 7408 as Melvina Johnson~~
No 3 1896 " " 7409
No 1 1896 " " 14713 as ~~ Johnson
No 1 also on 1897 Chickasaw roll Page 84 Pontotoc Co
~~No 2 also on Chickasaw roll, Pontotoc county, page 47 as Melvina Johnson~~
No 3 " " " " " " " " " Robert Johnson
Election to be enrolled as Choctaws Nov 10/02
June 7, 1900

Date of Application for Enrollment. Sept 1 1898

RESIDENCE: Chickasaw Nation ~~COUNTY.~~ **Choctaw Nation** **Choctaw Roll** *(Not Including Freedmen)* CARD NO.
POST OFFICE: Center, Ind. Ter. FIELD NO. 8

Dawes' Roll No.	NAME	Relationship to Person First Named	AGE	SEX	BLOOD	TRIBAL ENROLLMENT Year	County	No.
DEAD	~~Long, Veda~~ DEAD		~~20~~	~~F~~	~~1/16~~		~~Chickasaw Dist~~	CCR #2 244

No 1 hereon dismissed under order of the commission to the Five Civilized Tribes of March 31, 1905.

No 1 on 1893 roll Atoka Co p. 98 No 962 as [illegible]m Vida Brinkley.

Wife of Charley Long, a non-citizen. Choc D.57

CANCELLED

Applicant died prior to the ratification of the Choctaw - Chickasaw agreement on Sept. 25 1902

TRIBAL ENROLLMENT OF PARENTS

Name of Father	Year	County	Name of Mother	Year	County
~~Alfred Brinkley~~	~~Dead~~	~~non-citizen~~	~~Ester Brinkley~~	~~Dead~~	~~Choctaw roll~~

~~On 1896 roll as Victor B. Osborne~~
~~Page 254, No 10033, Chick Dist~~

No 1 Died Feby 19, 1900 proof of death filed April 8, 1902
~~No 1 Evidence of divorce from her former husband A.M. Osborn filed with Choctaw No 857 Nov. 18, 1902~~

Date of Application for Enrollment. Sept 1, 1898

Choctaw By Blood Enrollment Cards 1898-1914

RESIDENCE: Chickasaw Nation ~~COUNTY.~~
POST OFFICE: Dalberg Ind. Ter Pontotoc Co.

Choctaw Nation — **Choctaw Roll** *(Not Including Freedmen)* CARD NO. FIELD NO. 9

Dawes' Roll No.		NAME		Relationship to Person First Named	AGE	SEX	BLOOD	TRIBAL ENROLLMENT Year	County	No.
IW1393	1	Berry, George	42	First Named	38	M	I.W.	1896	Chickasaw Dist	14367
21	2	" Nancy	32	wife	28	F	Full		" "	CCR #2 83
22	3	" Turner	11	son	7	M	1/2		" "	CCR #2 83
23	4	" Roscoe	9	"	5	"	1/2		" "	CCR #2 83
14473	5	" Jesse	5	"	1	"	1/2		" "	CCR #2 83
24	6	" Walter Milburn	2	son	1mo	M	1/2			

ENROLLMENT OF NOS. 2,3,4 and 6 HEREON APPROVED BY THE SECRETARY OF INTERIOR Dec. 12 1902

ENROLLMENT OF NOS. 5 HEREON APPROVED BY THE SECRETARY OF INTERIOR May 20 1903

~~Nos 2, 3 4 and 5 were placed on Choctaw Census Rolls Sept 1, 1898 by Citizenship committee~~ (No 2 inserted)

11/13/02 P.O. Roff I.T.

TRIBAL ENROLLMENT OF PARENTS

	Name of Father	Year	County	Name of Mother	Year	County
1	S. V. Berry		non citizen	Sarah Berry		non citizen
2	Pittman Hays			Lizzie Scoper		
3	No.1			No.2		
4	No.1			No.2		
5	No.1			No.2		
6	No.1			No.2		

~~No 2 1896 Chickasaw Dist 1733~~
~~No 3 1896 " " 1734~~
No 4 1896 " " 1735
No 1 1896 " " 14367 as Geo W Berry
No 6 Enrolled Aug 6th 1900
~~No 5 Proof of birth received and filed Sept 11, 1902~~
For child of Nos 1 & 2 N.B. (Apr 26, 1906) Card No 100
" " " " " " (Mar 3-1905) " " 50

ENROLLMENT OF NOS. ~ 1 ~ HEREON APPROVED BY THE SECRETARY OF INTERIOR Jun 12 1905

#1 to 5 Date of application for Enrollment Sept 1/98

RESIDENCE: Chickasaw Nation ~~COUNTY~~.
POST OFFICE: Wayne, Ind. Ter

Choctaw Nation

Choctaw Roll *(Not Including Freedmen)*

CARD NO.
FIELD NO. 10

Dawes' Roll No.		NAME	Relationship to Person First Named	AGE	SEX	BLOOD	TRIBAL ENROLLMENT Year	County	No.
25	1	Gallamore, Eva P 28		24	F	Full		Chickasaw Dist	CCR #2 215
26	2	" Cecil 9	Son	5	M	1/2		" "	CCR #2 215
27	3	" Zada 7	Dau	3	F	1/2		" "	CCR #2 215
28	4	" Lucile 1	Dau	1wk	F	1/2			
IW1054	5	" Elonzo W 37	Husb	34	M	I.W.			
	6								
	7	ENROLLMENT OF NOS. 1,2,3 and 4 HEREON APPROVED BY THE SECRETARY OF INTERIOR Dec. 12 1902							
	8								
	9								
	10	ENROLLMENT OF NOS. ~ 5 ~ HEREON APPROVED BY THE SECRETARY OF INTERIOR Nov 16 1904							
	11								
	12								
	13								
	14								
	15								
	16	P.O. Albuquerque N.M.	12/6/02						
	17	P.O. Purcell I.T. 4/6/04							

TRIBAL ENROLLMENT OF PARENTS

	Name of Father	Year	County	Name of Mother	Year	County
1	John Donnelly	Dead	Choctaw	Henrietta La Flora	Dead	Choctaw
2	Walter Gallamore		non-citizen	No 1		
3	Walter Gallamore		" "	"		
4	E.W. Gallamore			No 1		
5	J. W. Gallamore	Dead	non citizen	Nancy Gallamore	Dead	non-Citz

No 1 1896 Chickasaw Dist 5029 as Eva Pursell Galmor[sic]
No 2 1896 " " 5030 " Cecil C "
No 3 1896 " " 5031 " Ida "
~~No 4 born Nov. 19, 1901; Enrolled Nov 26, 1901~~
Husband of No 1 on Choctaw D 267

~~No 5 transferred from Choctaw card #8-267 Oct 31, 1904: See decision of Oct 15, 1904.~~

#1 to 3
~~Date of Application~~ for Enrollment. Sept 1 - 1898

RESIDENCE: Chickasaw Nation ~~County~~ Pontotoc Co.
POST OFFICE: Ada Ind Ter

Choctaw Nation

Choctaw Roll (*Not Including Freedmen*)

CARD NO.
FIELD NO. 11

Dawes' Roll No.	NAME	Relationship to Person First Named	AGE	SEX	BLOOD	TRIBAL ENROLLMENT Year	County	No.
IW 1394	1 Broughton, Lee		25	M	I.W.	1896	Chickasaw Dist	14355
~~29~~	2 ~~Ida B~~ Died prior to September 25 1902	~~wife~~	~~23~~	~~F~~	~~1/8~~			CCR #2 81

ENROLLMENT OF NOS. 2 HEREON APPROVED BY THE SECRETARY OF INTERIOR Dec. 12 1902

ENROLLMENT OF NOS. ~ 1 ~ HEREON APPROVED BY THE SECRETARY OF INTERIOR Jun 12 1905

No 2 1896 Chickasaw Dist 2033

No 1 on 1896 roll as L. T. Broughton
No 2 Died July 11 1895; proof of death filed Nov 14 1902

~~No 2 died July 11, 1895; Enrollment cancelled by Department July 8 1904~~

TRIBAL ENROLLMENT OF PARENTS

	Name of Father	Year	County	Name of Mother	Year	County
1	John Broughton		non citizen	Lida Broughton		non citizen
2	~~Jack Barnett~~		" "	~~Lizzie Barnett~~	~~1896~~	~~Atoka~~

Sept. 1898
Date of Application for Enrollment.

RESIDENCE: Chickasaw Nation COUNTY.
POST OFFICE: Center, Ind. Ter.

Choctaw Nation — **Choctaw Roll** *(Not Including Freedmen)* — CARD NO. / FIELD NO. 12

Dawes' Roll No.		NAME	Relationship to Person First Named	AGE	SEX	BLOOD	TRIBAL ENROLLMENT Year	County	No.
	1	Roper, Zora	Named	29	F	1/4	U.S.	Court Cent Dist D	#101
	2	" Belle F.	Dau	9	"	1/8	" "	" D "	" "
	3	" Rhoda L.	"	7	"	1/8	" "	" D "	" "
	4	" Amanda P.	"	4	"	1/8	" "	" D "	" "
	5	" Joseph W.	Son	2	M	1/8	" "	" D "	" "
	6	" Rufus M.	"	1Mo	"	1/8	" "	" " "	" "
	7	" William Henry	"	1Mo	M	1/8			

No 7 Enrolled December 15, 1900.

Nos 1 to 5 incl. denied by Com 96 Case #850

Nos 1 to 5 inclusive were admitted by U.S. Court, Central District Ind. Ter. So. McAlester I.T. Jany 19th 1898: Court Case #101 Zora P. Lewis et al.

P.O. address: Bebee I.T. May 29, 1902.

Judgement[sic] of U.S. Ct admitting No 1 to 5 incl. vacated and set aside by Decree of Choctaw-Chickasaw Citizenship Court Dec. 17, 1903.

Nos 1 to 5 incl. in C.C.C.C. Case #58

No 1,2,3,4,5 Denied citizenship by the Choctaw and Chickasaw Citizenship Court Decr 3 04

58 M

TRIBAL ENROLLMENT OF PARENTS

	Name of Father	Year	County	Name of Mother	Year	County
1	Simon J. Cowart	Dead	non citizen	Rhoda T. Lewis	Dead	Choctaw Indian
2	H.C. Roper		" "	No 1		
3	" " "		" "	No.1		
4	" " "		" "	No.1		
5	" " "		" "	No.1		
6	" " "		" "	No.1		
7	" " "		" "	No.1		

6 - 7 Dismissed
Jan 21 1905

Date of Application for Enrollment. Sept 2/98

Choctaw By Blood Enrollment Cards 1898-1914

RESIDENCE: Chickasaw Nation ~~COUNTY~~.
POST OFFICE: Maxwell Ind Ter

Choctaw Nation — **Choctaw Roll** *(Not Including Freedmen)* — CARD NO. FIELD NO. 13

Dawes' Roll No.		NAME	Relationship to Person First Named	AGE	SEX	BLOOD	TRIBAL ENROLLMENT Year	County	No.
	1	~~Tabor Angeline~~	~~First Named~~	~~31~~	~~F~~	~~1/4~~	~~U.S.~~	~~Court Cent Dist~~ D	~~Case #101~~
	2	~~" Willie~~	~~Son~~	~~12~~	~~M~~	~~1/8~~	~~" "~~	~~" " "~~ D	~~" #101~~
	3	~~" Ben~~	~~"~~	~~6~~	~~"~~	~~1/8~~	~~" "~~	~~" " "~~ D	~~" 101~~
	4	~~" Herschel L~~	~~"~~	~~4~~	~~"~~	~~1/8~~	~~" "~~	~~" " "~~ D	~~" 101~~
	5	~~Adams, Ruthe~~	~~Dau~~	~~2 mo~~	~~F~~	~~1/8~~			
	6	~~Tabor, Leona~~	~~Dau~~	~~20 mo~~	~~F~~	~~1/8~~			
	7								
	8	No 1 Denied by CCCC Angelina Adams or Angelina Tabor							
	9	or Angeline Tabor							
	10								
	11	Nos 1 to 4 inclusive denied by Com- 96 Case #820							
#5 & 6	12	Dismissed — Nos 1 to 4 inclusive were admitted by U.S. Court Central District Ind Ter ~~So McAlester I.T. Jany 19 1898: Court Case #101 Zora P. Lewis et al.~~							
	13	Jan 19 1905 — ~~No 1 is now the wife of John J. Adams a non citizen: March 1st 1901~~							
	14	No 5 Enrolled March 1st 1901							
	15	No 1 is the mother of Leona Tabor on Choctaw card #R.292							
	16								
	17	P.O. Address is now Bebee I.T.							

TRIBAL ENROLLMENT OF PARENTS

	Name of Father	Year	County	Name of Mother	Year	County
1	~~David Leard~~		~~non citizen~~	~~Susanna [Early?]~~	~~Dead~~	~~Choctaw Indian~~
2	~~Sherman Tabor~~		~~" "~~	~~No.1~~		
3	~~" "~~		~~" "~~	~~No.1~~		
4	~~" "~~		~~" "~~	~~No.1~~		
5	~~J.J. Adams~~		~~" "~~	~~No.1~~		
6	~~Sherman Tabor~~		~~" "~~	~~No.1~~		
7	~~No 6 transferred from Choctaw card #R292 Aug 7, 1902~~					
8	~~No 6 Born Jany 11, 1897: enrolled on this card Aug. 7, 1902.~~					
9	Judgement[sic] of U.S. Court admitting Nos 1 to 4 incl. vacated and set aside by Decree of					
10	Choctaw-Chickasaw Citizenship Court Dec. 17 '02					
10	~~Nos 1 to 4 in C.C.C.C. Case #58~~					
11	~~See Pet. #C-130~~					
12						
13						
14						
15						Sept 2/98
16						Date of Application for Enrollment.
17	Duplicate record bound.					

1,2,3,4 Denied citizenship by the Choctaw and Chickasaw Citizenship Court

RESIDENCE: Chickasaw Nation ~~COUNTY~~.
POST OFFICE: Center, Ind. Ter

Choctaw Nation

Choctaw Roll (*Not Including Freedmen*)

CARD NO.
FIELD NO. **14**

Dawes' Roll No.		NAME	Relationship to Person First Named	AGE	SEX	BLOOD	TRIBAL ENROLLMENT Year	County	No.
	1	~~Leard, Joseph H~~	~~Named~~	~~24~~	~~M~~	~~1/4~~	~~U.S.~~	~~Court Cent Dist~~ D	~~Case #101~~
	2	~~" Belle~~	~~Wife~~	~~22~~	~~F~~	~~I.W.~~	~~" "~~	~~" D "~~	~~" 101~~
	3	~~" Madison~~	~~Bro~~	~~21~~	~~M~~	~~1/4~~	~~" "~~	~~" D "~~	~~" 101~~
	4	~~" Jack~~	~~"~~	~~18~~	~~"~~	~~1/4~~	~~" "~~	~~" D "~~	~~" 101~~
	5	~~Early, Maud~~	~~1/2 Sist~~	~~15~~	~~F~~	~~1/4~~	~~" "~~	~~" D "~~	~~" 101~~
	6	~~" Hugh~~	~~1/2 Bro~~	~~12~~	~~M~~	~~1/4~~	~~" "~~	~~" D "~~	~~" 101~~
	7	~~Leard, Frank David~~	~~Nephew~~	~~4mo~~	~~M~~	~~1/8~~			
	8	~~Venable, Elihu~~	~~son of No 5~~	~~1 yr~~	~~M~~	~~1/8~~			

No 3 Denied by CCCC as "Madison Leard or Madison L Leard"
No 5 " " " " "Maude Early"
~~Judgement[sic] of U.S. Court admitting Nos 1 to 6 inclusive vacated and set aside~~
by Decree of Choc. Chic. Citizenship Court Decr 17 '02
Nos 1 to 6 inclusive C.C.C.C. 58
#7 - 8 - Dismissed
~~Jan 19 1909~~

See Pet #C-130
Duplicate record bound

TRIBAL ENROLLMENT OF PARENTS

	Name of Father	Year	County	Name of Mother	Year	County
1	~~David Leard~~		~~non citizen~~	~~Susanna Early~~	~~Dead~~	~~Choctaw Indian~~
2	~~Dave Gwinn~~		~~" "~~	~~Polly Gwinn~~		~~non citizen~~
3	~~David Leard~~		~~" "~~	~~Susanna Early~~	~~Dead~~	~~Choctaw Indian~~
4	~~" "~~		~~" "~~	~~" "~~	~~"~~	~~" "~~
5	~~Bill Early~~	~~Dead~~	~~" "~~	~~Susanna Early~~	~~Dead~~	~~Choctaw Indian~~
6	~~" "~~	~~"~~	~~" "~~	~~" "~~	~~"~~	~~" "~~
7	~~No 3~~			~~Eliza Leard~~		~~non citz~~
8	~~John Venable~~		~~non citizen~~	~~No 5~~		

Nos 1 to 6 inclusive denied by Com-96 Case #850
Nos 1 to 6 inclusive were admitted by US Court Central District Ind Ter So McAlester I.T.
~~Jany 19, 1898 Court Case #101 Zora P. Lewis et al~~
~~No 7 Enrolled February 28, 1901~~
No 3 is now the husband of Eliza Leard Evidence of marriage filed this date February 28 1901
No 5 is now the wife of J.M. Venable a non citizen. Evidence of marriage filed Aug 29, 1901
~~No 8 Enrolled Aug 29 1901~~

1,2,3,4,5,6 Denied citizenship by the Choctaw and Chickasaw Citizenship Court Dec 3 '04 28M

Sept 2/98
~~Date of Application~~
for Enrollment.

Choctaw By Blood Enrollment Cards 1898-1914

RESIDENCE: Chickasaw Nation ~~COUNTY~~ **Choctaw Nation** **Choctaw Roll** *(Not Including Freedmen)* CARD NO.

POST OFFICE: Center Ind. Ter. FIELD NO. 15

Dawes' Roll No.	NAME	Relationship to Person First Named	AGE	SEX	BLOOD	TRIBAL ENROLLMENT Year	County	No.
~~DP~~	~~Stewart, Sarah I.~~	~~Named~~	~~24~~	~~F~~	~~1/8~~	~~U.S.~~	~~Ct. Cent. Dist.~~	~~56~~
	~~" Wynona Elizabeth~~	~~Dau.~~	~~3mo.~~	~~F~~	~~1/8~~			
	~~" Knox~~	~~Dau[sic]~~	~~2wk.~~	~~M~~	~~1/8~~			

No 1 is the wife of John B. Stewart on Choctaw card #D1. See also Card 977 Doubtful

~~Jun 5, 1902 DECISION PREPARED as to Nos. 2 & 3~~

No 1 is a duplicate of Sarah I. Steward, Choctaw card #D 977

~~No 1 cancelled from this card Dec 9, 1904.~~

No 1 appears as an I.W. 7D977.

Wife of John B. Stewart Doubtful card No 1, Choctaw Nation.

~~No 1 denied by Dawes Comm. in 96 case #1196. No appeal to C.C.C.C.~~

~~No 1 admitted a citizen by blood by U.S. Court, Central Dist. Ind. Ter.~~

So. McAlester, I.T. Aug 30, 1897; Court case #56 G.F.King et al.

No 3 born Feby 5, 1902; Enrolled Fab[sic]. 11, 1902

CANCELLED

No.1 transferred to Choctaw D 977 and

No.2 and 3 transferred to Choctaw #5877 Dec 9, 1904

TRIBAL ENROLLMENT OF PARENTS

Name of Father	Year	County	Name of Mother	Year	County
~~G.F. King~~		~~NonCitizen~~	~~Lizzie King~~		~~NonCit.~~
~~John B. Stewart~~			~~No.1~~		
~~" " "~~			~~No.1~~		

Protest of attorneys for Choctaw and Chickasaw Nations filed July 29, 1903, to enrollment

~~of No 2 & 3. Original record and protest forwarded Department Aug 7, 1903.~~

~~Dec 1, 1904: Decision of Commission of July 20, 1903~~

enrolling Nos 2 & 3 affirmed by Sect. of Interior No.2 enrolled May 24, 1900

No 2 & 3 transferred to Choctaw card #5877 Dec 9, 1904.

Sept 2, 98

Date of Application ~~for Enrollment.~~

RESIDENCE: Chickasaw Nation ~~XXXXXX~~
POST OFFICE: Center, Ind. Ter.

Choctaw Nation

Choctaw Roll *(Not Including Freedmen)*

CARD NO.
FIELD NO. **16**

Dawes' Roll No.		NAME	Relationship to Person First Named	AGE	SEX	BLOOD	TRIBAL ENROLLMENT Year	County	No.
	1	~~Newton, Helen V.~~	~~Named~~	~~42~~	~~F~~	~~1/4~~	~~U.S.~~	~~Court Cen. Dist. Case~~	~~#11~~
	2	~~" , Daniel S~~	~~Son~~	~~15~~	~~M~~	~~1/8~~	~~" "~~	~~" " " "~~	~~"11~~
	3	~~" , Clarence C.~~	~~"~~	~~11~~	~~M~~	~~1/8~~	~~" "~~	~~" " " "~~	~~"11~~
	4	~~" , James L.~~	~~"~~	~~9~~	~~M~~	~~1/8~~	~~" "~~	~~" " " "~~	~~"11~~
	5	~~" , Eva L.~~	~~Dau.~~	~~5~~	~~F~~	~~1/8~~	~~" "~~	~~" " " "~~	~~"11~~
	6								
	7								
	8	No.1 to 5 denied by Com. in case #1142							
	9	~~No.1 to 5 inclusive admitted as citizens by blood by U.S.Court Central District~~							
		~~So. McAlester I.T. August 26, 1897, Court Case #11.~~							
	10	Judge of U.S. Court admitting No.1 to 5 inclusive and vacated and set aside by							
	11	Decree of Choctaw-Chickasaw Cit. Ct. Dec. 17, 02							
	12	No.1 to 5 incl. in C.C.C.C. #71.							
	13								
	14								
	15								
	16								
	17								

ALL DENIED CITIZENSHIP BY CHOCTAW AND CHICKASAW CITIZENSHIP COURT CCCC CASE # 71M October 20, 1904.

TRIBAL ENROLLMENT OF PARENTS

	Name of Father	Year	County	Name of Mother	Year	County
1	~~Ben Jones~~	~~Dead~~	~~Choctaw Ind.~~	~~Mary Ann Jones~~	~~Dead~~	~~Non-Citz.~~
2	~~Isaac M. Newton~~		~~NonCitizen~~	~~No.1~~		
3	~~" " "~~		~~" "~~	~~No.1~~		
4	~~" " "~~		~~" "~~	~~No.1~~		
5	~~" " "~~		~~" "~~	~~No.1~~		
6						
7						
8						
9						
10						
11						
12						
13						
14						
15						Date of Application
16						~~for Enrollment.~~ Sept 2, 1898
17						

RESIDENCE: Tobucksy COUNTY. **Choctaw Nation** Choctaw Roll (*Not Including Freedmen*) CARD NO.
POST OFFICE: South McAlester Ind Ter FIELD NO. 17

Dawes' Roll No.	NAME	Relationship to Person First Named	AGE	SEX	BLOOD	TRIBAL ENROLLMENT Year	County	No.
~~30~~	1 ~~Folsom, Lyman~~ Died Prior to September 25, 1902.	~~Named~~ First	~~52~~	~~M~~	~~Full~~		~~Tobucksy~~	CCR #2 ~~17~~
	2							
	3					1896 Tobucksy 4006 as Lyman Fulsom		
	4							
	5							
	6							
	7							
	8	Husband of Phoebie Folsom Chickasaw Card No 84.						
	9							
	10	No 1 died before Sept. 25, 1902. Enrollment cancelled by Department May 2 1906						
	11							
	12							
	13							
	14							
	15							
	16							
	17							

ENROLLMENT OF NOS. 1 HEREON APPROVED BY THE SECRETARY OF INTERIOR Dec. 12 1902

TRIBAL ENROLLMENT OF PARENTS

Name of Father	Year	County	Name of Mother	Year	County
1 ~~Idom Folsom~~	~~Dead~~	~~Atoka~~		~~Dead~~	~~Choctaw roll~~
2					
3					
4					
5					
6					
7					
8					
9					
10					
11					
12					
13					
14					
15					Sept 2/98
16					Date of Application for Enrollment.
17					

RESIDENCE: Chickasaw Nation ~~COUNTY~~.
POST OFFICE: Oakman Ind. Ter.

Choctaw Nation

Choctaw Roll *(Not Including Freedmen)*

CARD NO.
FIELD NO. 18

Dawes' Roll No.	NAME	Relationship to Person First Named	AGE	SEX	BLOOD	TRIBAL ENROLLMENT Year	County	No.
31	1 Folsom, Ethel	Named	10	F	1/4		Chickasaw Dist	CCR #2 194
IW1395	2 Denney, Ida	Mother	32	"	I.W.			
	3				1896 Chickasaw Dist 4580 as Ethel Fulsom			

ENROLLMENT OF NOS. 1 HEREON APPROVED BY THE SECRETARY OF INTERIOR Dec. 12 1902

ENROLLMENT OF NOS. ~2~ HEREON APPROVED BY THE SECRETARY OF INTERIOR Jun 12 1905

No 2 formerly wife of Jerry Folsom, a recognized and enrolled citizen by blood of the Choctaw Nation, final roll #6438, Choctaw card #2224

TRIBAL ENROLLMENT OF PARENTS

Name of Father	Year	County	Name of Mother	Year	County
1 Jerry Folsom		Sugar Loaf	No.2 Mary Ida Scroggins		non citizen

No 2 originally listed for enrollment on Choctaw card #10 - 743 transferred to this card May 15, 1905. See decision of March 28, 1905
For child[ren] of No 2 see N.B. (Apr 26 '06) #1112

Date of Application for Enrollment. Sept 2/98

17 No.2 P.O. Francis I.T. 3/28/05

RESIDENCE: Tobucksy COUNTY. **Choctaw Nation** **Choctaw Roll** *(Not Including Freedmen)* CARD NO.
POST OFFICE: Tandy Ind. Ter. FIELD NO. 19

Dawes' Roll No.		NAME	Relationship to Person First Named	AGE	SEX	BLOOD	TRIBAL ENROLLMENT Year	County	No.
32	1	Johnston, Jane	First Named	33	F	1/2	1896	Tobucksy	6648
33	2	" Albert	Son	19	M	1/4	1896	"	6649
34	3	" Edmund H.	"	14	"	1/4	1896	"	6650
~~35~~	4	Died prior to September 25, 1902. ~~" Jack~~	~~"~~	~~11~~	~~"~~	~~1/4~~	~~1896~~	~~"~~	~~6651~~
36	5	" Allie	Dau	8	F	1/4	1896	"	6652
~~37~~	6	Died prior to September 25, 1902. ~~" Blanche~~	~~"~~	~~5~~	~~"~~	~~1/4~~	~~1896~~	~~"~~	~~6653~~
38	7	" Myrtle	"	3	"	1/4	1896	"	6654

ENROLLMENT OF NOS. 1,2,3,4,5,6 and 7 HEREON APPROVED BY THE SECRETARY OF INTERIOR Dec. 12 1902

Jane Johnston on Choctaw Roll as Mary J Johnson wife of B.F. Johnston Chickasaw Roll Card No 103.

No 4 died Oct 25, 1899 No.6 died June 19, 1900: Enrollment cancelled by Department July 8 1904

~~All of family on Roll as Johnson (also on Choctaw Census Record No 2 Page 280)~~

TRIBAL ENROLLMENT OF PARENTS

	Name of Father	Year	County	Name of Mother	Year	County
1	Fish-a-pus-ley	Dead	Choctaw Roll	Betsey Martindale	Dead	Choctaw roll
2	B.F. Johnston		Chickasaw roll	No 1		
3	" " "		" "	No 1		
4	~~" " "~~		~~" "~~	~~No 1~~		
5	" " "		" "	No 1		
6	~~" " "~~		~~" "~~	~~No 1~~		
7	" " "		" "	No 1		

Jack Johnston on Roll as Jackson Johnson
No 4 Died Oct 25, 1899: proof of death filed Nov. 12, 1902
No 6 Died June 19, 1900: proof of death filed Nov. 12, 1902

P.O. Roff, I.T.

Date of Application for Enrollment. Sept 3/98

RESIDENCE: Chickasaw Nation ~~COUNTY~~.
POST OFFICE: Stonewall Ind Ter

Choctaw Nation

Choctaw Roll *(Not Including Freedmen)*

CARD NO.
FIELD NO. **20**

Dawes' Roll No.	NAME	Relationship to Person First Named	AGE	SEX	BLOOD	TRIBAL ENROLLMENT Year	County	No.
IW539	1 Hensley Robert L 58	First Named	54	M	I.W.		Living in Chickasaw Dist. Choctaw I.M. Roll	Page 47
	2							
	3							
	4							
	5							
	6							
	7							
	8							
	9							
	10							
	11							
	12							
	13							
	14							
	15							
	16							
	17							

~~12/19/98 not found on 1896 Choctaw roll.~~

Wife of No 1 was Phoeba Goins Hensley on 1893 Choctaw pay roll:
Chickasaw district: page 27: #272.
See copy of letter filed herewith.

ENROLLMENT
OF NOS. ~ 1 ~ HEREON
APPROVED BY THE SECRETARY
OF INTERIOR Feb 8 1904

TRIBAL ENROLLMENT OF PARENTS

	Name of Father	Year	County	Name of Mother	Year	County
1	Samuel Hensley	Dead	non citizen	Mary Hensley	Dead	non citizen
2						
3						
4						
5						
6						
7						
8						
9						
10						
11						
12						
13						
14						
15						
16						
17						

Date of Application for Enrollment. Sept 3/98

RESIDENCE: Chickasaw Nation XXXXX
POST OFFICE: Stonewall, Ind. Ter.

Choctaw Nation

Choctaw Roll
(Not Including Freedmen)

CARD NO.
FIELD NO. 21

Dawes' Roll No.	NAME	Relationship to Person First Named	AGE	SEX	BLOOD	TRIBAL ENROLLMENT Year	County	No.
	1 Cochran, W.L.	First Named	64	M	I.W.		Int.Choc. residing in Chic Dist	IC roll Pg 19

2 White Card Oct 1898

Also admitted by Dawes Commission Case No. 962, Dawes Comm. Record "C".

CANCELLED

TRIBAL ENROLLMENT OF PARENTS

Name of Father	Year	County	Name of Mother	Year	County
1 A.O. Cochran	Dead	~~Non~~Citizen	Frances B. Cochran	Dead	NonCitz.

Sept. 3, 98

Date of Application for Enrollment.

RESIDENCE: Chickasaw Nation ~~COUNTY~~.
POST OFFICE: Conway Ind. Ter

Choctaw Nation

Choctaw Roll (Not Including Freedmen)

CARD NO.
FIELD NO. 22

Dawes' Roll No.	NAME	Relationship to Person First Named	AGE	SEX	BLOOD	TRIBAL ENROLLMENT Year	County	No.
Granted	1 Nelson Chilley	First Named	42	M	Full	1893	Choc. residing in Chic Dist	439

~~Name is on Chickasaw roll Pontotoc C; Page 47; Transferred to Choctaw roll by Dawes Commission.~~
Father of children on card No.121 Chickasaw roll.
NO.1 on 1893 Choctaw roll, Chickasaw District, Page 46, No.439.

CANCELLED
and transferred to Chickasaw card NO.1704
Apr. 7, 1904

TRIBAL ENROLLMENT OF PARENTS

Name of Father	Year	County	Name of Mother	Year	County
1 Nelson	Dead	Choctaw Roll	La-po-te-ma	Dead	Choc. roll

Date of Application for Enrollment.

Choctaw By Blood Enrollment Cards 1898-1914

RESIDENCE: Chickasaw Nation ~~XXXXX~~ COUNTY **Choctaw Nation** **Choctaw Roll** (Not Including Freedmen) CARD NO.
POST OFFICE: Waupanucka Ind. Ter. FIELD NO. 23

Dawes' Roll No.		NAME	Relationship to Person First Named	AGE	SEX	BLOOD	TRIBAL ENROLLMENT Year	County	No.
Void	1	~~Francis, B.L.~~	~~Named~~	~~40~~	~~M~~	~~I.W.~~			
"	2	~~" , Katie~~	~~wife~~	~~24~~	~~F~~	~~1/2~~			
"	3	~~" , Percy~~	~~son~~	~~2~~	~~M~~	~~1/4~~			
"	4	~~" , Bertram~~	~~son~~	~~18d~~	~~M~~	~~1/4~~			
	5								
	6								
	7								
	8								
	9								

10 Marriage licence[sic] to be forwarded to Muskogee Office. Received Sept. 12, 98

11

12 B.L. Francis on Chickasaw Roll, Intermarried Roll Page 81.
~~Katie " " " " , Pontotoc Co. " Page 59.~~
13 Percy " " " " " " " " " as Pearcy
14 All transferred to Choctaw roll by Dawes Comm.
No.4 enrolled August 31, 1901.
15 ~~Evidence of birth of No.3 received and filed March 6, 1902.~~

16

17

CANCELLED
and transferred to Chickasaw card #1583, Oct. 10, 1902

TRIBAL ENROLLMENT OF PARENTS

	Name of Father	Year	County	Name of Mother	Year	County
1	~~Miller, Francis~~		Non Citzen[sic]	~~Mary A. Francis~~		~~NonCitz.~~
2	~~Solomon Goforth~~	1897	Chic. residing in Choc.N'2n.D	~~Caroline Goforth~~	~~Dead~~	~~Choc. Roll~~
3	~~No.1~~			~~No.2~~		
4	~~No.1~~			~~No.2~~		
5						
6						
7						
8						
9						
10						
11						
12						
13						
14						
15	P.O. Owl, I.T. 11/20/02.				Date of Application for Enrollment.	
16						
17						

RESIDENCE: Chickasaw Nation XXXXX
POST OFFICE: Waupanuka Ind. Ter.

Choctaw Nation

Choctaw Roll (Not Including Freedmen)

CARD NO.
FIELD NO. 24

Dawes' Roll No.	NAME	Relationship to Person First Named	AGE	SEX	BLOOD	TRIBAL ENROLLMENT Year	County	No.
Void	1 Goforth, Eli P.	Named	41	M	3/8			
"	2 " , Sophina	wife	36	F	Full			
"	3 " , Charlotte	dau	14	"	3/4			
"	4 " , Bessie	"	12	"	"			
"	5 " , Odelia	"	10	"	"			
"	6 " , Solomon	son	8	M	"			
"	7 " , William	"	6	"	"			
"	8 " , Grover C.	"	4	"	"			
"	9 " , E.P. Jr.	"	3	"	"			
"	10 "DEAD, Louvina	dau.	1	F	"			
"	11 " , Louisa	mother	67	F	"	1893	Blue	534
"	12 " DEAD, Francis E.	dau.	2mo.	F	"			
"	13 " , Ruth	"	2mo.	F	"			

No 1,2,3,4,5,6,7,8,9,10,12 and 13 transferred to Chickasaw card No. 1584 Oct. 11, 1902

All are Choctaws found on Chickasaw Roll Page 57 and transferred to Choctaw roll by Dawes Comm.
No.13 Born March 11, 1902, enrolled May 26, 1902.
No.12 enrolled Oct. 6,99

TRIBAL ENROLLMENT OF PARENTS

	Name of Father	Year	County	Name of Mother	Year	County
1	Wm. Goforth	Dead	Chickasaw roll	Louisa Goforth		Choc. resid in Chic. Dist
2	Robison Mahaley	"	Choctaw roll	Melvina	Dead	Choc. roll
3	No.1			No.2		
4	No.1			No.2		
5	No.1			No.2		
6	No.1			No.2		
7	No.1			No.2		
8	No.1			No.2		
9	No.1			No.2		
10	No.1			No.2		
11	Dan McCoy	Dead	Choctaw Roll	Rebecca	Dead	Choc. roll
12	No.1			No.2		
13	No.1			No.2		
14						
15						
16						
17						

CANCELLED
and No.11 transferred to Chickasaw card #1584 Sept. 12, 1903

RESIDENCE: Chickasaw Nation ~~COUNTY~~.
POST OFFICE: Conway Ind Ter.

Choctaw Nation

Choctaw Roll (Not Including Freedmen)

CARD NO.
FIELD NO. 25

Dawes' Roll No.		NAME	Relationship to Person First Named	AGE	SEX	BLOOD	TRIBAL ENROLLMENT Year	County	No.
void	1	Perry Annie	First Named	24	F	1/2		Choctaw residing in Chickasaw Dist	
void	2	" Tandy F	Son	7	M	1/4		" " "	
void	3	" Juanita	Dau	4	F	1/4		" " "	
void	4	" Minnie	"	2	"	1/4		" " "	
void	5	" Lillie	"	6mo	"	1/4		" " "	
void	6	" Roxy	Dau	4mo	F	1/4			
void	7	" Theodore Mosely	Son	3mo	M	1/4			

No 1 is the ~~husband~~ wife of Geo H Perry on Chickasaw card #127

All of above parties except Lillie are on Chickasaw Roll Page 47, transferred to Choctaw roll by Dawes Com.
Tandy F. Perry on Chickasaw Roll as Andy F. Perry
Juanita " " " " " Jannita "
Evidence of birth of No 5 received and filed, Feby 28, 1902.
No 6 Enrolled July 14, 1900
No 7 Born June 22, 1902. enrolled Sept 19, 1902

CANCELLED

Transferred to Chickasaw Card #1585 Oct 11, 1902

TRIBAL ENROLLMENT OF PARENTS

	Name of Father	Year	County	Name of Mother	Year	County
1	Tandy Walker	1897	Chickasaw Roll	Adeline Wade	Dead	Choctaw Roll
2	Geo H. Perry		" "	No.1		
3	" " "		" "	No.1		
4	" " "		" "	No.1		
5	" " "		" "	No.1		
6	" " "		" "	No.1		
7	" " "		" "	No.1		

Date of Application for Enrollment.
Sept 3/98

RESIDENCE: Chickasaw Nation ~~COUNTY~~.
POST OFFICE: Viola, Ind. Ter.

Choctaw Nation

Choctaw Roll
(Not Including Freedmen)

CARD NO.
FIELD NO. **26**

Dawes' Roll No.		NAME	Relationship to Person First Named	AGE	SEX	BLOOD	TRIBAL ENROLLMENT		
							Year	County	No.
Void	1	~~Cravatt, Allen W.~~		~~42~~	~~M~~	~~1/2~~			
	2								
	3	Husband of Katie Cravatt, Chickasaw Roll Card No.139.							
	4	Allen W. Cravatt is on Chickasaw Roll, Pontotoc County Page 54: transferred							
	5	to Choctaw Roll by Dawes Com.							
	6								
	7								
	8								
	9								
	10								
	11								
	12								
	13								
	14								
	15								
	16								
	17								

TRIBAL ENROLLMENT OF PARENTS

	Name of Father	Year	County	Name of Mother	Year	County
1	~~Wm Cravatt~~	~~Dead~~	~~Chickasaw Roll~~	~~Bicey~~	~~Dead~~	~~Choctaw Roll~~
2						
3						
4						
5						
6						
7						
8						
9						
10						
11						
12						
13						
14						
15						
16						
17						

CANCELLED

Transferred to Chickasaw Card #586
Oct 11, 1902

Date of Application for Enrollment.
Sept 3/98

RESIDENCE: Chickasaw Nation COUNTY.
POST OFFICE: Newton Ind. Ter

Choctaw Nation

Choctaw Roll *(Not Including Freedmen)*

CARD NO.
FIELD NO. 27

Dawes' Roll No.	NAME	Relationship to Person First Named	AGE	SEX	BLOOD	TRIBAL ENROLLMENT Year	County	No.
1055	1 West, Thomas J.	First Named	60	M	I.W.		Choc. residing in Chic. Dist	Choc. IR. 118
39	2 " , Robert	son	18	M	1/8		" " "	CCR #2 489
40	3 Scroggins, Geo Thomas	G-son	6	"	1/16		" " "	CCR #2 434
41	4 Bryant, Mary	Dau.	20	F	1/8		" " "	CCR #2 82
42	5 " , Amy	G-dau	6mo	F	1/16		" " "	CCR #2 82
43	6 " , Willie Lillian	G-dau	1yr	F	1/16			
44	7 " , Frank Thomas	G-son	3mo	M	1/16		" " "	
	8 ENROLLMENT							
	9 OF NOS. 2,3,4,5,6,7 HEREON APPROVED BY THE SECRETARY							
	10 OF INTERIOR Dec. 12, 1902							
	11 No.7 born Jan 21, 1902, enrolled April 19, 1902							
	12 ~~For child of No 4 see NB (Apr.26,1906)No.189)~~							
	13 ENROLLMENT							
	14 OF NOS. 1 HEREON APPROVED BY THE SECRETARY				Child of No.2 on NB(Apr26,06) card 285.			
	15 OF INTERIOR Nov 16, 1904				Children of No1 on NB(Apr26,06) card 1225			
	16 No.2 is the husband of Liddy West on Choctaw Card #D614-7-5895							
	17 No.1 married in 1860 No.1[sic]							

TRIBAL ENROLLMENT OF PARENTS

Name of Father	Year	County	Name of Mother	Year	County
1 James West	Dead	NonCitizen	Betsy West	Dead	NonCitz.
2 No.1			Isabel West	"	Choc. Roll
3 George Scroggins		NonCitizen	Nellie Scroggins	"	Choc. Residing in Chic. Dist
4 No.1			Isabel West	"	Choc. Roll
5 Lou Bryant		NonCitizen	No.4		
6 W.A. Bryant		" "	No.4		
7 " " "		" ".	No.4		
8 No.2			Lydia West	Born	Oct. 14, 1905
9 ~~No.3 on Choctaw roll as Geo. P.~~					
10 No.4 "	"	" " May West Bryant	No.4 Born 4/28/05		
11 Evidence of marriage between No.4 and W.A. Bryant filed July 9, 1902					
12 ~~No.1 1896 Chickasaw Dist 15196 as Tom J. West~~			Evidence of birth of No.5 received and filed		
~~No2 1896 " " 14171~~			~~Notify Bingham & Wipple of~~		~~Apr.19,1902~~
13 No3 1896 " " 11773 as Geo.P.Scroggins			decision 3/1/04		#1-5
14 No.4 1896 " " 14170 "Mary West					Date of Application for Enrollment.
15 No.6 enrolled July 9, 1901 For child of No2 see NB(Mar3,1905) card No34					Sept. 5,08
16					
17 P.O. Francis I.T.					

RESIDENCE: Chickasaw Nation ■ **Choctaw Nation** **Choctaw Roll** (Not Including Freedmen) CARD NO.
POST OFFICE: Newton, Ind. Ter FIELD NO. 28

Dawes' Roll No.	NAME	Relationship to Person First Named	AGE	SEX	BLOOD	TRIBAL ENROLLMENT Year	County	No.
207	1 Chandler, James R 34	First Named	30	M	I.W.		Choc. Residing in Chic. Dist	ClntR 19
45	2 " , Nettie 25	wife	21	F	1/8		" " "	CCR #2 127
46	3 " , William T. 8	son	4	M	1/16		" " "	"
47	4 " , James E. 5	"	1 ½	M	1/16		" " "	"
48	5 " , Lory Elvy 3	dau	1mo	F	1/16		" " "	
49	6 " , Iva Ethel 1	"	2mo	F	1/16			

ENROLLMENT OF NOS. 2,3,4,5,6 HEREON APPROVED BY THE SECRETARY OF INTERIOR Dec. 12, 1903

ENROLLMENT OF NOS. 1 HEREON APPROVED BY THE SECRETARY OF INTERIOR Sept 12, 1903

~~No.6 born Dec 5,1901: Enrolled Feb.7,02~~

Evidence of birth of Nos 3&4 received and filed Feb.7,1902 No.5 enrolled Oct 6,99

P.O. Francis, I.T.

TRIBAL ENROLLMENT OF PARENTS

	Name of Father	Year	County	Name of Mother	Year	County
1	S.G. Chandler		NonCitz.	Elizabeth Chandler		NonCitz
2	Thos. J. West	1897	Choc Residing in Chic. Dist	Isabel West	Dead	Choc. roll
3	No.1			No 2		
4	No.1			No.2		
5	No.1			No.2		
6	No.1			No.2		

~~No 1 1896 Chickasaw Dist. 14436 as Jas.R. Chandlin~~

For child of Nos. 1&2, see NB(Apr.26,1906) dcard No.198

~~12/19/98 Nos. 2,3,&4 not found on 1896 Choctaw roll.~~

For child of Nos. 1&2 see NB(March 3,1905)#4

No.2 also on 1893 payroll, Page 13, No 130 Chickasaw Dist. as Nettie Chandler Jan 20,1900

Date of Application for Enrollment.

~~For Nos 1-4 incl. Sept 5,98~~

Choctaw By Blood Enrollment Cards 1898-1914

RESIDENCE: Chickasaw Nation ~~COUNTY~~ **Choctaw Nation** **Choctaw Roll** *(Not Including Freedmen)* CARD NO.
POST OFFICE: Center, Ind. Ter. FIELD NO. 29

Dawes' Roll No.	NAME	Relationship to Person First Named	AGE	SEX	BLOOD	TRIBAL ENROLLMENT Year	County	No.
Void	1 ~~Cofer, Bettie~~	~~Named~~	~~26~~	~~F~~	~~1/2~~			
Void	2 ~~" , Andrew Jackson~~	~~son~~	~~9~~	~~M~~	~~1/4~~			
Void	3 ~~" , Emma Lena~~	~~dau.~~	~~7~~	~~F~~	~~1/4~~			
Void	4 ~~" , Geo. Edward~~	~~son~~	~~3~~	~~M~~	~~1/4~~			
Void	5 ~~" , Jesse Freeman~~	~~"~~	~~5mo~~	~~M~~	~~1/4~~			
Void	6 ~~" ,Virgil Lee~~	~~"~~	~~2mo~~	~~M~~	~~1/4~~			

7 Surname on Chickasaw roll "Coffer"
8 All above parties except Jesse Freeman are on Chickasaw roll, Pontotoc County Page 41
9 transferred to Choctaw roll by Dawes Comm.
10 No 2 on Chickasaw roll as A.J.
~~No 3 on Chickasaw roll as E.L.~~
11 ~~No.4 on Chickasaw roll as Edward~~
12 No.6 enrolled May 24, 1900
13 Evidence of birth of No.5 received and filed July 25, 1902

CANCELLED
Transferred to Chickasaw card No.1587
Oct 11, 1902

TRIBAL ENROLLMENT OF PARENTS

	Name of Father	Year	County	Name of Mother	Year	County
1	~~Geo. Johnson~~	~~Dead~~	~~Chick. roll~~	~~Elizabeth Cocheron~~[sic]	~~1896~~	~~Atoka Pg 70~~ CCR#[?]
2	~~G. F. Cofer~~		~~NonCitizen~~	~~No.1~~		
3	~~" " "~~		~~" "~~	~~No.1~~		
4	~~" " "~~		~~" "~~	~~No.1~~		
5	~~" " "~~		~~" "~~	~~No.1~~		
6	~~" " "~~		~~" "~~	~~No.1~~		

Choctaw By Blood Enrollment Cards 1898-1914

RESIDENCE: Chickasaw Nation ~~COUNTY~~. POST OFFICE: Allen, Ind Ter.

Choctaw Nation — **Choctaw Roll** *(Not Including Freedmen)* — CARD NO. FIELD NO. **30**

Dawes' Roll No.		NAME	Relationship to Person First Named	AGE	SEX	BLOOD	TRIBAL ENROLLMENT Year	County	No.
50	1	Jackson, Abby	First Named	16	F	1/2		Atoka	CCR #2 306
51	2	" Adeline	Sister	15	"	1/2		"	CCR #2 306
	3	ENROLLMENT							
	4	OF NOS. 1 and 2 HEREON APPROVED BY THE SECRETARY							
	5	OF INTERIOR Dec. 12 1902							
	6					No 1	1896	Atoka	7328
	7					No 2	1896	"	7327
	8						as Adaline Jackson		
	9								
	10	For child of No.1 see Chick N.B.(March 3,1905) #536							
	11								
	12								
	13								
	14								
	15								
	16								
	17								

TRIBAL ENROLLMENT OF PARENTS

	Name of Father	Year	County	Name of Mother	Year	County
1	York Jackson		Chick Freedman	Sibbey Jackson	Dead	Choctaw Roll
2	" "		" "	" "	"	" "
3						
4						
5						
6						
7						
8						
9						
10						
11						
12						
13						
14						
15						
16					Date of Application for Enrollment.	Sept 5/98
17						

RESIDENCE: Chickasaw Nation COUNTY.
POST OFFICE: Newton, Ind. Ter.

Choctaw Nation

Choctaw Roll *(Not Including Freedmen)*

CARD NO.
FIELD NO. 31

Dawes' Roll No.	NAME	Relationship to Person First Named	AGE	SEX	BLOOD	TRIBAL ENROLLMENT Year	County	No.
DEAD	1 ~~West, Albert~~	~~Named~~	~~26~~	~~M~~	~~1/8~~		~~Choc. residing in Chic. Dist~~	~~CCR #2 489~~
52	2 " , Allen	Son	5	M	1/16		" " "	CCR #2 489
53	3 " , Mary Etta	Dau	3	F	1/16		" " "	CCR #2 489
54	4 " , Albert Harley	Son	5mo	M	1/16			
55	5 " , Pearly	Dau	5mo	F	1/16			
IW 1056	6 Henson, Virginia	Wife	25	F	IW			

ENROLLMENT OF NOS. 2,3,4,5 HEREON APPROVED BY THE SECRETARY OF INTERIOR Dec. 12, 1902

ENROLLMENT OF NOS. 6 HEREON APPROVED BY THE SECRETARY OF INTERIOR Nov 16, 1904

Virginia West, wife of No.1 and mother of 2,3,4,&5 on Choctaw card #D613

No. 1 Hereon Dismissed Under Order Of The Commission To The Five Civilized Tribes of Mar 31, 1905.

No.6 transferred from Choctaw card #D 613, Oct 31, 1904: See decision of Oct. 15, 1904.

TRIBAL ENROLLMENT OF PARENTS

	Name of Father	Year	County	Name of Mother	Year	County
1	~~Thos. J. West~~		~~Choc. residing in Chic. Dist~~	~~Isabel West~~	~~Dead~~	~~Choc. roll~~
2	No.1			Virginia West		NonCitz
3	No.1			" "		" "
4	No.1			" "		" "
5	No.1			" "		" "
6	Lawson Nichols	Dead	NonCitizen	Mary Nichols		" "

~~No1 1896 Chickasaw Dist. 14166~~
~~No2 1896 " " 14168~~
No.3 1896 " " 14169 as Mary E. West
Evidence of birth of No.4 received and filed Aug. 6, 1900
~~No1 died Nov. 21, 1900. Proof of death filed Jan. 29, 1901~~
~~Evidence of marriage of No.1 and Virginia West to be supplied.~~
Filed Jan 29, 1901.

Date of Application for Enrollment.
Sept. 5, 98

RESIDENCE: Chickasaw Nation ~~xxxxx~~ **Choctaw Nation** Choctaw Roll (Not Including Freedmen) CARD NO.
POST OFFICE: Newton, Ind. Ter. FIELD NO. 32

Dawes' Roll No.		NAME	Relationship to Person First Named	AGE	SEX	BLOOD	TRIBAL ENROLLMENT Year	County	No.
56	1	West, James	First Named	25	M	18		Choc. residing in Chic. Dist	CCR #2 489
	2								
	3	ENROLLMENT					1896	Chic. Dist	14167
	4	OF NOS. 1 HEREON APPROVED BY THE SECRETARY							
	5	OF INTERIOR Dec. 12, 1902							
	6								
	7								
	8	2 children of No.1 on NB card (April 26,06) No.296							
	9								
	10								
	11								
	12								
	13								
	14								
	15								
	16								
	17								

TRIBAL ENROLLMENT OF PARENTS

	Name of Father	Year	County	Name of Mother	Year	County
1	Thos. J. West		Choc. residing ~~in Chic. Dist~~	Isabel West	Dead	Choc. roll
2						
3						
4				Carrie Ethel West Born Oct. 2, 1905		
5						
6	No 1 [sic]					
7						
8						
9						
10						
11						
12						
13						
14						
15				Date of Application for Enrollment.		
16						Sept. 5, 98
17	P.O. Oakman I.T. May	16, '06				

RESIDENCE: Chickasaw Nation ~~XXXXX~~
POST OFFICE: Ada Ind. Ter.

Choctaw Nation

Choctaw Roll (*Not Including Freedmen*)

CARD NO.
FIELD NO. 33

Dawes' Roll No.	NAME	Relationship to Person First Named	AGE	SEX	BLOOD	TRIBAL ENROLLMENT Year	County	No.
57	1 Shelby, Rebecca	First Named	49	F	Full		Tobucksy	CCR #2 422
IW 165	2 Allen, Zachariah	Husb.	54	M	IW	1896	"	11296

ENROLLMENT OF NOS. 1 HEREON APPROVED BY THE SECRETARY OF INTERIOR Dec. 12, 1902

No.2 transferred form[sic] Choctaw card #D 59
See decision of May 5, 1903

No.1 now the wife of Z.D.Allen, Choc. D 59 11/10/02

ENROLLMENT OF NOS. 2 HEREON APPROVED BY THE SECRETARY OF INTERIOR Jun 13, 1903

TRIBAL ENROLLMENT OF PARENTS

Name of Father	Year	County	Name of Mother	Year	County
1 Zelic Harrison	Dead	Choctaw roll	Elizabeth Harrison	1896	Atoka
2 Zachariah Allen	"	NonCitizen	Nancy Allen	Dead	Non-Citz.

Date of Application for Enrollment. Sept. 5, 98

Choctaw By Blood Enrollment Cards 1898-1914

RESIDENCE: Chickasaw Nation ~~COUNTY~~
POST OFFICE: Pontotoc Ind. Ter.

Choctaw Nation

Choctaw Roll (Not Including Freedmen)

CARD NO.
FIELD NO. 34

Dawes' Roll No.		NAME	Relationship to Person First Named	AGE	SEX	BLOOD	TRIBAL ENROLLMENT Year	County	No.
58	1	Anderson, Lizzie 44		40	F	Full		Jack Fork	CCR #2 21
59	2	" , Reuben 16	son	12	M	1/2		" "	CCR #2 21
60	3	" , Margaret 11	dau	7	F	1/2		" "	CCR #2 21

ENROLLMENT ~~OF NOS.~~ 1, 2, 3 ~~HEREON~~ APPROVED BY THE SECRETARY OF INTERIOR Dec. 12, 1902

No 1 1896 Jack Fork 528
No 2 1896 " " 529
No3 1896 " " 530 as Maggie Anderson

TRIBAL ENROLLMENT OF PARENTS

	Name of Father	Year	County	Name of Mother	Year	County
1	Isum Fletcher	Dead	Choctaw roll	Rachael Fletcher	Dead	Jack Fork
2	Sampson Anderson		Chick. "	No.1		
3	" "		" "	No.1		

~~No.1 wife of Sampson Anderson, Chickasaw roll card No.205.~~
No.3 on Choctaw roll as Maggie

Date of Application for Enrollment.
Sept. 5, 98

RESIDENCE: Chickasaw Nation ~~XXXXX~~ **Choctaw Nation** **Choctaw Roll** *(Not Including Freedmen)* CARD NO.
POST OFFICE: Pontotoc Ind. Ter. FIELD NO. 35

Dawes' Roll No.	NAME	Relationship to Person First Named	AGE	SEX	BLOOD	TRIBAL ENROLLMENT Year	County	No.
61	1 Anderson, Elsie 46		42	F	Full		Choc. residing in Chic. Dist	CCR #2 21
	2							
	3					1896	Jack Fork	512
	4							
	5							
	6							
	7 On Choctaw Roll as "Eliza" wife of Wm.B. Anderson, Chickasaw roll card No.206							
	8							
	9							
	10							
	11							
	12							
	13							
	14							
	15							
	16							
	17							

ENROLLMENT OF NOS. 1 HEREON APPROVED BY THE SECRETARY OF INTERIOR Dec. 12, 1902

TRIBAL ENROLLMENT OF PARENTS

Name of Father	Year	County	Name of Mother	Year	County
1 Min-ta-ham-by	Dead	Choctaw roll	Kittie	Dead	Choc. roll
2					
3					
4					
5					
6					
7					
8					
9					
10					
11					
12					
13					
14					
15					
16					
17					

Date of Application for Enrollment.
Sept 5/98

RESIDENCE: Atoka COUNTY. **Choctaw Nation** Choctaw Roll (*Not Including Freedmen*) CARD NO.
POST OFFICE: Owl Ind. Ter. FIELD NO. **36**

Dawes' Roll No.		NAME	Relationship to Person First Named	AGE	SEX	BLOOD	TRIBAL ENROLLMENT Year	County	No.
62	1	Frazier, Solomon		33	M	Full		Atoka	CCR #2 191
	2								
	3	ENROLLMENT OF NOS. 1 HEREON					1896		4487
	4	APPROVED BY THE SECRETARY OF INTERIOR Dec. 12, 1902							
	5								
	6								
	7	Husband of Kiliza Frazier, Chickasaw roll card No.210							
	8								
	9								
	10								
	11								
	12								
	13								
	14								
	15								
	16								
	17								

TRIBAL ENROLLMENT OF PARENTS

	Name of Father	Year	County	Name of Mother	Year	County
1	Stanton Frazier	Dead	Choctaw roll		Dead	Choc. roll
2						
3						
4						
5						
6						
7						
8						
9						
10						
11						
12						
13						
14						
15						
16				Date of Application for Enrollment.		Sept. 5, 98
17						

RESIDENCE: Jack Fork COUNTY. POST OFFICE: Tuskahoma Ind. Ter.

Choctaw Nation — Choctaw Roll (Not Including Freedmen) — CARD NO. FIELD NO. 37

Dawes' Roll No.		NAME	Relationship to Person First Named	AGE	SEX	BLOOD	Tribal Enrollment Year	Tribal Enrollment County	Tribal Enrollment No.
63	1	Calvin, Joshua		40	M	Full		Jack Fork	CCR #2 123
64 DIED PRIOR TO SEPT 25 1902	2	~~" , Willis~~	~~son~~	~~17~~	~~"~~	~~"~~		~~" "~~	~~"~~
SEE 1974	3	~~" , Isabelle~~	~~dau.~~	~~15~~	~~F~~	~~"~~		~~" "~~	~~"~~
65 DIED PRIOR TO SEPT 25 1902	4	~~" , Edwin~~	~~son~~	~~10~~	~~M~~	~~"~~		~~" "~~	~~"~~
66	5	" , Ben	"	7	M	"		" "	"

ENROLLMENT OF NOS. 1,2,4,5 HEREON APPROVED BY THE SECRETARY OF INTERIOR Dec. 12, 1902

For child of No.1 see NB(Mar 3,1905) Card #39

No 2 died April 1902; No 4 died Nov 30,1899. Enrollment cancelled by Dept. July 8,1904

No.3 on Choctaw roll as "Sibby"

No 1 1896 Jacks Fork 3022
~~No 2 " " " 3024~~
No 3 " " " 3025
No 4 " " " 3026
No 5 " " " 3027 as Benjamin Calvin

~~No.3 transferred to Card No.1974 with husband 5/23/99~~

~~No 2 died April 1902, proof of death filed Dec 13, 1902~~
~~No 4 died Nov 30, 1899 " " " " " " "~~

TRIBAL ENROLLMENT OF PARENTS

	Name of Father	Year	County	Name of Mother	Year	County
1	Ta-tub-by	Dead	Choctaw roll		Dead	Choc. roll
2	~~No.1~~			~~Lucy~~	~~"~~	~~Jack Fork~~
3	~~No.1~~			~~Lucy~~	~~"~~	~~" "~~
4	~~No.1~~			~~Lucy~~	~~"~~	~~" "~~
5	No.1			Lucy	"	" "

Date of Application for Enrollment. Sept 6, 98

RESIDENCE: Chickasaw Nation ~~COUNTY~~. **Choctaw Nation** Choctaw Roll (Not Including Freedmen) CARD NO.
POST OFFICE: Roff, Ind. Ter. FIELD NO. 38

Dawes' Roll No.		NAME	Relationship to Person First Named	AGE	SEX	BLOOD	TRIBAL ENROLLMENT Year	County	No.
IW487	1	Suddath, Thomas M 39	First Named	29	M	IW			
67	2	" Elizabeth Roff 24	wife	20	F	1/4		Choctaw residing Chickasaw Dist	CCR #2 416
68	3	" Ralph M 3	son	3mo	M	1/8			
69	4	" Pauline 1	dau	3wks	F	1/8			
	5	ENROLLMENT							
	6	OF NOS. 2,3 and 4 HEREON APPROVED BY THE SECRETARY							
	7	OF INTERIOR Dec. 12, 1902							
	8								
	9	ENROLLMENT							
	10	OF NOS. ~ 1 ~ HEREON APPROVED BY THE SECRETARY							
	11	OF INTERIOR Dec. 24, 1903							
	12								
	13	No 2 on 1896 roll as Elizabeth Raulph Page 284, No 11034, Chick. Dist							
	14	No.4 Enrolled June 22, 1901							
	15	For child of Nos. 1 & 2 see N.B. (March 3rd 1905) #3							
	16								
	17								

TRIBAL ENROLLMENT OF PARENTS

	Name of Father	Year	County	Name of Mother	Year	County
1	M.M. Suddath		non citizen	Sarah Suddath		non citizen
2	Joe Roff		Choctaw Roll	David Ann Roff	dead	Choctaw Roll
3	No 1			No 2		
4	No 1			No.2		
5						
6						
7						
8						
9						
10						
11						
12						
13						#1&2
14				Date of Application for Enrollment.		Sept. 6/ 98
15				No.3 Enrolled Aug 9/99		
16						
17						

RESIDENCE: Chickasaw Nation ~~COUNTY~~ **Choctaw Nation** **Choctaw Roll** (Not Including Freedmen) CARD NO.
POST OFFICE: Roff, Ind. Ter. FIELD NO. 39

Dawes' Roll No.		NAME	Relationship to Person First Named	AGE	SEX	BLOOD	TRIBAL ENROLLMENT Year	County	No.
70	1	Roff, Andrew V.	First Named	26	M	1/4		Choc. residing in Chic. Dist	CCR #2 416
~~71~~	2	~~" , Cleo Estelle~~	~~Dau~~	~~6wks~~	~~F~~	~~1/8~~			
IW1517	3	" , Pearl	Wife	20	F	I.W.			

ENROLLMENT OF NOS. 1, 2 HEREON APPROVED BY THE SECRETARY OF INTERIOR Dec. 12, 1902

ENROLLMENT OF NOS. 3 HEREON APPROVED BY THE SECRETARY OF INTERIOR March 14, 1906

For child of Nos. 1&3 see NB(March 3, 1905) #1349
No.1 also on 1896 Choctaw census roll page 284
No.11032 as Andrew V. Raulph
~~No.1 is now husband of Pearl Roff, non citizen. Evidence~~
of marriage filed Oct. 3, 1901

No.2 enrolled Oct 3, 1901
No.2 died July 18, 1902. Proof of death filed Nov. 12, 1902.
No.2 died July 18, 1902. Enrollment cancelled by Department July 8, 1904
~~No.3 placed on this card, Sept. 28, 1905, in accordance with order of the Commissioner~~
to the Five Civilized Tribes of that date holding application was made written prescribed by Act of Congress approved July 1, 1902 (32 Stat. 641).
Former wife of No.1 on Choc. card #6054

For child of Nos. 1 & 3 see NB (Apr. 26,06) card #469

TRIBAL ENROLLMENT OF PARENTS

	Name of Father	Year	County	Name of Mother	Year	County
1	Joe Roff (IW)		Choctaw roll	David Ann Roff	Dead	Choc. roll
2	~~No.1~~			~~Pearl Roff~~		~~NonCitz.~~
3	Frank Moore		NonCitizen	Penney Moore		" "

No 3 GRANTED
Nov. 4, 1905

PO Lula I.T. 3/21/06

Date of Application for Enrollment.
Sept. 6, 98

RESIDENCE: Chickasaw Nation ~~COUNTY~~ **Choctaw Nation** **Choctaw Roll** (Not Including Freedmen) CARD NO.
POST OFFICE: Roff, Ind. Ter. FIELD NO. **40**

Dawes' Roll No.		NAME	Relationship to Person First Named	AGE	SEX	BLOOD	TRIBAL ENROLLMENT Year	County	No.
72	1	Roff, William D. 28		24	M	1/4		Choc. residing in Chic. Dist	CCR #2 416
IW1057	2	" , Joe 54	Father	54	M	I.W.		" " "	C.I.roll 96

ENROLLMENT OF NOS. 1 HEREON APPROVED BY THE SECRETARY OF INTERIOR ....

ENROLLMENT OF NOS. 2 HEREON APPROVED BY THE SECRETARY OF INTERIOR ....

For child of No.1 see NB (Apr. 26,06) Card # 509.

No.1 also on 1896 Choctaw census roll page 284 No.11033 as W.D. Raulph.
No.2 on 1896 Chickasaw Dist. 15012 as Joe B. Roff p-399.
No.2 first marriage to David Anna Walls, Choctaw woman in 1871.
No.2 second marriage to Lillie Braley, white " in 1886.
No.2 third " " Mary McGallian, white " in 1890
Certificate of marriage to David Anna Walls filed Nov. 25, 98
See Choctaw card R-727 for children of No.3

No.2 transferred from Choctaw card #D-15, Oct. 31, 1904. See decision of Oct. 15, 1904.

TRIBAL ENROLLMENT OF PARENTS

	Name of Father	Year	County	Name of Mother	Year	County
1	Joe Roff (I.W.)		Choctaw roll	David Ann Roff	Dead	Choc. roll
2	Charles L. Roff		NonCitizen	Elizabeth Roff	"	NonCitz.
3	No.1			Dottie Roff	Born	Dec 28 05

Date of Application for Enrollment. Sept. 6, 98

No.4 P.O. Tishomingo 8/24/04

RESIDENCE: Atoka COUNTY. **Choctaw Nation** **Choctaw Roll** *(Not Including Freedmen)* CARD NO.
POST OFFICE: Oconee, Ind. Ter. FIELD NO. 41

Dawes' Roll No.	NAME	Relationship to Person First Named	AGE	SEX	BLOOD	TRIBAL ENROLLMENT Year	County	No.
73	1 Guynes, William	First Named	30	M	1/2	1893	Atoka	Page 392
	2							
	3							
	4							
	5							
	6							
	7							
	8							
	9							
	10							
	11							
	12							
	13							
	14							
	15							
	16 No.1 P.O. Ardmore I.T	10/1/04						
	17							

ENROLLMENT OF NOS. 1 HEREON APPROVED BY THE SECRETARY OF INTERIOR Dec 12/1902

No1 also on 1896 Choc. Census roll #2, Atoka, page 211.
Husband of Margaret Guynes, Chickasaw roll card No. 230.

TRIBAL ENROLLMENT OF PARENTS

Name of Father	Year	County	Name of Mother	Year	County
1 John Guynes	Dead	Non-Citizen	Amanda Guynes	Dead	Choc. roll
2					
3					
4					
5					
6					
7					
8					
9					
10					
11					
12					
13					
14					
15					
16					
17					

Date of Application for Enrollment. Sept. 6, 98

RESIDENCE: Atoka COUNTY. POST OFFICE: Lehigh Ind. Ter.

Choctaw Nation — Choctaw Roll (Not Including Freedmen) — CARD NO. FIELD NO. 42

Dawes' Roll No.	NAME	Relationship to Person First Named	AGE	SEX	BLOOD	TRIBAL ENROLLMENT Year	County	No.
74	1 James, Henry C. 61		57	M	1/2		Atoka	CCR #2 305
IW 806	2 James, Orlener (36)	wife	36	F	I.W.			

ENROLLMENT OF NOS. 1 HEREON APPROVED BY THE SECRETARY OF INTERIOR Dec. 12, 1902

1896 Atoka 7299 as Henry James

ENROLLMENT OF NOS. 2 HEREON APPROVED BY THE SECRETARY OF INTERIOR May 21, 1904

Father of 3 children, Chickasaw Roll, Card No. 247
No.1 is husband of Orlener James on Choctaw card #835

No 2 transferred from Choctaw card D 835 April 15.
See decision of March 15, 1904

TRIBAL ENROLLMENT OF PARENTS

Name of Father	Year	County	Name of Mother	Year	County
1 Benj. James	Dead	Non-citizen	Mary James	Dead	Choc. roll
2 J.W. Collins		" "	Nancy Collins	"	Non-citz.

Date of Application for Enrollment.

Sept. 6, 98

RESIDENCE: Chickasaw Nation ~~COUNTY~~.
POST OFFICE: Hunton Ind. Ter.

Choctaw Nation — **Choctaw Roll** (Not Including Freedmen) — CARD NO. — FIELD NO. 43

Dawes' Roll No.	NAME	Relationship to Person First Named	AGE	SEX	BLOOD	TRIBAL ENROLLMENT Year	County	No.
15151	1 Moran, Marmaduke Y 56	First Named	52	M	1/8		Choctaw residing in ~~Chickasaw Dist~~	CCR #2 358
15152	2 " George M 27	son	23	"	1/16		" "	CCR #2 358
15558	3 Simmons, Maude B 20	dau	16	F	1/16		" "	CCR #2 358
15153	4 Nix, Lucinda E 18	"	14	"	1/16		" "	CCR #2 359
15559	5 Simmons, Fay 2	grand dau	1mo	F	1/32			
15154	6 Nix, Mable C. 2	grand dau	2mo	F	1/32			
15560	7 Simmons, Wallace 1	gr. son	3wks	M	1/32			

8
9 Nos 1 and 2 admitted by Act of Choctaw Council approved Nov. 3, 1879
~~No.1 has one son James, not named in Act of Council~~
10 No3 is now the wife of O.E. Simmons, a non citizen
11 No5 Enrolled, November 19th 1900
12 Evidence of marriage between No3 and O.E. Simmons, a non-citizen filed
December 5 1900 For child of No4 see N.B.(Mar 3-1905) card No.21
13 ~~No4 is now the wife of N.C. Nix a non-citizen. Evidence of marriage to be~~
14 supplied. Received and filed May 17, 1901
15 No6 Enrolled May 6, 1901
16 No7 Born July 11, 1902: Enrolled Aug 2, 1902.
17

ENROLLMENT OF NOS. 3,5 and 7 HEREON APPROVED BY THE SECRETARY OF INTERIOR Sep 11 1904

TRIBAL ENROLLMENT OF PARENTS

Name of Father	Year	County	Name of Mother	Year	County
1 Charles Moran	dead	non-citizen	Elizabeth Moran	1896	Blue
2 No.1			Catherine Moran	dead	~~Choctaw residing~~ in Chickasaw Dist
3 No.1			" "	"	" "
4 No.1			" "	"	" "
5 O.E. Simmons		non-citizen	No 3		
6 N.C. Nix		" "	No 4		
7 O.E. Simmons		" "	No 3		

8
9 No 1 in Act of Choctaw Council as Marm a-duke Moran
10 No.2 in Act of Choctaw Council as George Moran
~~No1 on 1894 Choctaw roll, Kiamitia County page 119~~
11 ~~No2 " " " " " " " "~~

ENROLLMENT ~~OF NOS. 1,2-4 and 6~~ HEREON APPROVED BY THE SECRETARY OF INTERIOR Mar. 26, 1904.

Date of Application for Enrollment. Sept. 6/98

No 4 P.O. Jesse I.T. 3/8/05

RESIDENCE: Chickasaw Nation ~~County~~
POST OFFICE: Jesse, Ind. Ter.

Choctaw Nation — Choctaw Roll (Not Including Freedmen) — CARD NO. — FIELD NO. 44

Dawes' Roll No.	NAME	Relationship to Person First Named	AGE	SEX	BLOOD	TRIBAL ENROLLMENT Year	County	No.
15162	1 Thompson, Sarah 22	First Named	18	F	1/16		Choc. residing in Chic. Dist	CCR #2 452
15163	2 " , George L. 2	Son	2wk.	M	1/32			

ENROLLMENT OF NOS. 1, 2 HEREON APPROVED BY THE SECRETARY OF INTERIOR March 26, 1904

Wife of G.P. Thompson white man
~~Daughter of Catherine Moran who was admitted by Act of Council approved Nov. 3, 1879.~~
(See Choctaw card No. 43)

No.2 enrolled Aug. 6, 1900

No.1 on Choctaw census roll No.2 1896, page 452 as Sarah Moran Thompson
~~No.1 is the daughter of Marmaduke Moran who was admitted by act of Choctaw Council, approved Nov. 3, 1879.~~

TRIBAL ENROLLMENT OF PARENTS

Name of Father	Year	County	Name of Mother	Year	County
1 Marmaduke Y. Moran		Choc. residing in Chic. Dist	Catherine Moran	Dead	Choc. residing in Chickasaw Dist
2 Geo. B. Thompson		NonCitizen	No.1		

~~For child of No.1 see NB (Mar 3, 1905) Card # 57~~
" " " " " " " (April 26, 06) " 190

Date of Application for Enrollment. Sept. 6/98

RESIDENCE: Chickasaw Nation ~~XXXXX~~
POST OFFICE: Hunton, Ind. Ter

Choctaw Nation

Choctaw Roll (Not Including Freedmen)

CARD NO.
FIELD NO. 45

Dawes' Roll No.		NAME		Relationship to Person First Named	AGE	SEX	BLOOD	TRIBAL ENROLLMENT Year	County	No.
15159	1	Brady, Selina	28	First Named	24	F	1/16		Choc. residing in Chic. Dist	CCR #2 31
15160	2	" , Bruce M	4	son	11mo	M	1/32			
15161	3	" , Robert Golston	2	son	6wks	M	1/32			
IW 1058	4	" , Robert G.	30	Husb.	30	M	IW			

ENROLLMENT OF NOS. 1,2,3 HEREON APPROVED BY THE SECRETARY OF INTERIOR March 26, 1904

Wife of R.G.brady[sic], white man on Choctaw card #D 482
Selina Brady, nee Moran, admitted by Act of Council Nov. 3, 1897
~~No.1 is on Choctaw census roll No.2, 1896, page 81 as Selina Moran Brady~~
Address now seems to be Jesse I.T. 10/11/1900
No 3 enrolled Oct 12, 1900

ENROLLMENT OF NOS. 4 HEREON APPROVED BY THE SECRETARY OF INTERIOR Nov. 16, 1904

TRIBAL ENROLLMENT OF PARENTS

	Name of Father	Year	County	Name of Mother	Year	County
1	Marmaduke U[sic] Moran		Choc. residing in Chic. Dist	Catherine Moran	Dead	Choc. residing in Chic. Dist
2	R.G. Brady		Non-citizen	No.1		
3	" " "		" "	No.1		
4	Saml. B. Brady	Dead	" "	Elizabeth Brady		U.S. Citz.

No.1 on 1893 Choctaw roll Kiamutia County; page 119 as Selina Moran
No4 transferred from Choctaw card #D-482, Oct 31, 1904: see decision of Oct 15, 1904
For child of No.1 see NB(Apr 26, 06) No. 808
~~" " " No1&4 " " (Mar 3,05) " 163~~

#1
Date of Application for Enrollment. Sept. 6.98

~~No 2 enrolled Dec 14, 99~~

RESIDENCE: Chickasaw Nation ~~XXXXX~~
POST OFFICE: Ada Ind. Ter.

Choctaw Nation

Choctaw Roll (Not Including Freedmen)

CARD NO.
FIELD NO. 46

Dawes' Roll No.		NAME	Relationship to Person First Named	AGE	SEX	BLOOD	TRIBAL ENROLLMENT Year	County	No.
15640	1	Allen, Mary I. 23	First Named	19	F	1/16		Choc. residing in Chic. Dist	CCR #2 24
15641	2	" , Evi Catherine 6	Dau.	2	"	1/32		" "	CCR #2 24
15642	3	" , Jesse Edger 2	Son	2mo	M	1/32			
15643	4	" , Randel M. 4	Son	6mo	M	1/32			

ENROLLMENT OF NOS. 1,2,3,4 HEREON APPROVED BY THE SECRETARY OF INTERIOR Dec 1, 1904

On Choctaw roll as Mary Moran Allen
Daughter of Marmaduke Y. Moran, see Choctaw card No. 43
No.2 admitted in 96 case #1129
~~Husband and one child on Choctaw card No. 3288, Aug.7, 99.~~

Moran family said to be admitted by Act of Council Aug.7,99
Procure certified copy of Act before enrolling. Aug. 7,99
No.3 Enrolled June 8, 1901.

TRIBAL ENROLLMENT OF PARENTS

	Name of Father	Year	County	Name of Mother	Year	County
1	Marmaduke Y. Moran		Choc. residing in Chic. Dist	Catherine Moran	Dead	Chocresidin-g inChic. Dist
2	John C. Allen		NonCitizen	No.1		
3	" " "		" "	No.1		
4	" " "		" "	No.1		

No.4 originally enrolled on Choctaw card No. 3288 Aug. 7, 1899 and transferred to this card Oct. 28, 1902

No.1 born Aug. 7, 1878. See copy of letter filed with records in this case.
For children of No.1 see NB (March 3, 1905L #730.

Date of Application for Enrollment. 1&2 Sept. 6.98.

P.O. Brady I.T. 12/12/02

RESIDENCE: Chickasaw Nation ~~XXXXX~~
POST OFFICE: Pontotoc, Ind. Ter.

Choctaw Nation

Choctaw Roll *(Not Including Freedmen)*

CARD NO.
FIELD NO. 47

Dawes' Roll No.	NAME		Relationship to Person First Named	AGE	SEX	BLOOD	TRIBAL ENROLLMENT Year	County	No.
75	1 Anderson, Mack	24		20	M	1/2		Jack Ford	CCR #2 21
76	2 " , Ella Fry	27	wife	23	F	1/2		Blue	CCR #2 188
77	3 " , Nora	3	dau.	4mo	"	1/2			
78	4 " , Samuel	2	son	2mo	M	1/2			
79	5 " , Rogers[sic]M	1	son	3mo	M	1/2			

ENROLLMENT
OF NOS. 1,2,3,4 & 5 HEREON
APPROVED BY THE SECRETARY
OF INTERIOR ....

~~No.1 1896 Jacks Fork 531~~
No2 1896 Blue 4396 as Ella Fry
No4 enrolled December 3, 1900
~~No5 Born April 2, 1902; Enrolled June 20, 1902.~~
~~For child of Nos.1&2 see NB(March 3, 1905) #1067~~

TRIBAL ENROLLMENT OF PARENTS

	Name of Father	Year	County	Name of Mother	Year	County
1	Sampson Anderson	1897	Pontotoc	Lizzie Anderson		Choc. residing in Chic. Dist
2	Wm. Fry		Blue	Vicey		Blue
3	No.1			No.2		
4	No.1			No.2		
5	No.1			No.2		

1&2
Date of Application for Enrollment.
Sept. 6,98

0[sic] No3 enrolled Oct 6.99

P.O. Connersville[sic] I.T. 4/12/05

RESIDENCE: Chickasaw Nation ~~XXXXXX~~ **Choctaw Nation** **Choctaw Roll** CARD NO.
POST OFFICE: Stonewall, Ind. Ter. *(Not Including Freedmen)* FIELD NO. **48**

Dawes' Roll No.	NAME	Relationship to Person First Named	AGE	SEX	BLOOD	TRIBAL ENROLLMENT Year	County	No.
80	1 Kemp, Sophia Virginia		11	F	1/2		Choc. residing in Chic. Dist	CCR #2 325
	2					1896	Jack Fork	7660
	3							
	4							
	5							
	6	On 1896 roll as Sophia B. Kemp						
	7							
	8							
	9							
	10							
	11							
	12							
	13							
	14							
	15							
	16							
	17							

ENROLLMENT
OF NOS. 1 HEREON
APPROVED BY THE SECRETARY
OF INTERIOR Dec 12, 1902

TRIBAL ENROLLMENT OF PARENTS

	Name of Father	Year	County	Name of Mother	Year	County
1	Dixon Kemp	Dead	Red River	Sarah Kemp		NonCitizen
2						
3						
4						
5						
6						
7						
8						
9						
10						
11						
12						
13						
14						
15						
16						
17						

Date of Application for Enrollment. Sep. 6,98

RESIDENCE: Tobucksy COUNTY. **Choctaw Nation** **Choctaw Roll** *(Not Including Freedmen)* CARD NO.
POST OFFICE: Tandy, Ind. Ter FIELD NO. 49

Dawes' Roll No.	NAME	Relationship to Person First Named	AGE	SEX	BLOOD	TRIBAL ENROLLMENT Year	County	No.
81	1 Johnston Lucretia 37	First Named	33	F	1/2		Tobucksy	CCR #2 280
82	2 " George W 18	son	14	M	3/8		"	"
~~83~~	3 ~~" Richard 14~~ Died prior to September 25, 1902	~~"~~	~~10~~	~~"~~	~~3/8~~		~~"~~	~~"~~
84	4 " Myrtle Belle 13	dau	9	F	3/8		"	"
85	5 " Amelia May 11	"	7	"	3/8		"	"
	6							
	7 ENROLLMENT OF NOS. 1,2,3,4 and 5 HEREON APPROVED BY THE SECRETARY OF INTERIOR Dec 12, 1902							
	8							
	9							
	10							
	11							
	12 No3 died June 7, 1901. Enrollment cancelled by Department, July 8-1904							
	13 No 1 wife of William Johnston Chickasaw Roll Card No. 259							
	14							
	15							
	16							
	17							

TRIBAL ENROLLMENT OF PARENTS

Name of Father	Year	County	Name of Mother	Year	County
1 Fisher Pusley	dead	Choctaw Roll		dead	Choctaw roll
2 William Johnston	1897	Chick residing in Choctaw N.1st Dist	No 1		
3 ~~" "~~	~~1897~~	~~" "~~	~~No 1~~		
4 " "	1897	" "	No 1		
5 " "	1897	" "	No 1		
6					
7 No1 1896 Tobucksy 6655 as Lucretia Johnson					
8 No2 1896 " 6657 " George "					
~~No3 1896 " 6658 " Richard "~~					
9 No4 1896 " 6659 " Myrtle "					
10 No5 1896 " 6660 " Amanda M "					
11 No 3 died June 7, 1901; proof of death filed Nov 12,1902					
12					
13					
14					
15				Date of Application for Enrollment.	
16				Sept 6/98	
17 P. O. Roff I.T. 11/10/02					

Choctaw By Blood Enrollment Cards 1898-1914

RESIDENCE: Chickasaw Nation ~~COUNTY~~.
POST OFFICE: Hurd Ind Ter

Choctaw Nation

Choctaw Roll (*Not Including Freedmen*) CARD NO. FIELD NO. 50

Dawes' Roll No.		NAME		Relationship to Person First Named	AGE	SEX	BLOOD	TRIBAL ENROLLMENT Year	County	No.
IW 59	1	McDaniel, William	48		44	M	I.W.		Atoka	C I Roll 77
86	2	" Lucetta	30	wife	26	F	1/2		"	CCR #2 373
87	3	" Laura	14	dau	10	"	1/4		"	"
88	4	" Alice	12	"	8	"	1/4		"	"
89	5	" Robert	11	Son	7	M	1/4		"	"
90	6	" William	9	"	5	"	1/4		"	"
91	7	" Jesse	8	"	4	"	1/4		"	"
92	8	" Annie	5	Dau	6mo	F	1/4		"	"
~~93~~	9	Died prior to September 25, 1902 ~~" Mary Artemissa~~	~~2~~	~~Dau~~	~~2mo~~	~~F~~	~~1/4~~			
94	10	" Lula	1	Dau	2mo	F	1/4			
	11	Aug 10/99 As to								
	12	marriage of parents of No2 see testimony of S.								
	13	E. Lewis attached to								
	14	card No 3345.								
	15	~~No1 admitted as an intermarried citizen in 1896, Choctaw case #82~~								
	16	no appear.								
	17									

ENROLLMENT OF NOS. 2,3,4,5,6,7,8,9 and 10 HEREON APPROVED BY THE SECRETARY OF INTERIOR Dec. 12, 1902

No10 born Dec. 28, 190" Enrolled Feby 10, 1902
~~Evidence of birth of No8 received and filed Feby 14, 1902~~

ENROLLMENT OF NOS. ~1~ HEREON APPROVED BY THE SECRETARY OF INTERIOR Jun 13 1903

No9 Enrolled May 24, 1900

TRIBAL ENROLLMENT OF PARENTS

	Name of Father	Year	County	Name of Mother	Year	County
1	Samuel McDaniel		non citizen	Annie McDaniel	dead	non citizen
2	Isaac McClure	dead	Choctaw roll	Laura McClure	"	" "
3	No1			No2		
4	No1			No2		
5	No1			No2		
6	No1			No2		
7	No1			No2		
8	No1			No2		
9	~~No1~~			~~No2~~		
10	No1			No2		
11	No1 1896 Atoka 14878 Proof of death of No9 to be supplied					
12	No2 1896 " 9448 as Lucretia McDanial					
13	~~No3 1896 " 9452 " Laura "~~					
13	~~No4 1896 " 9453 " Alice "~~					
14	No5 1896 " 9449 " Robert "					
15	No6 1896 " 9450 " William "					
15	~~No7 1896 " 9451 " Jessie "~~					
16						
17	P.O. address Tyrola, I.T.			For child of Nos 1&2 see NB (Mar 3'05) #557		

~~#1 to 8~~
Date of Application for Enrollment.
~~Sept 6/98~~

No9 died April 27-1900- Enrollment cancelled by Department July 8, 1904

RESIDENCE: Chickasaw Nation ~~XXXXX~~ **Choctaw Nation** **Choctaw Roll** (Not Including Freedmen) CARD NO.
POST OFFICE: Allen Ind. Ter. FIELD NO. 51

Dawes' Roll No.	NAME	Relationship to Person First Named	AGE	SEX	BLOOD	TRIBAL ENROLLMENT Year	County	No.
DEAD	1 Fry, Elijah DEAD	First Named	37	M	1/2		Choc. residing in Chic. Dist	CCR #2 ~~188~~
Void	2 ~~" , Mary~~	~~wife~~	~~17~~	~~F~~	~~Full~~		~~" " "~~	~~CCR #2 402~~
Void	3 ~~Peyton, Philip~~	~~Bro in law~~	~~21~~	~~M~~	~~"~~		~~" " "~~	~~"~~
	4				No1	1896	Blue 4416	
	5 ~~No1 DISMISSED~~				No.2	1896	" 10499 as Mary	Payton
	6 Feb. 28, 1907				~~No.3~~	~~1896~~	~~" 10498 as Philip~~	~~Payton~~
	7							
	8							
	9							
	10							
	11							
	12							
	13							
	14							
	15							
	16							
	17							

~~No 2 & 3 have been placed on Card No 2813~~

No 2 has been deserted by No.1 and asked that she and her brother be placed on seperate[sic] cards from that of her husband.
~~Change made June 19, 99~~

Proof of death requested 7/3/05

TRIBAL ENROLLMENT OF PARENTS

	Name of Father	Year	County	Name of Mother	Year	County
1	Jim Fry	Dead	Chickasaw roll	Winnie Fry	Dead	Choc. roll
2	~~Daniel Peyton~~		~~Blue~~	~~Sophie Peyton~~	"	~~Blue~~
3	~~" "~~		~~"~~	~~" "~~	~~"~~	~~"~~
4						
5						
6						
7						
8						
9						
10						
11						
12						
13						
14						
15						
16						
17						

Date of Application ~~for Enrollment.~~ ~~Sept. 6, 98~~

RESIDENCE: Atoka COUNTY. **Choctaw Nation** **Choctaw Roll** *(Not Including Freedmen)* CARD NO.
POST OFFICE: Conway Ind. Ter. FIELD NO. 52

Dawes' Roll No.	NAME	Relationship to Person First Named	AGE	SEX	BLOOD	TRIBAL ENROLLMENT Year	County	No.
95	1 Goer, William 42	First Named	38	M	1/2		Atoka	CCR #2 212
	2							
	3 ENROLLMENT OF NOS. 1 HEREON					1896	Atoka	4968
	4 APPROVED BY THE SECRETARY							
	5 OF INTERIOR Dec. 12, 1902							
	6							
	7 Husband of Mary Goer, Chickasaw roll, Crad[sic] No. 276							
	8							
	9							
	10							
	11							
	12							
	13							
	14							
	15							
	16							
	17							

TRIBAL ENROLLMENT OF PARENTS

Name of Father	Year	County	Name of Mother	Year	County
1 Will Goer	Dead	NonCitizen	Jane Goer	Dead	Choc. roll
2					
3					
4					
5					
6					
7					
8					
9					
10					
11					
12					
13					
14					
15					
16			Date of Application for Enrollment.		Sept. 7/98
17					

RESIDENCE: Tobucksy COUNTY. POST OFFICE: Kiowa, Ind. Ter.

Choctaw Nation

Choctaw Roll *(Not Including Freedmen)* CARD No. FIELD No. 53

Dawes' Roll No.	NAME	Relationship to Person First Named	AGE	SEX	BLOOD	TRIBAL ENROLLMENT Year	County	No.
96	1 Colbert, Mary E. 23	First Named	19	F	1/4		Tobueksy[sic]	CCR #2 464
97	2 " , Theodore W Jr 3	Son	1 wk	M	1/8			
98	3 " , Velma 1	Dau.	3mo	F	1/8			
	4							
	5					1896	Tobucksy	13018
	6							

ENROLLMENT OF NOS. 1, 2 & 3 HEREON APPROVED BY THE SECRETARY OF INTERIOR Dec. 12, 1902

On Choctaw roll as Mary E. Ward wife of Theodore Colbert, Chickasaw roll, card No. 283.

No.2 Affidavit of birth to be supplied: Recd Oct. 6, 99
No3 Born Nov. 22, 1901: enrolled Feby, 24, 1902

For child of No.1 see NB(March 3, 1905) Card #71

No 2 enrolled Sept. 4, 99

TRIBAL ENROLLMENT OF PARENTS

	Name of Father	Year	County	Name of Mother	Year	County
1	Charles Ward		Tobueksy[sic]	Mollie Ward (IW)	Dead	Tobueksy
2	Theodore Colbert Sr.		Chic. Roll	No.1		
3	" " "		" "	No.1		

Date of Application for Enrollment. #1 Sept. 7, 98

RESIDENCE: Atoka COUNTY. **Choctaw Nation** **Choctaw Roll** (Not Including Freedmen) CARD NO.
POST OFFICE: Guertie Ind. Ter FIELD NO. **54**

Dawes' Roll No.		NAME	Relationship to Person First Named	AGE	SEX	BLOOD	TRIBAL ENROLLMENT Year	County	No.
99	1	Lawrence, S.S. 56		52	M	1/4		Atoka	CCR #2 341
	2								
	3	ENROLLMENT OF NOS. 1 HEREON APPROVED BY THE SECRETARY OF INTERIOR Dec. 12, 1902							
	4						1896	Atoka	8291
	5								
	6								
	7								
	8								
	9	Father of Anna Isabelle Lawrence, Chickasaw Roll, Card No. 286							
	10	Husband of Sinie " " " " " 286							
	11								
	12								
	13								
	14								
	15								
	16								
	17								

TRIBAL ENROLLMENT OF PARENTS

	Name of Father	Year	County	Name of Mother	Year	County
1	David Lawrence	Dead	NonCitizen	Mary Fisher	Dead	Choctaw roll
2						
3						
4						
5						
6						
7						
8						
9				Date of Application for Enrollment.	Sept. 7, 98	
10						
11						
12						
13						
14						
15						
16						
17						

RESIDENCE: Chickasaw Nation COUNTY. **Choctaw Nation** **Choctaw Roll** *(Not Including Freedmen)* CARD NO.
POST OFFICE: Roff, Ind. Ter. FIELD NO. 55

Dawes' Roll No.		NAME	Relationship to Person First Named	AGE	SEX	BLOOD	TRIBAL ENROLLMENT Year	County	No.
Refus-ed	1	~~Jones, Clay H.~~	~~Named~~	~~27~~	~~M~~	~~I.W.~~		~~Choc. residing in Chic. Dist~~	~~C I Roll 53~~
100	2	" , Pearl	wife	21	F	1/8			CCR #2 309
DEAD	3	~~" , Anna Madge~~ DEAD	~~dau.~~	~~15mo~~	~~F~~	~~1/16~~			
101	4	" , Charles R.	son	3mo	M	1/16			

ENROLLMENT OF NOS. 2 and 4 HEREON APPROVED BY THE SECRETARY OF INTERIOR Dec. 12, 1902

~~No. 3 HERON[sic] DISMISSED UNDER ORDER OF THE COMMISSION TO THE FIVE CIVILIZED TRIBES OF MARCH 31, 1905~~

~~No2 1896 Chickasaw Dist. 7370 as Zukkie Pearl Jones~~
~~No.2 on Choctaw roll as Zueleika P. Jones~~
No.4 Enrolled Sept. 22, 1900
No.3 is dead. See letter of No.1 filed Aug. 11, 1900
No. 3 died April 13, 1899; proof of death filed Nov. 14, 1902.
~~No.1 Refused: see Decision of July 30, 1903.~~

TRIBAL ENROLLMENT OF PARENTS

	Name of Father	Year	County	Name of Mother	Year	County
1	~~Rufus Jones~~		~~NonCitizen~~	~~Emily Jones~~	~~Dead~~	~~Non-Citz.~~
2	Joe Roff		Choc. residing in Chic. Dist	Anna Roff	"	Choc. residing in Chic. Dist
3	~~No.1~~			~~No 2~~		
4	No.1			No.2		

~~Decision of Commission refusing enrollment of No.1 affirmed by Secty. of Interior,~~
Nov. 14, 1903 (I.T.D. 7280-1903)
Nov. 30, 1903 Applicant and attorneys for Choctaw and Chickasaw nations[sic] notified of Departmental action

Date of Application for Enrollment. ~~Sept. 7.98~~

P.O. Bokchito, I.T. 1/3/03

RESIDENCE: Chickasaw Nation ~~xxxxx~~ **Choctaw Nation** **Choctaw Roll** (*Not Including Freedmen*) CARD NO.
POST OFFICE: Waupanuka Ind. Ter. FIELD NO. **56**

Dawes' Roll No.		NAME	Relationship to Person First Named	AGE	SEX	BLOOD	TRIBAL ENROLLMENT Year	County	No.
102	1	Riley, Joanna	First Named	9	F	3/8		Choc. residing in Chic. Dist	CCR #2 415
	2								
	3	ENROLLMENT					1896	Atoka	10989
	4	OF NOS. 1 HEREON APPROVED BY THE SECRETARY							
	5	OF INTERIOR Dec. 12, 1902							
	6								
	7	10989 Choctaw 1896 roll shows Mrs. Sallie Howell is the guardian is No.1							
	8								
	9								
	10								
	11								
	12								
	13								
	14								
	15								
	16								
	17								

TRIBAL ENROLLMENT OF PARENTS

	Name of Father	Year	County	Name of Mother	Year	County
1	Joseph H. Riley	Dead	Choctaw roll	Sally Howell		NonCitz.
2						
3						
4						
5						
6						
7				Date of Application		
8				for Enrollment.		Sept. 7,98
9						
10						
11						
12						
13						
14						
15						
16						
17						

Choctaw By Blood Enrollment Cards 1898-1914

RESIDENCE: Chickasaw Nation COUNTY. **Choctaw Nation** **Choctaw Roll** (*Not Including Freedmen*) CARD NO.
POST OFFICE: Palmer, Ind. Ter. FIELD NO. 57

Dawes' Roll No.	NAME	Relationship to Person First Named	AGE	SEX	BLOOD	TRIBAL ENROLLMENT Year	County	No.
103	1 McClung, Wm. Oscar	First Named	28	M	1/16		Choc. residing in Chic. Dist	CCR #2 375
IW1059	2 " " Willie	wife	32	F	IW			C. I. Roll 77
104	DIED PRIOR TO SEPT 25 1902 3 ~~" " Lena~~	~~dau.~~	~~3~~	~~"~~	~~1/32~~			CCR #2 375
105	4 " " , Clarence M.	son	1	M	1/32			
106	5 " " , Fannie Dell	dau.	3mo	F	1/32			

ENROLLMENT OF NOS. 1,3,4 & 5 HEREON APPROVED BY THE SECRETARY OF INTERIOR Dec. 12, 1902

~~No.1 1896 Chickasaw Dist 9499 as Oscar McClung~~
No.2 1896 " " 14884
No.3 1896 " " 9504

Evidence of marriage of Nos.1 and 2 and evidence of birth of No.4; received and filed Aug. 18, 1900

ENROLLMENT OF NOS. 2 HEREON APPROVED BY THE SECRETARY OF INTERIOR Nov. 16, 1904

TRIBAL ENROLLMENT OF PARENTS

	Name of Father	Year	County	Name of Mother	Year	County
1	L.M. McClung (IW)		Choc. residing in Chic. Dist	Emma McClung		Choc. residing in Chic. Dist
2	Howard	Dead	NonCitizen	Lizzie Howard		NonCitz.
3	~~No.1~~			~~No.2~~		
4	No.1			No.2		
5	No.1			No.2		

~~Take no further action relative to the~~ enrollment of No2. Protest of Choctaw and Chickasaw Nations, Jun 23, 1904.

~~No.3 Died March 25, 1899, proof of death filed Oct. 20, 1902~~
No.3 died March 25, 1899: Enrollemnt[sic] cancelled by Department July 8, 1904.

Date of Application for Enrollment. Sept. 7, 98

No 5 enrolled May 24, 1900

P.O. Rush Springs I.T. 1/3/03

RESIDENCE: Chickasaw Nation ~~COUNTY~~: XXXXX
POST OFFICE: Palmer, Ind. Ter.

Choctaw Nation

Choctaw Roll (Not Including Freedmen)

CARD NO.
FIELD NO. 58

Dawes' Roll No.		NAME	Relationship to Person First Named	AGE	SEX	BLOOD	TRIBAL ENROLLMENT Year	County	No.
IW	1	Carr, Daniel H.		51	M	IW		Choc. residing in Chic. Dist	ClRoll 19
107	2	" , Lillie McClung	wife	25	F	1/16		" " "	CCR #2 125
108	3	" , James Henry	son	9	M	1/32		" " "	"
109	4	" , Wesley	"	7	M	1/32		" " "	"
110	5	" , Annie	dau.	1mo	F	1/32			
111	6	" , George William	son	1mo	M	1/32			

ENROLLMENT OF NOS. 2,3,4,5 & 6 HEREON APPROVED BY THE SECRETARY OF INTERIOR ....

No1 admitted by Act of Council, Dec. 24, 1889; also admitted by Dawes Commission, case No. 1259.

ENROLLMENT OF NOS. 1 HEREON APPROVED BY THE SECRETARY OF INTERIOR ....

TRIBAL ENROLLMENT OF PARENTS

	Name of Father	Year	County	Name of Mother	Year	County
1	Andrew Carr	Dead	NonCitizen	Annie Carr	Dead	NonCitz.
2	L.M. McClung (IW)		Choc. residing in Chic. Dist	Emmer[sic] McClung		Choc. residing in Chic. Dist
3	No.1			No.2		
4	No.1			No.2		
5	No.1			No.2		
6	No.1			No.2		

No 1 1896 Chick. Dist, 14437 as D.H. Carr
No.2 1896 " " 3109
No.3 1896 " " 3110 as Henry Carr
No.4 1896 " " 3111
No.6 born Nov. 9, 1901: Enrolled Dec 2, 1901
For child of Nos. 1 and 2 see NB(March 3, 1905) #741

#1 to 4 incl.
Date of Application for Enrollment. Sept. 7,98

No 5 enrolled Oct 6,99

RESIDENCE: Chickasaw Nation ~~COUNTY~~.
POST OFFICE: Roff, Ind Ter

Choctaw Nation

Choctaw Roll *(Not Including Freedmen)*

CARD NO.
FIELD NO. 59

Dawes' Roll No.	NAME	Relationship to Person First Named	AGE	SEX	BLOOD	TRIBAL ENROLLMENT Year	County	No.
112	1 Taylor, John 28	First Named	24	M	1/8		Choctaw residing in Chickasaw Dist	CCR #2 452
IW 1599	2 " Cora	wife	21	F	I.W.			
	3					1896	Chickasaw Dist	12550
	4							
	5							
	6							
	7							
	8							
	9							
	10							
	11							
	12							
	13							
	14							
	15							
	16							
	17							

ENROLLMENT
OF NOS. 1 HEREON
APPROVED BY THE SECRETARY
OF INTERIOR Dec. 12, 1902

ENROLLMENT
OF NOS. ~ 2 ~ HEREON
APPROVED BY THE SECRETARY
OF INTERIOR Feb. 12, 1907

~~For child of No.1 See N.B.(Apr. 26, 1906) card No. 191~~
" " " " " " " (March 3, 1905) " " 801

No2 placed hereon under order of the Commissioner to the Five Civilized Tribes ~~of Dec. 21-1906 holding that application was made for her enrollment within the time provided by the Act of Congress approved April 26-1906~~

TRIBAL ENROLLMENT OF PARENTS

Name of Father	Year	County	Name of Mother	Year	County
1 Jackson Taylor	dead	Wolf	Rebecca Croso[sic] Taylor	Dead	Wolf
2 Brandon	dead	Non Citz	Brandon	Dead	non citz
3					
4					
5					
6					
7					
8					
9					
10					
11					
12					
13					
14					
15					
16			Date of Application for Enrollment.		Sept. 7/98
17					

RESIDENCE: Chickasaw Nation ~~xxxxx~~
POST OFFICE: Roff Ind. Ter.

Choctaw Nation

Choctaw Roll *(Not Including Freedmen)*

CARD NO.
FIELD NO. **60**

Dawes' Roll No.		NAME	Relationship to Person First Named	AGE	SEX	BLOOD	TRIBAL ENROLLMENT		
							Year	County	No.
IW188	1	Cushman, Charles A	Named	32	M	IW		Choc. residing in Chic. Dist	
113	2	" , Artie M	wife	22	F	1/8		" " "	CCR #2 127
~~114~~	3	~~" , Bettie Lee~~	~~dau~~	~~4~~	~~F~~	~~1/16~~		~~" " "~~	~~"~~
~~115~~	4	~~" , Oliver Edgar~~	~~son~~	~~3~~	~~M~~	~~1/16~~		~~" " "~~	
116	5	" , Earnest	"	5mo	M	1/16			
117	6	" , Elvira	dau	6wk	F	1/16			
118	7	" , Glenn	son	3wk	M	1/16			

ENROLLMENT OF NOS. 2,3,4,5,6 &7 HEREON APPROVED BY THE SECRETARY OF INTERIOR Dec. 12, 1902

No.2 on Choctaw Roll as Artie Jones Cushman
No.3 " " " " Betsey "
~~No.4 " " " " Oliver "~~

~~No.3 died June 27, 1899; No.4 died June 26, 1899. Enrollment cancelled by Department July 8, 1904.~~

ENROLLMENT OF NOS. 1 HEREON APPROVED BY THE SECRETARY OF INTERIOR Dec. 24, 1903

TRIBAL ENROLLMENT OF PARENTS

	Name of Father	Year	County	Name of Mother	Year	County
1	O.P. Cushman		NonCitizen	Harriet Cushman	Dead	NonCitz.
2	Jackson Taylor		Wolf	Rebecca Cross Taylor		Wolf
3	~~No.1~~			~~No.2~~		
4	~~No.1~~			~~No. 2~~		
5	No.1			No.2		
6	No.1			No.2		
7	No.1			No.2		

Date of Application for Enrollment.
Sept. 7/98

~~No.2 1896 Chickasaw Dis. 3112 as C. Jones Cushman~~
~~No.3 1896 " " 3113 as Betsy "~~
No4 1896 " " 3114 as Oliver "

For child of No.1&2 see NB(Mar 3, 05) #362

No.7 Born June 14, 1902: Enrolled July 3, 1902
~~No.6 Enrolled November 12, 1900~~

~~No3 Died June 27, 1899; proof of death filed Nov. 14, 1902~~

~~Evidence of birth of No.5 received and filed Feby. 13, 1902~~ ~~N.4 died June 26, 1899; proof of death filed Nov. 14, 1902~~

RESIDENCE: Chickasaw Nation ~~XXXXX~~ **Choctaw Nation** **Choctaw Roll** *(Not Including Freedmen)* CARD No.
POST OFFICE: Victor, Ind. Ter. FIELD No. **61**

Dawes' Roll No.		NAME		Relationship to Person First Named	AGE	SEX	BLOOD	TRIBAL ENROLLMENT Year	County	No.
15034	1	Victor, Alfred	59	First Named	55	M	1/4		Choc. residing in Chic. Dist	CCR #2 455
	2							1893	Chickasaw Dist.	Page 63
	3									
	4	No.1 also on 1897 Chickasaw roll, page 81 as an								
	5	intermarried Chickasaw Dec. 5, 1900								
	6									
	7									
	8	No.1 is husband of Mary J. Victor, Choctaw card No. 3262								
	9									
	10									
	11									
	12									
	13									
	14	ENROLLMENT OF NOS. 1 HEREON								
	15	APPROVED BY THE SECRETARY								
	16	OF INTERIOR Feb. 16, 1904								
	17									

TRIBAL ENROLLMENT OF PARENTS

	Name of Father	Year	County	Name of Mother	Year	County
1	John Victor	Dead	NonCitizen	Ellen Victor	Dead	Red River
2						
3						
4						
5						
6						
7						
8						
9						
10						
11						
12						
13						
14						
15	~~Franks I.T.~~					
16	Roff I.T. 6/19/03			Date of Application for Enrollment.		
17						Sept. 7, 1898

RESIDENCE: Chickasaw Nation ~~County~~.
POST OFFICE: Waupanuka, I.T.

Choctaw Nation

Choctaw Roll *(Not Including Freedmen)*

CARD NO.
FIELD NO. **62**

Dawes' Roll No.		NAME	Relationship to Person First Named	AGE	SEX	BLOOD	TRIBAL ENROLLMENT Year	County	No.
void	1	James, McKee	Named	48	M	1/2			
void	2	" Rhoena	wife	40	F	Full			
void	3	" Edward W.	son	19	M	3/4			
void	4	" Mary Ann	Dau	18	F	3/4			
void	5	" Benj. D.	son	14	M	3/4			
void	6	" Frank	"	12	"	3/4			
void	7	" Jesse	"	10	"	3/4			
void	8	" Elsie A.	Dau	17	F	3/4	1893	Atoka	566
	9								
	10								
	11	Sept.4, '99, No.4 has been placed on Card No. 1551 with husband, Stephen L. Taylor.							
	12	Nos. 1,2,3,5,6 and 7 transferred to Chickasaw card #1588=Oct. 11, 1902.							
	13	No.8 transferred to Chickasaw card #1588, May 14, 1903.							
	14								
	15								
	16								
	17								

CANCELLED

And transferred to Chickasaw Card #1588 May 14, 1903.

TRIBAL ENROLLMENT OF PARENTS

	Name of Father	Year	County	Name of Mother	Year	County
1	Robison James	Dead	Chickasaw Roll	Mary James	Dead	Gaines
2	David Perkins		Choctaw "	Elsie Perkins		Blue
3	No. 1			No. 2		
4	No. 1			No. 2		
5	No. 1			No. 2		
6	No. 1			No. 2		
7	No. 1			No. 2		
8	No. 1			No. 2		
9	All above on Chickasaw Roll, Pontotoc Co. P.51 transferred to Choctaw Roll,					
10	by Dawes Commission					
11	No.3 on Chickasaw Roll as Edward					
12	No.4 " " " " Mary					
12	No.7 " " " " Jessie					
13	No.8 on 1893 Pay Roll, P.54, No. 566, Atoka					
14	County, as Elsy Ann James					
15	No.8 Enrolled Sept 21, 1899.					Date of Application for Enrollment.
16						Sept 7,98
17						

RESIDENCE: Tobucksy COUNTY. **Choctaw Nation** **Choctaw Roll** *(Not Including Freedmen)* CARD NO.
POST OFFICE: ~~Stewart~~, Ind. Ter Stuart FIELD NO. **63**

Dawes' Roll No.	NAME	Relationship to Person First Named	AGE	SEX	BLOOD	TRIBAL ENROLLMENT Year	County	No.
119	Wade, Icey [44]	First Named	40	F	1/2		Tobucksy	CCR #2 463
120	Wright, Frances [21]	Dau.	17	F	1/2			"
121	" , Palmar[sic] [3]	Gr.son	2 3/4	M	3/4			
122	" , Mary [1]	Gr.dau	9mo	F	3/4			
	ENROLLMENT OF NOS. 1,2,3,4 HEREON APPROVED BY THE SECRETARY OF INTERIOR Dec. 12, 1902				No.1	1896	Tobucksy	12998
					No 2	1896	"	12999

No.1 wife of Alemos F. Wade, Chickasaw roll card No. 321

No.2 is the wife of Eslam Wright on Choctaw card # 4656
No.3 Born Nov. 24, 1899; enrolled Aug.6, 1902
No.4 Born Nov. 11, 1901; enrolled Aug 6, 1902

TRIBAL ENROLLMENT OF PARENTS

	Name of Father	Year	County	Name of Mother	Year	County
1		Dead	Chickasaw Roll		Dead	Choc. roll
2	Alemos F. Wade		" "	No.1		
3	Eslam Wright	1896	Atoka	No.2		
4	" "	1896	"	No.2		

Date of Application for Enrollment. ~~Nos.1&2~~
Sept. 7/98

RESIDENCE: Atoka COUNTY. **Choctaw Nation** Choctaw Roll (Not Including Freedmen) CARD NO.
POST OFFICE: Guertie, Ind. Ter FIELD NO. 64

Dawes' Roll No.	NAME	Relationship to Person First Named	AGE	SEX	BLOOD	TRIBAL ENROLLMENT Year	County	No.
Void	1 ~~Leader, Susan~~		~~29~~	~~F~~	~~Full~~		~~Atoka~~	CCR #2 342
	2							
	3					1896	Atoka	8331
	4							
	5							
	6							
	7							
	8 Transferred to Card 4814. Sept. 15th, 1899							
	9							
	10							
	11							
	12							
	13							
	14							
	15							
	16							
	17							

CANCELLED

TRIBAL ENROLLMENT OF PARENTS

Name of Father	Year	County	Name of Mother	Year	County
1 ~~Tecumseh Leader~~	~~Dead~~	~~Atoka~~	~~Salina Leader~~	~~Dead~~	~~Atoka~~
2					
3					
4					
5					
6					
7					
8					
9					
10					
11					
12					
13					
14					
15					
16					
17					

Date of Application for Enrollment.
Sept. 7,98

RESIDENCE: Chickasaw Nation ~~COUNTY~~ XXXXX **Choctaw Nation** **Choctaw Roll** *(Not Including Freedmen)* CARD NO.
POST OFFICE: Stonewall Ind. Ter. FIELD NO. 65

Dawes' Roll No.		NAME	Relationship to Person First Named	AGE	SEX	BLOOD	TRIBAL ENROLLMENT Year	County	No.
	1	~~Byrd, Susan F.~~	~~Named~~	~~54~~	~~F~~	~~1/2~~		Choc. Residing in Chic. Dist	~~CCR #2 82~~
	2								
	3								
	4								
	5								
	6								
	7								
	8								
	9								
	10								
	11								
	12								
	13								
	14								
	15								
	16								
	17								

CANCELLED

Wife of William L. Byrd, Chickasaw roll card No. 323

Dec. 5,99. Also on 1896 roll as Susan Boyd
Page 49, No. 2024, Chick. Dist.

~~No.1 also on Chickasaw roll, Page 80 as~~
Susan F. Byrd June 5, 1900

TRIBAL ENROLLMENT OF PARENTS

	Name of Father	Year	County	Name of Mother	Year	County
1	~~David Folsom~~	~~Dead~~	~~Choctaw roll~~	~~Jane Folsom~~	~~Dead~~	~~Choc. roll~~
2						
3						
4						
5						
6						
7						
8						
9						
10						
11						
12						
13						
14						
15						
16						
17						

CANCELLED

Transferred to Chickasaw card #1665 Feb. 25, 1903

Date of Application for Enrollment. Sept. 7,98

RESIDENCE: Tobucksy COUNTY. **Choctaw Nation** Choctaw Roll *(Not Including Freedmen)* CARD NO.
POST OFFICE: Stewart, Ind. Ter. FIELD NO. 66

Dawes' Roll No.	NAME	Relationship to Person First Named	AGE	SEX	BLOOD	TRIBAL ENROLLMENT Year	County	No.
123	1 Ott, Carney		23	M	3/4		Tobucksy	CCR #2 386
	2							
	3					1896	Tobucksy	9918

ENROLLMENT
OF NOS. 1 HEREON
APPROVED BY THE SECRETARY
OF INTERIOR Dec. 12, 1902

Husband of Eliza Wade Ott, Chickasaw roll, Card No. 327.

~~For child of No.1 see NB (Apr 26/06) card #766~~
" " " " " Chick. NB(Mar 3,05) card #516.

TRIBAL ENROLLMENT OF PARENTS

Name of Father	Year	County	Name of Mother	Year	County
1 Alfred Ott		Gaines	Icey Wade		Tobucksy

Date of Application for Enrollment. Sep. 7,98

RESIDENCE: Atoka COUNTY. **Choctaw Nation** **Choctaw Roll** (Not Including Freedmen) CARD NO.
POST OFFICE: Allen Ind. Ter. FIELD NO. 67

Dawes' Roll No.	NAME	Relationship to Person First Named	AGE	SEX	BLOOD	TRIBAL ENROLLMENT Year	County	No.
14474	1 Wolfe, Rachel 49	First Named	45	F	Full		Atoka	CCR #2 486
VOID.	2 " , Alum	Son	12	M	1/2			
VOID.	3 " , Chiminayne	Dau	10	F	1/2			
	4							
	5				No 1	1896	Atoka	14027

ENROLLMENT
OF NOS. 1 HEREON
APPROVED BY THE SECRETARY
OF INTERIOR MAY 20 1903

No.1 wife of Mose Wolfe, Chickasaw Roll, Card No 329
Nos 2 and 3 on Chickasaw roll, Pontotoc County, Page 97, transferred to Choctaw roll by Dawes Commission
No.3 on Chickasaw Roll, as "Chimmie"

TRIBAL ENROLLMENT OF PARENTS

Name of Father	Year	County	Name of Mother	Year	County
1 Sun-tom-by	Dead	Choctaw Roll		Dead	Choctaw Roll
2 Mose Wolfe		Chickasaw Roll	No. 1		
3 " "		" "	No. 1		

Date of Application for Enrollment. Sept. 7/98

Choctaw By Blood Enrollment Cards 1898-1914

RESIDENCE: Chickasaw Nation ~~xxxxx~~
POST OFFICE: Waldon, Ind. Ter.

Choctaw Nation

Choctaw Roll (Not Including Freedmen)

CARD NO.
FIELD NO. 68

Dawes' Roll No.	NAME	Relationship to Person First Named	AGE	SEX	BLOOD	TRIBAL ENROLLMENT Year	County	No.
D.P.	1 ~~Carter, Lawrence~~ Florence	First Named	~~24~~	~~M~~	~~1/4~~		~~Choc. residing in Chic. Dist~~	~~CCR #2 127~~

Granted as Chickasaw transfer to Chickasaw card

No1 also on 1896 Chickasaw roll, page 86, Pickens County as Lawrence Carter
He is a full brother of Ida Womack, Choctaw card #190.
~~No.1 as Florence Carter on 1893 Chick. roll No.2, page 53~~
See affidavit of 9/15/04

TRIBAL ENROLLMENT OF PARENTS

Name of Father	Year	County	Name of Mother	Year	County
1 ~~Eli Carter~~	~~Dead~~	~~NonCitizen~~	~~Mary Carter~~	~~Dead~~	~~Chic. resd. in Choc. Dist~~

CANCELLED and transferred to Chickasaw card #1779, Oct. 31, 1904

~~Date of Application for Enrollment.~~ Sept. 8, 98

Take no further action relative to enrollment of No.1. Protest of Attys. for Choctaw & Chickasaw ~~Nations Jan. 23, 1904~~

Choctaw By Blood Enrollment Cards 1898-1914

RESIDENCE: Atoka COUNTY.
POST OFFICE: Oconee Ind. Ter.

Choctaw Nation

Choctaw Roll *(Not Including Freedmen)*

CARD NO.
FIELD NO. 69

Dawes' Roll No.	NAME	Relationship to Person First Named	AGE	SEX	BLOOD	TRIBAL ENROLLMENT Year	County	No.
124	1 Perkins, Albert	First Named	24	M	Full	1893	Atoka	Pg. 86 #853
	2							
	3							
	4							
	5							
	6							
	7							
	8							
	9							
	10							
	11							
	12							
	13							
	14							
	15							
	16							
	17							

ENROLLMENT
OF NOS. 1 HEREON
APPROVED BY THE SECRETARY
OF INTERIOR Dec 12, 1902

Husband of Jane Perkins, Chickasaw roll, card No. 354
No.1 also on 1896 CCR#2, page 403
Duplication of Choctaw card # 3966

TRIBAL ENROLLMENT OF PARENTS

	Name of Father	Year	County	Name of Mother	Year	County
1	Simon Perkins	Dead	Blue		Dead	Atoka
2						
3						
4						
5						
6						
7						
8						
9						
10						
11						
12						
13						
14						
15						
16						
17						

Date of Application for Enrollment. Sep. 8,98

RESIDENCE: Atoka COUNTY. **Choctaw Nation** Choctaw Roll (Not Including Freedmen) CARD NO.
POST OFFICE: Citra, I.T. FIELD NO. 70

Dawes' Roll No.	NAME	Relationship to Person First Named	AGE	SEX	BLOOD	TRIBAL ENROLLMENT Year	County	No.
125	1 Meshontambi, Louisa [47]	First Named	43	F	Full	1896	Atoka	8851
126	2 " Francis [18]	Dau	14	"	3/4	1893	Chick Dist.	412

ENROLLMENT OF NOS. 1 and 2 HEREON APPROVED BY THE SECRETARY OF INTERIOR Dec 12 1902

No.1 on 1896 roll as Lewis Mishontambe
No.2 " 1893 Pay Roll, Chickasaw Dist
Page 42 No. 412 as Sis Mishontambe.

TRIBAL ENROLLMENT OF PARENTS

	Name of Father	Year	County	Name of Mother	Year	County
1	Meshontambi	Dead	Atoka		Dead	Choctaw Roll
2	Abel Peter	"	Chick. Roll	No. 1		

Date of Application for Enrollment.
Sept. 8/98

RESIDENCE: Atoka COUNTY. **Choctaw Nation** **Choctaw Roll** *(Not Including Freedmen)* CARD NO.
POST OFFICE: Coalgate, Ind. Ter. FIELD NO. 71

Dawes' Roll No.	NAME	Relationship to Person First Named	AGE	SEX	BLOOD	TRIBAL ENROLLMENT Year	County	No.
127	1 England, Hannah	First Named	20	F	1/8		Atoka	CCR #2 162
	2 " , George	husb.	26	M	IW			
	3							
	4					1896	Atoka	3818

ENROLLMENT OF NOS. 1 HEREON APPROVED BY THE SECRETARY OF INTERIOR Dec. 12, 1902

ENROLLMENT OF NOS. 2 HEREON APPROVED BY THE SECRETARY OF INTERIOR Jun 13, 1903

Also on Choctaw Census record No.1 Page 92
Wife of George England, U.S. Citizen
~~No.1 is the wife of George England on Choctaw card # D 419~~
No 2 transferred from Choctaw card #D419. See decision of May 1, 1903.

No.1 Descendant of Mary M. Spain who was admitted by act of Choctaw Council of Oct. 31, 1877.

TRIBAL ENROLLMENT OF PARENTS

Name of Father	Year	County	Name of Mother	Year	County
1 William Spain	Dead	Choctaw Roll	Louisa Spain		NonCitz.
2 B.F. England		Non-Citz.	Ellen England		" "

Date of Application for Enrollment. Sept. 8, 98

RESIDENCE: Atoka COUNTY.
POST OFFICE: Guertie, Ind. Ter

Choctaw Nation

Choctaw Roll *(Not Including Freedmen)*

CARD NO.
FIELD NO. 72

Dawes' Roll No.	NAME	Relationship to Person First Named	AGE	SEX	BLOOD	TRIBAL ENROLLMENT Year	County	No.
128	1 Leader, Morris	First Named	40	W[sic]	Full		Atoka	CCR #2 343
	2							
	3					1896	Atoka	8340
	4							
	5							
	6							
	7							
	8							
	9							
	10							
	11							
	12							
	13							
	14							
	15							
	16							
	17							

ENROLLMENT
OF NOS. 1 HEREON
APPROVED BY THE SECRETARY
OF INTERIOR Dec. 12, 1902

Husband of Susan Leader, Chickasaw Roll Card No. 357

TRIBAL ENROLLMENT OF PARENTS

	Name of Father	Year	County	Name of Mother	Year	County
1	Tecumseh Leader	Dead	Atoka	Salina		Atoka
2						
3						
4						
5						
6						
7						
8						
9						
10						
11						
12						
13						
14						
15						
16						
17						

Date of Application for Enrollment. Sept. 8/98

RESIDENCE: Chickasaw Nation XXXXX
POST OFFICE: Purcell Ind. Ter.

Choctaw Nation

Choctaw Roll *(Not Including Freedmen)*

CARD NO.
FIELD NO. 73

Dawes' Roll No.	NAME	Relationship to Person First Named	AGE	SEX	BLOOD	TRIBAL ENROLLMENT Year	County	No.
129	1 Murray, Alzira		49	F	1/8		Choc. residing in Chic. Dist	CCR #2 359
130	2 " , Erin	Dau	17	F	1/16		" " "	"
131	3 " , Lula	"	15	F	1/16		" " "	"
~~132~~	4 ~~" , Ila~~	~~"~~	~~12~~	~~F~~	~~1/16~~		~~" " "~~	~~"~~
~~133~~	5 ~~" , Mamie~~	~~"~~	~~9~~	~~F~~	~~1/16~~		~~" " "~~	~~"~~
	6							
	7							
	8							
	9							
	10							
	11							
	12							
	13							
	14							
	15							
	16							
	17							

ENROLLMENT
OF NOS. 1,2,3,4,5 HEREON
APPROVED BY THE SECRETARY
OF INTERIOR Dec. 12, 1905

No.1 1896 Chickasaw Dist 8945 as Mrs. Eliza Murray
No.2 1896 " " 8946 as Aaron "
No 3 1896 " " 8947 as Lula "
No.4 1896 " " 8948 as Ida "
No.5 1896 " " 8949 as Mamie "
~~No. 4 died Jany.4, 1901. Proof of death filed Oct. 23, 1902.~~
No.5 died Jany.4, 1901 Proof of death filed Oct 23, 1902

Nov.4 died Jan.11 1901; No.5 Jan. 4, 1901:Enrollment cancelled by Department July 8,1904.

TRIBAL ENROLLMENT OF PARENTS

	Name of Father	Year	County	Name of Mother	Year	County
1	John McCoy	Dead	NonCitizen	Sophie McCoy	Dead	Choc. roll
2	Frank Murray	"	"	No.1		
3	" "	"		" "		
4	~~" "~~	~~"~~		~~No.1~~		
5	~~" "~~	~~"~~		~~No.1~~		
6						
7						
8						
9						
10						
11						
12						
13						
14						
15						
16					Sept.	12/98
17						

RESIDENCE: Chickasaw Nation COUNTY.
POST OFFICE: Erin Springs, Ind. Ter.

Choctaw Nation

Choctaw Roll (*Not Including Freedmen*)

CARD NO.
FIELD NO. **74**

Dawes' Roll No.		NAME	Relationship to Person First Named	AGE	SEX	BLOOD	TRIBAL ENROLLMENT Year	County	No.
134	1	McCaughey, Emmet 55	First Named	51	M	1/8		Chic. residing in Choc. Dist	CCR #2 375
W1060	2	" " , Annie M 41	wife	37	F	IW		" " "	CIRoll 77
135	3	" " , John 25	son	21	M	1/16		" " "	CCR #2 375
136	4	" " , Ethel 17	dau	13	F	1/16		" " "	"
137	5	" " , Leliah 16	"	12	F	1/16		" " "	"
138	6	" " , Sophia 14	"	10	F	1/16		" " "	"
139	7	" " , Emmet Jr 12	son	8	M	1/16		" " "	"
140	8	" " , Annie 10	dau	6	F	1/16		" " "	"
141	9	" " , Loraine 3	"	4	F	1/16		" " "	"
142	10	" " , Claude E. 1	son	3wk	M	1/16		" " "	"

11 No.1 1896 Chickasaw Dist. 9515 as Emmet McCoy
12 No2 1896 " " 14888 as Annie M.L.McConghey
13 ~~No.3 1896 " " 9516 " John McCoy~~
14 ~~No.4 1896~~ " " ~~9517~~ " ~~Ethel~~ "
No.5 1896 " " 9518 " Delilah "
15 No.6 1896 " " 9519 " Sophia "
16 ~~No.7 1896 " " 9520 " Emmit " Jr.~~
17 ~~No.8 1896~~ " " ~~9521~~ " ~~Annie~~ "
No.9 1896 " " 9522 " Lorena McCoy

ENROLLMENT OF NOS. 1,3,4,5,6,7,8,9,10 HEREON APPROVED BY THE SECRETARY OF INTERIOR Dec. 12, 1902

TRIBAL ENROLLMENT OF PARENTS

	Name of Father	Year	County	Name of Mother	Year	County
1	John McCaughey	Dead	NonCitzen[sic]	Sophie McCuaghey[sic]	Dead	Choc. roll
2	Frank M. See		" "	Atlanta See	"	NonCitzen[sic]
3	No.1			Alice McCaughey	"	" "
4	No.1			Sallie McCuaghey[sic]	"	" "
5	No.1			" "	"	" "
6	No.1			" "	"	" "
7	No.1			" "	"	" "
8	No.1			No. 2	"	" "
9	No.1			No.2		
10	No.1			No.2		

11 See testimony of No.1 taken Oct. 20, 1902
12 No 2 Hold up

ENROLLMENT OF NOS. 2 HEREON ~~APPROVED BY THE SECRETARY~~ OF INTERIOR Nov. 16, 1904

14 No.10 Born May 18, 1902: enrolled May 27, 02.

Date of Application for Enrollment. Sept. 12,98

17 P.O. Lindsay I.T. 3/5/03

RESIDENCE: Chickasaw Nation XXXXX
POST OFFICE: Pauls Valley, Ind. Ter.

Choctaw Nation

Choctaw Roll (*Not Including Freedmen*)

CARD NO.
FIELD NO. 75

Dawes' Roll No.	NAME	Relationship to Person First Named	AGE	SEX	BLOOD	TRIBAL ENROLLMENT Year	County	No.
143	1 Williams, Newt 32	First Named	28	M	1/4		Choc. residing in Chic. Dist	CCR #2 489
IW1242	2 " , Abbie 24	wife	20	F	IW			CIRoll 118

ENROLLMENT OF NOS. 1 HEREON APPROVED BY THE SECRETARY OF INTERIOR Dec. 12' 02

No.1 1896 Chickasaw Dist. 14164 as Newt Williams
No.2 1896 " " 15203 as Abbey "

ENROLLMENT OF NOS. 2 HEREON APPROVED BY THE SECRETARY OF INTERIOR Dec. 30, 1904

TRIBAL ENROLLMENT OF PARENTS

Name of Father	Year	County	Name of Mother	Year	County
1 Chris Williams	Dead	Chick. Roll	Rhoda Williams	Dead	Choc. roll
2 Jim Branum		NonCitizen	Malinda Branum		NonCitz.

Date of Application for Enrollment. Sept. 12,98

RESIDENCE: Chickasaw Nation XXXXXX
POST OFFICE: Purcell, Ind. Ter.

Choctaw Nation

Choctaw Roll (Not Including Freedmen)

CARD NO.
FIELD NO. 76

Dawes' Roll No.	NAME	Relationship to Person First Named	AGE	SEX	BLOOD	TRIBAL ENROLLMENT Year	County	No.
144	1 Taylor, Nettie 30	First Named	20	F	1/2		Choc. residing in Chick. Dist	CCR #2 452

ENROLLMENT
OF NOS. 1 HEREON
APPROVED BY THE SECRETARY
OF INTERIOR Dec. 12, 1902

1896 Chickasaw Dist. 12572 as Nettie V. Taylor

Known in religion as Sister Mary Olivia

TRIBAL ENROLLMENT OF PARENTS

	Name of Father	Year	County	Name of Mother	Year	County
1	Jackson Taylor	Dead	Choc. Roll	Emaline Taylor		NonCitz.

Date of Application for Enrollment. Sept. 12,98

RESIDENCE: Chickasaw Nation ~~COUNTY~~.
POST OFFICE: Fox, Ind. Ter.

Choctaw Nation

Choctaw Roll (Not Including Freedmen)

CARD NO.
FIELD NO. 77

Dawes' Roll No.	NAME	Relationship to Person First Named	AGE	SEX	BLOOD	TRIBAL ENROLLMENT Year	County	No.
14173	1 Burkes, John G. 56		52	M	1/4			
14174	2 " John G. Jr. 22	son	18	"	1/8			
14175	3 Lowe, Ella I. 17	dau	13	F	1/8	ENROLLMENT		
14176	4 Burkes, Lillie B. 16	"	12	"	1/8	OF NOS. 1 2 3 4 5 6 7 8 9 10 HEREON	APPROVED BY THE SECRETARY	
14177	5 " , Myrtle J. 14	"	10	"	1/8	OF INTERIOR Apr. 11, 1903		
14178	6 " , Lelia A. 11	"	7	"	1/8			
14179	7 " , Mary Ellen 9	"	5	"	1/8			
14180	8 " , Ben Ager 7	son	3	M	1/8			
14181	9 " , Maudie Vinita 4	dau	3mos	F	1/8			
14182	10 " , Charley McClellan Jr. 1	son	7wks	M	1/16			

11 All admitted by Dawes Com. Case No. 908 and no appeal taken. Evidence of birth of
12 No.9 received and filed Aug 18, 1900. No.3 is now the wife of Boyd M Lowe on
~~Choctaw card #D726. Evidence of marriage filed therein May 19, 1902.~~ For child of
13 No.3 see NB(Mar 3-05) #522. ~~No1 is husband of Alice V.R. Burkes on Choctaw card~~
14 # ~~#D812~~ Oct. 15, 1902 - 7-5874 Dec. 15, 1904.
15 No.2 is now the husband of Sarah P. Burkes-non citizen. Evidence of marriage filed
~~Nov. 1, 1902~~
16 ~~No.10 Born Sept. 20, 1902, Enrolled Nov. 1, 1902~~
17 For children of No4 see NB(Mar 3-05) card No 655 & Apr 26-06) card #295.

TRIBAL ENROLLMENT OF PARENTS

	Name of Father	Year	County	Name of Mother	Year	County
1	Jim Burkes	Dead	non citizen	Elizabeth Burkes	Dead	Choctaw Indian
2	No 1			Vilaney Burkes	"	non citizen
3	No 1			Alice "		" "
4	No 1			Alice "		" "
5	No 1			Alice "		" "
6	No 1			Alice "		" "
7	No 1			Alice "		" "
8	No 1			Alice "		" "
9	No 1			Alice "		" "
10	No.2			Sarah P. Burkes		non citizen

11 No.2 is husband of Sarah P. Burkes on Choctaw card 5989.

Date of Application for Enrollment. ~~Sept. 19/98.~~

14 PO No 4 Bailey IT 4/3/05

17 P.O. of No2 Marlow Ind Ty

No 9 Enrolled on Sept. 23/98

RESIDENCE: Chickasaw Nation xxxxxx
POST OFFICE: Arthur, Ind. Ter. 12/13/04

Choctaw Nation

Choctaw Roll (Not Including Freedmen)

CARD NO.
FIELD NO. 78

Dawes' Roll No.	NAME	Relationship to Person First Named	AGE	SEX	BLOOD	TRIBAL ENROLLMENT Year	County	No.
145	1 Little, Lucy Wadkins 24	First Named	20	F	1/2		Choc. residing in Chic. Dist	CCR #2 488
146	2 " , Moma 3	dau.	2mo.	F	1/4			
147	3 " , Frederick T. 1	son	2wks	M	1/4			
	4 " , William A.	husb.	28	M	I.W.	1896	Chick. Dist.	14143

ENROLLMENT OF NOS. 1, 2, 3 HEREON APPROVED BY THE SECRETARY OF INTERIOR Dec. 12, 1902

~~On Choctaw roll as Lucy Watkins~~
Wife of William A. Little, Choctaw card D.39
No. 3 Born July 21, 1902; enrolled Aug. 1, 1902
No.4 transferred from Choctaw card #D39. See decision ~~of May 5, 1903~~
For child of Nos. 1&4 see NB(Apr. 26, 1906) Card No.210
" " " " " " " (Mar.3, 1905) " No.6

ENROLLMENT OF NOS. 4 HEREON APPROVED BY THE SECRETARY OF INTERIOR ~~Jan. 13, 1903~~

No.2 enrolled Oct 6,99

TRIBAL ENROLLMENT OF PARENTS

	Name of Father	Year	County	Name of Mother	Year	County
1	Fred Wadkins		Choc. residing in Chic. Dist	Nancy Wadkins	Dead	NonCitz.
2	W.A. Little		White man	No.1		
3	" " "		" "	No.1		
4	John Little		NonCitizen	Eliza Little		NonCitz.

Date of Application for Enrollment. ~~Sept. 12,98~~

~~P.O. Velma I.T. 2/18/04~~

RESIDENCE: Chickasaw Nation ~~xxxxx~~
POST OFFICE: Pauls Valley

Choctaw Nation

Choctaw Roll *(Not Including Freedmen)*

CARD NO.
FIELD NO. 79

Dawes' Roll No.	NAME	Relationship to Person First Named	AGE	SEX	BLOOD	TRIBAL ENROLLMENT Year	County	No.
Void	1 ~~Conner, James O.~~	~~Named~~	~~41~~	~~M~~	~~I.W.~~			
Void	2 ~~" , Ada B.~~	~~wife~~	~~37~~	~~F~~	~~1/2~~			
Void	3 ~~Shelton, Myrtle C.~~	~~step-dau~~	~~12~~	~~F~~	~~1/4~~			
	4							
	5							
	6							
	7							

8 No.1 Chickasaw roll, Pickens Co, Page 78. Transferred to Choctaw roll by Dawes Com.
~~No.2 " " " " " 14. " " " " " " "~~
9 ~~No.3 " " " " " 14 " " " " " " "~~
10 No.2 also " " " " 96 " " " " " " "
11 No.1 on Chickasaw roll as James O'Conner, admitted by Dawes Com. Case No. 35
~~No.2 " " " " Ida B. Bonner[sic]~~
12 ~~No.3 " " " " Myrtle Shelton~~
13 No.2 " " " " Ada O'Conner

CANCELLED

Transferred to Chickasaw card No. 1590 Oct. 11, 1902

TRIBAL ENROLLMENT OF PARENTS

Name of Father	Year	County	Name of Mother	Year	County
1 ~~Thos. H. Conner~~		~~Non-citizen~~	~~Elizabeth A. Conner~~		~~NonCitz.~~
2 ~~Calvin Colbert~~	~~Dead~~	~~Chickasaw roll~~	~~Emma Colbert~~	~~Dead~~	~~Choc. Roll~~
3 ~~Dr. Shelton~~		~~NonCitizen~~	~~No.2~~		

~~Date of Application~~ for Enrollment. Sept. 12,98

Choctaw By Blood Enrollment Cards 1898-1914

RESIDENCE: Chickasaw Nation ~~COUNTY~~.
POST OFFICE: Guertie, Ind. Ter.

Choctaw Nation

Choctaw Roll *(Not Including Freedmen)*
CARD NO.
FIELD NO. **80**

Dawes' Roll No.		NAME	Relationship to Person First Named	AGE	SEX	BLOOD	TRIBAL ENROLLMENT Year	County	No.
Void	1	~~Hathaway, Willie M.~~		~~18~~	~~F~~	~~1/8~~		~~Choc. residing in Chic Dist~~	~~CCR #2 260~~
	2								
	3								
	4								
	5								
	6	Transferred from original 96 roll on Sept. 12, 98							
	7								
	8								
	9								
	10								
	11								
	12								
	13								
	14								
	15								
	16								
	17								

TRIBAL ENROLLMENT OF PARENTS

	Name of Father	Year	County	Name of Mother	Year	County
1	~~Charlie Hathaway~~	~~Dead~~	~~Non-citizen~~	~~Celia Hathaway~~	~~Dead~~	~~Choc. roll~~
2						
3						
4						
5						
6						
7						
8						
9						
10						
11					Date of Application for Enrollment.	Sept. 12,98
12						
13						
14						
15						
16						
17						

CANCELLED

Duplicate of No.2 on Choctaw card 3272 Sept 3, 1902

RESIDENCE: Chickasaw Nation XXXXXX
POST OFFICE: Pauls Valley, Ind. Ter.

Choctaw Nation — **Choctaw Roll** *(Not Including Freedmen)*

CARD NO.
FIELD NO. 81

Dawes' Roll No.	NAME	Relationship to Person First Named	AGE	SEX	BLOOD	TRIBAL ENROLLMENT Year	County	No.
148	1 Gardner, Zachariah 73	First Named	69	M	1/2		Chic. residing in Choc. Dist	CCR #2 215
149	2 " , Levina 60	wife	60	F	1/2		" " "	"
	3 ENROLLMENT							
	4 OF NOS. 1 and 2 HEREON							
	5 APPROVED BY THE SECRETARY OF INTERIOR Dec. 12 '02							
	6							
	7				No.1	1896	Chickasaw Dist.	5021
	8				No.2	1896	" "	5022
	9							
	10							
	11							
	12							
	13							
	14							
	15							
	16							
	17							

TRIBAL ENROLLMENT OF PARENTS

	Name of Father	Year	County	Name of Mother	Year	County
1	Isaac Gardner	Dead	Choctaw roll	Rebecca Gardner	Dead	Choc. roll
2	McKinney	"	" "	McKinney	"	" "
3						
4						
5						
6						
7						
8						
9						
10						
11						
12						
13						
14						
15						Date of Application for Enrollment.
16						Sept. 12,98
17						

RESIDENCE: Chickasaw Nation ~~COUNTY~~
POST OFFICE: Atlee, Ind. Ter

Choctaw Nation

Choctaw Roll *(Not Including Freedmen)*

CARD NO.
FIELD NO. 82

Dawes' Roll No.	NAME	Relationship to Person First Named	AGE	SEX	BLOOD	TRIBAL ENROLLMENT Year	County	No.
15035	1 Steward, Lige 30	First Named	26	M	1/8		Choc. residing in Chic Dist	CCR #2 435
	2							
	3							
	4							
	5							
	6							
	7							
	8 On 1893 Leased District payment Roll Kianutia County Page 116 No. 42 as Lige Stewart							
	9 On Choctaw roll as L.D. Steward							
	10							
	11							
	12							
	13							
	14							
	15							
	16							
	17							

ENROLLMENT OF NOS. 1 HEREON APPROVED BY THE SECRETARY OF INTERIOR Feb. 16, 1904

TRIBAL ENROLLMENT OF PARENTS

Name of Father	Year	County	Name of Mother	Year	County
1 Steuard	Dead	NonCitizen	Palmyra Steuard	Dead	Choc. roll
2					
3					
4					
5					
6					
7					
8					
9					
10					
11					
12					
13					
14					
15					
16				Date of Application for Enrollment.	Sept. 12,98
17 P.O. Tishomingo IT. 5/26/03		Atlee I.T. 8/8/03			

RESIDENCE: Chickasaw Nation ~~XXXXX~~
POST OFFICE: Puray, Ind. Ter.

Choctaw Nation

Choctaw Roll (Not Including Freedmen)

CARD NO.
FIELD NO. 83

Dawes' Roll No.	NAME	Relationship to Person First Named	AGE	SEX	BLOOD	TRIBAL ENROLLMENT Year	County	No.
~~150~~	DIED PRIOR TO SEPT 25, 1902 1 ~~Gibson, Ruben~~		~~55~~	~~M~~	~~1/2~~		~~Jack Fork~~	CCR #2 ~~213~~
151	2 " , Nicey	wife	53	F	1/2		" "	"
~~152~~	DIED PRIOR TO SEPT 25, 1902 3 ~~" , Robert E. Lee~~	~~son~~		~~M~~	~~1/2~~		" "	"

ENROLLMENT OF NOS. 1, 2, 3 HEREON APPROVED BY THE SECRETARY OF INTERIOR Dec. 12, 1902

No.1 1896 Jacks Fork 4992 as Reuben Gibson
No.2 1896 " " 4993
~~No3 1896 " " 4995 " Lee Gibson~~

No.1 died March 18, 1902; No3 died March 10, 1902:
Enrollment cancelled by Department July 8, 1904

No.3 on Choctaw roll as Lee Gibson.

TRIBAL ENROLLMENT OF PARENTS

Name of Father	Year	County	Name of Mother	Year	County
1 ~~James Gibson~~	~~Dead~~	~~Choctaw roll~~	~~Maria Gibson~~	~~Dead~~	~~Choc. roll~~
2 George Waters	"	Chick. roll		"	" "
3 ~~No.1~~			~~No.2~~		

Date of Application for Enrollment. 9-12-98

RESIDENCE: Chickasaw Nation ~~COUNTY~~ **Choctaw Nation** **Choctaw Roll** *(Not Including Freedmen)* CARD NO.
POST OFFICE: Purdy, Ind. Ter. FIELD NO. 84

Dawes' Roll No.	NAME	Relationship to Person First Named	AGE	SEX	BLOOD	TRIBAL ENROLLMENT Year	County	No.
153	1 Gibson, Silas [37]	First Named	33	M	3/4		Choc. residing in Chic. Dist	CCR #2 216
	2							
	3					1896	Chick. Dist.	5041
	4							
	5							
	6							
	7							
	8							
	9							
	10							
	11							
	12							
	13							
	14							
	15							
	16							
	17							

ENROLLMENT OF NOS. 1 HEREON APPROVED BY THE SECRETARY OF INTERIOR Dec. 12, 1902

Husband of Minnie Gibson, Chickasaw roll, card No. 389

For child of No.1 see Chickasaw NB(March 3, 1905) #47

TRIBAL ENROLLMENT OF PARENTS

	Name of Father	Year	County	Name of Mother	Year	County
1	Isaac Gibson	Dead	Choc roll	Lucinda Gibson	Dead	Choc. roll
2						
3						
4						
5						
6						
7						
8						
9						
10						
11						
12						
13						
14						
15						
16						
17						

Date of Application for Enrollment.
Sept. 12,98

Choctaw By Blood Enrollment Cards 1898-1914

RESIDENCE: Chickasaw Nation ~~COUNTY~~ **Choctaw Nation** **Choctaw Roll** *(Not Including Freedmen)* CARD NO.
POST OFFICE: Wynnewood, Ind. Ter. FIELD NO. 85

Dawes' Roll No.	NAME	Relationship to Person First Named	AGE	SEX	BLOOD	TRIBAL ENROLLMENT Year	County	No.
15561	1 Yates, Laura 41	Named	36	F	1/8		Choc. residing in Chick. Dist	CCR #0[sic] 34
	2							
	3							
	4 Take no further action relative to the							
	5 enrollment of No.1. Protest of Attys							
	6 ~~for Choctaw and Chickasaw Nations~~ ~~Jan 23, '04 Protest withdrawn by~~							
	7 M M^c & C 5/19/04							
	8							
	9							
	10	Is she not Lorena Conradda[sic] 1893 Blue 248						
	11	On Choctaw roll as Miss Laura Conrade[sic], Choctaw Census						
	12	~~Record No.0 Page 34, No. 353~~ ~~No.1 is now wife of Ellis Yates, non-citizen. Evidence of~~						
	13	marriage filed Oct. 23, 1902.						
	14	See testimony of No.1 taken October 20, 1902						
	15							
	16							
	17							

TRIBAL ENROLLMENT OF PARENTS

Name of Father	Year	County	Name of Mother	Year	County
1 Henry Conrady		White man	Harriet Lattey		Blue
2					
3					
4					
5					
6					
7					
8					
9					
10					
11					
12					
13					
14 Pauls Valley I.T.					
15					
16			Date of Application for Enrollment.		
17					Sept. 12,98

Choctaw By Blood Enrollment Cards 1898-1914

RESIDENCE: Chickasaw Nation ~~County.~~
POST OFFICE: Wynnewood, Ind. Ter.

Choctaw Nation

Choctaw Roll (*Not Including Freedmen*) CARD NO. FIELD NO. **86**

Dawes' Roll No.		NAME		Relationship to Person First Named	AGE	SEX	BLOOD	TRIBAL ENROLLMENT Year	County	No.
154	1	Gay, Caroline	22		18	F	1/16		Blue	CCR #2 401
DEAD	2	~~" , Ollie Burney~~ DEAD		~~son~~	~~2mo~~	~~M~~	~~1/32~~			
155	3	" , Sylvia Katy	3	dau.	3mo	F	1/32			
14475	4	" , Press Clifton	1	son	1mo	M	1/32			

ENROLLMENT OF NOS. 1 & 3 HEREON APPROVED BY THE SECRETARY OF INTERIOR Dec. 12, 1902

No 1 1896 Blue 10495 as Callie Palmer

No.1 on Choctaw roll as Carollie Palmer
No.3 Enrolled July 2, 1900
~~P.O. address is now Pauls Valley I.T.~~
~~Oct. 16, 1900~~

ENROLLMENT ~~OF NOS.~~ 4 ~~HEREON~~ APPROVED BY THE SECRETARY OF INTERIOR May 20, 1902

~~No. 2 HEREON DISMISSED UNDER ORDER OF THE COMMISS-~~
IN TO THE FIVE TRIBES OF
MARCH 31, 1905

TRIBAL ENROLLMENT OF PARENTS

	Name of Father	Year	County	Name of Mother	Year	County
1	Fred Palmer		NonCitizen	Laura Conrady		~~Choc. resd. in Chic. Dist.~~
2	~~Henry Gay~~		" "	~~No.1~~		
3	Headrich W. Gay		" "	No.1		
4	" " "		" "	No.1		

No.1 also on 1896 Choctaw census roll: page 271: no. 10614
as Cala Palmer
~~Evidence of death of No.2 received and filed Feby. 11, 1902~~
No.2 died Sept. 20, 1901
No.4 born Aug 18, 1902, enrolled Sept. 25, 1902

Date of Application for Enrollment. Sept. 12.98

RESIDENCE: Chickasaw Nation ~~XXXXX~~ **Choctaw Nation** **Choctaw Roll** (*Not Including Freedmen*) CARD NO.

POST OFFICE: Wynnewood, Ind. Ter. FIELD NO. **87**

Dawes' Roll No.	NAME		Relationship to Person First Named	AGE	SEX	BLOOD	TRIBAL ENROLLMENT Year	County	No.
156	1 Hensley, Elzira	42	First Named	38	F	1/8		Choc. residing in Chic. Dist.	CCR #2 255
157	2 " , Columbus	23	son	19	M	1/16		" " "	"
~~**158**~~	3 ~~" , John~~ DIED PRIOR TO SEPT 25, 1902		~~"~~	~~15~~	~~"~~	~~1/16~~		~~" " "~~	~~"~~
159	4 " , Willie	17	"	13	"	1/16		" " "	"
160	5 " , Ida	14	dau.	10	F	1/16		" " "	"
161	6 " , Guss	12	son	8	M	1/16		" " "	"
162	7 " , Walter	7	"	3	M	1/16		" " "	"
	8 " , Rosabelle Lee	9	dau.	5	F	1/16	1896	Chic. Dist.	CCR #0 35No.361

9 No.3 died Feb.14,1899:Enrollment cancelled by Department July 8, 1904

10–11 ENROLLMENT OF NOS. 1,2,3,4,5,6,7 HEREON APPROVED BY THE SECRETARY OF INTERIOR Dec. 12, 1902

12 No.3 died Feb.14,1899; proof of

13 death filed Oct. 25. 1902.

15–16 ENROLLMENT OF NOS. 8 HEREON APPROVED BY THE SECRETARY OF INTERIOR May 22, 1903

No.1 1896 Chick.Dist. 6160 as Elsie Hensley
No.2 1896 " " 6162 as Columbus Husley
No.3 1896 " " 6163 " John "
No.4 1896 " " 6164 " Willie "
No.5 1896 " " 6165 " Ida "
No.6 1896 " " 6166 " Guess "
No.7 1896 " " 6167 " Walter "
No.8 on Choctaw Census record No.0 Page 35, No.361
No8 also on 1893 pay roll Chick.Dist.Page 26 #266 as
Laura Hensley see also affidavit of No.1 as to
change of given name filed Sept 18, 1902 OK W^m^O.B.

TRIBAL ENROLLMENT OF PARENTS

	Name of Father	Year	County	Name of Mother	Year	County
1	Henry Conrady		White man	Hariet[sic] Lattey		Blue
2	Wm. Hensley	Dead	NonCitizen	No.1		
3	~~" "~~	~~"~~	~~" "~~	~~No.1~~		
4	" "	"	" "	No.1		
5	" "	"	" "	No.1		
6	" "	"	" "	No.1		
7	" "	"	" "	No.1		
8	" "	"	" "	No.1		
9						
10						
11				No.8 born Feby.2, 1893	Date of Application for Enrollment.	
12						
13	For child of No.2 see NB(Apr.26,06)				Sept. 12, 98	
14	card #396					
15			For child of No.5 see NB(Mar.3,05) Card #13			
16			" " " No.2 " " " (" " " # 865			
17	No5 P.O. Spencerville I.T. 12/13/04					

RESIDENCE: Chickasaw Nation ~~COUNTY~~.
POST OFFICE: Arthur, Ind. Ter.

Choctaw Nation

Choctaw Roll (Not Including Freedmen)

CARD NO.
FIELD NO. 88

Dawes' Roll No.	NAME	Relationship to Person First Named	AGE	SEX	BLOOD	TRIBAL ENROLLMENT Year	County	No.
163	1 Watkins Frederick 56		52	M	1/2		Choctaw residing in Chickasaw District	CCR #2 488
dead	2 ~~" Louisa dead~~	~~wife~~	~~52~~	~~F~~	~~I.W.~~			C.I.Roll 118

ENROLLMENT OF NOS. 1 HEREON APPROVED BY THE SECRETARY OF INTERIOR Dec. 12, 1902

No1 1896 Chickasaw Dist. 14142 as Fred Watkins
No2 1896 " " 15204 " Lou "

No 2 hereon dismissed under order of the Commission to the five[sic] civilized[sic] tribes[sic] of March 31, 1905.

No2 on Choctaw roll as Lou Watkins
No2 Died March 14, 1902 proof of death filed Oct. 23, 1902

For child of No2 see N.B. (March 3-1905) card #8

TRIBAL ENROLLMENT OF PARENTS

	Name of Father	Year	County	Name of Mother	Year	County
1	George Watkins	dead	non citizen	Hannah Watkins	Dead	Choctaw roll
2	~~Copeland~~	"	" "	~~Copeland~~	"	~~non citizen~~

Date of Application for Enrollment. Sept. 12/98

RESIDENCE: Chickasaw Nation XXXXX
POST OFFICE: Erin Springs, Ind. Ter.

Choctaw Nation

Choctaw Roll *(Not Including Freedmen)*

CARD NO.
FIELD NO. 89

Dawes' Roll No.	NAME	Relationship to Person First Named	AGE	SEX	BLOOD	TRIBAL ENROLLMENT Year	County	No.
164	1 McCaughey J.C. 46	First Named	42	M	1/8		Choc. residing in Chic. Dist.	CCR #2 375
	2							
	3							
	4					1896 Chick. Dist.	9514 as Jno L. McCoy	
	5							
	6							
	7							
	8	On roll as John L. McCaughey also known as Major.						
	9							
	10							
	11							
	12							
	13							
	14							
	15							
	16							
	17							

ENROLLMENT OF NOS. ....HEREON APPROVED BY THE SECRETARY OF INTERIOR Dec. 12, 1902

TRIBAL ENROLLMENT OF PARENTS

Name of Father	Year	County	Name of Mother	Year	County
1 John McCaughey	Dead	NonCitizen	Sophia McCaughey	Dead	Choc. roll
2					
3					
4					
5					
6					
7					
8					
9			Date of Application for Enrollment.		Sept. 12,98
10					
11					
12					
13					
14					
15					
16					
17					

RESIDENCE: Chickasaw Nation ~~County~~.
POST OFFICE: McGee, Ind. Ter.

Choctaw Nation — Choctaw Roll (Not Including Freedmen) — CARD NO. — FIELD NO. 90

Dawes' Roll No.	NAME	Relationship to Person First Named	AGE	SEX	BLOOD	TRIBAL ENROLLMENT Year	County	No.
IW540	1 Leewright Minor 56	First Named	50	M	I.W.		Choctaw residing in Chickasaw District	CIRoll 66
165	2 " Fidy 52	wife	48	F	1/16		" "	CCR #2 489
166	3 " Pearl 14	dau	10	"	1/32		" "	"
167	4 " Lizzie 11	"	7	"	1/32		" "	"
168	5 Hibdon Fannie 24	Step Dau	20	"	1/32		" "	CCR #2 258
169	6 Worley Annie 21	" "	17	"	1/32		" "	"
170	7 Hibdon Henry 19	" son	15	M	1/32		" "	"
171	8 Worley, Floyd Lonzo 1	son of No 6	2 mo	M	1/64		" "	

ENROLLMENT OF NOS. 2,3,4,5,6,7 and 8 HEREON APPROVED BY THE SECRETARY OF INTERIOR Dec. 12 1902

For child of No 2 see N.B. (Mar 3-1905) card No. 28.

12 For child of No.7 see N B. (Apr 25 06) card #388.
13 No 7 is the husband of Emma Lively Hibdon on ~~Choctaw card #D815, Oct 21 1902~~ 7-5869.
14 No5 is now named Morrison.
15 No5 P.O. Byars I.T. 3/23/05.
16 For children of No 5 see NB (Mar 3-1905) #23
17 " child " " 6 " " " #443

ENROLLMENT OF NOS. ~ 1 ~ HEREON APPROVED BY THE SECRETARY OF INTERIOR Feb. 8-1904

TRIBAL ENROLLMENT OF PARENTS

Name of Father	Year	County	Name of Mother	Year	County
1 B.T. Leewright	dead	non citizen	Milain Leewright	dead	non citizen
2 Thos T. Spain	"	" "	Mary Spain	"	Choctaw roll
3 No 1			No 2		
4 No 1			No 2		
5 Clay Hibdon	dead	non citizen	No 2		
6 " "	"	" "	No 2		
7 " "	"	" "	No 2		
8 J.A. Worley		" "	No 6		
		No.7	Emma Lively[sic] Hibbon[sic] Born Sep 15-05		

9 No.2 daughter of Mary M Spain who was admitted by Act of Choctaw Council of Oct 31,1879
10 No2 1896 Chickasaw Dist 14184 as Fedia Lee Wright
11 No3 1896 " " 14188 " Pearl " "
~~No4 1896 " " 14189 " Eliza "~~
12 ~~No5 1896 " " 6174 " Nancy Hibden~~
13 No6 1896 " " 6176 " Annie "
14 No7 1896 " " 6175 " Henry "
15 ~~No1 1896 " " 15198 " Murrow L. Wright~~

Date of Application for Enrollment.
No 1 enrolled Sept 15/98
all others Sept 12/98

16 No6 is the wife of Jesse A Worley on Choctaw card #D531. Evidence of marriage filed with
17 papers in Choctaw card #D531. No8 Born Feby 4, 1902 enrolled April 19 1902

RESIDENCE: Chickasaw Nation ~~COUNTY~~.
POST OFFICE: Wynnewood, Ind Ter.

Choctaw Nation

Choctaw Roll *(Not Including Freedmen)*

CARD NO.
FIELD NO. 91

Dawes' Roll No.		NAME	Relationship to Person First Named	AGE	SEX	BLOOD	TRIBAL ENROLLMENT Year	County	No.
VOID.	1	Walner Lula	Named	32	F	1/4			
VOID.	2	" Susan V.	Dau	14	"	1/8			
VOID.	3	" Acca.	"	12	"	1/8			
VOID.	4	" Julia	"	10	"	1/8			
VOID.	5	" Hugh	Son	5	M	1/8			
	6								
	7								
	8	All on Chickasaw Roll Pontotoc County Page 60, transferred to Choctaw roll							
	9	by Dawes Com.							
	10	No 1 wife of John H Walner, Chickasaw Roll Case #390							
	11								
	12								
	13								
	14								
	15								
	16								
	17								

CANCELLED

To Chickasaw Card #1597
Oct. 13 1902

TRIBAL ENROLLMENT OF PARENTS

	Name of Father	Year	County	Name of Mother	Year	County
1	Wiley Stewart	Dead	non citizen	Nancy F. Stewart		Blue
2	John H Walner	1897	Pontotoc County Chickasaw Roll	No 1		
3	" " "	1897	" "	No 1		
4	" " "	1897	" "	No 1		
5	" " "	1897	" "	No 1		
6						
7						
8						
9						
10				Date of Application		
11				for Enrollment.		Sept 12/98
12						
13						
14						
15						
16						
17						

Choctaw By Blood Enrollment Cards 1898-1914

RESIDENCE: Chickasaw Nation ~~COUNTY~~. **Choctaw Nation** **Choctaw Roll** *(Not Including Freedmen)* CARD NO.
POST OFFICE: Erin Springs Ind. Ter. FIELD NO. **92**

Dawes' Roll No.		NAME		Relationship to Person First Named	AGE	SEX	BLOOD	TRIBAL ENROLLMENT Year	County	No.
IW60	1	Jenkins, John L.	34	First Named	30	M	I.W.		Choctaw residing in Chickasaw District	C I Roll 53
172	2	" Mary	30	wife	26	F	1/32		" "	CCR #2 309
173	3	" John Leonard		son	7	M	1/64		" "	"
174	4	" Seth	9	"	5	"	1/64		" "	"
175	5	" Claude	7	"	3	"	1/64		" "	"
176	6	" Lee	4	"	7mo	"	1/64			
177	7	" Clarance	1	"	2mo	"	1/64			
	8	ENROLLMENT								
	9	OF NOS. 2,3,4,5,5 and 7 HEREON APPROVED BY THE SECRETARY								
	10	OF INTERIOR DEC 12 1902								
	11	ENROLLMENT OF NOS. 1 HEREON			No1	1896	Chickasaw Dist		14710 as Jno L Jinkins	
	12	APPROVED BY THE SECRETARY			No2	1896	"	"	7395	
	13	OF INTERIOR JUN 13 1903			No3	1896	"	"	7396 as Lemon Jenkins	
	14				~~No4~~	~~1896~~	~~"~~	~~"~~	~~7397~~	
	15				~~No5~~	~~1896~~	"	"	~~7398~~	
	16				No.7 Enrolled Aug 9 1901.					
	17									

TRIBAL ENROLLMENT OF PARENTS

	Name of Father	Year	County	Name of Mother	Year	County
1	Wm Jenkins	Dead	non citizen	Mary Jenkins	Dead	non citizen
2	James Hazel	"	Choctaw Roll		Dead	" "
3	No 1			No 2		
4	No 1			No 2		
5	No 1			No 2		
6	No 1			No 2		
7	No 1			No 2		
8						
9						
10						
11						
12						
13						~~#1 to 5 in~~
14				Date of Application for Enrollment.		
15						Sept. 12/98
16				No 6 Enrolled Oct 6/99		
17	Sulphur I.T.					

RESIDENCE: Tobucksy COUNTY.
POST OFFICE: Calvin Ind. Ter.

Choctaw Nation

Choctaw Roll
(Not Including Freedmen)

CARD NO.
FIELD NO. 93

Dawes' Roll No.	NAME		Relationship to Person First Named	AGE	SEX	BLOOD	TRIBAL ENROLLMENT		
							Year	County	No.
IW 61	Eaton, Robert L.	36	First Named	32	M	I.W.		Tobucksy	
178	" Belle	24	wife	20	F	5/8		"	CCR #2 154
179	" Ruby Pearl	7	dau	3	"	5/16		"	"
180	" Sunnie	1	dau	6wks	F	5/16			

ENROLLMENT
OF NOS. 2, 3 and 4 HEREON
APPROVED BY THE SECRETARY
OF INTERIOR Dec. 12 1902

No 2 1896 Tobucksy 3697 as Belle Easton
No 3 1896 " 3698 " Rubie "
No 4 Enrolled Sept. 18, 1901

No 1 admitted in 1890 Choctaw case #1172[?]

ENROLLMENT
OF NOS. ~ 1 ~ HEREON
APPROVED BY THE SECRETARY
OF INTERIOR Jun 13 1903

TRIBAL ENROLLMENT OF PARENTS

Name of Father	Year	County	Name of Mother	Year	County
Joel Eaton		non citizen	Cornelia Eaton	Dead	non citizen
Calvin Perry	18[sic]	Tobucksy	Phoebe Perry		Tobucksy
No1			No2		
No1			No2		

~~# 1 to 3~~
Date of Application for Enrollment.
~~Sept. 12/98~~

Roff I.T.

RESIDENCE: Tobucksy COUNTY. **Choctaw Nation** Choctaw Roll (Not Including Freedmen) CARD NO.
POST OFFICE: Newburg, Ind. Ter. FIELD NO. 94

Dawes' Roll No.		NAME		Relationship to Person First Named	AGE	SEX	BLOOD	TRIBAL ENROLLMENT Year	County	No.
181	1	Burris, Hampton	40	First Named	36	M	3/4		Tobucksy	CCR #1 23
IW856	2	" Rebecca	25	wife	22	F	I.W.		"	IC Roll 7
182	3	" Odie	9	son	5	M	3/8		"	CCR #1 23
	4									
	5									
	6						No 1	1896	Tobucksy	867
	7						No 2	1896	"	868
	8						No 3	1896	"	869
	9									
	10									
	11									
	12									
	13									
	14									
	15									
	16									
	17									

ENROLLMENT OF NOS. 1 and 3 HEREON APPROVED BY THE SECRETARY OF INTERIOR Dec 12 1902

ENROLLMENT OF NOS. ~ 2 ~ HEREON APPROVED BY THE SECRETARY OF INTERIOR Aug -3 - 1904

TRIBAL ENROLLMENT OF PARENTS

	Name of Father	Year	County	Name of Mother	Year	County
1	Ben Burris	dead	Tobucksy	Sallie Burris	dead	Tobucksy
2	Thos Sparks	"	non citizen	Margaret Sparks		non citizen
3	No1			No2		
4						
5						
6						
7						
8						
9						
10						
11						
12						
13						
14						
15						
16						
17						

Date of Application for Enrollment. Sept. 12/98

RESIDENCE: Chickasaw Nation ~~COUNTY~~.
POST OFFICE: Wynnewood Ind. Ter.

Choctaw Nation — Choctaw Roll (Not Including Freedmen) — CARD NO. / FIELD NO. 95

Dawes' Roll No.	NAME	Relationship to Person First Named	AGE	SEX	BLOOD	TRIBAL ENROLLMENT Year	County	No.
183	1 McMenamin, F.P. 34	First Named	30	M	1/2		Choctaw residing in Chickasaw District	CCR #2 375
IW 62	2 " Laura Lee 30	wife	26	F	I.W.		" "	C.I.Roll 77
14477	3 " Michael McK. 7	son	3	M	1/4	1896	" " 9492	CCR #2 374
14478	4 " Mary Elizabeth 6	dau	2	F	1/4		" "	CCR #2 375
14479	5 " Roy Francis 4	son	1mo	M	1/4			

ENROLLMENT OF NOS. 1 HEREON APPROVED BY THE SECRETARY OF INTERIOR DEC 12 1902

No 1 1896 Chickasaw Dist 9505 as F.P. McNaman
No 2 1896 " " 14885 " Lavina L. McMinamin
No 3 1896 " " 9492 " Michael "

ENROLLMENT OF NOS. 3,4 & 5 HEREON APPROVED BY THE SECRETARY OF INTERIOR MAY 20 1903

Evidence of birth of Nos 4 and 5 received and filed Aug. 18, 1900

ENROLLMENT OF NOS. ~ 2 ~ HEREON APPROVED BY THE SECRETARY OF INTERIOR JUN 13 1903

No2 on Chickasaw roll as Levina L. Admitted by Dawes Com. Case No 1327.
Marriage license and certificate in Dawes Com office with papers in " " "

TRIBAL ENROLLMENT OF PARENTS

	Name of Father	Year	County	Name of Mother	Year	County
1	M. McMenamin (I.W.)		Choctaw residing in Chickasaw District	Harriet McMenamin	Dead	Choctaw Roll
2	D.M. Huddleson		noncitizen	Ivagine Huddleson		noncitizen
3	No 1			No 2		
4	No 1			No 2		
5	No 1			No 2		

Date of Application for Enrollment.
Sept. 12/98

RESIDENCE: Chickasaw Nation ~~COUNTY.~~
POST OFFICE: Roberson Ind Ter

Choctaw Nation

Choctaw Roll (Not Including Freedmen)

CARD NO.
FIELD NO. 96

Dawes' Roll No.	NAME		Relationship to Person First Named	AGE	SEX	BLOOD	TRIBAL ENROLLMENT Year	County	No.
184	1 Riddle, William	48		44	M	1/2	1893	Choctaw residing in Chickasaw District	page 50 476
I.W. 807	2 " Henrietta	39	wife	35	F	I.W.	1896	" "	C I Roll 96
185	3 " Ella	17	Dau	13	F	1/4	1893	" "	page 50 478
186	4 " Mary Belle	12	"	8	F	1/4	1893	" "	page 50 480
187	5 " Arthur Lee	10	son	6	M	1/4	1893	" "	page 50 481
188	6 " Robert	18	"	14	"	1/4	1893	" "	page 50 477
~~189~~	DIED PRIOR TO SEPTEMBER 25, 1902 7 ~~" Carry~~		~~dau~~	~~1mo~~	~~F~~	~~1/4~~			
~~190~~	DIED PRIOR TO SEPTEMBER 25, 1902 8 ~~" Calley~~		~~"~~	~~1mo~~	~~"~~	~~1/4~~			

9 ~~N°s 1-3-4-5&6 identified from 1893 Pay Roll~~
10 ~~N^o1 appears as Wm Riddle N° 476~~
11 N^o4 " " Mary " 480
12 N° 5 " " Authur " 481
~~N° 6 " " Robe " 477~~
13 ~~Chickasaw District~~

ENROLLMENT OF NOS. 1,3,4,5,6,7 and 8 HEREON APPROVED BY THE SECRETARY OF INTERIOR DEC 12 1902

For child of Nos1&2 see NB(March 3, 1905) card #598

ENROLLMENT OF NOS. 2 HEREON APPROVED BY THE SECRETARY OF INTERIOR MAY 21 1904

17 P.O. Wynnewood

TRIBAL ENROLLMENT OF PARENTS

	Name of Father	Year	County	Name of Mother	Year	County
1	Ed. Riddle	Dead	Choctaw Roll	Juicy Riddle	Dead	Choctaw Roll
2	W.-M. McCarly		Non citizen	Mary McCarly		non citizen
3	No 1			(No2) Henrietta Riddle		white woman
4	No 1			(No2) " "		" "
5	No 1			(No2) " "		" "
6	No 1			(No2) " "		" "
7	~~No 1~~			~~" "~~		~~" "~~
8	~~No 1~~			~~" "~~		~~" "~~

9 No2 1896 Chickasaw Dist 15006 as Etta M Riddle
~~No1 husband of Henrietta Riddle Choctaw Doubtful card No 15~~ This notation evidently an error.
10 No3 on Choctaw Roll as Ellen Riddle
11 No4 " " " Mary "
12 No5 " " " Arthur "
~~No2 " " " Etta M "~~
13 Nos 7&8 are twins
14 Nos 1-3-4-5&6 also on 1896 C.C.R.#2 page 417
15 No7 died 1899 No8 died 1899
16 For child of No 3 see NB (Apr26-06) Card #507
17 " " " " " " " (Mar4-05) " #590

No7 died in 1899; proof of death filed October 25, 1902
~~No8 died in 1899; proof of death filed October 25, 1902~~

Date of Application for Enrollment. Sept. 12/98

Enrollment cancelled by Department July 8-1904

RESIDENCE: Chickasaw Nation ~~COUNTY~~.
POST OFFICE: Wynnewood Ind Ter

Choctaw Nation

Choctaw Roll (Not Including Freedmen)

CARD NO.
FIELD NO. 97

Dawes' Roll No.	NAME	Relationship to Person First Named	AGE	SEX	BLOOD	TRIBAL ENROLLMENT Year	County	No.
191	1 Gardner James W. 43	First Named	49	M	3/8		Choctaw residing in Chickasaw District	CCR #2 215
IW619	2 " Emely 58	wife	54	F	I.W.		" "	C.I.Roll 39
192	3 " James Dolphin 18	son	14	M	3/16		" "	CCR #2 215

ENROLLMENT OF NOS. 1 and 3 HEREON APPROVED BY THE SECRETARY OF INTERIOR DEC 12 1902

ENROLLMENT OF NOS. 2 HEREON APPROVED BY THE SECRETARY OF INTERIOR MAR 26 1904

No1 1896 Chickasaw Dist 5024 as James Gardner
No2 1896 " " 14587
No3 1896 " " 5025 as Jas D. Gardner jr
No1 on Choctaw roll as James Gardner
No2 Admitted by Dawes Commission in 1896 as an intermarried citizen: Choctaw Card #1011: No appeal.
Affidavits of Zachariah Gardner and others as to marriage between Nos 1 and 2 filed Jany. 3, 1903.
No2 See judgement[sic] of Dec 10" 1903. Admitted.
For child of No.3 see NB (Mar.3,1905) #555

TRIBAL ENROLLMENT OF PARENTS

	Name of Father	Year	County	Name of Mother	Year	County
1	Isaac Gardner	Dead	Choctaw Roll	Rebecca Gardner	Dead	Choctaw Roll
2	Cornwall	"	noncitizen	Cornwall	"	noncitizen
3	No1			No2		

Date of Application for Enrollment.
Sept. 12/98

RESIDENCE: Chickasaw Nation ~~COUNTY~~.
POST OFFICE: Wynnewood, Ind Ter

Choctaw Nation

Choctaw Roll *(Not Including Freedmen)*

CARD NO.
FIELD NO. **98**

Dawes' Roll No.	NAME	Relationship to Person First Named	AGE	SEX	BLOOD	TRIBAL ENROLLMENT Year	County	No.
193	1 Stewart Charles F 48	First Named	44	M	1/4		Choctaw residing in Chickasaw District	CCR #1 304
	2							
	3							
	4							
	5							
	6	1896 Chickasaw Dist 11771 as Chas F. Steward						
	7							
	8							
	9							
	10 Husband of Josephine Stewart, Chickasaw Roll, Card No 393							
	11							
	12 No 1 Son of Nancy Stewart admitted by U.S. Indian Agent Oct 12, 1889.							
	13							
	14							
	15							
	16							
	17							

ENROLLMENT
~~OF NOS.~~ 1 ~~HEREON~~
APPROVED BY THE SECRETARY
OF INTERIOR DEC 12 1902

TRIBAL ENROLLMENT OF PARENTS

	Name of Father	Year	County	Name of Mother	Year	County
1	Wiley Stewart	Dead	noncitizen	Nancy Stewart		Blue
2						
3						
4						
5						
6						
7						
8						
9						
10						
11						
12						
13						
14						
15						
16				Date of Application for Enrollment.		Sept. 13/98
17						

RESIDENCE: Chickasaw Nation ~~COUNTY~~.
POST OFFICE: Wynnewood Ind Ter

Choctaw Nation

Choctaw Roll *(Not Including Freedmen)*

CARD NO.
FIELD NO. **99**

Dawes' Roll No.	NAME	Relationship to Person First Named	AGE	SEX	BLOOD	TRIBAL ENROLLMENT Year	County	No.
194	1 Stewart Nancy 70	First Named	66	F	1/2		Blue	CCR #1 299
	2					1896	Blue	11596
	3							
	4							
	5							
	6							
	7							
	8							
	9							
	10							
	11							
	12							
	13							
	14							
	15							
	16							
	17							

ENROLLMENT
~~OF NOS.~~ 1 ~~HEREON~~
APPROVED BY THE SECRETARY
OF INTERIOR DEC 12 1902

No 1 admitted by U.S. Indian Agent Oct. 12, 1889

TRIBAL ENROLLMENT OF PARENTS

	Name of Father	Year	County	Name of Mother	Year	County
1	Sam Fulsom	Dead	Choctaw Roll		Dead	Choctaw Roll
2						
3						
4						
5						
6						
7						
8						
9						
10						
11						
12						
13						
14						
15						
16						
17						

Date of Application ~~for Enrollment.~~ Sept. 13/97

RESIDENCE: Chickasaw Nation ~~COUNTY~~.
POST OFFICE: Center Ind Ter

Choctaw Nation

Choctaw Roll (Not Including Freedmen)

CARD NO.
FIELD NO. 100

Dawes' Roll No.		NAME	Relationship to Person First Named	AGE	SEX	BLOOD	TRIBAL ENROLLMENT Year	County	No.
195	1	Overstreet, Jane B. 25	First Named	21	F	Full		Choctaw residing in Chickasaw District	CCR #2 81
DEAD	2	~~" Clarence~~ DEAD	~~Son~~	~~1~~	~~M~~	~~1/2~~			
196	3	" Minnie	dau	4 ½mo	F	1/2			
	4	ENROLLMENT							
	5	OF NOS. 1 and 3 HEREON APPROVED BY THE SECRETARY					1896	Chickasaw Dist	2026
	6	OF INTERIOR Dec 12 1902							
	7	No 1 on Choctaw Roll as Mary Jane Bond, wife of Charley Overstreet U.S. Citizen.							
	8								
	9	Statement taken as to death of No 2							
	10	June 7, 1900							
	11								
	12	No.2 hereon dismissed under order of							
	13	the Commissioner to the Five Civilized							
	14	Tribes of March 31, 1905.				No 1 now Jane Brumley 4/19/07			
	15								
	16								
	17								

TRIBAL ENROLLMENT OF PARENTS

	Name of Father	Year	County	Name of Mother	Year	County
1	Sampson Bond	Dead	Choctaw Roll	Melvina Johnson		Choctaw residing in ~~Chickasaw District~~
2	~~Charley Overstreet~~		~~non citizen~~	~~No 1~~		
3	" "		" "	"		
4						
5						
6						
7						
8						
9						
10						
11						
12						
13						~~Date of Application~~
14						for Enrollment.
15						Sept. 13/98
16				No 3 Enrolled Jany 17, 1900		
17	P.O. Bebee[sic] I.T. 4/6/06					

Choctaw By Blood Enrollment Cards 1898-1914

RESIDENCE: Chickasaw Nation ~~COUNTY~~.
POST OFFICE: Wynnewood Ind Ter

Choctaw Nation

Choctaw Roll (Not Including Freedmen)

CARD NO.
FIELD NO. 101

Dawes' Roll No.		NAME		Relationship to Person First Named	AGE	SEX	BLOOD	TRIBAL ENROLLMENT Year	County	No.
IW 2	1	Cobb, Ben	37		33	M	I.W.		Choctaw residing in Chickasaw District	C.I.Roll 19
197	2	" Maud O.	24	wife	20	F	1/8		" "	CCR #2 388
198	3	" Mary Eilene	5	dau	1	"	1/16			
199	4	" Lois	3	"	4mo	"	1/16			
200	5	" Maude	1	"	2wks	F	1/16			

ENROLLMENT OF NOS. 2,3,4, and 5 HEREON APPROVED BY THE SECRETARY OF INTERIOR Dec 12 1902

No2 1896 Blue 10012 as Maud Owens

ENROLLMENT OF NOS. ~ 1 ~ HEREON APPROVED BY THE SECRETARY OF INTERIOR Jun 13 1903

No 2 on Choctaw roll as Maud Owens

~~No 4 enrolled Dec 19/99 Affidavit irregular~~ and returned for correction.

TRIBAL ENROLLMENT OF PARENTS

	Name of Father	Year	County	Name of Mother	Year	County
1	S.J. Cobb		non citizen	Rebecca Cobb	Dead	non citizen
2	Oliver P. Owens		" "	M.E. Cooper		Blue
3	No 1			No 2		
4	No 1			No 2		
5	No 1			No 2		

Evidence of birth of Nos 3 and 4 received and filed Aug 6th 1900

No5 Born June 9th 1902; Enrolled June 23rd 1902
~~See additional testimony of No1 taken October 20, 1902.~~

#1 to 3
Date of Application for Enrollment.
Sept. 13/98

RESIDENCE: Chickasaw Nation ~~COUNTY~~.
POST OFFICE: Wynnewood Ind Ter.

Choctaw Nation

Choctaw Roll (*Not Including Freedmen*)

CARD NO.
FIELD NO. **102**

Dawes' Roll No.		NAME	Relationship to Person First Named	AGE	SEX	BLOOD	TRIBAL ENROLLMENT Year	County	No.
201	1	Cooper, Mary Emaline	First Named	46	F	1/4		Blue	CCR #2 118
202	2	Randolph, Minnie	Dau	24	"	1/8		"	"
203	3	Randolph, Wirt Aubrey	Grandson	4mo	M	1/16			
IW1200	4	" Wirt	Husband of No2	31	M	IW			
	5	ENROLLMENT				No1	1896	Blue	2878
	6	OF NOS. 1, 2 and 3 HEREON APPROVED BY THE SECRETARY				No2	1896	"	2879
	7	OF INTERIOR DEC 12 1902							
	8	ENROLLMENT				No1 on Choctaw roll as Emma E. Cooper			
	9	OF NOS. ~4~ HEREON APPROVED BY THE SECRETARY			~~As to remarriage see No.4 testimony~~	No2 is the wife of Wirt Randolph on			
	10	OF INTERIOR DEC 13 1904				Choctaw Card D-499			
	11								
	12	No1 Daughter of Nancy Stewart who was admitted by U.S. Indian Agent Oct 12 1889							
	13	Marriage license and certificate to Minnie Cooper under Chick law filed May 28, 1900							
	14								
	15		No3 Enrolled May 24, 1900.						
	16								
	17								

TRIBAL ENROLLMENT OF PARENTS

	Name of Father	Year	County	Name of Mother	Year	County
1	Wiley Stewart	Dead	non citizen	Nancy Stewart		Blue
2	George Cooper	"	" "	No1		
3	Wirt Randolph		" "	No2		
4	Jas. T. Randolph		" "	Martha Randolph		Non-Cit.
5						
6						
7						
8						
9						
10						
11						
12	~~No.4 originally listed for enrollment on Choctaw card #D-499 - Sept 14/99. See decision of~~					
13	~~Nov. 9, 1904.~~					
14	No.4 transferred from Choc. card #D-499 Nov. 26, 1904.					
15						
16				~~Date of Application for Enrollment.~~		~~Sept. 13/98~~
17						

RESIDENCE: Chickasaw Nation ~~COUNTY~~.
POST OFFICE: Rush Spring Ind Ter

Choctaw Nation

Choctaw Roll *(Not Including Freedmen)*

CARD NO.
FIELD NO. 103

Dawes' Roll No.		NAME	Relationship to Person First Named	AGE	SEX	BLOOD	TRIBAL ENROLLMENT Year	County	No.
VOID.	1	~~Reynolds Charles A~~	~~Named~~	~~34~~	~~M~~	~~I.W.~~			
VOID.	2	~~" Katie~~	~~wife~~	~~25~~	~~F~~	~~1/2~~			
VOID.	3	~~" Willie~~	~~son~~	~~9~~	~~M~~	~~1/4~~			
VOID.	4	~~" Frank~~	~~"~~	~~7~~	~~"~~	~~1/4~~			
VOID.	5	~~" Seldan~~	~~"~~	~~5~~	~~"~~	~~1/4~~			
VOID.	6	~~" Ethel A.~~	~~Dau~~	~~4~~	~~F~~	~~1/4~~			
VOID.	7	DEAD ~~Lillie May~~	~~"~~	~~15mo~~	~~"~~	~~1/4~~			

8 No 1 on Chickasaw Roll Pickens Co Page 79 transferred to Choctaw Roll by Dawes Com.
Nos 2,3,4,5&6 " " " " " " 24 " " " " " " "
10 No7 " " " " " " 86 " " " " " " "

No 1 admitted as an intermarried Chickasaw and Nos 2-3-4-5
and is as[sic] Chickasaws by blood by Dawes Commission in 1896
in Chickasaw Case #77: no appeal

CANCELLED

Transferred to Chickasaw Card No 1599
Oct 17 1902

TRIBAL ENROLLMENT OF PARENTS

	Name of Father	Year	County	Name of Mother	Year	County
1	~~J.B. Reynolds~~		~~non citizen~~	~~Louisa Reynolds~~		~~non citizen~~
2	~~Levi Perry~~	~~Dead~~	~~Chickasaw Roll~~	~~Ellen Perry~~	~~Dead~~	~~Choctaw Roll~~
3	~~No1~~			~~No2~~		
4	~~No1~~			~~No2~~		
5	~~No1~~			~~No2~~		
6	~~No1~~			~~No2~~		
7	~~No1~~			~~No2~~		

11 No 1 married out

Date of Application for Enrollment. ~~Sept. 13/98~~

RESIDENCE: Chickasaw Nation ~~COUNTY~~.
POST OFFICE: Erin Springs Ind Ter.

Choctaw Nation

Choctaw Roll *(Not Including Freedmen)*

CARD NO.
FIELD NO. **104**

Dawes' Roll No.		NAME	Relationship to Person First Named	AGE	SEX	BLOOD	TRIBAL ENROLLMENT Year	County	No.
IW857	1	Carson Jerry 56		52	M	I.W.		Choctaw residing in Chickasaw District	C.I. Roll 19
204	2	See Hibernia 25	Dau	21	F	1/16		" "	CCR #2 126
205	3	Carson Cora 23	"	19	"	1/16		" "	"
206	4	" Rose 19	"	15	"	1/16		" "	"
207	5	" James 17	Son	13	M	1/16		" "	"
208	6	" Juanita	Dau	10	F	1/16		" "	"
209	7	" Milton 11	Son	7	M	1/16		" "	"
210	8	See Lula 1	Gr Dau	2mo	F	1/32			
211	9	" Ollie 1	G.Dau	1mo	F	1/32			
IW168	10	" Charles W	husband of No2	28	M	I.W.			
	11	~~Nos 2 to 7 inclusive on Choctaw roll as Cossin~~							
	12	No6 " " " " Jenette Cossin							
	13	No. 2 on Choctaw as Heberna Cossin							
	14								
	15	See testimony of N°1 taken October 20, 1902.							
	16	See testimony of Noah Lael taken October 20, 1902							
	17	For child of Nos 2 & 10 see NB (Mar 3-1905) #72.							

ENROLLMENT OF NOS.2,3,4,5,6,7,8 and 9 HEREON APPROVED BY THE SECRETARY OF INTERIOR

TRIBAL ENROLLMENT OF PARENTS

	Name of Father	Year	County	Name of Mother	Year	County
1	Lindsey Carson	Dead	non citizen	Mary Carson		non citizen
2	No1			Lula Carson	Dead	Choctaw residing in Chickasaw District
3	No1			" "		" "
4	No1			" "		" "
5	No1			" "		" "
6	No1			" "		" "
7	No1			" "		" "
8	Chas See			No2		
9	No2 is now the wife of Charles W See Choctaw Card D.441 June 4, 1900			No2		
10	Father of Nº10 is F.M. See noncitz Mother of Nº10 is Adeline See non-citz.					
11	No1 1896 Chickasaw Dist 14444			No.9 born Dec. 3, 1901: Enrolled Jan, 7, 1902,		
12	No2 1896 " " 3119			Father of No.9 Chas See non-citz.		
13	~~No3 1896 " " 3120~~					
14	~~No4 1896 " " 3121~~					
15	No5 1896 " " 3122			No8 enrolled 6/5/1900		Date of Application for Enrollment. Sept. 13/98
16	No6 1896 " " 3123					
17	~~No7 1896 " " 3124~~					

ENROLLMENT OF NOS. ~ 10 ~ HEREON APPROVED BY THE SECRETARY OF INTERIOR JUN 13 1903

ENROLLMENT OF NOS. ~ 1 ~ HEREON APPROVED BY THE SECRETARY OF INTERIOR AUG 3 1904

RESIDENCE: Chickasaw Nation ~~COUNTY.~~
POST OFFICE: Purcell, Ind Ter.

Choctaw Nation

Choctaw Roll (*Not Including Freedmen*)

CARD NO.
FIELD NO. 105

Dawes' Roll No.	NAME	Relationship to Person First Named	AGE	SEX	BLOOD	TRIBAL ENROLLMENT Year	County	No.
212	1 Dunn Salina 69	First Named	65	F	1/8		Choctaw residing in Chickasaw District	CCR #2 151
DEAD	2 ~~" Alfred DEAD~~	~~Son~~	~~38~~	~~M~~	~~1/16~~		~~" "~~	~~"~~

ENROLLMENT OF NOS. 1 HEREON APPROVED BY THE SECRETARY OF INTERIOR DEC 12 1902

No. 2 HEREON DISMISSED UNDER ORDER OF THE COMMISSION TO THE FIVE CIVILIZED TRIBES OF MARCH 31, 1905.

~~No1 1896 Chickasaw Dist 3670 as Selina Dunn~~
No2 1896 " " 3669

No2 Died Nov[r] 12th 1901: Evidence of Death filed July 14th 1902.

TRIBAL ENROLLMENT OF PARENTS

Name of Father	Year	County	Name of Mother	Year	County
1 Allen Yates	Dead	non citizen	Emily Yates	Dead	Choctaw Roll
2 ~~Wm M. Dunn~~	~~"~~	~~" "~~	~~No1~~		

Date of Application for Enrollment. Sept. 13/98

RESIDENCE: Chickasaw Nation ~~COUNTY~~.
POST OFFICE: Purcell Ind Ter.

Choctaw Nation

Choctaw Roll *(Not Including Freedmen)*

CARD NO.
FIELD NO. **106**

Dawes' Roll No.	NAME	Relationship to Person First Named	AGE	SEX	BLOOD	TRIBAL ENROLLMENT Year	County	No.
213	1 Harris Rosa L. 36	First Named	32	F	1/16		Atoka	CCR #2 254
214	2 " Alfred M. 14	Son	11	M	1/32		"	"
IW620	3 " Jonas R 63	Hus	63	M	I.W.	1896	Chick Dist	14674

ENROLLMENT
~~OF NOS.~~ 1 and 2 ~~HEREON~~
APPROVED BY THE SECRETARY
OF INTERIOR DEC 12 1902

ENROLLMENT
OF NOS. 3 HEREON
~~APPROVED BY THE SECRETARY~~
OF INTERIOR MAR 26 1904

~~No1 1896 Atoka 6002 as Mrs Rosa Harris~~
No2 1896 " 6003 " Alfred "
No1 1896 Chick Dist 6216 as Rosie Harris
No2 1896 " " 6217
~~No3 on 1896 roll as J.R. Harris~~
No1 wife of J.R. Harris; U.S. Citizen
No3 transferred from Choctaw card #3107 Oct 8, 1903

TRIBAL ENROLLMENT OF PARENTS

Name of Father	Year	County	Name of Mother	Year	County
1 Wm M. Dunn	Dead	noncitizen	Salina Dunn		Choctaw residing in Chickasaw Dist
2 J.R. Harris		" "	No1		
3 Harvey H. Harris	Dead	" "	Eliza Harris	Dead	noncitizen

#1 & 2
Date of Application ~~for Enrollment.~~ Sept. 13/98

RESIDENCE: Chickasaw Nation ~~COUNTY~~.
POST OFFICE: Purcell Ind Ter.

Choctaw Nation

Choctaw Roll *(Not Including Freedmen)*

CARD NO.
FIELD NO. 107

Dawes' Roll No.	NAME	Relationship to Person First Named	AGE	SEX	BLOOD	TRIBAL ENROLLMENT Year	County	No.
VOID.	1 ~~Perry Joseph~~	~~Named~~	~~39~~	~~M~~	~~1/2~~			
VOID.	2 ~~" Matilda~~	~~wife~~	~~39~~	~~F~~	~~1/4~~			
VOID.	3 ~~" Charles E.~~	~~son~~	~~16~~	~~M~~	~~3/8~~			
VOID.	4 ~~" Joel F.~~	~~"~~	~~15~~	~~"~~	~~3/8~~			
VOID.	5 ~~" Lela A.~~	~~dau~~	~~13~~	~~F~~	~~3/8~~			
VOID.	6 ~~" James W.~~	~~son~~	~~5~~	~~M~~	~~3/8~~			
VOID.	7 ~~" Clemmie May~~	~~Dau~~	~~3~~	~~F~~	~~3/8~~			
VOID.	8 ~~" Mildred Catherine~~	~~"~~	~~7mo~~	~~"~~	~~3/8~~			
	9							

10 All on Chickasaw Roll, Pontotoc County, Page 62, transferred to Choctaw roll by Dawes Com.
11 No2 " " " as Matila
12 No7 " " " " C.M.
13 Evidence of birth of No8 received and filed Feby. 15, 1902.
14
15
16
17

CANCELLED

Transferred to Chickasaw Card No. 592 Oct. 11, 1902.

TRIBAL ENROLLMENT OF PARENTS

	Name of Father	Year	County	Name of Mother	Year	County
1	~~Morgan Perry~~	~~Dead~~	~~Chickasaw Roll~~	~~Elizabeth Perry~~	~~Dead~~	~~Choctaw roll~~
2	~~Charles E Eastman~~	~~"~~	~~non citizen~~	~~Betsey Eastman~~	~~"~~	~~" "~~
3	~~No1~~			~~No2~~		
4	~~No1~~			~~No2~~		
5	~~No1~~			~~No2~~		
6	~~No1~~			~~No2~~		
7	~~No1~~			~~No2~~		
8	~~No1~~			~~No2~~		

Date of Application for Enrollment Sept. 13/98

RESIDENCE: Chickasaw Nation ~~COUNTY~~.
POST OFFICE: Davis, Ind Ter.

Choctaw Nation

Choctaw Roll
(Not Including Freedmen)

CARD NO.
FIELD NO. 108

Dawes' Roll No.	NAME	Relationship to Person First Named	AGE	SEX	BLOOD	TRIBAL ENROLLMENT Year	County	No.
215	1 Grant Thomas Jr 26	First Named	24	M	1/8		Choctaw residing in Chickasaw District	CCR #2 215
IW 1275	2 " Mardie 21	Wife	21	F	I.W.			
	3					1896	Chickasaw Dist	5012

ENROLLMENT OF NOS. 1 HEREON APPROVED BY THE SECRETARY OF INTERIOR DEC 12 1902

No1 is now the husband of Mardie Grant on Choctaw Card #D800 Sept 23, 1902
~~On Sept. 21, 1902 No.2 was married to No.1~~

No.2 originally listed for enrollment on Choctaw Card D-800 Sept 23, 1902 transferred to this card Jan. 2, 1905. See decision of Jan 12, 1905.
~~Record as to enrollment of No2 forwarded Department Mar. 14, 1906~~
Record returned. See opinion of Assistant Attorney General of March 15, 1906 in case of Omer R. Nicholson
For children of Nos 1 and 2 see NB (Mar 3 1905) #514

ENROLLMENT OF NOS. 2 HEREON APPROVED BY THE SECRETARY OF INTERIOR MAR 14 1905

TRIBAL ENROLLMENT OF PARENTS

Name of Father	Year	County	Name of Mother	Year	County
1 Thomas Grant	1897	Chic. residing in Pickens Co	Margaret Grant	Dead	Choctaw residing in Chickasaw District
2 Stephen Box		noncitizen	Winifred Box		noncitizen
17 P.O. Arbuckle 3/25/05			Date of Application for Enrollment.		Sept. 13/98

RESIDENCE: Chickasaw Nation ~~COUNTY~~.
POST OFFICE: White Bead, Ind Ter.

Choctaw Nation

Choctaw Roll *(Not Including Freedmen)*

CARD NO.
FIELD NO. **109**

Dawes' Roll No.	NAME	Relationship to Person First Named	AGE	SEX	BLOOD	TRIBAL ENROLLMENT Year	County	No.
216	1 Burnett Catherine C. 53	First Named	49	F	Full		Choctaw residing in Chickasaw District	CCR #2 82
IW1243	2 " John L 34	Husband	34	M	IW			
	3					1896	Chickasaw Dist	2034

ENROLLMENT OF NOS. 1 HEREON APPROVED BY THE SECRETARY OF INTERIOR DEC 12 1902

ENROLLMENT ~~OF NOS. 2 HEREON~~ APPROVED BY THE SECRETARY OF INTERIOR DEC 30 1904

No.2 Admitted by Dawes Commission in 1896 in Choctaw case #884, as an intermarried citizen. Appeal taken and appeal dismissed. See new Choctaw ~~Citizenship docket No.2, Page 361 Citizenship case #884.~~
~~No.2 originally listed for enrollment Nov. 14, 1902 on Choctaw card #D-824:~~ transferred to this card Dec. 15, 1904. See decision of Nov. 28, 1904.

TRIBAL ENROLLMENT OF PARENTS

	Name of Father	Year	County	Name of Mother	Year	County
1	John Campbell	Dead	Choctaw Roll	Annie Dennis	Dead	Choctaw Roll
2	John J. Burnett		Non citizen	Nancy Burnett	"	non citizen

Date of Application for Enrollment.
Sept. 13/98

Choctaw By Blood Enrollment Cards 1898-1914

RESIDENCE: Chickasaw Nation ~~COUNTY.~~
POST OFFICE: Wynnewood Ind Ter.

Choctaw Nation

Choctaw Roll (Not Including Freedmen)

CARD NO.
FIELD NO. **110**

Dawes' Roll No.	NAME	Relationship to Person First Named	AGE	SEX	BLOOD	TRIBAL ENROLLMENT Year	County	No.
IW960	1 Casey, Wiley P 29	First Named	25	M	I.W.			
15562	2 " Julia Ann W 24	wife	20	F	1/4		Choctaw residing in ~~Chickasaw District~~	CCR #2 489
15563	3 " Pushamataha 2	son	2wk	M	1/8	Born Oct 11, 1900		
	4 ENROLLMENT							
	5 OF NOS. 2 and 3 HEREON APPROVED BY THE SECRETARY							
	6 OF INTERIOR Sep 22 1904		No2	1896	Chickasaw	Dist	14180 as Julia Walker	
	7 ENROLLMENT		"	1893	"	"	Page 67 " " " No 619	
	8 OF NOS. ~ 1 ~ HEREON APPROVED BY THE SECRETARY							
	9 OF INTERIOR Sep 22 1904							
	10 No2 admitted by Dawes Commission Case No 1015, and no appeal taken							
	11 No2 on Choctaw roll as Julia Walker							
	12 ~~No3 Enrolled Oct 25th 1900~~							
	13 ~~No2 on Creek card field No 3749 as Julia Casey~~ Enroll No2 as Choctaw - not on final Creek roll							
	14 Nos 1,2,3 See Decision of May 28 '04							
	15							
	16 ~~For children of Nos 1 & 2 See N.B. (March 3rd 1905) Card No1.~~							
	17							

TRIBAL ENROLLMENT OF PARENTS

	Name of Father	Year	County	Name of Mother	Year	County
1	W.D. Casey		non citizen	Sarah E. Casey		non citizen
2	Wm Walker	Dead	San Bois	Mary F Gatling		" "
3	No1			No2		
4						
5						
6						
7						
8						
9						
10						
11						
12						
13						
14						
15						
16					Date of Application for Enrollment.	
17	Roff I.T.					Sept. 13/98

RESIDENCE: Chickasaw Nation COUNTY.
POST OFFICE: Davis Ind Ter.

Choctaw Nation

Choctaw Roll (Not Including Freedmen)

CARD NO.
FIELD NO. **111**

Dawes' Roll No.		NAME	Relationship to Person First Named	AGE	SEX	BLOOD	TRIBAL ENROLLMENT Year	County	No.
217	1	Howell, Thomas P. 53	First Named	49	M	1/8		Choctaw residing in Chickasaw District	CCR #2 259
IW955	2	" Henrietta ✳ 41	wife	37	F	I.W.		" "	CI Roll 47
218	3	" Thomas P. jr 14	son	10	M	1/16		" "	CCR #2 259
219	4	" Laura 11	dau	7	F	1/16		" "	"
220	5	" Vivian 9	"	5	"	1/16		" "	"
221	6	" Gladys 7	"	3	"	1/16		" "	"

ENROLLMENT OF NOS. 1,3,4,5 and 6 HEREON APPROVED BY THE SECRETARY OF INTERIOR Dec 12 1902

ENROLLMENT OF NOS. ~~ 2 ~~ HEREON APPROVED BY THE SECRETARY OF INTERIOR Aug 20 1904

✳No 2 Admitted by C.C.C.C Case 101T as an intermarried citizen June 22 1904 as Nettie Howell

No 2 admitted by U.S. Court Southern District, Ardmore I.T. March 11th 1898 in Court Case #147 as Nettie Howell
No 5 on Choctaw roll as Viney Howell
No 2 Denied by Dawes Com '96 Case #413 as Nettie Howell

Evidence of marriage of Nos 1 and 2 filed Oct 19, 1900.

TRIBAL ENROLLMENT OF PARENTS

	Name of Father	Year	County	Name of Mother	Year	County
1	Calvin H Howell (I.W.)	Dead	Eagle	Rhoda Howell		Choctaw residing in Chickasaw District
2	George W. Wright	"	non citizen		Dead	non citizen
3	No 1			No 2		
4	No 1			No 2		
5	No 1			No 2		
6	No 1			No 2		

No1 1896 Chickasaw Dist 6197 as T.F Howell
No2 1896 " " 14669
No3 1896 " " 6201 as F.L. Howell
No4 1896 " " 6202
No5 1896 " " 6203 as Viny Howell
No6 1896 " " 6204 " Glalis "
No1 is father of Daisy and Calvin H Howell on Chickasaw Card #402.
Judgement[sic] of U.S. Court admitting No2 vacated and set aside by Decree of Choctaw-Chickasaw Cit. Court Dec 16 '02

No2 in C.C.C.C. Case #101T and in 121T.

Date of Application for Enrollment. Sept. 13/98

RESIDENCE: Chickasaw Nation ~~COUNTY~~.
POST OFFICE: Paola Ind. Ter.

Choctaw Nation

Choctaw Roll (Not Including Freedmen)

CARD NO.
FIELD NO. 112

Dawes' Roll No.		NAME	Relationship to Person First Named	AGE	SEX	BLOOD	TRIBAL ENROLLMENT Year	County	No.
IW541	1	Florence, Robert C. 54	First Named	50	M	I.W.		Choctaw residing in Chickasaw District	CCR #0 56
222	2	" Mary Jane 44	wife	40	F	3/8		" "	CCR #2 194
See 4565	3	~~" Lucy A.~~	~~Dau~~	~~21~~	~~"~~	~~3/16~~		~~" "~~	~~"~~
223	4	" Charley 23	Son	19	M	3/16		" "	"
224	5	" Zach A. 20	"	16	M	3/16		" "	"
225	6	" Lena	Dau	11	F	3/16		" "	CCR #3 21
226	7	" Fannie	"	8	"	3/16		" "	"
	8	ENROLLMENT							
	9	OF NOS. 2,4,5,6 and 7 HEREON APPROVED BY THE SECRETARY							
	10	OF INTERIOR DEC 12 1902							
	11	ENROLLMENT							
	12	OF NOS. ~~ 1 ~~ HEREON APPROVED BY THE SECRETARY							
	13	OF INTERIOR FEB -8 1904							
	14	No1 on Choctaw Census Roll No.0. Page 56. No. 70.							
	15	No6 " " Pay " No3 " 21 " 204 1893 Chick. Dist.							
		~~No7 " " " " No3 " 21 " 205 1893 Chick. Dist.~~							
	16	No2 " " Roll as Mary G Florence							
	17								

TRIBAL ENROLLMENT OF PARENTS

	Name of Father	Year	County	Name of Mother	Year	County
1	Wm Florence	Dead	noncitizen	Lucy Ann Florence	Dead	noncitizen
2	George Gardner	"	Choctaw residing in Chickasaw District	Phoebe Gardner	"	Choctaw residing in Chickasaw District
3	~~No1~~			~~No2~~		
4	No1			No2		
5	No1			No2		
6	No1			No2		
7	No1			No2		
8						
9		No2 1896 Chickasaw Dist 4574 as Mary G Florence				
10		No3 1896 " " 4575				
11		~~No4 1896 " " 4576~~				
		No5 1896 " " 4577 as Zack Ann Florence				
12						
13						
14						
15						Date of Application for Enrollment.
16						Sept. 13/98
17						

RESIDENCE: Chickasaw Nation ~~COUNTY~~.
POST OFFICE: Paola, Ind Ter.

Choctaw Nation

Choctaw Roll *(Not Including Freedmen)*

CARD NO.
FIELD NO. 113

Dawes' Roll No.	NAME	Relationship to Person First Named	AGE	SEX	BLOOD	TRIBAL ENROLLMENT Year	County	No.
227	1 Wright, John W. 16	First Named	12	M	1/16		Choctaw residing in Chickasaw District	CCR #2 489
	2							
	3 ENROLLMENT					1896	Chickasaw Dist	14156
	4 OF NOS. 1 HEREON APPROVED BY THE SECRETARY							
	5 OF INTERIOR DEC 12 1902					On Choctaw roll as John Wright		
	6							
	7							
	8 Make inquiry as to marriage of John W Wright and Mary E Wright now M^c^Fadden							
	9 6/6/02 For evidence of marriage of John W and Mary E Wright see 7-D-321.							
	10							
	11							
	12							
	13							
	14							
	15							
	16							
	17							

TRIBAL ENROLLMENT OF PARENTS

Name of Father	Year	County	Name of Mother	Year	County
1 John W. Wright	Dead	Choctaw residing in Chickasaw District	Mary E Wright		non citizen
2					
3					
4					
5					
6					
7					
8					
9					
10					
11					
12					
13					
14					
15					Date of Application for Enrollment.
16					Sept. 13/98
17					

RESIDENCE: Chickasaw Nation ~~COUNTY~~.
POST OFFICE: Pauls Valley, Ind Ter.

Choctaw Nation

Choctaw Roll (Not Including Freedmen)

CARD NO.
FIELD NO. 114

Dawes' Roll No.	NAME	Relationship to Person First Named	AGE	SEX	BLOOD	TRIBAL ENROLLMENT Year	County	No.
14183	1 Hibdon, Jesse 11	First Named	7	M	1/32	1896	Chick Dist	6168
14184	2 " Charlie 8	Bro	4	"	1/32	1896	" "	6169
IW 1061	3 Magner, Eula H.	Mother	29	F	IW			

ENROLLMENT OF NOS. 1 and 2 HEREON APPROVED BY THE SECRETARY OF INTERIOR APR 11 1903

ENROLLMENT OF NOS. 3 HEREON APPROVED BY THE SECRETARY OF INTERIOR NOV 16 1904

~~Both admitted by Dawes Com Case No 1415 and no appeal taken~~
No1 " " " " as Jessie.
No3 " " " " Case #1415; no appeal.
~~No1 on 1896 Choctaw roll, Chick Dist, Page 150, No 6168 as Jessee Hibbon~~
~~No2 " 1896 " " " " " 150 " 6169 " Charlie "~~

No3 transferred from Choctaw card #D-329, Oct. 31, 1904: See decision of Oct 15, 1904
For children of No3 see NB (Apr 26 '06) #1150.

TRIBAL ENROLLMENT OF PARENTS

	Name of Father	Year	County	Name of Mother	Year	County
1	Charles Hibdon	Dead	Choctaw residing in ~~Chickasaw District~~	Eula Magner		non citizen
2	" "	"	" "	" "		" "
3	Jas. K. Jackson		non-citizen	Cornelia Jackson		non-citizen

Date of Application for Enrollment.
~~Date of application for enrollment Sept. 13/98~~

RESIDENCE: Chickasaw Nation ~~COUNTY.~~
POST OFFICE: Purcell, Ind Ter

Choctaw Nation

Choctaw Roll *(Not Including Freedmen)*

CARD NO.
FIELD NO. 115

Dawes' Roll No.		NAME	Relationship to Person First Named	AGE	SEX	BLOOD	TRIBAL ENROLLMENT Year	County	No.
IW 1062	1	Suttle, Merriman W 62	Named	58	M	I.W.			
	2								
	3								
	4								
	5								
	6								
	7								
	8								
	9								
	10								
	11								
	12								
	13								
	14								
	15								
	16								
	17								

ENROLLMENT
OF NOS. ~~~ 1 ~~~ HEREON
APPROVED BY THE SECRETARY
OF INTERIOR NOV 16 1904

Admitted by Dawes Commission Case No 1070 and no appeal taken

Marriage license and certificate on file in office of Dawes Com to be attached to this card

TRIBAL ENROLLMENT OF PARENTS

	Name of Father	Year	County	Name of Mother	Year	County
1	James Suttle	Dead	non citizen	Eliza Suttle		non citizen
2						
3						
4						
5						
6						
7						
8						
9						
10						
11						
12						
13						
14						
15						
16						
17						

Date of Application for Enrollment. Sept. 13/98

RESIDENCE: Chickasaw Nation COUNTY.
POST OFFICE: Pauls Valley Ind. Ter.

Choctaw Nation

Choctaw Roll (Not Including Freedmen)

CARD NO.
FIELD NO. 116

Dawes' Roll No.	NAME	Relationship to Person First Named	AGE	SEX	BLOOD	TRIBAL ENROLLMENT Year	County	No.
IW 1468	~~Vincent, Charley S~~ 31	~~First Named~~	~~27~~	~~M~~	~~I.W.~~		~~Choctaw residing in Chickasaw District~~	~~CD Roll #2 111~~
228	" Lena 24	wife	20	F	1/2		" "	~~CCR #2 455~~
229	" Nona 7	Dau	3	"	1/4		" "	
230	" Mahautie 5	"	1 1/2	"	1/4		" "	
231	" Monnie 1	Dau	6mo	F	1/4			

ENROLLMENT OF NOS. 2,3,4 and 5 HEREON APPROVED BY THE SECRETARY OF INTERIOR Dec. 12, 1902

ENROLLMENT OF NOS. One HEREON APPROVED BY THE SECRETARY OF INTERIOR Aug 22 1905

No 3 on Choctaw roll as Hannah

No1 1896 Chickasaw Dist 15137 as Charles I Vincent
No2 1896 " " 12635
No3 1896 " " 12636 as Hannah Vincent

No1 restored to roll by Departmental authority of January 19, 1909 (File 5-51)

~~Enrollment of No.1 cancelled by order of Dept. March 4, 1907~~

TRIBAL ENROLLMENT OF PARENTS

Name of Father	Year	County	Name of Mother	Year	County
~~Garland Vincent~~	~~Dead~~	~~non citizen~~	~~Martha Vincent~~		~~non citizen~~
Wm Riddle	"	Chickasaw Roll	Margaret Riddle	Dead	Choctaw Roll
No1			No2		
No1			No2		
No1			No2		

No1 See Dawes Commission Record 1896 Case 251
No1 was denied by Dawes Commission in 1896
Choctaw Case #251. No appeal.
~~Evidence of birth of No4 received and filed Feby 24, 1902~~
~~No5 Born Aug. 22, 1901; enrolled Feby 24, 1902~~

For child of Nos 1 & 2 see NB (Apr. 26 '06) Card No 217
" " " " " " " " (March 3, 1905) " " 785

Date of Application for Enrollment. ~~Sept. 13/98~~

P.O. Womack I.T. Oct 23/02 1905

RESIDENCE: Chickasaw Nation ~~COUNTY~~.
POST OFFICE: Paola, Ind. Ter.

Choctaw Nation — **Choctaw Roll** (Not Including Freedmen) — CARD NO. — FIELD NO. 117

Dawes' Roll No.		NAME		Relationship to Person First Named	AGE	SEX	BLOOD	TRIBAL ENROLLMENT Year	County	No.
IW63	1	Williams, Isaac W.	35	First Named	31	M	I.W.		Choctaw residing in Chickasaw District	CI Roll 118
232	2	" Georgianna N	33	wife	29	F	1/2		" "	CCR #2 489
233	3	" Walter K	13	son	9	M	1/4		" "	"
234	4	" Lorena	10	Dau	6	F	1/4		" "	"
235	5	" Mamie	6	"	2	"	1/4			
236	6	" Leona M.	3	"	2mo	"	1/4			

ENROLLMENT OF NOS. 2,3,4,5 and 6 HEREON APPROVED BY THE SECRETARY OF INTERIOR DEC 12 1902

~~No1 1896 Chickasaw Dist 15197 as I.W. William~~
No2 1896 " " 14186 as Georgiana William
No3 1896 " " 14190
~~No4 1896 " " 14191~~
~~Evidence of birth of No.5 filed Jan. 28, 1902.~~

See testimony of Nº1 as to his status as an intermarried citizen on Sept. 25, 1902, taken at Pauls Valley I.T. Oct. 21, 1902.

ENROLLMENT OF NOS. ~~~ 1 ~~~ HEREON APPROVED BY THE SECRETARY OF INTERIOR JUN 13 1903

TRIBAL ENROLLMENT OF PARENTS

	Name of Father	Year	County	Name of Mother	Year	County
1	Thos Williams	Dead	non citizen	Elizabeth Williams		non citizen
2	Edward Nail	"	Blue	Beckey Nail	Dead	Blue
3	No1			No2		
4	No1			No2		
5	No1			No2		
6	No1			No2		

No 6 Enrolled Dec 14/99

1 to 5
Date of Application for Enrollment.
Sept. 13/98

Purcell, I.T. 10/21/02

RESIDENCE: Chickasaw Nation ~~COUNTY~~.
POST OFFICE: Pauls Valley Ind. Ter.

Choctaw Nation

Choctaw Roll *(Not Including Freedmen)*

CARD NO.
FIELD NO. **118**

Dawes' Roll No.		NAME	Relationship to Person First Named	AGE	SEX	BLOOD	TRIBAL ENROLLMENT Year	County	No.
IW 542	1	Carrier, Joe G. 69	First Named	65	M	I.W.		Choctaw residing in Chickasaw District	C.I. Roll 19

ENROLLMENT OF NOS. ~~~ 1 ~~~ HEREON APPROVED BY THE SECRETARY OF INTERIOR FEB -8 1904

1896 Chickasaw Dist 14434 as Joe G. Conner

Admitted by Dawes Commission Case No. 478 and no appeal taken.

TRIBAL ENROLLMENT OF PARENTS

	Name of Father	Year	County	Name of Mother	Year	County
1	Joseph Carrier	Dead	non citizen	Louiza Carrier	Dead	non citizen

Date of Application for Enrollment. Sept. 13/98

P.O. White-Bead I.T.

RESIDENCE: Chickasaw Nation ~~COUNTY~~. **Choctaw Nation** **Choctaw Roll** *(Not Including Freedmen)* CARD NO.
POST OFFICE: Hart, Ind. Ter. FIELD NO. 119

Dawes' Roll No.		NAME		Relationship to Person First Named	AGE	SEX	BLOOD	TRIBAL ENROLLMENT Year	County	No.
237	1	Spain, Thomas G.	50	First Named	46	M	1/16	1896	Choctaw residing in Chickasaw District	11762
IW 3	2	" Elizabeth	45	wife	41	F	I.W.	1896	" "	15077
See 3411	3	~~" Andrew~~		~~Son~~	~~20~~	~~M~~	~~1/32~~	~~1896~~	" "	~~11763~~
DEAD	4	~~" David B~~ DEAD		"	~~19~~	"	~~1/32~~	~~1896~~	" "	~~11764~~
See 4747	5	~~" Mary Ann~~		~~Dau~~	~~17~~	~~F~~	~~1/32~~	~~1896~~	" "	~~11766~~
238	6	" Thomas H	19	Son	15	M	1/32	1896	" "	11765
239	7	" Sidney B	17	"	13	"	1/32	1896	" "	11767
240	8	" Elizabeth	13	Dau	9	F	1/32	1896	" "	11768
241	9	" Emma P	11	"	7	"	1/32	1896	" "	11769
242	10	now Wilson " Nellie May	10	"	6	"	1/32	1896	" "	11770
243	11	" James R	8	Son	4	M	1/32	1896	" "	11771
~~244~~	12	DIED PRIOR TO SEPTEMBER 25, 1902 ~~Willie Lee~~		~~Son~~	~~6mo~~	~~M~~	~~1/32~~			

13 No4 hereon dismissed under order of the
14 Commission to the Five Civilized Tribes
15 ~~of March 31 1905~~
15 ~~No3 has been placed on Card 3411 with~~
16 his wife Aug 15/99
17 No2 Enrolled December 15, 1900

No4 on Choctaw roll as T. B. Spain
~~No5 " " " " Margaret A "~~
~~No9 " " " " Emma "~~
No10 " " " " Nellie "
No6 " " " " Thos. B. "
~~No11 " " " " Isom "~~

For child of No6 see N.B. (Mar 3 1905) Card #9
" children " 5 " " #608 and (Apr 26 '06) 280

TRIBAL ENROLLMENT OF PARENTS

	Name of Father	Year	County	Name of Mother	Year	County
1	Thos. D, Spain	Dead	non citizen	Mary M. Spain	Dead	Blue
2	Steve Cantrell		" "	Sally Cantrell	"	non citizen
3	~~No1~~			~~No2~~		
4	~~No1~~			~~No2~~		
5	~~No1~~			No2		
6	No1			No2		
7	No1			No2		
8	No1			No2		
9	No1			No2		
10	No1			No2		
11	No1			No2		
12	~~No1~~			~~No2~~		

ENROLLMENT OF NOS. 1 6 7 8 9 10 11 & 12 HEREON APPROVED BY THE SECRETARY OF INTERIOR Dec 12, 1902

ENROLLMENT OF NOS. 2 HEREON APPROVED BY THE SECRETARY OF INTERIOR June 13 1903

~~No1 Son of Mary M.~~ Spain who was admitted by Act of Choctaw Council of Oct 31, 1877
No2 admitted in 1896 as an ~~intermarried citizen by Dawes~~ Commission: Choctaw Case #823 no appeal

13 No7 is now the husband of Minnie Lee Spain on Choctaw Card #5905
14 No5 is wife of William T Jones Choctaw card #4747 Sept 24 1902
~~No4 died June 15, 1900: see testimony of Nov 14, 1901~~
15 ~~Maggie Spain wife of No4 on Choctaw #D680~~
16 No12 died May 19, 1902. Proof of death filed Oct 27, 1902.
17 Harrisburg I.T. 10/23/02

Date of Application for Enrollment. Sept. 13/98

No12 died May 19-1902: Enrollment cancelled by Department July 8, 1904.

RESIDENCE: Chickasaw Nation ~~County~~. POST OFFICE: Purcell, Ind. Ter.

Choctaw Nation

Choctaw Roll (Not Including Freedmen) CARD NO. FIELD NO. 120

Dawes' Roll No.		NAME	Relationship to Person First Named	AGE	SEX	BLOOD	TRIBAL ENROLLMENT Year	County	No.
245	1	Freeny, Ben 43	First Named	39	M	1/16		Choctaw residing in Chickasaw District	CCR #2 195
IW543	2	" Era 27	wife	23	F	I.W.		" "	C.I. Roll 33
14480	3	" Robert 5	son	1	M	1/32		" "	CCR #2 195
246	4	" Lonnie Clay 3	son	2mo	M	1/32			

ENROLLMENT OF NOS. 1 and 4 HEREON APPROVED BY THE SECRETARY OF INTERIOR DEC 12 1902

ENROLLMENT OF NOS. 3 HEREON APPROVED BY THE SECRETARY OF INTERIOR MAY 20 1903

No1 1896 Chickasaw Dist 4590 as Benjamin Freeny

No4 Enrolled May 24, 1900.

~~Is not No2 same Ary (or Arry) Freeny on 1896 Choctaw Census roll page 387 #14554?~~

ENROLLMENT OF NOS. ~~2~~ HEREON APPROVED BY THE SECRETARY OF INTERIOR FEB -8 1904

TRIBAL ENROLLMENT OF PARENTS

	Name of Father	Year	County	Name of Mother	Year	County
1	Robert Freeny	Dead	non citizen	Sallie Freeny	Dead	Towson
2	G.C. Gage		" "		"	non citizen
3	No1			No2		
4	No1			No2		
5					Born	3-29-05

See testimony of №1 taken October 17, 1902

N°3 Proof of birth received and filed Nov. 11, 1902

~~Certified copy of decree of divorce of Eva Holt from Harry Holt filed April 6, 1903~~

For child of Nos 1&2 see N.B. (March 3-1905) Card No 7

~~3/8/2 " " " " " " " " Minor (April 26, 1906) " " 658~~

#1 to 3

PO Bradley I.T. 12/22/04

Date of Application for Enrollment. Sept 13/98

RESIDENCE: Chickasaw Nation ~~COUNTY.~~ **Choctaw Nation** **Choctaw Roll** CARD NO.
POST OFFICE: Paola Ind Ter. *(Not Including Freedmen)* FIELD NO. **121**

Dawes' Roll No.		NAME		Relationship to Person First Named	AGE	SEX	BLOOD	TRIBAL ENROLLMENT Year	County	No.
247	1	Camp, Joe A.	32		28	M	1/16		Choctaw residing in Chickasaw District	CCR #2 125
IW696	2	" Allie	30	wife	26	F	I.W.			C.I. Roll 19
15036	3	" Hoover	8	son	4	M	1/32			CCR #0 33
248	4	" Joe A jr	4	"	1/2	"	1/32			
~~249~~	5	DIED PRIOR TO SEPTEMBER 25, 1902 ~~" Mary Rhody~~	1	~~Dau~~	~~6mo~~	~~F~~	~~1/32~~			

ENROLLMENT OF NOS. 1,4 and 5 HEREON APPROVED BY THE SECRETARY OF INTERIOR DEC 12 1902

ENROLLMENT OF NOS. ~~ 3 ~~ HEREON APPROVED BY THE SECRETARY OF INTERIOR FEB 16 1904

ENROLLMENT OF NOS. ~~~ 2 ~~~ HEREON APPROVED BY THE SECRETARY OF INTERIOR MAY -7 1904

No2 on Choctaw roll as Alice W. Camp
No3 " " Census No 0 Page 33 No. 337

No1 1896 Chickasaw Dist 3088 as Joseph A Camp
No2 1896 " " 1441 " Alice W. "
~~Evidence of birth of No4 filed Oct 13th 1900~~
~~No5 Enrolled June 4th, 1901~~
№3 Proof of birth received and filed Oct 28, 1902

№5 Died May 21, 1902, proof of death filed Oct. 28, 1902.

TRIBAL ENROLLMENT OF PARENTS

	Name of Father	Year	County	Name of Mother	Year	County
1	Jos. B. Camp (I.W.)		Choctaw residing in Chickasaw District	Mary Camp		Choctaw residing in Chickasaw District
2	W.J. Wallace		non citizen	Lottie Wallace		non citizen
3	No1			No2		
4	No1			No2		
5	~~No1~~			~~No2~~		

No2 See Decision of March 2, 1904.
No.5 died May 21, 1902 Enrollment cancelled by Department July 4, 1904

#1 to 4
Date of Application for Enrollment.
Sept. 13/95

For child of Nos 1&2 see NB (March 3, 1905) #983 & 1537

RESIDENCE: Chickasaw Nation ~~County~~.
POST OFFICE: Pauls Valley Ind. Ter.

Choctaw Nation

Choctaw Roll (Not Including Freedmen)

CARD NO.
FIELD NO. **122**

Dawes' Roll No.	NAME	Relationship to Person First Named	AGE	SEX	BLOOD	TRIBAL ENROLLMENT Year	County	No.
IW 784	1 Garvin, S. J. ✱ (58)	First Named	54	M	I.W.		Choctaw residing in Chickasaw District	C.I.Roll 39
250	2 " Susan 47	wife	43	F	1/4		" "	CCR #2 215
See 3266	3 ~~" Robert~~	~~son~~	~~23~~	~~M~~	~~1/8~~		~~" "~~	~~"~~
251	4 " John 24	"	20	"	1/8		" "	"
252	5 Mays, Birdy 21	Dau	17	F	1/8		" "	"
253	6 Garvin, Vivian 12	"	8	"	1/8		" "	"
254	7 Mays, S.J. 1	G. Son	3mo	M	5/64		" "	

ENROLLMENT OF NOS. 2,4,5,6 and 7 HEREON APPROVED BY THE SECRETARY OF INTERIOR DEC 12 1902

No1 admitted by U.S. Court Southern District Indian territory [sic] as an intermarried citizen December 22nd 1897: ~~Court Case #239 Denied-96~~

~~No6 on Choctaw roll as Vinie Garvin~~

~~✱Decision of U.S. Court Southern District Dec 22 1897 Vacated and set aside by~~ Decree of Choctaw and Chickasaw Citizenship Court: Dec. 17, 1902: Admitted as an intermarried Choctaw by Citizenship Court Jan 14, 1904 Case #127

Aug 7/99 No3 has been placed on Card No. 3266 with wife

~~No 7 Enrolled Aug 8, 1901.~~

ENROLLMENT OF NOS. 1 HEREON APPROVED BY THE SECRETARY OF INTERIOR MAY 9 1904

TRIBAL ENROLLMENT OF PARENTS

Name of Father	Year	County	Name of Mother	Year	County
1 John Garvin	Dead	non citizen	Mary Garvin	Dead	non citizen
2 Wm Moncreath	"	Choctaw Roll	Margaret Moncreath		Choctaw residing in Chickasaw District
3 ~~No1~~			~~No2~~		
4 No1			No2		
5 No1			No2		
6 No1			No2		
7 T.G. Mays		Chickasaw roll	No5		

~~No1 1896 Chickasaw Dist 14584 as Samuel J Garvin~~
No2 1896 " " 5010 " Susan Moncrief "
~~No3 1896 " " 5014~~
~~No4 1896 " " 5015~~
No5 1896 " " 5013 as Briddy Garvin
No6 1896 " " 5016 " Vinie "
No5 is now the wife of T.G.Mayes on Chickasaw Card #415 Evidence of marriage requested ~~8/8/01 -Filed Aug 22, 1901~~

For child of No5 on Chickasaw NB (Apr 26/06) Card #136
~~" " " " " Chick NB (Mar 3-05) " #334~~

Date of Application for Enrollment.
Sept. 13/98

RESIDENCE: Chickasaw Nation ~~COUNTY.~~
POST OFFICE: Purcell, Ind. Ter.

Choctaw Nation **Choctaw Roll** (Not Including Freedmen) CARD NO. FIELD NO. 123

Dawes' Roll No.	NAME	Relationship to Person First Named	AGE	SEX	BLOOD	TRIBAL ENROLLMENT Year	County	No.
14185	1 Sacra, Clemmie G. 43	First Named	39	F	1/4		Choctaw residing in Chickasaw District	CCR #2 434
14186	2 " Bettie 22	Dau	18	"	1/8		" "	"
14187	3 " Lucy 20	"	16	"	1/8		" "	"
14188	4 " John 16	Son	12	M	1/8		" "	"
14189	5 " Agnes 12	Dau	8	F	1/8		" "	"
14190	6 " Clemmie 10	"	6	"	1/8		" "	"
	7							
	8 Broaddus is now the name of No2							

No1 is the wife of R.C. Sacra on Choctaw Card #453, and Nos 2 to 6 inclusive are his children

ENROLLMENT
OF NOS. 1 2 3 4 5 and 6 HEREON
APPROVED BY THE SECRETARY
OF INTERIOR APR 11 1903

TRIBAL ENROLLMENT OF PARENTS

Name of Father	Year	County	Name of Mother	Year	County
1 Dr J Davis	Dead	non citizen	Effie Davis	Dead	Choctaw Roll
2 R.C. Sacra		White man	No1		
3 " " "		" "	No1		
4 " " "		" "	No1		
5 " " "		" "	No1		
6 " " "		" "	No1		

No1 1896 Chickasaw Dist 11790 as Clamce Secry
No2 1896 " " 11791 " Betty "
No3 1896 " " 11792 " Lucy "
No4 1896 " " 11793 " John "
No5 1896 " " 11794 " Agnes "
No6 1896 " " 11795 " Clement "
Nos1 to 6 inclusive were admitted as citizens by blood by Dawes Commission: Choctaw Case #830: No appeal.

For children of No2 see NB (March 3-1905) Card #14

Date of Application for Enrollment. Sept. 13/98

RESIDENCE: Chickasaw Nation ~~COUNTY~~.
POST OFFICE: Tussy Ind. Ter.

Choctaw Nation

Choctaw Roll *(Not Including Freedmen)*

CARD NO.
FIELD NO. **124**

Dawes' Roll No.		NAME		Relationship to Person First Named	AGE	SEX	BLOOD	TRIBAL ENROLLMENT Year	County	No.
IW 1063	1	Gray, George	44		40	M	I.W.		Choctaw residing in Chickasaw District	C.I. Roll 39
DEAD	2	~~" Viney~~	DEAD	~~wife~~	~~29~~	~~F~~	~~1/2~~		~~" "~~	CCR #2 ~~216~~
255	3	" James	17	Son	13	M	1/4		" "	"
256	4	" Nora	13	Dau	9	F	1/4		" "	"
257	5	" William	11	Son	7	M	1/4		" "	"
258	6	" Gideon	9	"	5	"	1/4		" "	"
259	7	" Rosa	5	Dau	1	F	1/4		" "	"
~~260~~	8	DIED PRIOR TO SEPTEMBER 25, 1902 ~~Albert~~		~~Son~~	~~6mo~~	~~M~~	~~1/4~~		~~" "~~	~~"~~

ENROLLMENT OF NOS. 3,4,5,6,7 and 8 HEREON ~~APPROVED BY THE SECRETARY~~ OF INTERIOR Dec 12 1902

ENROLLMENT OF NOS. ~~ 1 ~~ HEREON APPROVED BY THE SECRETARY OF INTERIOR Nov 16 1904

~~No2 hereon dismissed under order of the Commission to the Five Civilized Tribes of March 31, 1900.~~

No8 died June 19-1900: Enrollment cancelled by Department Sept 16 1904

No1 married July '01 under U.S. License ~~to Mary Gary a non-citizen~~

TRIBAL ENROLLMENT OF PARENTS

	Name of Father	Year	County	Name of Mother	Year	County
1	Wm Gray		non citizen	Elizabeth Gray	Dead	non citizen
2	~~Geo. Gardner~~	~~Dead~~	~~Choctaw Roll~~	~~Phoebe Gardner~~	"	~~Choctaw roll~~
3	No1			No2		
4	No1			No2		
5	No1			No2		
6	No1			No2		
7	No1			No2		
8	~~No1~~			~~No2~~		

~~No1 1896 Chickasaw Dist 14591 as George Grey~~
No2 1896 " " 5053
No3 1896 " " 5054
~~No4 1896 " " 5055~~
~~No5 1896 " " 5056~~
No6 1896 " " 5057

No2 died April 3d 1900: Proof of death filed Feby 13, 1902.
Evidence of birth of No7 received and filed March 25, 1902.
No8 Died June 19, 1900, proof of death filed Oct. 23, 1902

No8 Enrolled Dec 19/99 Affidavit irregular and returned for correction. Filed Jany 17/1900.

Date of Application for Enrollment. Sept. 13/98

Choctaw By Blood Enrollment Cards 1898-1914

RESIDENCE: Chickasaw Nation ~~COUNTY~~.
POST OFFICE: Tussy, Ind. Ter.

Choctaw Nation

Choctaw Roll *(Not Including Freedmen)*

CARD NO.
FIELD NO. 125

Dawes' Roll No.	NAME	Relationship to Person First Named	AGE	SEX	BLOOD	TRIBAL ENROLLMENT Year	County	No.
~~261~~	1 ~~Davis, Alex~~		~~21~~	~~M~~	~~1/4~~		~~Choctaw residing in Chickasaw District~~	~~CCR #2 151~~
262	2 Underwood, Thomas [20]	1/2 Bro	16	"	1/4		" "	CCR #2 ~~453~~
					No1	1896	Chickasaw Dist	3668
					No2	1896	" "	12589

ENROLLMENT OF NOS. 1 and 2 HEREON APPROVED BY THE SECRETARY OF INTERIOR DEC 12 1902

No1 Died Dec. 28, 1898, proof of death filed Oct. 23, 1902.

No1 died Dec. 20-1898. Enrollment cancelled by Department July 8-1894

For child of No2 see NB (Apr 26 '06) Card No 1195.
" " " " " " " (March 3,1905) " " 597

TRIBAL ENROLLMENT OF PARENTS

Name of Father	Year	County	Name of Mother	Year	County
1 ~~John Davis~~	~~Dead~~	~~non citizen~~	~~Harriet Davis~~ ^ Underwood	~~Dead~~	Choctaw residing in ~~Chickasaw District~~
2 Thos Underwood	"	" "	" ^ ~~Underwood~~ Davis	"	" "

Date of Application for Enrollment. Sept. 13/98

RESIDENCE: Chickasaw Nation ~~County~~.
POST OFFICE: McGee, Ind. Ter.

Choctaw Nation

Choctaw Roll (Not Including Freedmen)

CARD NO.
FIELD NO. 126

Dawes' Roll No.		NAME		Relationship to Person First Named	AGE	SEX	BLOOD	TRIBAL ENROLLMENT Year	County	No.
263	1	Byford, Ellen	64	First Named	60	F	Full		Jack Fork	CCR #2 344
IW 858	2	" , H. M.	54	Hus.	54	M	I.W.			
	3							1896	Jacks Ford	8378

ENROLLMENT OF NOS. 1 HEREON APPROVED BY THE SECRETARY OF INTERIOR DEC 12 1902

ENROLLMENT OF NOS. ~~ 2 ~~ HEREON APPROVED BY THE SECRETARY OF INTERIOR AUG 3 1904

No1: the wife of H.M. Byford, on Choctaw Card D17. married Sept 8th 1898.

No.2 transferred from Choctaw card D-17 June 12-1904 See decision of May 27-1904.

TRIBAL ENROLLMENT OF PARENTS

	Name of Father	Year	County	Name of Mother	Year	County
1	Jim Lewis	Dead	Choctaw Roll	Silbert Lewis	Dead	Choctaw Roll
2	Wm Byford	Dead	non-citizen	Mary Byford	Dead	non-citizen

Date of Application for Enrollment. Sept. 13/98

RESIDENCE: Chickasaw Nation ~~COUNTY~~.
POST OFFICE: Purcell Ind. Ter.

Choctaw Nation

Choctaw Roll (Not Including Freedmen)

CARD NO.
FIELD NO. 127

Dawes' Roll No.	NAME	Relationship to Person First Named	AGE	SEX	BLOOD	TRIBAL ENROLLMENT Year	County	No.
I.W.4	1 Conner, F.L. 32	First Named	29	M	I.W.		Choctaw residing in Chickasaw District	C.I. Roll 19
264	2 " Effie May 24	wife	20	F	1/8		" "	CCR #2 126
265	3 " Alberta 4	Dau	4mos	"	1/16			
266	4 " Henry Merle 2	Son	6w	M	1/16			

ENROLLMENT OF NOS. 2,3 and 4 HEREON APPROVED BY THE SECRETARY OF INTERIOR DEC 12 1902

ENROLLMENT OF NOS. 1 HEREON APPROVED BY THE SECRETARY OF INTERIOR JUN 13 1903

No1 1896 Chickasaw Dist 14445 as FL. Cornor
No2 1896 " " 3124 " Effie Secry Conner

No2 on Choctaw roll as Effie S. Conner.
~~Affidavit of birth of Alberta to be furnished~~
Evidence of birth of No3 received and filed Aug 6,1900

No1 admitted by Dawes Commission in 1896 as an intermarried citizen: No appeal.
No4 Enrolled January 18, 1901.

TRIBAL ENROLLMENT OF PARENTS

	Name of Father	Year	County	Name of Mother	Year	County
1	H.S. Conner	Dead	non citizen	Mary J. Conner	Dead	non citizen
2	R.C. Sacra		" "	Clemmie G Sacra		Choctaw residing in Chickasaw District
3	No1			No2		
4	No1			No2		

Date of Application for Enrollment. Sept. 13/98

RESIDENCE: Chickasaw Nation ~~COUNTY~~.
POST OFFICE: Purcell Ind. Ter.

Choctaw Nation — **Choctaw Roll** (*Not Including Freedmen*) — CARD NO. — FIELD NO. 128

Dawes' Roll No.	NAME	Relationship to Person First Named	AGE	SEX	BLOOD	TRIBAL ENROLLMENT Year	County	No.
267	1 Muncrief, Sam 52	First Named	48	M	1/8	1896	Choctaw residing in Chickasaw District	8956
IW544	2 " Virginia 47	wife	43	F	I.W.	1896	" "	14848
268	3 " Walter L 25	son	19	M	1/16	1896	" "	8957
269	4 " Georgia 20	Dau	16	F	1/16	1896	" "	8958
270	5 " Sammie Myrtle 14	"	10	"	1/16	1896	" "	8959
14191	6 " Linney 8	"	4	"	1/16	1896	" "	8960
14481	7 " Gracie 6	"	3	"	1/16			
IW1064	8 " Olivia 24	Wife of No.3	24	"	I.W.			

ENROLLMENT OF NOS. ~~~ 7 ~~~ HEREON APPROVED BY THE SECRETARY OF INTERIOR MAY 20 1903

ENROLLMENT OF NOS. 1,3,4 and 5 HEREON APPROVED BY THE SECRETARY OF INTERIOR DEC 12 1902

ENROLLMENT OF NOS. ~~ 2 ~~ HEREON APPROVED BY THE SECRETARY OF INTERIOR FEB -8 1904

ENROLLMENT OF NOS. 6 HEREON APPROVED BY THE SECRETARY OF INTERIOR APR 11 1903

~~No1 born Jan 28, 1850~~
No3 " Dec 23 1879
No4 " Apr 27, 1882
No5 " Dec 1, 1888
~~No6 " Nov 6, 1894~~
~~No7 " Dec 10, 1896~~

No8 transferred from Choctaw card #D-610: See decision of Oct. 15, 1904

No3 is the husband of Olivia Muncrief on Choctaw Card #D610.

TRIBAL ENROLLMENT OF PARENTS

	Name of Father	Year	County	Name of Mother	Year	County
1	Wm Muncrief	Dead	Choctaw Roll	Margaret Muncrief		Choctaw residing in Chickasaw District
2	Lige Dodson		non citizen		Dead	non citizen
3	No1			Margaret Muncrief	"	Choctaw residing in Chickasaw District
4	No1			" "	"	" "
5	No1			Josephine "	"	non citizen
6	No1			No2		
7	No1			No2		
8	Henry P. Clowney		Non-citizen	Clara A Clowney		non-citizen

ENROLLMENT OF NOS. 8 HEREON APPROVED BY THE SECRETARY OF INTERIOR NOV 16 1904

For child of Nos 3&8 see NB (March 3, 1905) #1359
" " " No 4 " " " " #1423

~~No5 on Choctaw roll as Jane~~
No6 " " " " Lucy
No.7 - affidavit of attending physician to be furnished. Received Sept 27/98.
~~Surname of all on Choctaw Roll Moncrief.~~
~~No6 was admitted in 1896 as a citizen by blood by Dawes Commission~~
Choctaw Case #1303: No appeal.
No3 also on 1896 roll as Walter Moncrief Page 225, No 8980, Chick Dist.

P.O. Wayne I.T. 10/23/02

#1 to 7 Date of Application for Enrollment. Sept 14/98

RESIDENCE: Chickasaw Nation ~~COUNTY~~.
POST OFFICE: Purcell, Ind. Ter.

Choctaw Nation

Choctaw Roll *(Not Including Freedmen)*

CARD NO.
FIELD NO. 129

Dawes' Roll No.		NAME	Relationship to Person First Named	AGE	SEX	BLOOD	TRIBAL ENROLLMENT Year	County	No.
VOID.	1	~~Hamblin, Charley M.~~	~~Named~~	~~23~~	~~M~~	~~1/8~~			
	5	On Chickasaw roll, Panola County, Page 5 transferred to Choctaw roll by Dawes Com.							

CANCELLED

Transferred to Chickasaw Card No. 1593 Oct. 13 1902

TRIBAL ENROLLMENT OF PARENTS

	Name of Father	Year	County	Name of Mother	Year	County
1	~~H.C. Hamblin~~		~~noncitizen~~	~~Mollie Hamblin~~	~~Dead~~	~~Choctaw Roll~~

Date of Application for Enrollment. Sept. 14/98

RESIDENCE: Chickasaw Nation ~~COUNTY~~.
POST OFFICE: Purcell, Ind. Ter

Choctaw Nation

Choctaw Roll (*Not Including Freedmen*)

CARD NO.
FIELD NO. 130

Dawes' Roll No.		NAME	Relationship to Person First Named	AGE	SEX	BLOOD	TRIBAL ENROLLMENT Year	County	No.
IW 515	1	Trueblood, A.H. 35	First Named	26	M	I.W.		Choctaw residing in Chickasaw District	C.I. Roll 107
271	2	" Mary J. 28	wife	24	F	1/4		" "	CCR #2 452
14192	3	" Roy G. 9	Son	5	M	1/8		" "	"
14193	4	" Bryan Sewell 6	"	2	"	1/8		" "	"
272 ✓	5	" Sam Muncrief 4	"	5mos	"	1/8			
273	6	" Albert H. jr. 3	"	3mo	M	1/8			
274	7	" Pauline 1	Dau	1Mo	F	1/8			

8 See testimony of Nº1 taken October 22, 1902

9 For child of Nos. 1 and 2 see N.B. (Mar 3 '05) #444

ENROLLMENT OF NOS. 2,5,6 and 7 HEREON APPROVED BY THE SECRETARY OF INTERIOR Dec 12 1902

ENROLLMENT OF NOS. 3 and 4 HEREON APPROVED BY THE SECRETARY OF INTERIOR Apr 11, 1903

10 No.5 affidavit of attending physician to be furnished. Received Sept 21/98

11 Nos 1-3 and 4 admitted by Dawes Com Case No 284 and no appeal taken

12 Nº7 Born April 12, 1902: enrolled May 13, 1902.

13 No1 1896 Chickasaw Dist 15120 as A.H. Trueblood.

No2 1896 " " 12573 " Mary I. "

14 No3 1896 " " 12574 " Roy G. "

15 No4 1896 " " 12575 " Bryan L "

ENROLLMENT OF NOS. ~~ 1 ~~ HEREON APPROVED BY THE SECRETARY OF INTERIOR Feb -3 1904

16 Evidence of birth of No5 received and filed Aug. 6, 1900.

No6 Enrolled May 24, 1900.

17

TRIBAL ENROLLMENT OF PARENTS

	Name of Father	Year	County	Name of Mother	Year	County
1	A.H. Trueblood	Dead	non-citizen	Caroline Trueblood	Dead	non citizen
2	Sam Muncrief		Choctaw residing in Chickasaw District	Margaret Muncrief	"	Choctaw residing in Chickasaw District
3	No1			No2		
4	No1			No2		
5	No1			No2		
6	No1			No2		
7	No1			No2		
8						
9						
10						
11						
12						
13						
14						
15						
16						
17					Date of Application for Enrollment.	Sept. 14/98.

RESIDENCE: Chickasaw Nation ~~COUNTY~~.
POST OFFICE: Purcell, Ind. Ter.

Choctaw Nation — **Choctaw Roll** *(Not Including Freedmen)* — CARD NO. — FIELD NO. 131

Dawes' Roll No.	NAME	Relationship to Person First Named	AGE	SEX	BLOOD	TRIBAL ENROLLMENT Year	County	No.
275	1 Morse, Mabel 17	First Named	13	F	1/4		Choctaw residing in Chickasaw District	CCR #2 359
	2							
	3					1896	Chickasaw Dist	8961
	4							
	5							
	6							
	7							
	8							
	9							
	10							
	11							
	12							
	13							
	14							
	15							
	16							
	17							

ENROLLMENT OF NOS. 1 HEREON APPROVED BY THE SECRETARY OF INTERIOR DEC 12 1902

For child of No1 see NB (Apr 26-06) Card #760

TRIBAL ENROLLMENT OF PARENTS

Name of Father	Year	County	Name of Mother	Year	County
1 James M Morse		white man	Henrietta Morse	Dead	Blue
2 Floyd Morgan		" "	No1	Born	Mch 26-05
3					
4					
5					
6					
7					
8					
9					
10					
11					
12					
13					
14					
15					
16					
17					

Father, James M. Morse on Choctaw Doubtful Card No D.18.
#I.W. 1162

Date of Application for Enrollment. Sept. 14/98

RESIDENCE: Chickasaw Nation ~~COUNTY~~.
POST OFFICE: Whitebead, Ind. Ter

Choctaw Nation

Choctaw Roll *(Not Including Freedmen)*

CARD NO.
FIELD NO. **132**

Dawes' Roll No.	NAME	Relationship to Person First Named	AGE	SEX	BLOOD	TRIBAL ENROLLMENT Year	County	No.
IW 546	1 Burch, James E 35	First Named	31	M	I.W.		Choctaw residing in Chickasaw District	C.I. Roll 11
14194	2 " Raymond G. 9	Son	5	"	1/32		" "	CCR #2 82
	3							
	4							
	5							
	6							
	7							
	8							
	9							
	10							
	11							
	12							
	13							
	14							
	15							
	16							
	17							

ENROLLMENT
OF NOS. 2 HEREON
APPROVED BY THE SECRETARY
OF INTERIOR APR 11 1903

ENROLLMENT
OF NOS. ~~~1~~~ HEREON
APPROVED BY THE SECRETARY
OF INTERIOR FEB -8 1904

No1 1896 Chickasaw Dist 14352 as Ed Birch
No2 1896 " " 5017 " Burde Garvin
No 1 and 2 admitted by Dawes Commission in 1896. No appeal.
No1 on Choctaw roll as Ed. Burch Choctaw Case #882

TRIBAL ENROLLMENT OF PARENTS

Name of Father	Year	County	Name of Mother	Year	County
1 Jesse E Burch		non citizen	Mary A Burch		non citizen
2 No1			Lizzie "	Dead	Choctaw residing in Chickasaw District
3					
4					
5					
6					
7					
8					
9					
10					
11					
12					
13					
14					
15					
16					
17					

Date of Application for Enrollment.

Date of application for enrollment Sept. 14/98

RESIDENCE: Chickasaw Nation ~~COUNTY~~.
POST OFFICE: Roberson, Ind. Ter.

Choctaw Nation

Choctaw Roll (Not Including Freedmen)

CARD NO.
FIELD NO. 133

Dawes' Roll No.	NAME	Relationship to Person First Named	AGE	SEX	BLOOD	TRIBAL ENROLLMENT Year	County	No.
276	1 Winters, Clifton E 23	Named	19	M	1/4		Choctaw residing in Chickasaw District	CCR #2 489

ENROLLMENT
OF NOS. 1 HEREON
APPROVED BY THE SECRETARY
OF INTERIOR DEC 12 1902

1896 Chickasaw Dist 14183 as Clifton Winters

For child of No1 see NB (Apr 26-06) Card #696

TRIBAL ENROLLMENT OF PARENTS

Name of Father	Year	County	Name of Mother	Year	County
1 Charles Winters		non citizen	Sophie Winters	Dead	Choctaw Roll

Date of Application for Enrollment.
Sept. 14/98

RESIDENCE: Chickasaw Nation ~~COUNTY~~.
POST OFFICE: Washita Ind. Ter.

Choctaw Nation

Choctaw Roll *(Not Including Freedmen)*

CARD NO.
FIELD NO. 134

Dawes' Roll No.		NAME	Relationship to Person First Named	AGE	SEX	BLOOD	TRIBAL ENROLLMENT Year	County	No.
IW 208	1	McMenamin, Michael 74	First Named	70	M	I.W.		Choctaw residing in Chickasaw District	C.I. Roll 77
	2								
	3								
	4								
	5					1896 Chickasaw Dist 14891 as McMinaman			
	6	ENROLLMENT OF NOS. 1 HEREON APPROVED BY THE SECRETARY OF INTERIOR SEP 12 1903							
	7								
	8								
	9	Admitted by Dawes Com. Case No 1267 and no appeal taken.							
	10	~~Marriage license and certificate to be furnished~~ - Oct 5/98 marriage license							
	11	and certificate on file in office of Dawes Commission, Muskogee Ind. Ter.							
	12								
	13	Once married to Choctaw woman and divorced. Certified copy of divorce ~~proceedings to be supplied~~ - Received Oct 5/98 ~~ D 28.							
	14	No1 is the husband of Emma McMenama on Choctaw card #D28							
	15								
	16								
	17								

TRIBAL ENROLLMENT OF PARENTS

	Name of Father	Year	County	Name of Mother	Year	County
1	Frank McMenania	Dead	non citizen	Mary McMenania	Dead	non citizen
2						
3						
4						
5						
6						
7						
8						
9						
10						
11						
12						
13						
14						
15						
16				Date of Application for Enrollment.		Sept. 14/98
17						

RESIDENCE: Chickasaw Nation ~~COUNTY~~. POST OFFICE: Wynnewood Ind Ter.

Choctaw Nation — **Choctaw Roll** (Not Including Freedmen) — CARD NO. FIELD NO. 135

Dawes' Roll No.	NAME	Relationship to Person First Named	AGE	SEX	BLOOD	TRIBAL ENROLLMENT Year	County	No.
VOID.	1 Jennings Henrietta L	First Named	42	F	1/4			
VOID.	2 " Daisy	Dau	18	"	1/8			
VOID.	3 " Thenia	"	17	"	1/8			
VOID.	DEAD 4 " Kutchentubby	Son	15	M	1/8			
VOID.	5 " Lovica	Dau	13	F	1/8			
VOID.	6 " Alvers	Son	10	M	1/8			
VOID.	7 " James	"	8	"	1/8			
VOID.	8 " John	"	5	"	1/8			
VOID.	9 " R.W.	Husband	42	"	I.W.			

10 Correct name of No5 as Lovica

12 No1 on Chickasaw roll as H.L. Jennings.
13 No3 " " " " Themia "
14 No4 " " " " D. J. "
No7 " " " " Jane "
15 No1 wife of R.W. Jennings, Choctaw Doubtful Card No. D.19.
16 All on Chickasaw roll, Pontotoc Co. Page 60 transferred to Choctaw roll by Dawes Com No 9 on Chickasaw roll, Page 80
17 No9 transferred from Card No D.19 Nov 26/98

CANCELLED

Transferred to Chickasaw Card #1595 Oct 13, 1902

TRIBAL ENROLLMENT OF PARENTS

	Name of Father	Year	County	Name of Mother	Year	County
1	Jim Colbert	Dead	Chickasaw Roll	Themius Colbert		Atoka
2	R.W. Jennings		(No 9)	No1		
3	" " "		" "	No1		
4	" " "		" "	No1		
5	" " "		" "	No1		
6	" " "		" "	No1		
7	" " "		" "	No1		
8	" " "		" "	No1		
9	John Jennings	Dead	noncitizen	Elmira Jennings		noncitizen

Date of Application for Enrollment. Sept. 14/98

RESIDENCE: Chickasaw Nation ~~COUNTY~~.
POST OFFICE: Wynnewood, Ind. Ter.

Choctaw Nation

Choctaw Roll (Not Including Freedmen)

CARD NO.
FIELD NO. 136

Dawes' Roll No.		NAME		Relationship to Person First Named	AGE	SEX	BLOOD	TRIBAL ENROLLMENT Year	County	No.
277	1	Mackey E.M.	40	First Named	36	M	1/2		Choctaw residing in Chickasaw District	CCR #2 374
IW1396	2	" Wayne Lee	33	Wife	29	F	I.W.		" "	C.I.Roll 77
278	3	" Missouri Lee	13	Dau	9	"	1/4		" "	CCR #2 374
279	4	" Louis	11	Son	7	M	1/4		" "	"
280	5	" Elum	9	"	5	"	1/4		" "	"
281	6	" Dolph	3	"	4mo	"	1/4			

ENROLLMENT OF NOS. 1 3 4 5 and 6 HEREON APPROVED BY THE SECRETARY OF INTERIOR DEC 12 1902

July 20 1903 Record and decision refusing enrollment of No.2 for *(illegible)* Secy of Interior

No2 Refused. See Decision of July 20, 1903.
April 8, 1905: Decision of Commission of July 20, 1903 refusing No.2 reversed by Secty of Interior; and Commission directed to enroll her as an intermarried Choctaw.
For child of Nos1&2(Apr26'06) Card #389
" " " " " " (Mar 8-05) " #829

ENROLLMENT OF NOS. ~~ 2 ~~ HEREON APPROVED BY THE SECRETARY OF INTERIOR JUN 12 1905

No6 Enrolled Dec 14/99

TRIBAL ENROLLMENT OF PARENTS

	Name of Father	Year	County	Name of Mother	Year	County
1	Elum Mackey	Dead	Blue	Catherine Mackey	Dead	Blue
2	Doc Hill	"	non citizen	Sarah Hill		non citizen
3	No1			No2		
4	No1			No2		
5	No1			No2		
6	No1			No2		

No2 on Choctaw roll as Wayne Lee McMackey
No3 " " " " Missouri "
No4 " " " " Louis "
No5 " " " " E.
See testimony of No1 taken October 20, 1902.

No1 1896 Chickasaw Dist 9491 as E.M. McKey
No2 1896 " " 14883 " Wayne L McMackey
No3 1896 " " 9495 " Missouri McKey
No4 1896 " " 9496 " Louis "
No5 1896 " " 9497 " E "

#1 to 5
Date of Application for Enrollment.
Sept. 14/98

RESIDENCE: Chickasaw Nation ~~COUNTY~~. **Choctaw Nation** **Choctaw Roll** *(Not Including Freedmen)* CARD NO.
POST OFFICE: Duncan, Ind. Ter. FIELD NO. 137

Dawes' Roll No.	NAME	Relationship to Person First Named	AGE	SEX	BLOOD	TRIBAL ENROLLMENT Year	County	No.
15336	1 Dibrell, Charles 25		21	M	1/16		Choctaw residing in Chickasaw District	CCR #2 152
IW 1065	2 " Allie 22	Wife	18	F	I.W.			
15337	3 " Carl Washington 4	Son	2wks	M	1/32			
15338	4 " Clyde B. 1	Son	4Mo	M	1/32			

ENROLLMENT OF NOS. 1-3-4 HEREON APPROVED BY THE SECRETARY OF INTERIOR MAY 9 1904

ENROLLMENT OF NOS. ~~~~ 2 ~~~~ HEREON APPROVED BY THE SECRETARY OF INTERIOR NOV 16 1904

No1 1896 Chickasaw Dist 3674 as Charley Diberl
Evidence of birth of #3 received and filed Aug 6, 1900

No3 Enrolled Oct 17/98
Nº4 Born April 23, 1902: enrolled Aug 28, 1902.

No1 admitted by Dawes Commission in 96 Case #298 Jas A Tucker et al appeal as to head of case only. No appeal as to others. Appeal affirmed.

Mother of Nº1 is Nancy Tucker on Choctaw Card #5273

TRIBAL ENROLLMENT OF PARENTS

	Name of Father	Year	County	Name of Mother	Year	County
1	Joe Dibrell	Dead	Choctaw residing in ~~Chickasaw District~~	Nancy Dibrell		noncitizen
2	Geo Tucker		non citizen	Manda Tucker		" "
3	No1			No2		
4	No1			No2		

Date of Application for Enrollment. #1 to 3 ~~Sept. 14/98~~

RESIDENCE: Chickasaw Nation ~~COUNTY~~.
POST OFFICE: Wynnewood Ind Ter

Choctaw Nation

Choctaw Roll (*Not Including Freedmen*)

CARD NO.
FIELD NO. 138

Dawes' Roll No.		NAME		Relationship to Person First Named	AGE	SEX	BLOOD	TRIBAL ENROLLMENT Year	County	No.
282	1	Grant, Charley M	28	First Named	24	M	1/16		Choctaw residing in Chickasaw District	CCR #2 215
IW 5	2	" Alice	29	Wife	25	F	I.W.		" "	C.I. Roll 39
14482	3	" Margaret	8	Dau	4	"	1/32		" "	CR #2 215
14483	4	" Alma	6	Dau	2	"	1/32		" "	"

ENROLLMENT OF NOS. 1 HEREON ~~APPROVED BY THE SECRETARY~~ OF INTERIOR DEC 12 1902

ENROLLMENT OF NOS. 3 & 4 HEREON APPROVED BY THE SECRETARY ~~OF INTERIOR~~ MAY 20 1903

No1 1896 Chickasaw Dist 5011 as Charles Grant
~~No2 1896 " " 14586~~
~~No3 1896 " " 5018~~
No4 1896 " " 5019 as Almond Grant

~~J.A. Camp of Paola Ind. Ter. testifies under oath that he was present at the marriage of Charley M Grant to Alice Mayrant at Woodville in June 1892.~~

ENROLLMENT ~~OF NOS.~~ 2 HEREON APPROVED BY THE SECRETARY OF INTERIOR JUN 13 1903

TRIBAL ENROLLMENT OF PARENTS

	Name of Father	Year	County	Name of Mother	Year	County
1	Tom Grant	1897	Pickens	Margaret Grant	Dead	Choctaw residing in Chickasaw District
2	John Mayrant	Dead	non citizen	Sinnie Mayrant		non citizen
3	No1			No2		
4	No1			No2		

No2 was admitted by Dawes Commission in 1896 as an intermarried citizen: Choctaw case #261: no appeal;
~~No.2 was admitted as Mrs. Chas. M. Grant~~
No 3 & 4 admitted by Dawes Com in 1896. No appeal.
For child of Nos 1 & 2 see NB (March 3, 1905) #1160.

~~Date of Application~~ for Enrollment. Sept. 14/98

RESIDENCE: Chickasaw Nation ~~COUNTY.~~
POST OFFICE: Davis, Ind. Ter.

Choctaw Nation

Choctaw Roll (Not Including Freedmen)

CARD NO.
FIELD NO. 139

Dawes' Roll No.	NAME	Relationship to Person First Named	AGE	SEX	BLOOD	TRIBAL ENROLLMENT Year	County	No.
IW209	1 Hoover, D. H. 39	First Named	35	M	I.W.		Choctaw residing in Chickasaw District	C.I. Roll 47
283	2 " Rosa Camp 27	Wife	23	F	1/16		" "	CCR #2 258
284	3 " Thelma 7	Dau	3	"	1/32		" "	"

ENROLLMENT OF NOS. 2 and 3 HEREON APPROVED BY THE SECRETARY OF INTERIOR DEC 12 1902

ENROLLMENT OF NOS. 1 HEREON APPROVED BY THE SECRETARY OF INTERIOR SEP 12 1903

No1 on Choctaw roll as Henry Hoover
No3 " " " " Thelson "

No1 1896 Chickasaw Dist 14664 as Henry Hoover
No2 1896 " " 6177 " Rose Camp Homer
No3 1896 " " 6182 " Thelson Homer
~~No1 admitted by Dawes Com in 1896 No appeal Case 1359~~

TRIBAL ENROLLMENT OF PARENTS

	Name of Father	Year	County	Name of Mother	Year	County
1	David Hoover (I.W.)	Dead	non citizen	Cynthia Hoover		non citizen
2	Bradford Camp		Choctaw residing in Chickasaw District	Mary Camp		Choctaw residing in Chickasaw District
3	No1			No2		

Date of Application for Enrollment. Sept. 14/98

RESIDENCE: Chickasaw Nation ~~COUNTY~~.
POST OFFICE: Pauls Valley, Ind. Ter.

Choctaw Nation

Choctaw Roll *(Not Including Freedmen)*

CARD NO.
FIELD NO. **140**

Dawes' Roll No.		NAME	Relationship to Person First Named	AGE	SEX	BLOOD	TRIBAL ENROLLMENT Year	County	No.
14484	1	Cunningham, West L. [36] (Mc Gee)		32	M	1/32		Choctaw residing in Chickasaw District	CCR #2 125
IW 1066	2	" Lella Myrtle [27]	Wife	23	F	I.W.			
14485	3	" Sarah Ella [2]	Dau	1mo	F	1/64			

ENROLLMENT OF NOS. 1 & 3 HEREON APPROVED BY THE SECRETARY OF INTERIOR MAY 20 1903

No1 1896 Chickasaw Dist 3096 as West I. Cunningham

ENROLLMENT OF NOS. ~~~ 2 ~~~ HEREON APPROVED BY THE SECRETARY OF INTERIOR NOV 16 1904

Nov 26/98 Citizenship of Sarah C. Hulett, mother of No.1 (See Choctaw Card No. D27) in question

No3 Enrolled Oct 18th 1900.

No 1 admitted by act of Choctaw Council of Oct. 21, 1885

For children of Nos 1&2 see NB (Mar 3-1905) Card No. 63.

TRIBAL ENROLLMENT OF PARENTS

	Name of Father	Year	County	Name of Mother	Year	County
1	Jno A Cunningham	Dead	non citizen	Sarah C Cunningham (now Hewlett)		Choctaw residing in ~~Chickasaw District~~
2	Selanus Dill		" "	Mary Ellen Dill		noncitizen
3	No1			No2		

#1&2

Date of Application for Enrollment. Sept. 14/98

RESIDENCE: Chickasaw Nation ~~COUNTY~~.
POST OFFICE: Purcell, Ind. Ter.

Choctaw Nation — **Choctaw Roll** (Not Including Freedmen) — CARD NO. — FIELD NO. **141**

Dawes' Roll No.	NAME	Relationship to Person First Named	AGE	SEX	BLOOD	TRIBAL ENROLLMENT Year	County	No.
285	1 Autry, Emma 32	First Named	28	F	1/8		Choctaw residing in Chickasaw District	CCR #2 22
~~286~~	~~2 " Alvah 15~~	~~Son~~	~~11~~	~~M~~	~~1/16~~		" "	"
287	3 " Hester 12	Dau	8	F	1/16		" "	"
14919	4 " Edgar 8	Son	4	M	1/16		" "	"
DEAD	~~5 " Nelson~~	~~"~~	~~3mo~~	~~M~~	~~1/16~~			
14486	6 " Tams 1	Son	2Mo	M	1/16			

ENROLLMENT OF NOS. 1 2 and 3 HEREON APPROVED BY THE SECRETARY OF INTERIOR Dec 12 1902

No1 on Choctaw roll as Emma Autrey
No2 " " " " Alva "

No5 affidavit of attending physician to be furnished. Received Sept 27/98.

Nº4 Born Sept 24, 1894, proof of birth filed April 10, 1903.

ENROLLMENT OF NOS. 6 HEREON APPROVED BY THE SECRETARY OF INTERIOR May 20 1903

ENROLLMENT OF NOS. ~~4~~ HEREON APPROVED BY THE SECRETARY OF INTERIOR Oct 15 1903

No5 hereon dismissed under order of the Commission to the Five Civilized Tribes of March 31, 1905.

TRIBAL ENROLLMENT OF PARENTS

Name of Father	Year	County	Name of Mother	Year	County
1 Stephen Coaknall	Dead	Choctaw Roll	Annie Coaknall	Dead	Choctaw Roll
~~2 Wm S. Autry~~		~~white man~~	~~No 1~~		
3 " " "		" "	No 1		
4 " " "		" "	No 1		
~~5 " " "~~		~~" "~~	~~No 1~~		
6 " " "		" "	No 1		

No1 1896 Chickasaw Dist 537 as Emma Autrey

No1 on 1893 Choc. payroll #3 as Emma Autrey #20
No2 " " " " " #3 " Alva " #21
~~No3 " " " " " #3 " Hester " #22~~

Nº6 Born Aug. 5, 1902, enrolled Oct. 15, 1902

As to No 4. See testimony of William S Autry, husband of No 1, taken Oct. 22, 1902.

Nº5 died March 3, 1900. Proof of death filed Oct. 29, 1902.

P.O. Norman Okla 10/22/02

Date of Application for Enrollment. Sept 14/98

RESIDENCE: Chickasaw Nation ~~COUNTY~~.
POST OFFICE: Purdy, Ind. Ter.

Choctaw Nation

Choctaw Roll *(Not Including Freedmen)*

CARD NO.
FIELD NO. 142

Dawes' Roll No.	NAME	Relationship to Person First Named	AGE	SEX	BLOOD	TRIBAL ENROLLMENT Year	County	No.
288	1 Freeney, Susie Ann 10	First Named	6	F	1/16		Choctaw residing in Chickasaw District	CCR #2 195

ENROLLMENT OF NOS. 1 HEREON APPROVED BY THE SECRETARY OF INTERIOR DEC 12 1902

1896 Chickasaw Dist 4693 as Susan Freeney.

On Choctaw roll as Susan Freeney.

TRIBAL ENROLLMENT OF PARENTS

Name of Father	Year	County	Name of Mother	Year	County
1 John Freeney	Dead		Charlotte Stephens		non citizen

Date of Application for Enrollment. Sept. 14/98

RESIDENCE: Chickasaw Nation ~~COUNTY.~~ **Choctaw Nation** **Choctaw Roll** *(Not Including Freedmen)* CARD NO.
POST OFFICE: Wayne, Ind. Ter. FIELD NO. **143**

Dawes' Roll No.	NAME	Relationship to Person First Named	AGE	SEX	BLOOD	Year	County	No.
IW1067	1 Robinson, Sam P 42		38	M	I.W.		Choctaw residing in Chickasaw District	C.I.Roll 96
15172	2 " Cora 33	Wife	29	F	1/32		" "	CCR #2 417
15173	3 " Delany 17	Son	13	M	1/64		" "	"
15174	4 " Minnie 14	Dau	10	F	1/64		" "	"
15175	5 " Pearl	Dau	6	"	1/64		" "	"
DEAD	6 ~~" Eley Evert~~	~~Son~~	~~1mo~~	~~M~~	~~1/64~~			

7 See opinion of Atty Gen[1] of Feb 18 04 and letter of Secy of Interior of Feb 24-04 in case
8 of James M Buckholts et al 7-5738
~~No2 Grand-daughter of William Buckholts admitted by Supreme~~
9 "Buckholty Crowd" of Choctaw Nation Oct 1872

10 No. 6 HEREON DISMISSED UNDER ORDER OF THE COMMISSION TO THE FIVE
11 ~~CIVILIZED TRIBES OF MARCH 31, 1905.~~

No1 on Choctaw Roll as S.E. Robinson
No3 " " " " Delena
~~No4 " " " " Winnie~~
No5 " " " " Carl

12 ~~No6 died June 17, 1900, proof of~~
13 ~~death filed April 22, 1903.~~

14 No1 admitted as an intermarried citizen by Dawes Commission Choctaw Case #685. No appeal.
For child of Nos 1&2 see NB (Mar 3'05) #535

15 ENROLLMENT
~~OF NOS. 2-3-5-4 and 5~~ HEREON
16 APPROVED BY THE SECRETARY
OF INTERIOR MAY 9 1904

17 No6 Enrolled Nov 1/99

TRIBAL ENROLLMENT OF PARENTS

	Name of Father	Year	County	Name of Mother	Year	County
1	Sam Robinson	Dead	non citizen	Cynthia C Robinson		non citizen
2	Jim Buckholts		Blue	Nettie Buckholts (IW)		Blue
3	No1			No2		
4	No1			No2		
5	No1			No2		
6	~~No1~~			~~No2~~		

8 No1 1896 Chickasaw Dist 15010 as S.E. Robinson
9 No2 1896 " " 11063 " Cora Roberson
~~No3 1896 " " 11064 " Delena "~~
10 ~~No4 1896 " " 11065 " Winnie "~~
11 No5 1896 " " 11066 " Carl "

15 ENROLLMENT
OF NOS. ~~~ 1 ~~~ HEREON
16 APPROVED BY THE SECRETARY
OF INTERIOR NOV 16 1904

~~Date of Application~~ **for Enrollment.**
Sept. 14/98

17 Chickasha I.T. 10/22/02

RESIDENCE: Chickasaw Nation ~~COUNTY.~~
POST OFFICE: Whitebead, Ind. Ter.

Choctaw Nation

Choctaw Roll
(Not Including Freedmen)

CARD NO.
FIELD NO. 144

Dawes' Roll No.		NAME		Relationship to Person First Named	AGE	SEX	BLOOD	TRIBAL ENROLLMENT Year	County	No.
15564	1	Spain, David M.	44	First Named	40	M	1/8	1893	Choctaw residing in Chickasaw District	Page 56 #533
289	2	" Jubilee	17	Nephew	13	"	1/16		" "	CCR #0 35
IW 1276	3	" Cora M.	25	Wife		F	I.W.			

ENROLLMENT OF NOS. 2 HEREON APPROVED BY THE SECRETARY OF INTERIOR DEC 12 1902

On Nov. 30, 1901 No.3 married No.1 a recognized and enrolled citizen by blood of the Choc. Nation

No1 on Chickasaw Roll as D.M. Spain.

ENROLLMENT OF NOS. 1 HEREON APPROVED BY THE SECRETARY OF INTERIOR SEP 22 1904

No1 See Decision of May 31 '04

No1 Husband of Georgia D. Spain, Chickasaw Roll Card No.444
No1 on Chickasaw Intermarried roll, Page 77, transferred to Choctaw Roll by Dawes Commission
~~No2 also on 1896 roll, Chick Dist, Page 304, No 11760 as Juklin Spain.~~

Georgia D. Spain is dead and No.1 is now the husband of Cora M. Spain on Choctaw card #D.707. March 8, 1902.

TRIBAL ENROLLMENT OF PARENTS

	Name of Father	Year	County	Name of Mother	Year	County
1	Thos. D. Spain	Dead	non citizen	Mary M. Spain	Dead	Choctaw Roll
2	Jubil Spain	"	Choctaw Roll	Myrtle Spain	"	non citizen
3	William Jones		non citizens[sic]	Mary Jones		non citizen

~~No2 is now the husband of Martha E. Spain on Choctaw Card #D802~~ 7-5898 Sept 24, 1902
No2 is descendant of Mary M. Spain who wad admitted by act of Choctaw Council of Oct 31, 1877.
No1 is son of Mary M. Spain who was admitted by act of Council of Oct 31, 1877.
~~No1 was also admitted in same Act.~~
For child of No2 see NB (Mar 3-05) #78.

ENROLLMENT OF NOS. 3 HEREON APPROVED BY THE SECRETARY OF INTERIOR MAR 14 1905

No.3 originally listed for enrollment on Choctaw card D-707 Mar 8, 1902: transferred to this card Jan. 28, 1905. See decision of Jan. 12, 1905.

Date of Application for Enrollment. Sept. 14/98 #1&2

RESIDENCE: Chickasaw Nation ~~COUNTY~~.
POST OFFICE: Pauls Valley, Ind. Ter.

Choctaw Nation

Choctaw Roll *(Not Including Freedmen)*

CARD NO.
FIELD NO. **145**

Dawes' Roll No.	NAME	Relationship to Person First Named	AGE	SEX	BLOOD	TRIBAL ENROLLMENT Year	County	No.
VOID.	1 ~~Fleming, Willie Hampton~~	~~First Named~~	~~7~~	~~M~~	~~1/16~~		~~Choctaw residing in Chickasaw District~~	
	2							
	3							
	4							
	5 On Chickasaw Roll, Pickens Co. Page 29, as Hamp Flemming - transferred to							
	6 Choctaw roll by Dawes Com.							
	7							
	8							
	9							
	10							
	11							
	12							
	13							
	14							
	15							
	16							
	17							

CANCELLED

Transferred to Chickasaw Card #1596
Oct. 13, 1902

TRIBAL ENROLLMENT OF PARENTS

Name of Father	Year	County	Name of Mother	Year	County
1 ~~Wm B. Fleming~~	~~Dead~~	~~non citizen~~	~~Minnie Fleming~~		~~Choctaw residing in Chickasaw District~~
2					
3					
4					
5					
6					
7					
8					
9					
10					
11					
12					
13					
14					
15					
16			Date of Application for Enrollment.		~~Sept. 15/98~~
17					

RESIDENCE: Chickasaw Nation ~~COUNTY~~.
POST OFFICE: McGee, Ind. Ter.

Choctaw Nation

Choctaw Roll *(Not Including Freedmen)*

CARD NO.
FIELD NO. **146**

Dawes' Roll No.	NAME	Relationship to Person First Named	AGE	SEX	BLOOD	TRIBAL ENROLLMENT Year	County	No.
290	1 Shi, Isaac Garvin	First Named	8	M	3/8		Choctaw residing in Chickasaw District	CCR #2 434
	2							
	3		1896 Chickasaw Dist 11789 as Isaac G Shry					
	4							
	5							
	6	On Choctaw Roll as Isaac G. Shri						
	7							
	8							
	9							
	10							
	11							
	12							
	13							
	14							
	15							
	16							
	17							

ENROLLMENT
OF NOS. 1 HEREON
APPROVED BY THE SECRETARY
OF INTERIOR DEC 12 1902

TRIBAL ENROLLMENT OF PARENTS

Name of Father	Year	County	Name of Mother	Year	County
1 T.P. Shi M.D.		non citizen	Francis Shi	Dead	Nashoba
2					
3					
4					
5					
6					
7					
8					
9					
10					
11					
12					
13					
14					
15					
16					
17					

Date of Application for Enrollment. Sept. 15/98

RESIDENCE: Chickasaw Nation ~~COUNTY~~. **Choctaw Nation** **Choctaw Roll** *(Not Including Freedmen)* CARD NO.

POST OFFICE: Wynnewood, Ind. Ter. FIELD NO. **147**

Dawes' Roll No.	NAME	Relationship to Person First Named	AGE	SEX	BLOOD	TRIBAL ENROLLMENT Year	County	No.
DEAD	1 ~~Carter, Thomas~~	~~Named~~	~~36~~	~~M~~	~~1/8~~		~~Choctaw residing in Chickasaw District~~	~~CCR #2 127~~

No1 died March 6 1899. Evidence of death filed May 2, 1901.

No. 1 HEREON DISMISSED UNDER ORDER OF THE COMMISSION TO THE FIVE CIVILIZED TRIBES OF MARCH 31, 1905.

CANCELLED

Applicant died prior to the ratification of the Choctaw Chickasaw agreement on Sept. 25, 1902.

TRIBAL ENROLLMENT OF PARENTS

Name of Father	Year	County	Name of Mother	Year	County
1 ~~*(Illegible)* Carter~~	~~Dead~~	~~non citizen~~	~~Melvina Carter~~	~~Dead~~	~~Choctaw roll~~

Date of Application for Enrollment. Sept. 15/98

RESIDENCE: Chickasaw Nation ~~COUNTY~~.
POST OFFICE: Wynnewood, Ind. Ter.

Choctaw Nation

Choctaw Roll (Not Including Freedmen)

CARD NO.
FIELD NO. 148

Dawes' Roll No.		NAME	Relationship to Person First Named	AGE	SEX	BLOOD	TRIBAL ENROLLMENT Year	County	No.
IW210	1	Riggan, S.C. 31		27	M	I.W.		Choctaw residing in Chickasaw District	
291	2	" Edith 25	Wife	21	F	1/16		" "	CCR #2 125
292	3	" Vada 4	Dau	3mo	"	1/32			
293	4	" Burniece 2	Dau	2wk	F	1/32			

ENROLLMENT OF NOS. 2 3 and 4 HEREON APPROVED BY THE SECRETARY OF INTERIOR DEC 12 1902

ENROLLMENT OF NOS. 1 HEREON APPROVED BY THE SECRETARY OF INTERIOR SEP 12 1903

No2 1896 Chickasaw Dist 3104 as Lillie Carr.

No2 on Choctaw Roll as Lillie E. Carr
No4 Enrolled July 7, 1900.

Evidence of birth of No.3 received and filed Feby. 10, 1902

For child of Nos 1&2 see NB (Mar 3-1905) Card No 2[?]

TRIBAL ENROLLMENT OF PARENTS

	Name of Father	Year	County	Name of Mother	Year	County
1	Benj Riggan		non citizen	P. J. Riggan		non citizen
2	Jno E. Carr		Choctaw residing in Chickasaw District	Alice Carr I.W.		Choctaw residing in Chickasaw District
3	No1			No2		
4	No1			No2		

Date of Application for Enrollment. Sept. 15/98

RESIDENCE: Chickasaw Nation COUNTY.
POST OFFICE: Wynnewood Ind. Ter.

Choctaw Nation

Choctaw Roll (Not Including Freedmen)

CARD NO.
FIELD NO. 149

Dawes' Roll No.	NAME	Relationship to Person First Named	AGE	SEX	BLOOD	Tribal Enrollment: Year	Tribal Enrollment: County	Tribal Enrollment: No.
294	1 Carr, J.E. 53		49	M	1/8		Choctaw residing in Chickasaw District	CCR #2 125
IW859	2 " Alice C. (49)	Wife	45	F	I.W.		" "	C.I. Roll 19
295	3 Waide, Helen E. 22	Dau	18	"	1/16		" "	CCR #2 125
296	4 Deal, Ida Isabelle 18	"	14	"	1/16		" "	"
297	5 Carr, Beula C. 16	"	12	"	1/16		" "	"
298	6 " Bonnie O. 11	"	10	"	1/16		" "	"
299	7 Waide, Harrold L. 1	Grandson	1mo	M	1/32			
300	8 Deal, Faye 1	Grand Dau	2wks	F	1/32			

9 Father of No8 Frank Deal non citizen
10 Mother of No8 is No.4.
No8 born March 27, 1902
11 Enrolled April 8, 1902
12 See testimony of No1 taken October 20, 1902

No3 is now the wife of 4955 Whit M. Waide on Choctaw Card D 594 Dec 6 1900

No2 on Choctaw Roll as Alice H. Carr
No3 " " " " Hattie "
No4 " " " " Ida "
No6 " " " " Bonneo "

ENROLLMENT
OF NOS.1,3,4,5,6,7 and 8 HEREON
APPROVED BY THE SECRETARY
OF INTERIOR DEC 12 1902

TRIBAL ENROLLMENT OF PARENTS

	Name of Father	Year	County	Name of Mother	Year	County
1	J.H. Carr	Dead	non citizen	Harriet Carr	Dead	Choctaw Roll
2	W.M. Johnson	"	" "	Edith Johnson	"	non citizen
3	No1			No2		
4	No1			No2		
5	No1			No2		
6	No1			No2		
7	Whit M. Waide		non-citizen	No3		
8	[No information given.]					

No.7 born Jany 8, 1902: Enrolled Jany 30, 1902.

9 No1 1896 Chickasaw Dist 3099 as Jno E Conn
10 No2 1896 " " 14442 " Alice H Carr
11 No3 1896 " " 3105 " Hattie "
12 No4 1896 " " 3106 " Ida "
No5 1896 " " 3107 " Beula C "
13 No6 1896 " " 3108 " Bonner "

ENROLLMENT
OF NOS. 2 HEREON
APPROVED BY THE SECRETARY
OF INTERIOR AUG 3 1904

15 No4 is now the wife of Frank Deal non citizen. Evidence of marriage requested. Received and filed June 10, 1902.
16 For child of No4 see NB (Mar 4 '05) #653

17 Date of Application for Enrollment. Sept. 15/98
1 to 6

Choctaw By Blood Enrollment Cards 1898-1914

RESIDENCE: Chickasaw Nation ~~County~~.
POST OFFICE: Dolberg, Ind. Ter

Choctaw Nation

Choctaw Roll (*Not Including Freedmen*)

CARD NO.
FIELD NO. **150**

Dawes' Roll No.	NAME	Relationship to Person First Named	AGE	SEX	BLOOD	TRIBAL ENROLLMENT Year	County	No.
301	1 M^c^Daniel Leonadus 50	First Named	46	M	Full		Choctaw residing in Chickasaw District	CCR #2
IW 1068	2 " Mollie 39	wife	35	F	I.W.		" "	C.I. Roll 78

ENROLLMENT OF NOS. 1 HEREON APPROVED BY THE SECRETARY OF INTERIOR DEC 12 1902

ENROLLMENT OF NOS. ~~~~2~~~~ HEREON APPROVED BY THE SECRETARY OF INTERIOR NOV 16 1904

No1 on 1893 pay roll No.3 #436.
Evidence of marriage filed April 9, 1901.
Nos 1 and 2 have seperated[sic] See evidence filed 12/10/02.
~~No1 is now deceased see letter. No 3495-1910~~

Ayers & [Illegible] Atoka I.T. Attys for N°2

No2 lives at Stringtown I.T. 12/10/02

TRIBAL ENROLLMENT OF PARENTS

Name of Father	Year	County	Name of Mother	Year	County
1 Colwel M^c^Daniel	Dead	Choctaw Roll	Sallie M^c^Daniel	Dead	Choctaw Roll
2 George McCarty	"	non citizen		"	non citizen

Date of Application for Enrollment. Sept. 15/98

RESIDENCE: Chickasaw Nation ~~COUNTY~~.
POST OFFICE: Pauls Valley, Ind. Ter

Choctaw Nation

Choctaw Roll *(Not Including Freedmen)*

CARD NO.
FIELD NO. 151

Dawes' Roll No.	NAME	Relationship to Person First Named	AGE	SEX	BLOOD	TRIBAL ENROLLMENT Year	County	No.
VOID.	1 ~~Dennis, A.B.~~	~~Named~~	~~37~~	~~M~~	~~I.W.~~			
VOID.	2 ~~" DEAD Sallie~~	~~Wife~~	~~37~~	~~f~~	~~1/2~~			
VOID.	3 ~~" Jessie~~	~~Dau~~	~~13mo~~	~~F~~	~~1/4~~			
VOID.	4 ~~Ard, Emet~~	~~Step-Son~~	~~11~~	~~M~~	~~1/4~~			
VOID.	5 ~~" Maud Lena~~	~~" Dau~~	~~8~~	~~F~~	~~1/4~~			
VOID.	6 ~~" Albert Devro~~	~~" Son~~	~~5~~	~~M~~	~~1/4~~			

Nos 1 and 2 admitted by Dawes Com. Case No. 38, no appeal taken
Nos 2-4-5 and 6 on Chickasaw roll, Pickens County, Page 16 and 17, transferred by Dawes Com
~~No3 " " " " " " 86 registered under Act of Legislature~~
~~July 31/97 (Chick Roll Page 86)~~

Marriage papers on file with Daws[sic] Com. in Case No 38 Chickasaw Nation.
~~Certified copies of marriage license and certificate to be furnished~~
~~No5 on Chickasaw roll as Maude Ard~~
No6 " " " " Devora "
Nos 1-2-4-5 and 6 admitted as Chickasaws in 1896, Chickasaw Case #38

CANCELLED

Transferred to Chick Card No 1597 Oct 13, 1902

TRIBAL ENROLLMENT OF PARENTS

	Name of Father	Year	County	Name of Mother	Year	County
1	~~John Dennis~~	~~Dead~~	~~non citizen~~	~~Delilah Dennis~~	~~Dead~~	~~non citizen~~
2	~~Stone Thomas~~	~~"~~	~~Chickasaw Roll~~	~~Hettie Jenkins~~	~~"~~	~~Choctaw Roll~~
3	~~No 1~~			~~No 2~~		
4	~~Albert D Ard~~	~~Dead~~	~~non citizen~~	~~No 2~~		
5	~~" " "~~	~~"~~	~~"~~	~~No 2~~		
6	~~" " "~~	~~"~~	~~"~~	~~No 2~~		

Date of Application for Enrollment. ~~Sept. 15/98~~

RESIDENCE: Chickasaw Nation ~~COUNTY~~.
POST OFFICE: McGee, Ind. Ter.

Choctaw Nation

Choctaw Roll (*Not Including Freedmen*)

CARD NO.
FIELD NO. 152

Dawes' Roll No.		NAME		Relationship to Person First Named	AGE	SEX	BLOOD	TRIBAL ENROLLMENT Year	County	No.
15339	1	Bullock ✓ Lola	32	First Named	28	F	1/32			
15340	2	" ✓ Emma	14	Dau	10	"	1/64			
15341	3	" ✓ Beatrice	9	"	5	"	1/64			
15342	4	" ✓ Olive	7	"	2 1/2	"	1/64			
15343	5	" ✓ Jonathan	4	Son	4mo	M	1/64			
15344	6	" ✓ J. D. Jr.	1	Son	1mo	M	1/64			

Take no further action relative to enrollment of Nos 1 to 6 incl.

Protest by Atty for Choctaw and Chickasaw Nations Jan 23 '04.

Above protest overruled See Departmental letter of March 31, 1904.

ENROLLMENT
OF NOS. 1-2-3-4-5-6 HEREON
APPROVED BY THE SECRETARY
OF INTERIOR MAY 9 1904

TRIBAL ENROLLMENT OF PARENTS

	Name of Father	Year	County	Name of Mother	Year	County
1	Chas Simpson	Dead	non citizen	Amanda Simpson	Dead	Choctaw Indian
2	J.D. Bullock		" "	No 1		
3	" " "		" "	No 1		
4	" " "		" "	No 1		
5	" " "		" "	No 1		
6	" " "		" "	No 1		

All admitted by Dawes Com. Case No 632: No appeal as to these applicants.

~~No1 wife of J.D. Bullock, U.S. Citizen.~~

No5 - April 13/99

No 6 born Sept. 17, 1901: Enrolled Oct. 22d, 1901

~~P.O. Lindsay I.T. 3/23/04~~
P.O. Purcell I.T. 10/20/02 - 6/15-03
~~P.O. Wayne I.T. 1/3/03~~

Date of Application for Enrollment. Sept. 15/98

RESIDENCE: Chickasaw Nation ~~COUNTY~~.
POST OFFICE: Wynnewood, Ind. Ter.

Choctaw Nation

Choctaw Roll *(Not Including Freedmen)*

CARD NO.
FIELD NO. 153

Dawes' Roll No.	NAME	Relationship to Person First Named	AGE	SEX	BLOOD	TRIBAL ENROLLMENT Year	County	No.
302	1 Williams, Emma Lee 23	First Named	19	F	3/16		Choctaw residing in Chickasaw District	~~CCR #2~~ 489
303	2 " Ethel Lorraine 5	Dau	6mo	"	3/32			
304	3 " Benjamin D. 2	Son	2wks	M	3/32			

ENROLLMENT OF NOS. 1, 2 and 3 HEREON APPROVED BY THE SECRETARY OF INTERIOR DEC 12 1902

No1 1896 Chickasaw Dist 14185 as Emma Williams

No1 on Choctaw roll as Emma Williams
No2 affidavit of attending physician to be supplied. Received Oct 5/98
No3 Enrolled January 2, 1901.
~~Quantity of blood of Nos 1-2 & 3 ascertained from Choctaw Card #97.~~

TRIBAL ENROLLMENT OF PARENTS

Name of Father	Year	County	Name of Mother	Year	County
1 Jas. W. Gardner		Choctaw residing in ~~Chickasaw District~~	Emily Gardner (I.W)		Choctaw residing in ~~Chickasaw District~~
2 Owen T. Williams		non citizen	No 1		
3 " " "		" "	No 1		

Date of Application for Enrollment. Sept. 15/98

RESIDENCE: Chickasaw Nation ~~COUNTY~~.
POST OFFICE: Antioch, Ind. Ter.

Choctaw Nation

Choctaw Roll (Not Including Freedmen)

CARD NO.
FIELD NO. 154

Dawes' Roll No.		NAME	Relationship to Person First Named	AGE	SEX	BLOOD	TRIBAL ENROLLMENT Year	County	No.
14195	1	Guthrie Rebecca 39	First Named	35	F	1/4		Choctaw residing in Chickasaw District	CCR #2 215
14196	2	" Susie 11	Dau	7	"	1/8		" "	"
14197	3	" Charley 8	Son	4	M	1/8		" "	"
14583	4	" Edgar 6	"	2	"	1/8		" "	"
14584	5	" Mattie 6	Dau	2	F	1/8		" "	"
14198	6	" Rachel 1	Dau	1wk	F	1/8			
I.W. 6	7	" W. M.	Husband	37	M	I W			

ENROLLMENT OF NOS. 1 2 3 and 6 HEREON APPROVED BY THE SECRETARY OF INTERIOR APR 11 1903

ENROLLMENT OF NOS. 4 and 5 0 HEREON APPROVED BY THE SECRETARY OF INTERIOR MAY 20 1903

No1 wife of W.M. Guthrie, Choctaw Doubtful Card No D23.
Nos 1-2 and 3 admitted by Dawes Com. Case No 1006, and no appeal taken.
~~No6 Born July 9" 1902: Enrolled July 16" 1902~~

TRIBAL ENROLLMENT OF PARENTS

	Name of Father	Year	County	Name of Mother	Year	County
1	Wiley Johnson	Dead	non citizen	Amanda Johnson	Dead	Choctaw Roll
2	W. M. Guthrie		white man	No 1		
3	" " "		" "	No 1		
4	" " "		" "	No 1		
5	" " "		" "	No 1		
6	" " "		" "	No 1		

For child of Nos 1 and 7 see NB (Mar 3, 1905) #445

No7 admitted by Dawes Commission Case No 1006 and no appeal taken.
~~No1 1896 Chickasaw Dist 5026 as Rebecca Gurthry~~
~~No3 1896 " " 5028 " Charlie "~~
No4 1896 " " 5062
No5 1896 " " 5063
~~Nos 4 and 5 are twins.~~

ENROLLMENT OF NOS. 7 HEREON APPROVED BY THE SECRETARY OF INTERIOR JUN 13 1903

Date of Application for Enrollment.
~~Sept. 15/98~~

No7 transferred from Choctaw card D#23 March 20, 1903 See decision of March 4 1903

RESIDENCE: Chickasaw District ~~COUNTY~~.
POST OFFICE: Antioch Ind Ter.

Choctaw Nation

Choctaw Roll *(Not Including Freedmen)*

CARD NO.
FIELD NO. 155

Dawes' Roll No.	NAME		Relationship to Person First Named	AGE	SEX	BLOOD	TRIBAL ENROLLMENT Year	County	No.
14199	1 Hays, Andrew	22	First Named	18	M	1/8		Choctaw residing in Chickasaw District	CCR #2 259
14200	2 Ward, Mary	18	Sister	14	F	1/8		" "	"
14201	3 Hays, John	16	Bro	12	M	1/8		" "	"
14202	4 " William	14	"	10	"	1/8		" "	"

ENROLLMENT OF NOS. 1 2 3 and 4 HEREON APPROVED BY THE SECRETARY OF INTERIOR APR 11 1903

No 2 on Choctaw roll as May.

No1 on 1896 roll Chick Dist. Page 151, No. 6183
No2 " " " " " " 151 " 6184 as May Hays.
No3 " " " " " " 151 " 6185
No4 " " " " " " 151 " 6186

All admitted by Dawes Commission in 1896 case #1006. No appeal.
№2 is now the wife of A.F. Ward non-citizen Evidence of marriage filed Oct. 21, 1902.

~~For child of No2 see NB (March 3-1905) Card No 12.~~

TRIBAL ENROLLMENT OF PARENTS

Name of Father	Year	County	Name of Mother	Year	County
1 Thos. Hays	Dead	non citizen	Rebecca Guthrie		Choctaw residing in Chickasaw District
2 " "	"	" "	" "		" "
3 " "	"	" "	" "		" "
4 " "	"	" "	" "		" "
17 P.O. Dibble I.T. of No.2					Date of Application for Enrollment. Sept. 15/98

RESIDENCE: Chickasaw Nation ~~COUNTY~~.
POST OFFICE: Davis, Ind. Ter

Choctaw Nation

Choctaw Roll
(Not Including Freedmen)

CARD NO.
FIELD NO. 156

Dawes' Roll No.	NAME	Relationship to Person First Named	AGE	SEX	BLOOD	TRIBAL ENROLLMENT Year	County	No.
14487	1 Camp, Mary 51		48	F	1/4		Choctaw residing in Chickasaw District	CCR #2 126
IW 1069	2 " Joseph B. 63	Husband	63	M	I.W.		Choctaw residing in ~~Chickasaw District~~	C.I. Roll 19

ENROLLMENT OF NOS. 1 HEREON APPROVED BY THE SECRETARY OF INTERIOR MAY 20 1903

1896 Chickasaw Dist 3152 as Mary H Camp.

ENROLLMENT OF NOS. 2 HEREON APPROVED BY THE SECRETARY OF INTERIOR NOV 16 1904

Wife of J B. Camp Choctaw Doubtful Card No D.24

#1 - "Died prior to September 25, 1902; not entitled to land or money."
See Indian Office letter May 13, 1910. D.C. #$658-1910

No.2 admitted by Commission in 1896: case #726: no appeal.
No.2 transferred from Choctaw card #D-24, Oct. 31, 1904: See decision of Oct. 15, 1904.

TRIBAL ENROLLMENT OF PARENTS

Name of Father	Year	County	Name of Mother	Year	County
1 Calvin Howell	Dead	non citizen	Rhoda Howell		Choctaw residing in Chickasaw District
2 A.G. Camp	dead	non-citizen	Harriet Camp	dead	non-citizen

Date of Application for Enrollment. #1 Sept. 15/98

RESIDENCE: Chickasaw Nation ~~COUNTY~~.
POST OFFICE: Wynnewood, Ind. Ter.

Choctaw Nation

Choctaw Roll *(Not Including Freedmen)*

CARD NO.
FIELD NO. 157

Dawes' Roll No.	NAME	Relationship to Person First Named	AGE	SEX	BLOOD	TRIBAL ENROLLMENT Year	County	No.
305	1 Gardner, Benjamin 25	First Named	21	M	1/16		Choctaw residing in Chickasaw District	CCR #2 215
IW1070	2 Kemp, Rosa E 24	Wife	20	F	I.W.		" "	C.I. Roll 39
IW1653	3 Gardner, Maud T.	Wife	18	F	I.W.			

ENROLLMENT OF NOS. ~~1~~ HEREON APPROVED BY THE SECRETARY OF INTERIOR Dec 12 1902

ENROLLMENT OF NOS. ~~2~~ HEREON APPROVED BY THE SECRETARY OF INTERIOR Nov. 16 1904

ENROLLMENT OF NOS. ~~~ 3 ~~~ HEREON APPROVED BY THE SECRETARY OF INTERIOR Mar 2-1907

No. 1 1896 Chickasaw Dist. 5023 as Benjamin Gardner
No. 2 1896 " " 14588 " Rosie "

No.3 Granted Jan 30 1907

TRIBAL ENROLLMENT OF PARENTS

Name of Father	Year	County	Name of Mother	Year	County
1 J.W. Gardner		Choctaw residing in ~~Chickasaw District~~	Emily Gardner (IW)		Choctaw residing in Chickasaw District
2 R. Florence		non citizen	Josie Florence		non citizen
3 John Tennis Watts		non citz	Sarah Ann Eakes		non citz.

Nos 1 and 2 are divorced.
No 1 is now husband of Maude Watts, white woman
~~No 2 is now wife of Kemp. White man~~
No.3 placed hereon udner order of the Commissioner to the Five Civilized Tribes of Nov. 1-1906 holding that application was made for her enrollment within the time provided by the act of Congress approved Apr. 26-1906.

P.O. of No.2 Midland I.T. 1/10/03
No 2 Dibble I.T. 1/10/07

Date of Application for Enrollment. Sept. 15/98

RESIDENCE: Chickasaw Nation ~~COUNTY.~~
POST OFFICE: Purdy, Ind. Ter.

Choctaw Nation

Choctaw Roll *(Not Including Freedmen)*

CARD NO.
FIELD NO. 158

Dawes' Roll No.	NAME	Relationship to Person First Named	AGE	SEX	BLOOD	TRIBAL ENROLLMENT Year	County	No.
15551	1 Freeney, Benj. Andrew 15*	First Named	11	M	1/8		Choctaw residing in Chickasaw District	CCR #0 48
15552	2 " Martha Elizabeth 13*	Sister	9	F	1/8		" "	CCR #2 195
15553	3 " Mary Ada 10*	"	6	F	1/8		" "	"
	4							

(Case 34 evidently transferred to this docket)

Nos. 1,2 and 3 admitted by C.C.C.C. in Case #1317 May 24 '04 in the case of Mary Ann Thompson et al re- Choctaw & Chickasaw N.

No. 1 on Choctaw ^Census^ roll No. 0 Page 48, No. 645.

No. 1,2,3 admitted by Dawes Com. in 96 case 274
No. 2 1896 Chickasaw Dist 4591 as Martha E. Freeney.
No. 3 1896 " " 4591 " Mary A. "

See Count Card No. C. 76. The above parties are duplicate thereon. Aug 9/99

ENROLLMENT
OF NOS. 1,2 and 3 HEREON
APPROVED BY THE SECRETARY
OF INTERIOR Aug 20 1904

For child of No. 2 see NB (Ap 26-06) Card

TRIBAL ENROLLMENT OF PARENTS

	Name of Father	Year	County	Name of Mother	Year	County
1	Andrew G. Freeney	Dead	Choctaw residing in Chickasaw District	Mary Ann Thompson		non citizen
2	" " "	"	" "	" " "		" "
3	" " "	"	" "	" " "		" "
4	John Farres			No 2	Born	11-1-05

Nos. 1,2 and 3 are duplicate enrollment of Nos. 2,3 and 4 on Choctaw Card #5031 ^~~which duplicates on 5031 cancelled~~^

Nos. 1-2 and 3 were admitted by U.S. Court Central District Ind. Ter. To McAlester I.T. Aug 25, 1897; Court Case #227.

Nos. 1 and 2 are named in Court judgment as "Benjamin Andrew Thompson" and "Martha Elizabeth Thompson"

Judgement[sic] of U.S. Ct. admitting Nos. 1,2, and 3 vacated and set aside by Decree of ~~Choctaw-Chickasaw Cit. Court Decr 17 '06~~
Nos.1,2and 3 in C.C.C.C. #34 3/9/03.

Date of Application for Enrollment. Sept. 15/98

RESIDENCE: Chickasaw Nation ~~COUNTY~~.
POST OFFICE: Rush Springs, Ind. Ter.

Choctaw Nation

Choctaw Roll (Not Including Freedmen)

CARD NO.
FIELD NO. 159

Dawes' Roll No.		NAME		Relationship to Person First Named	AGE	SEX	BLOOD	TRIBAL ENROLLMENT Year	County	No.
15345	1	Gray, Ellen	44	First Named	40	F	1/4		Choctaw residing in Chickasaw District	CCR #2 216
15346	2	" Ella	19	Dau	15	"	1/8		" "	"
15347	3	" Laura	17	"	13	"	1/8		" "	"
15348	4	" Pearl	13	"	9	"	1/8		" "	"
15349	5	" Elmer	8	Son	4	M	1/8		" "	"
15350	6	" Clifford	6	"	3	"	1/8			
15351	7	" Charles E.	3	"	3mo	"	1/8			
IW1518	8	" John Calvin		Hus.	50	"	I.W.	~~1896~~	~~Chick. District~~	~~14589~~

ENROLLMENT OF NOS. 1-2-3-4-5-6-7 HEREON APPROVED BY THE SECRETARY OF INTERIOR May 9 1904

9 For child of No.3 see N.B(Mar 3'05)#541
10 Nos.2,3,4 and 5 were admitted in case #80 ~~Oct 25/99 All but Nos 1-6-7 were ad-~~
11 ~~mitted by Dawes Com. case No. 80.~~
12 Appealed as to J.C.Gray.
13 Husband of No1 and father of the children ~~on this card is John C. Grey on Choctaw~~
14 ~~card #D725.~~
15
16
17 All but Clifford &No.1 admitted by Dawes Com. Case No. 80 and no appeal taken

No2 on Choctaw roll as Ellen Gray
No3 " " " Janie "
No5 " " " Almer "
No6 - affidavit of midwife to be supplied - Received Oct 20/98.

~~No.8 was admitted as intermarried citizen by Dawes Commission in 1896 Choctaw case #86 and on appeal the U.S. Court Central Dist I.T. reversed this decision.~~

For child of No2 see N.B. (Apr. 26'06) Card #91

TRIBAL ENROLLMENT OF PARENTS

	Name of Father	Year	County	Name of Mother	Year	County
1	Baker	Dead	non-citizen	Sophia Beshears Baker	Dead	Choctaw Roll
2	John C. Gray		" "	No.1		
3	" " "		" "	No.1		
4	" " "		" "	No.1		
5	" " "		" "	No.1		
6	" " "		" "	No.1		
7	" " "		" "	No.1		
8	Henry Gray	~~Dead~~	~~non-citizen~~	Mary Gray		non citizen
9	Richard J Gray			No2		Born July 20-'05

No 8 restored to roll by Department [illegible] authority of January 19,1909 (File 5-51)

ENROLLMENT OF NOS. ~~8~~ HEREON APPROVED BY THE SECRETARY OF INTERIOR Mar 14, 1906

10 No.1 1896 Chickasaw Dist 5044
11 No.2 1896 " " 5045 " Ellen Gray
12 ~~No.3 1896 " " 5046 " Janie "~~
~~No.4 1896 " " 5047~~
13 No.5 1896 " " 5048 as Almeo Gray
14 ~~order of~~
15 ~~Enrollment of No.8 cancelled by order of Department March 5, 1907~~
16 No.8 transferred from D725 January 12 1906: See decision of Dec. 27,1905
17 No.2 P.O. Ninnekah, I.T. 5/4/'06 No.7 enrolled July 27/99

Date of Application for Enrollment. Sept. 15/98

Choctaw By Blood Enrollment Cards 1898-1914

RESIDENCE: Chickasaw Nation ~~COUNTY.~~ **Choctaw Nation** **Choctaw Roll** *(Not Including Freedmen)* CARD NO.

POST OFFICE: Center, Ind. Ter FIELD NO. **160**

Dawes' Roll No.		NAME	Relationship to Person First Named	AGE	SEX	BLOOD	TRIBAL ENROLLMENT Year	County	No.
VOID.	1	~~Bond, Galloway~~	~~First Named~~	~~17~~	~~M~~	~~3/4~~			
VOID.	2	~~" Jesse~~	~~Bro~~	~~15~~	~~"~~	~~3/4~~			
	3								
	4								
	5								
	6								
	7								
	8								
	9								
	10								
	11								
	12								
	13								
	14								
	15								
	16								
	17								

No 2 on Chickasaw roll as Jessie

Both on Chickasaw roll, Pontotoc County, Page 47, transferred to Choctaw Nation by Dawes Com.

CANCELLED

Transferred to Chick Card No 1598 Oct. 13, 1902

TRIBAL ENROLLMENT OF PARENTS

	Name of Father	Year	County	Name of Mother	Year	County
1	~~Sampson Bond~~	~~Dead~~	~~Choctaw Roll~~	~~Melvina Johnson~~		~~Choctaw residing in Chickasaw District~~
2	~~" "~~	~~"~~	~~" "~~	~~" "~~		~~" "~~
3						
4						
5						
6						
7						
8						
9						
10						
11						
12						
13						
14						
15						
16				Date of Application for Enrollment.		Sept. 15/98
17						

RESIDENCE: Chickasaw Nation ~~COUNTY~~. **Choctaw Nation** Choctaw Roll (Not Including Freedmen) CARD NO.
POST OFFICE: Ireton, Ind. Ter. FIELD NO. 161

Dawes' Roll No.	NAME	Relationship to Person First Named	AGE	SEX	BLOOD	TRIBAL ENROLLMENT Year	County	No.
306	1 Ireton, Henry 25	First Named	21	M	1/4		Choctaw residing in Chickasaw District	CCR #2 269
IW 1277	2 " Laura 28	Wife	24	F	I.W.		" "	C.I. Roll 48
~~307~~	3 DIED PRIOR TO SEPTEMBER 25, 1902 ~~" Mary C.~~	~~Dau~~	~~2mo~~	~~"~~	~~1/8~~			
308	4 " Cleopatra A.	Dau	1mo	F	1/8			

ENROLLMENT OF NOS. 1, 3 and 4 HEREON APPROVED BY THE SECRETARY OF INTERIOR DEC 12 1902

No1 1896 Chickasaw Dist 6349 as Henry Iraton

Marriage certificate to be furnished. Received Sept 16/98

~~No2 on C.C.R. No2 in pencil~~

No3 Enrolled Oct 6/99

ENROLLMENT OF NOS. 2 HEREON APPROVED BY THE SECRETARY OF INTERIOR MAR 14 1905

No.4 born Dec. 9th, 1901: Enrolled Jany. 16, 1902.

~~Nº 3 Died Feby 24, 1900, proof of death filed Oct. 20, 1902.~~

~~Nº 3 Died Feby 24, 1900. Enrollment cancelled by Department July 8, 1904.~~

TRIBAL ENROLLMENT OF PARENTS

	Name of Father	Year	County	Name of Mother	Year	County
1	John Ireton (I.W.)		~~Choctaw residing in Chickasaw District~~			~~Choctaw residing in Chickasaw District~~
2	G.G. Anderson		non-citizen			non citizen
3	~~No1~~			~~No2~~		
4	No1			No2		

For child of Nos 1&2 see N.B. (Apr. 26, '06) card No. 230.
" " " " " " " (March 3 1905) " " 735

Naples I.T. 10/20/02

Date of Application for Enrollment. Sept. 15/98

RESIDENCE: Chickasaw Nation ~~COUNTY.~~ **Choctaw Nation** **Choctaw Roll** *(Not Including Freedmen)* CARD NO.
POST OFFICE: Ara, Ind. Ter. FIELD NO. 162

Dawes' Roll No.		NAME		Relationship to Person First Named	AGE	SEX	BLOOD	TRIBAL ENROLLMENT Year	County	No.
309	1	Spain, S. Beauregard	40		36	M	1/16	1896	Choctaw residing in Chickasaw District	11754
I.W. 7	2	" Emma E.	36	Wife	32	F	I.W.	1896	" "	15075
310	3	" Ollie Lee	15	Dau	11	"	1/32	1896	" "	11756
311	4	" Maudie	11	"	7	"	1/32	1896	" "	11757
312	5	" Dora	9	"	5	"	1/32	1896	" "	11758
313	6	" Georgie D.	6	"	2	"	1/32	1896	" "	11759
314	7	" Mary Ann	4	"	1mo	"	1/32			

ENROLLMENT OF NOS. 1,3,4,5,6 and 7 HEREON APPROVED BY THE SECRETARY OF INTERIOR Dec 12 1902

No.1 on 1896 Choctaw Census roll as J. Benj. Spain
No.6 also on 1896 Choctaw roll as Benj. T. Spain: page 304: #11759
No.7 Evidence of Birth filed July 3rd 1902.

No.1 on Choctaw roll as J. Benjamin Spain
No.3 " " " " Ollie "
No.4 " " " " Mena "
No.6 " " " " Borgia D. "

ENROLLMENT OF NOS. 2 HEREON APPROVED BY THE SECRETARY OF INTERIOR Jun 13 1903

TRIBAL ENROLLMENT OF PARENTS

	Name of Father	Year	County	Name of Mother	Year	County
1	Thos. D. Spain	Dead	non citizen	Mary Spain	Dead	Choctaw Roll
2	Ned Jones		" "	Caroline Jones		non-citizen
3	No.1			No.2		
4	No.1			No.2		
5	No.1			No.2		
6	No.1			No.2		
7	No.1			No.2		

Marriage license and certificate to be supplied.
Certificate received Sept 16/98 - no certificate required.
No2 admitted as an intermarried citizen by Dawes Commission: Choctaw Case #804: no appeal.

Take no further action relative to allotment to No.2 Protest overruled by Department March 31-04
Protest of Attys for Choctaw and Chickasaw Nations
J 012304

No.1 son of Mary M. Spain who was admitted by act of Choctaw Council of Oct 31,1877
No.7 Enrolled Nov. 23/98

Date of application for enrollment 9/15/98

RESIDENCE: Chickasaw Nation ~~COUNTY~~.
POST OFFICE: Wynnewood, Ind. Ter.

Choctaw Nation

Choctaw Roll (Not Including Freedmen)

CARD NO.
FIELD NO. 163

Dawes' Roll No.	NAME	Relationship to Person First Named	AGE	SEX	BLOOD	TRIBAL ENROLLMENT Year	County	No.
I.W.489	1 Jones Frank		43	M	I.W.			
14488	2 " Salina Izzard 39	Wife	35	F	1/32		Choctaw residing in ~~Chickasaw District~~	CPR #3 33
14489	3 " Effies 17	Dau	13	"	1/64		" "	"
14490	4 " Georgia 15	"	11	"	1/64		" "	"
14491	5 " Burr 14	Son	10	M	1/64		" "	"
14492	6 " Della 12	Dau	8	F	1/64		" "	"
14493	7 " Sadie 10	"	6	"	1/64		" "	"
14203	8 " Una May 7	"	3	"	1/64	ENROLLMENT OF NOS. ~~~ 1 ~~~ HEREON APPROVED BY THE SECRETARY OF INTERIOR DEC 24 1903		
14494	9 " Bertie Page 4	Son	1mo	M	1/64			
DEAD	10 ~~" Minnie Etta~~	~~Dau~~	~~1mo~~	~~F~~	~~1/64~~			
14495	11 " Henry B. 1	Son	6mo	M	1/64			

12 ENROLLMENT OF NOS. 8 HEREON APPROVED BY THE SECRETARY OF INTERIOR APR 11 1903

Nos 1 and 8 admitted by Dawes Com Case No 1049 and no appeal taken

No7 on Choctaw roll as Sarah

14 For child of No4 see NB(Apr 26-06) Card #342

No 1 HEREON DISMISSED UNDER ORDER OF THE COMMISSION TO THE FIVE CIVILIZED TRIBES OF MARCH 31, 1905.

14 №11 Born Feby.8.1902; enrolled Aug 9,1902.

15 ~~№10 Died April 20,1901, proof of death filed Oct.23 1902~~

16 №8 Born Sept 11,1896; proof of birth filed Feby 17, 1903

17 No2 admitted by act of Council of Nov 3 1879 as Selena Izzard

TRIBAL ENROLLMENT OF PARENTS

Name of Father	Year	County	Name of Mother	Year	County
1 Levi Jones	Dead	non citizen	Catherine Jones		non citizen
2 George Izzard	"	" "	Sarah Izzard		Blue
3 No 1			No 2		
4 No 1			No 2		
5 No 1			No 2		
6 No 1			No 2		
7 No 1			No 2		
8 No 1			No 2		
9 No 1			No 2		
10 ~~No 1~~			~~No 2~~		
11 No 1			No 2		

12 No2 on Choctaw Pay Roll, No 3, Page 33, No 322

No.10 Enrolled March 20, 1901

13 No3 " " " " " 3 " 33 " 323

~~No4 " " " " " 3 " 33 " 324~~

14 No5 " " " " " 3 " 33 " 325

ENROLLMENT OF NOS. 2,3,4,5,6,7,9&11 HEREON APPROVED BY THE SECRETARY OF INTERIOR MAY 20 1903

15 No6 " " " " " 3 " 33 " 326

No7 " " " " " 3 " 33 " 327

16 ~~No9 enrolled March 6/99~~

#1 to 8

Date of Application for Enrollment.

Sept. 15/98

17 ~~For child of Nos 1&2 see NB (Apr 26 '06) Card #492~~

RESIDENCE: Chickasaw Nation ~~COUNTY.~~ **Choctaw Nation** Choctaw Roll (Not Including Freedmen) CARD NO.
POST OFFICE: Foster, Ind Ter FIELD NO. 164

Dawes' Roll No.	NAME	Relationship to Person First Named	AGE	SEX	BLOOD	TRIBAL ENROLLMENT Year	County	No.
315	1 Poff, Patsey 74	First Named	70	F	1/2		Choctaw residing in Chickasaw District	CCR #2 258
	2							
	3					1896	Chickasaw Dist	6178
	4							

ENROLLMENT OF NOS 1 HEREON APPROVED BY THE SECRETARY OF INTERIOR DEC 12 1902

On Choctaw Roll as Patsey Hall

№1 is the wife of David H. Poff on Choctaw card #D818, Oct. 20, 1902

TRIBAL ENROLLMENT OF PARENTS

	Name of Father	Year	County	Name of Mother	Year	County
1	Tom Martin	Dead	non-citizen		Dead	Choctaw Roll

Date of Application for Enrollment. Sept. 15/98

RESIDENCE: Chickasaw Nation ~~COUNTY.~~ **Choctaw Nation** **Choctaw Roll** *(Not Including Freedmen)* CARD NO.
POST OFFICE: Foster, Ind. Ter. FIELD NO. **165**

Dawes' Roll No.	NAME	Relationship to Person First Named	AGE	SEX	BLOOD	TRIBAL ENROLLMENT Year	County	No.
316	1 Hayes, Henry 49	First Named	45	M	3/4		Choctaw residing in Chickasaw District	CCR #2 259
~~317~~	2 ~~Isabelle~~ 59 Died prior to September 25, 1902	~~Wife~~	~~55~~	~~F~~	~~Full~~			

ENROLLMENT OF NOS. 1 and 2 HEREON APPROVED BY THE SECRETARY OF INTERIOR DEC 12 1902

No1 1896 Chickasaw Dist 6218
No2 1896 " " 6219 as Isabella Hay

№2 Died in March 1902, proof of death filed Oct. 23, 1902.

No 2 died March 1902 July 8, 1904[sic]

TRIBAL ENROLLMENT OF PARENTS

Name of Father	Year	County	Name of Mother	Year	County
1 Solomon Hays	Dead	Choctaw Roll	Beckey Hays	Dead	Choctaw Roll
2 ~~Wilson Belvin~~	~~Dead~~	~~" "~~	~~Sallie Belvin~~	~~"~~	~~" "~~

Date of Application for Enrollment. Sept. 15/98

RESIDENCE: Chickasaw Nation ~~COUNTY.~~
POST OFFICE: Foster, Ind. Ter.

Choctaw Nation

Choctaw Roll (*Not Including Freedmen*)

CARD NO.
FIELD NO. **166**

Dawes' Roll No.	NAME	Relationship to Person First Named	AGE	SEX	BLOOD	TRIBAL ENROLLMENT Year	County	No.
318	1 Pernell, Henry 20	First Named	16	M	3/4		Choctaw residing in Chickasaw District	CCR #2 405
319	2 " Thomas 18	Bro	14	"	3/4		" "	"
15028	3 Garrison, Isabelle Pernell 13	Sister	12	F	3/4	1893	" "	115
15029	4 Garrison, Mina Marana 1	Niece	2mo	F	3/4			

ENROLLMENT OF NOS. 1 and 2 HEREON APPROVED BY THE SECRETARY OF INTERIOR DEC 12 1902

ENROLLMENT OF NOS. 3 and 4 HEREON APPROVED BY THE SECRETARY OF INTERIOR OCT 15 1903

No1 1896 Chickasaw Dist 10621 as Henry Pursell
No2 1896 " " 10622 " Thomas "

Nº3 is now the wife of John E.S. Garrison a non-citizen. Evidence of marriage requested June 14, 1902. Filed June 24th 1902
Nº4 Born April 19, 1902: enrolled June 14, 1902.
For child of No 3 see NB (March 3, 1905) #1038

TRIBAL ENROLLMENT OF PARENTS

Name of Father	Year	County	Name of Mother	Year	County
1 Sim Pernell	Dead	Choctaw Roll	Sibbie Pernell	Dead	Choctaw residing in Chickasaw District
2 " "	"	" "	" "	"	" "
3 " "	"	" "	" "	"	" "
4 John E.S. Garrison		non-citizen	Nº 3		

#1 to 3
Date of Application ~~for Enrollment.~~ Sept. 15/98

RESIDENCE: Chickasaw Nation ~~COUNTY~~. **Choctaw Nation** Choctaw Roll (Not Including Freedmen) CARD NO.
POST OFFICE: Pauls Valley Ind Ter. FIELD NO. 167

Dawes' Roll No.	NAME	Relationship to Person First Named	AGE	SEX	BLOOD	TRIBAL ENROLLMENT Year	County	No.
IW490	1 Campbell, Hugh 59	First Named	55	M	I.W.		Choctaw residing in Chickasaw District	C.I. Roll 19
320	2 " Julia G. 45	Wife	41	F	3/4		" "	CCR #2 125
321	3 " Kate 27	Dau	23	"	3/8		" "	"
to 4730	4 ~~" Jennie~~	~~"~~	~~19~~	~~"~~	~~3/8~~		~~" "~~	~~"~~
322	5 " John 21	Son	17	M	3/8		" "	"
323	6 " Rebeeca 18	Dau	14	F	3/8		" "	"
324	7 " Amanda 15	"	11	"	3/8		" "	"
325	8 " Anita 13	"	9	"	3/8		" "	"
326	9 " Elizabeth 8	"	4	"	3/8		" "	"

ENROLLMENT OF NOS. 2,3,4,5,6,7,8 and 9 HEREON APPROVED BY THE SECRETARY OF INTERIOR DEC 12 1902

No4 is the wife of William E Reel Choctaw Card #4730
Nos 1 &9 admitted by Dawes Com 1896 case #773 no ap

ENROLLMENT OF NOS. ~~~ 1 ~~~ HEREON APPROVED BY THE SECRETARY OF INTERIOR DEC 24 1903

TRIBAL ENROLLMENT OF PARENTS

Name of Father	Year	County	Name of Mother	Year	County
1 John Campbell	Dead	non citizen	Catherine Campbell		non citizen
2 Silas Gardner	"	Choctaw roll	Hettie Gardner	Dead	Choctaw Roll
3 No 1			No 2		
4 ~~No 1~~			~~No 2~~		
5 No 1			No 2		
6 No 1			No 2		
7 No 1			No 2		
8 No 1			No 2		
9 No 1			No 2		

No1 1896 Chickasaw Dist 14433
No2 1896 " " 3080
No3 1896 " " 3082 as Katie Campbell
No4 1896 " " 3081 " Janie "
No5 1896 " " 3083
No6 1896 " " 3084
No7 1896 " " 3085
No8 1896 " " 3086 as Nila Campbell
No9 1896 " " 3087

Date of Application for Enrollment. Sept 15/98

Choctaw By Blood Enrollment Cards 1898-1914

RESIDENCE: Chickasaw Nation ~~COUNTY.~~
POST OFFICE: Purcell, Ind Ter

Choctaw Nation

Choctaw Roll *(Not Including Freedmen)*

CARD NO.
FIELD NO. 168

Dawes' Roll No.		NAME		Relationship to Person First Named	AGE	SEX	BLOOD	TRIBAL ENROLLMENT		
								Year	County	No.
327	1	Walker, Willie	35	First Named	31	M	1/2		Choctaw residing in Chickasaw District	CCR #2 481
328	2	" Edna May	8	Dau	4	F	1/4		" "	"
14496	3	" Laura E.	4	"	8mo	F	1/4			
14497	4	" Clara B	2	Dau	3mo	F	1/4			
IW 1627	5	" Mary		Wife	24	F	I.W.			
	6	ENROLLMENT								
	7	OF NOS. 1 and 2 HEREON								
	8	APPROVED BY THE SECRETARY OF INTERIOR DEC 12 1902					No 1	1896	Kiamitia	13759
	9	ENROLLMENT					No 2	1896	" "	13760
	10	OF NOS. 3 and 4 HEREON								
	11	APPROVED BY THE SECRETARY OF INTERIOR MAY 20 1903								
	12									
	13									
	14	ENROLLMENT OF NOS. 5 HEREON								
	15	APPROVED BY THE SECRETARY OF INTERIOR FEB 19 1907								
	16									
	17									

TRIBAL ENROLLMENT OF PARENTS

	Name of Father	Year	County	Name of Mother	Year	County
1	Green Walker		Kiamisha[sic]	Clarissa Walker		Kiamisha[sic]
2	No 1			Mary Walker		non citizen
3	No 1			" "		" "
4	No 1			" "		" "
5	Jim Hyter	dead		Katie Hyter		

No2 on Choctaw Roll as Etna M.
~~No3 affidavit of attending physician to be supplied~~ Received Dec 13/98
~~No4 Enrolled December 27, 1900~~
No5 placed hereon under order of the Commissioner to the Five Civilized Tribes of Oct-19-1906, holding that application was made for her enrollment within the time ~~provided by act of Congress approved April 26-1906 (34 Stats-137)~~

For children of Nos 1&2 see NB (Mar 3, 1905) #532

P.O. seems to be Okra I.T.
P O Wayne I.T. 1/5/05

GRANTED JAN 16 1907

#1 to 3 inc
Date of Application for Enrollment.
Sept. 15/98

RESIDENCE: Chickasaw Nation ~~COUNTY.~~ **Choctaw Nation** Choctaw Roll (Not Including Freedmen) CARD NO.
POST OFFICE: Purcell, Ind. Ter. FIELD NO. 169

Dawes' Roll No.		NAME		Relationship to Person First Named	AGE	SEX	BLOOD	TRIBAL ENROLLMENT Year	County	No.
14204	1	Hazel, Jonathan	51	First Named	47	M	1/16		Choctaw residing in Chickasaw District	CCR #2 259
IW491	2	" Eveline	45	Wife	42	F	I.W.		" "	C.I. Roll 47
14205	3	" Caroline M.	25	Dau	21	"	1/32		" "	CCR #2 259
14206	4	" Arthur	21	Son	17	M	1/32		" "	"
14207	5	" Alberta	19	Dau	15	F	1/32		" "	"
14208	6	" Lemar	17	Son	13	M	1/32		" "	"
14209	7	" George	12	"	8	"	1/32		" "	"
See 4587	8	~~" Seth~~		~~Nephew~~	~~24~~	~~"~~	~~1/32~~			

ENROLLMENT OF NOS. 1 3 4 5 6 and 7 HEREON APPROVED BY THE SECRETARY OF INTERIOR Apr 11 1903

No. 8 transferred to Choctaw Card #4587 9/6/99
~~No. 1-2-3-4-5-6-7 admitted by Dawes Com. 1896~~
~~No appeal. Choctaw Case No. 1339.~~

ENROLLMENT OF NOS. ~~~ 2 ~~~ HEREON APPROVED BY THE SECRETARY OF INTERIOR Dec 24 1903

For child of No 4 see NB (Mar.3-05) Card #162.

TRIBAL ENROLLMENT OF PARENTS

	Name of Father	Year	County	Name of Mother	Year	County
1	Seth Hazel	Dead	non citizen	Caroline Hazel	Dead	Choctaw residing in Chickasaw District
2	A.D. Irwin		" "	Elizabeth Irwin	"	noncitizen
3	No 1			No 2		
4	No 1			No 2		
5	No 1			No 2		
6	No 1			No 2		
7	No 1			No 2		
8	~~James P. Hazel~~	~~Dead~~	~~Choctaw Roll~~	~~Jane Hazel~~	~~Dead~~	~~non citizen~~

No.1 1896 Chickasaw Dist 6209
No.2 1896 " " 14671 as Everline I. Hazel
~~No.3 1896 " " 6210 " Carrie "~~
~~No.4 1896 " " 6212~~
No.5 1896 " " 6213 as Albertie Hazel
No.6 1896 " " 6214 " Lemon "
~~No.7 1896 " " 6215~~
~~No.8 1896 " " 6208~~

Date of Application for Enrollment.
Sept. 15/98

P.O. Erin Springs

RESIDENCE: Chickasaw Nation ~~COUNTY.~~ **Choctaw Nation** Choctaw Roll (Not Including Freedmen) CARD NO.
POST OFFICE: Fox, Ind. Ter. FIELD NO. 170

Dawes' Roll No.		NAME	Relationship to Person First Named	AGE	SEX	BLOOD	TRIBAL ENROLLMENT Year	County	No.
14210	1	Burkes, William M [27]	First Named	23	M	1/8			
IW 1600	2	" Maud Ella	Wife	22	F	I.W.			
	3								
	4								
	5								
	6								
	7								
	8								
	9								
	10								
	11								
	12								
	13								
	14								
	15								
	16								
	17								

ENROLLMENT OF NOS. 1 HEREON APPROVED BY THE SECRETARY OF INTERIOR APR 11 1903

ENROLLMENT OF NOS. ~~~ 2 ~~~ HEREON APPROVED BY THE SECRETARY OF INTERIOR FEB 12 1907

Admitted by Dawes Com. Case No 908 and no appeal taken.

~~No2 placed hereon under order of the Commissioner to the Five Civilized Tribes of Nov 15-1906; holding that application was made for her~~ enrollment within the time provided by the act of Congress approved April 26-1906.

For child of No1 see N B. (Mar 3-1905) Card #79.

TRIBAL ENROLLMENT OF PARENTS

	Name of Father	Year	County	Name of Mother	Year	County
1	John G Burks			Mollie Burkes	Dead	non citizen
2	Jesse Davis	dead	Non Citz	Nettie Byrd		non citz.
3						
4						
5						
6						
7						
8						
9						
10						
11						
12						
13						
14						
15						
16						
17	P.O. Wilburton 7/14/06					

Date of Application for Enrollment. Sept. 19/98

RESIDENCE: Chickasaw Nation ~~COUNTY.~~
POST OFFICE: Purcell, Ind. Ter.

Choctaw Nation

Choctaw Roll *(Not Including Freedmen)*

CARD NO.
FIELD NO. **171**

Dawes' Roll No.	NAME		Relationship to Person First Named	AGE	SEX	BLOOD	TRIBAL ENROLLMENT Year	County	No.
IW192	1 Smith, Joseph P.	32	First Named	28	M	I.W.			
329	2 " Elizabeth	23	Wife	19	F	1/32		~~Choctaw residing in Chickasaw District~~	~~CCR #2 257~~
330	3 " Lois Hazel	3	Dau	4mos	F	1/64			
	4								
	5					No 2	1896	Chickasaw Dist	6211

ENROLLMENT OF NOS. 2 and 3 HEREON APPROVED BY THE SECRETARY OF INTERIOR DEC 12 1902

ENROLLMENT OF NOS. ~~~ 1 ~~~ HEREON APPROVED BY THE SECRETARY OF INTERIOR DEC 24 1903

No2 on Choctaw roll as Elizabeth Hazel.

No3 Enrolled May 24, 1900.

For children of Nos 1&2 see NB (Mar 3-1905) Card No 15.

TRIBAL ENROLLMENT OF PARENTS

	Name of Father	Year	County	Name of Mother	Year	County
1	J. I. Smith		non citizen	Lou M. Smith		non citizen
2	John N Hazel		~~Choctaw residing in Chickasaw District~~	Eveline Hazel (I.W.)		~~Choctaw residing in Chickasaw District~~
3	No1			No2		

Date of Application for Enrollment. ~~Sept. 15/98~~

RESIDENCE: Chickasaw Nation ~~COUNTY.~~ **Choctaw Nation** **Choctaw Roll** (Not Including Freedmen) CARD NO.
POST OFFICE: Hart, Ind. Ter. FIELD NO. 172

Dawes' Roll No.		NAME	Relationship to Person First Named	AGE	SEX	BLOOD	TRIBAL ENROLLMENT Year	County	No.
~~331~~	1	~~Carpenter, Amazon~~ 25	~~Named~~	~~21~~	~~F~~	~~1/32~~		~~Choctaw residing in Chickasaw District~~	~~CCR #2 119~~
332	2	" Nettie May 10	Dau	6	"	1/64		" "	"
333	3	" Joe Cornelius 9	Son	5	M	1/64		" "	"
334	4	" Ollie 6	Dau	2	F	1/64		" "	"
15352	5	" Thomas 5	Son	10mo	M	1/64		" "	"
335	6	" Mabel 2	Dau	5mo	F	1/64			
	7	ENROLLMENT							
	8	OF NOS. 1 2 3 4 and 6 HEREON APPROVED BY THE SECRETARY							
	9	OF INTERIOR Dec 12 1902							
	10	No 1 is decendant[sic] of Mary M. Spain who was admitted by act of Oct. 31 1877							
	11	No.3 on Choctaw roll as Cornelius							
	12	No.5 " " " " J.T.							
	13	ENROLLMENT							
	14	OF NOS. ~~ 5 ~~ HEREON APPROVED BY THE SECRETARY							
	15	OF INTERIOR May 9 1904							
	16	No.1 died March 10, 1902: Enrollment cancelled by Department July 8-1904							
	17								

TRIBAL ENROLLMENT OF PARENTS

	Name of Father	Year	County	Name of Mother	Year	County
1	~~Thos. G. Spain~~		~~Choctaw residing in Chickasaw District~~	~~Elizabeth Spain~~ (I.W.)		~~Choctaw residing in Chickasaw District~~
2	Joe Carpenter		non citizen	No. 1		
3	" "		" "	No. 1		
4	" "		" "	No. 1		
5	" "		" "	No. 1		
6	" "		" "	No. 1		
7	No.1 1896 Blue 2901 as Emmerson Carpenter.					
8	No.2 1896 " 2902 " Meka May "					
9	No.3 1896 " 2903 " Cornelius "					
10	~~No.4 1896 " 2904~~					
10	No.6 Enrolled December 15, 1900					
11	No.1 Died 10 March, 1902. Proof of death filed Oct 27, 1902					
12	№5 Born Dec. 13 1897. See affidavit of Lou Bowers filed Jany 19, 1904					
13						
14						#1 to 5 inc
15						Date of Application for Enrollment.
16						
17	P.O. Harrisburg			Date of application for enrollment		~~Sept. 16/98~~

RESIDENCE: Chickasaw Nation ~~COUNTY.~~ **Choctaw Nation** **Choctaw Roll** *(Not Including Freedmen)* CARD NO.
POST OFFICE: Davis, Ind. Ter. FIELD NO. 173

Dawes' Roll No.		NAME		Relationship to Person First Named	AGE	SEX	BLOOD	TRIBAL ENROLLMENT Year	County	No.
I.W. 860	1	Butterly, Nicholas	51		48	M	I.W.		Choctaw residing in Chickasaw District	C.I. Roll 11
336	2	" Fannie H.	46	Wife	42	F	1/16		" "	CCR #2 81
337	3	" John	21	Son	17	M	1/32		" "	CCR #2 81
338	4	" Everett	18	"	14	"	1/32		" "	CCR #2 81
339	5	" Ellen	15	Dau	11	F	1/32		" "	CCR #2 81
340	6	" Rhoda	15	"	11	"	1/32		" "	CCR #2 81
341	7	" William	10	Son	6	M	1/32		" "	CCR #2 81

ENROLLMENT OF NOS. 2,3,4,5,6 and 7 HEREON APPROVED BY THE SECRETARY OF INTERIOR Dec. 12 1902

ENROLLMENT OF NOS. 1 HEREON APPROVED BY THE SECRETARY OF INTERIOR Aug 3 1904

Eviden[sic] Affidavit of Mat Wolf as to marriage between Nos 1 and 2 filed Oct. 25, 1902

TRIBAL ENROLLMENT OF PARENTS

	Name of Father	Year	County	Name of Mother	Year	County
1	Thos. Butterly		non citizen	Eliza Butterly	Dead	non citizen
2	Calvin Howell	Dead	" "	Rhoda Howell		Choctaw residing in Chickasaw District
3	No.1			No.2		
4	No.1			No.2		
5	No.1			No.2		
6	No.1			No.2		
7	No.1			No.2		

No.1 1896 Chickasaw Dist 14354 as Nicholas Buttery
No.2 1896 " " 2025 " Henry H. "
~~No.3 1896 " " 2027 " John Buddy~~
No.4 1896 " " 2028 " Everett "
No.5 1896 " " 2029 " Ellen "
No.6 1896 " " 2030 " Rhoda "
~~No.7 1896 " " 2031 " William "~~

Date of Application for Enrollment. Sept. 16/98

RESIDENCE: Chickasaw Nation ~~COUNTY.~~
POST OFFICE: Davis, Ind. Ter.

Choctaw Nation

Choctaw Roll (*Not Including Freedmen*)

CARD NO.
FIELD NO. **174**

Dawes' Roll No.		NAME	Relationship to Person First Named	AGE	SEX	BLOOD	TRIBAL ENROLLMENT Year	County	No.
342	1	Howell, Rhoda 90	First Named	86	F	1/8		Choctaw residing in Chickasaw District	CCR #2 259
	2								
	3						1896	Chickasaw Dist	6199
	4								
	5								
	6								
	7								
	8								
	9								
	10								
	11								
	12								
	13								
	14								
	15								
	16								
	17								

ENROLLMENT OF NOS. 1 HEREON APPROVED BY THE SECRETARY OF INTERIOR DEC 12 1902

TRIBAL ENROLLMENT OF PARENTS

	Name of Father	Year	County	Name of Mother	Year	County
1	-- Pitchlynn	Dead	non citizen		Dead	Choctaw Roll
2						
3						
4						
5						
6						
7						
8						
9						
10						
11						
12						
13						
14						
15						
16						
17						

Date of Application for Enrollment. Sept. 16/98

RESIDENCE: Chickasaw Nation ~~COUNTY~~.
POST OFFICE: Davis, Ind. Ter.

Choctaw Nation — **Choctaw Roll** *(Not Including Freedmen)*

CARD NO.
FIELD NO. 175

Dawes' Roll No.	NAME	Relationship to Person First Named	AGE	SEX	BLOOD	TRIBAL ENROLLMENT Year	County	No.
DEAD	1 ~~Howell, John T.~~ DEAD	~~First Named~~	~~60~~	~~M~~	~~1/16~~		~~Choctaw residing in Chickasaw District~~	~~CCR #2 250~~
	2							
	3					1896	Chickasaw Dist	6198
	4							
	5							
	6							
	7							
	8							
	9							
	10							
	11							
	12							
	13							
	14							
	15							
	16							
	17							

No. 1 HEREON DISMISSED UNDER ~~ORDER OF THE COMMISSION TO THE FIVE~~ CIVILIZED TRIBES OF MARCH 31, 1905

No 1 on Choctaw roll as John Howell
Also on 1897 Chickasaw Roll, Page 29,
Tishomingo Co. as John Howell.
~~No. 1 died Feby 15, 1900. Proof of death filed Oct. 25, 1902.~~

CANCELLED

Applicant died prior to the ratification of the Choctaw Chickasaw agreement on Sept. 25, 1902.

TRIBAL ENROLLMENT OF PARENTS

	Name of Father	Year	County	Name of Mother	Year	County
1	~~Calvin Howell~~	~~Dead~~	~~non citizen~~	~~Rhoda Howell~~		~~Choctaw residing in Chickasaw District~~
2						
3						
4						
5						
6						
7						
8						
9						
10						
11						
12						
13						
14						
15						
16						
17						

Date of Application ~~for Enrollment.~~ ~~Sept. 16/98~~

Choctaw By Blood Enrollment Cards 1898-1914

RESIDENCE: Chickasaw Nation ~~COUNTY.~~ **Choctaw Nation** Choctaw Roll *(Not Including Freedmen)* CARD NO.
POST OFFICE: Whitebead, Ind. Ter. FIELD NO. **176**

Dawes' Roll No.		NAME	Relationship to Person First Named	AGE	SEX	BLOOD	TRIBAL ENROLLMENT Year	County	No.
343	1	Spain, Frank 35	First Named	31	M	1/32		Choctaw residing in Chickasaw District	CCR #2 433
I.W. 493	2	" Hattie E. 26	Wife	22	F	I.W.		" "	C.I. Roll 102
344	3	" Ruby M. 8	Dau	4	"	1/64		" "	CCR #2 433
~~345~~	4	DIED PRIOR TO SEPTEMBER 25, 1902 ~~" Jas. Samuel 5~~	~~Son~~	~~8mo~~	~~M~~	~~1/64~~			
346	5	" Leah Ima 3	Dau	4mo	F	1/64			
14498	6	" Franklin G. 1	Son	6wks	M	1/64			

ENROLLMENT OF NOS. 1,3,4 and 5 HEREON APPROVED BY THE SECRETARY OF INTERIOR Dec 12 1902

ENROLLMENT OF NOS. ~~ 2 ~~ HEREON APPROVED BY THE SECRETARY OF INTERIOR Dec 24, 1903

ENROLLMENT OF NOS. 6 HEREON APPROVED BY THE SECRETARY OF INTERIOR May 20 1903

No.4 died Sept. 16, 1901: Enrollment cancelled by Department Sept 16-1904

~~No.4 Died Sept 26, 1901. Proof of death filed Oct. 28, 1902~~

No.1 descendant of Mary M Spain who was admitted by act of Choctaw Council of Oct. 31, 1877

~~No3 on Choctaw Roll as Buby~~

No4 0 affidavit of attending physician to be supplied. Received Sept 16/98.

Marriage license and certificate lost See affidavit attached.

TRIBAL ENROLLMENT OF PARENTS

	Name of Father	Year	County	Name of Mother	Year	County
1	Philander Spain	Dead	Choctaw Roll	Margaret A. Myers		non citizen
2	S.A. Montgomery		non citizen	Martha A Montgomery		" "
3	No. 1			No.2		
4	~~No. 1~~			~~No.2~~		
5	No. 1			No.2		
6	No. 1			No.2		

No.1 1896 Chickasaw Dist 11755

No.2 1896 " " 15076

~~No.3 1896 " " 11761 as Buby Spain~~

No.2 admitted as an intermarried citizen by Dawes Commission in 1896: Choctaw Case #785: no appeal

No.5 Enrolled May 24, 1900

~~No. 6 Born Aug. 16, 1902. enrolled Sept. 25, 1902.~~

Date of Application for Enrollment. Sept. 16/98

P.O. Fleetwood I.T. 10/24/02

RESIDENCE: Chickasaw Nation ~~COUNTY~~. POST OFFICE: Purcell, Ind. Ter.

Choctaw Nation — Choctaw Roll (Not Including Freedmen) — CARD NO. — FIELD NO. 177

Dawes' Roll No.		NAME		Relationship to Person First Named	AGE	SEX	BLOOD	Tribal Enrollment Year	County	No.
I.W. 861	1	Lindsay, Lewis	40	First Named	37	M	I.W.		Choctaw residing in Chickasaw District	C.I. Roll 66
347	2	" Juanita	31	Wife	27	F	1/8		" "	CCR #2 344
348	3	" Jessie	11	Dau	7	"	1/16		" "	"
349	4	" Fannie	8	"	4	"	1/16		" "	"
350	5	" John	5	Son	10mo	M	1/16			
351	6	" Guy	3	"	1mo	"	1/16			
352	7	" Mamie	1	Dau	2wk	F	1/16			

ENROLLMENT OF NOS. 2,3,4,5 6 and 7 HEREON APPROVED BY THE SECRETARY OF INTERIOR DEC 12 1902

No1 on Choctaw Roll as Louis Lindsay
No2 " " " " Waretta " (Sometimes called Pidgeon)
~~No3 " " " " Fisher "~~

ENROLLMENT ~~OF NOS. 1 HEREON~~ APPROVED BY THE SECRETARY OF INTERIOR AUG 3 1904

See affidavits relative to residence of N°s 1 and 2 at date of their marriage filed July 28, 1903
~~For child of Nos 1&2 see NB(March 3,1905) #570~~

TRIBAL ENROLLMENT OF PARENTS

	Name of Father	Year	County	Name of Mother	Year	County
1	John Lindsay	Dead	non citizen	Elively Lindsay	Dead	non citizen
2	Frank Murray	"	" "	Elzira Murray		Choctaw residing in Chickasaw District
3	No1			No2		
4	No1			No2		
5	No1			No2		
6	No1			No2		
7	No1			No2		

No1 1896 Chickasaw Dist 14794 as Louis Lindsy
No2 1896 " " 8411 " Waretta Lindsey
~~No3 1896 " " 8412 " Fisher "~~
~~No4 1896 " " 8413 " Fannie "~~
Evidence of birth of No5 received and filed Aug 22 1900
No6 Enrolled Oct. 6/99 No7 born Jan. 12, 1902: Enrolled Jan. 23, 1902.

#1 to 5 inc
Date of Application for Enrollment. Sept. 16/98

Lindsay 10/22/02

RESIDENCE: Chickasaw Nation ~~COUNTY.~~
POST OFFICE: Wynnewood, Ind. Ter.

Choctaw Nation — **Choctaw Roll** (*Not Including Freedmen*)

CARD NO.
FIELD NO. 178

Dawes' Roll No.		NAME	Relationship to Person First Named	AGE	SEX	BLOOD	TRIBAL ENROLLMENT Year	County	No.
I.W. 862	1	Richardson, S.O. (45)	First Named	41	M	I.W.		Choctaw residing in Chickasaw District	C.I. Roll 96
15176	2	" Lucinda Cordelia 31	Wife	27	F	1/32		" "	CCR #2 416
15177	3	" Fannie Elizabeth 10	Dau	6	"	1/64		" "	"
15178	4	" Panola 7	"	3	"	1/64		" "	"
15179	5	" Niete Jones 6	"	1 1/2	"	1/64			
15180	6	" Lela Buford 3	"	1mo	"	1/64			
15181	7	" Robert Devotie 2	Son	4mo	M	1/64			

See opinion of Atty Genl of Feb 18'04 and letter of Secy of Interior of Feb 24'04 in case of James M Buckholts et al 7-5738.

See testimony of №1 taken October 20, 1902

"Buckholts crowd"

No2 is the daughter of Rodham T Jones admitted by Supreme Court Choctaw Nation Oct, 1872.

No1 admitted by Dawes Com Case No 682 and no appeal taken
No2 on Choctaw roll as Delilah J.
No3 " " " " Vaney
No4 " " " " Pruda
No5 affidavit of attending physician to be supplied - Received Sept 26/98

ENROLLMENT OF NOS. 2-3-4-5-6-7 HEREON APPROVED BY THE SECRETARY OF INTERIOR MAY 9 1904

TRIBAL ENROLLMENT OF PARENTS

	Name of Father	Year	County	Name of Mother	Year	County
1	M.B. Richardson	Dead	non citizen	Fannie Richardson		non citizen
2	R.T. Jones		" "	Lizzie Jones		Blue
3	No1			No2		
4	No1			No2		
5	No1			No2		
6	No1			No2		
7	No1			No2		

No1 1896 Chickasaw Dist 15005
No2 1896 " " 11049
No3 1896 " " 11050
No4 1896 " " 11051

For children of Nos 1&2 see NB (Mar 3-05) #830

Evidence of birth No5 received & filed Aug 6-1900
No6 - May 24/99

No.7 Enrolled June 3, 1901

ENROLLMENT OF NOS. 1 HEREON APPROVED BY THE SECRETARY OF INTERIOR AUG 3 1904

Date of Application for Enrollment. Sept. 16/98

Choctaw By Blood Enrollment Cards 1898-1914

RESIDENCE: Chickasaw Nation ~~COUNTY.~~ **Choctaw Nation** **Choctaw Roll** *(Not Including Freedmen)* CARD NO.
POST OFFICE: Wynnewood Ind. Ter. FIELD NO. 179

Dawes' Roll No.		NAME	Relationship to Person First Named	AGE	SEX	BLOOD	TRIBAL ENROLLMENT Year	County	No.
15182	1	Jones, John Robert 38	First Named	34	M	1/32		Choctaw residing in Chickasaw District	CCR #2 302
I.W. 863	2	" Martha Ann 31	Wife	27	F	I.W.		" "	C.I. Roll 52
15183	3	" Sophronia Elizabeth 13	Dau	9	"	1/64		" "	CCR #2 302
15184	4	" William M 11	Son	7	M	1/64		" "	"
15185	5	" May Cordelia 9	Dau	5	F	1/64		" "	"
15186	6	" Walter A 7	Son	3	M	1/64		" "	"
15187	7	" Samuel C. 4	"	1mo	"	1/64			

See opinion of Atty Genl of Feb 18'04 and letter of Secy of Interior of Feb 24'04 in case of James M Buckholts et al 7-5738.

No1 son of Rodham T Jones admitted by Supreme Court Choctaw Nation Oct 1872
~~No1 1896 Blue 7190 as J.R. Jones~~
No2 1896 " 14705 " Martha A Jones
No2 admitted by Dawes Co Case No 1044 and no appeal taken
See testimony of No1 taken October 20, 1902
"Buckholts Crowd"

10/20/02
Father of No2 is R. Shirley-non-citizen
Mother " " 2 " Sophronia Shirley-non-citizen

TRIBAL ENROLLMENT OF PARENTS

	Name of Father	Year	County	Name of Mother	Year	County
1	R.T. Jones		non citizen	L.E. Jones		Blue
2	R. Shirley		" "	Sophronia Shirley		Non-Citizen
3	No1			No2		
4	No1			No2		
5	No1			No2		
6	No1			No2		
7	No1			No2		

ENROLLMENT OF NOS. 2 HEREON APPROVED BY THE SECRETARY OF INTERIOR AUG 3 1904

ENROLLMENT OF NOS. 1-3-4-5-6-7 HEREON APPROVED BY THE SECRETARY OF INTERIOR MAY 9 1904

No1 on Choctaw Roll as J.R.Jones
Marriage Certificate with Dawes Com Case 1044
~~No3 on Choctaw roll as S. Elizabeth Jones~~
~~No5 " " " " Mary C. "~~

No3 1896 Blue 7191 as S. Elizabeth Jones
No4 1896 " 7192 " Wm M. "
~~No5 1896 " 7193 " Mary C.~~ ✓ "
~~No6 1896 " 7194~~

~~No7 Born March 26, 1899, proof~~ of birth filed Oct. 9. 1903
No7. Apr 17/99✓

For child of No3 see NB (Apr26-06) Card #463

Certified copy of certificate of marriage between Nos 1 and 2 filed Aug 7, 1903

Date of Application for Enrollment. Sept. 16/98

RESIDENCE: Chickasaw Nation ~~COUNTY.~~
POST OFFICE: Johnson, Ind. Ter.

Choctaw Nation

Choctaw Roll *(Not Including Freedmen)*

CARD NO.
FIELD NO. 180

Dawes' Roll No.	NAME	Relationship to Person First Named	AGE	SEX	BLOOD	TRIBAL ENROLLMENT Year	County	No.
353	1 Stevenson, Rosa 12		8	F	1/4		Choctaw residing in Chickasaw District	CPR #3 55

ENROLLMENT
OF NOS. 1 HEREON
APPROVED BY THE SECRETARY
OF INTERIOR DEC 12 1902

On Choctaw Pay Roll No3 Page 55 No 525
Also on 1896 Roll, Page 304, No. 11740, Chick Dist, as Rosie P. Stephenson.

For child of No1 see NB (Apr 26-06) Card #393

TRIBAL ENROLLMENT OF PARENTS

Name of Father	Year	County	Name of Mother	Year	County
1 John Stevenson (I.W)	1897	Chickasaw Roll ~~Pickens County~~	Sarah C. Stevenson	Dead	Choctaw Roll

~~Date of Application~~ for Enrollment. Sept. 16/98

RESIDENCE: Chickasaw Nation ~~COUNTY.~~ **Choctaw Nation** **Choctaw Roll** *(Not Including Freedmen)* CARD NO.
POST OFFICE: Purcell, Ind. Ter. FIELD NO. **181**

Dawes' Roll No.		NAME	Relationship to Person First Named	AGE	SEX	BLOOD	TRIBAL ENROLLMENT Year	County	No.
	1	~~Jennings, Dora Lee~~	~~Named~~	~~33~~	~~F~~	~~1/16~~		~~Choctaw residing in Chickasaw District~~	~~CCR #2 304~~
15972	2	" Arthur 16	Son	12	M	1/32		" "	CCR #2 309
15973	3	" Clyde 13	"	9	M	1/32		" "	CCR #2 309
	4								

5 Nos (1) (2) and (3) denied by Com in '96 Case #1048
No.1 1896 Chickasaw Dist 7399
6 ~~No.2 1896 " " 7400~~
7 ~~No 3 1896 " " 7401~~

ENROLLMENT
~~OF NOS 2 and 3 HEREON~~
APPROVED BY THE SECRETARY
~~OF INTERIOR Jun 16 1906~~

9 DISMISSED
Sep 22 1904

11 Nos 2&3 GRANTED Feb. 27 1906

12 No1 DISMISSED Feb. 27 1906

15 ~~Enrollment of Nos 2 and 3 cancelled by order of Department March 4, 1907~~
16 Nos 2&3 restored to roll by Departmental au-
17 thority of January 19,1909. (File 5-51)

TRIBAL ENROLLMENT OF PARENTS

	Name of Father	Year	County	Name of Mother	Year	County
1	~~Jackson Lee~~	~~Dead~~	~~non citizen~~	~~Amanda Lee~~	~~Dead~~	~~Choctaw Indian~~
2	Andy Jennings		"	No. 1		
3	" "			No. 1		
4						

5 No.1 on 1893 pay roll, Choctaw Nation Chickasaw District page 31, #303.
6 No.2 " " " " " " " " #304.
7 No.3 " " " " " " " " #305.

9 Nos 1-2 and 3 admitted by U.S. Court, Southern District,
~~Ind. Ter. at Ardmore I.T. Dec 22d 1897 in Court Case #142.~~
10 ~~No.1 admitted as Dora P. Jennings~~
11 No.3 " " Clide Jennings
12 Husband of No.1 and father of Nos 2 and 3, on Choctaw Card #5046

15 Judgement[sic] of U.S. Court admitting Nos 1,2 and 3 vacated and set aside by Decree of
16 Choctaw-Chickasaw Cit Court Dec. 17-'02
17 ~~No appeal to C.C.C.C.~~

Date of Application for Enrollment. Sept. 16/98

Choctaw By Blood Enrollment Cards 1898-1914

RESIDENCE: Chickasaw Nation ~~COUNTY~~.
POST OFFICE: Roberson, Ind. Ter.

Choctaw Nation

Choctaw Roll *(Not Including Freedmen)*

CARD NO.
FIELD NO. **182**

Dawes' Roll No.		NAME		Relationship to Person First Named	AGE	SEX	BLOOD	TRIBAL ENROLLMENT Year	County	No.
354	1	Wright, Calvin C.	43	First Named	39	M	1/16		Choctaw residing in Chickasaw District	CCR #2 489
IW 8	2	" Belle	31	Wife	27	F	I.W.		" "	C.I. Roll 118
355	3	" Fannie	15	Dau	11	"	1/32		" "	CCR #2 489
356	4	" Mary	13	"	9	"	1/32		" "	"
357	5	" Arthur	11	Son	7	M	1/32		" "	"
358	6	" Nettie	9	Dau	5	F	1/32		" "	"
359	7	" Edward	7	Son	3	M	1/32		" "	"
360	8	" Eula	4	Dau	1mo	F	1/32			
361	9	" Vallie R.	1	Dau	3mo	F	1/32			
	10	No1 1896 Chickasaw Dist 14165 as C.C. Wright								
	11	No2 1896 " " 15199								
		~~No3 1896 " " 14172 as James Wright~~								
	12	~~No4 1896 " " 14173~~								
	13	No5 1896 " " 14174								
	14	No6 1896 " " 14175								
		~~No7 1896 " " 14176~~								
	15	~~Evidence of birth of No8 received and filed Aug.6 1900~~								
	16	No.3 on Choctaw Roll as James								
	17	No8- affidavit of attending physician to be supplied. Received Oct. 12/98								

TRIBAL ENROLLMENT OF PARENTS

	Name of Father	Year	County	Name of Mother	Year	County
1	Ashley Wright	Dead	non citizen	Arabella Wright	Dead	Choctaw residing in Chickasaw District
2	Gus Johnson	"	" "	Sarah Johnson		non citizen
3	No. 1			No. 2		
4	No. 1			No. 2		
5	No. 1			No. 2		
6	No. 1			No. 2		
7	No. 1			No. 2		
8	No. 1			No. 2		
9	No. 1			No. 2		

ENROLLMENT
OF NOS. 2 HEREON
APPROVED BY THE SECRETARY
OF INTERIOR Jun 13, 1903

No.9 Enrolled April 27, 1901

ENROLLMENT
OF NOS. 1 3 4 5 6 7 8 and 9 HEREON
APPROVED BY THE SECRETARY
OF INTERIOR Dec 12 1902

No.2 admitted as an intermarried citizen and No.7 as a citizen by blood, by Dawes Commission in 1896 Choctaw Case #517; no appeal

#1 to 8
Date of Application for Enrollment. Sept. 16/98

RESIDENCE: Chickasaw Nation ~~COUNTY.~~
POST OFFICE: Whitebead, Ind Ter

Choctaw Nation — Choctaw Roll (Not Including Freedmen) — CARD NO. / FIELD NO. 183

Dawes' Roll No.	NAME	Relationship to Person First Named	AGE	SEX	BLOOD	TRIBAL ENROLLMENT Year	County	No.
IW621	1 Fisher George W. 32	First Named	25	M	I.W.		Choctaw residing in Chickasaw District	C.I. Roll 33
362	2 " Emma 36	Wife	32	F	1/4		" "	CCR #2 194
363	3 " Walter Van 5	Son	14mos	M	1/8			
364	4 " Elizabeth Ellen 18	Step dau	14	F	1/8		Choctaw residing in Chickasaw District	CCR #2 405
365	5 Powers, Maide 16	" "	12	"	1/8		" "	"
366	6 " Vesta 14	" "	10	"	1/8		" "	"
~~367~~	~~7 Fisher Emily Bell~~ DIED PRIOR TO SEPTEMBER 25, 1902	~~Dau~~	~~2wks~~	~~"~~	~~1/8~~			
368	8 " Altha Frances 3	Dau	2mo	F	1/8			
369	9 " Emmett Van 5	Son of No4	3½ mo	M	1/16			

ENROLLMENT OF NOS. 2 3 4 5 6 7 7 and 9 HEREON APPROVED BY THE SECRETARY OF INTERIOR DEC 12 1902

No7 died May 27 1900; ~~proof of death filed October 25, 1902~~

ENROLLMENT OF NOS. 1 HEREON APPROVED BY THE SECRETARY OF INTERIOR MAR 26 1904

No4 on Choctaw roll as Eliza
No5 " " " " Myrtle
No6 " " " " Virtie
~~No4 is now the wife of JA Fisher a non citizen:~~
Evidence of marriage filed July 5 1901
No.9 Enrolled July 5, 1901.

For child of Nos 1&2 see NB (Mar 3rd 1905) #69

TRIBAL ENROLLMENT OF PARENTS

	Name of Father	Year	County	Name of Mother	Year	County
1	H. Fisher		non citizen	Emily Fisher		non citizen
2	Dave Harkins	Dead	Choctaw Roll	Isabelle Harkins	Dead	Atoka
3	No1			No2		
4	Eugene Powers		non citizen	No2		
5	" "		" "	No2		
6	" "		" "	No2		
7	~~No1~~			~~No2~~		
8	No1			No2		
9	J.A. Fisher		non citizen	No4		

No1 1896 Chickasaw Dist 14547
No2 1896 " " 4579
~~No4 1896 " " 10615~~
No5 1896 " " 10616
No6 1896 " " 10617
No7 Enrolled Mar 21/99
~~No8 Enrolled June 18, 1901.~~

For child of No4 See NB (Apr 26-06) Card #598
" " " " " " " " (Mar 3-05) " #591
For child of No5 see NB (Mar 3 1905) #507
" children " No6 " " " #508

P O Chicasha[sic] IT 3/21/05

Date of Application for Enrollment. #1 to 6 Sept. 16/98

RESIDENCE: Chickasaw Nation ~~COUNTY.~~ **Choctaw Nation** **Choctaw Roll** (Not Including Freedmen) CARD NO.
POST OFFICE: Foster, Ind. Ter. FIELD NO. **184**

Dawes' Roll No.	NAME	Relationship to Person First Named	AGE	SEX	BLOOD	TRIBAL ENROLLMENT Year	County	No.
IW 9	1 Childs, F.H. 46	First Named	42	M	I.W.		Choctaw residing in Chickasaw District	C.I. Roll 19
370	2 " Newton Nelson 12	Son	8	"	1/4		" "	CCR #2 125
371	3 " Mina Adelia 10	Dau	6	F	1/4		" "	"
	4							
	5				No1	1896	Chickasaw Dist	14432
	6				No2	1896	" "	3102
	7				No3	1896	" "	3103

ENROLLMENT OF NOS. 2 and 3 HEREON APPROVED BY THE SECRETARY OF INTERIOR DEC 12 1902

ENROLLMENT OF NOS. ~~~ 1 ~~~ HEREON APPROVED BY THE SECRETARY OF INTERIOR JUN 13 1903

No2 on Choctaw Roll as Newton
No3 " " " " Delilah
No1 admitted as an intermarried citizen in 1896
by Dawes Commission: Choctaw Case #735: No appeal

TRIBAL ENROLLMENT OF PARENTS

	Name of Father	Year	County	Name of Mother	Year	County
1	H.O. Childs		non citizen	S.A. Childs		non citizen
2	No1			Sibbie Childs	Dead	Choctaw residing in Chickasaw District
3	No1			" "	"	" "

Date of Application for Enrollment. Sept. 16/98

RESIDENCE: Chickasaw Nation ~~COUNTY~~. **Choctaw Nation** **Choctaw Roll** *(Not Including Freedmen)* CARD NO.
POST OFFICE: Foster Ind. Ter. FIELD NO. 185

Dawes' Roll No.	NAME	Relationship to Person First Named	AGE	SEX	BLOOD	TRIBAL ENROLLMENT Year	County	No.
372	1 Nelson, Sim 32	First Named	28	M	1/2		Kiamitia	CCR #2 382
IW 1244	2 " Ella 17	Wife	17	F	I.W.			
	3					1896	Kiamitia	9742

ENROLLMENT OF NOS. 1 HEREON APPROVED BY THE SECRETARY OF INTERIOR DEC 12 1902

ENROLLMENT OF NOS. ~2~ HEREON APPROVED BY THE SECRETARY OF INTERIOR DEC 30 1904

No1 is the husband of Ella Nelson on Choctaw Card #D817. Oct. 20, 1902
~~No2 originally lister for enrollment Oct. 20, 1902 on Choctaw Card #D-817 transferred to this card Dec. 15, 1904. See decision of Nov. 26, 1904.~~
For child of No2 see NB (Apr 26 '06) #1164.

TRIBAL ENROLLMENT OF PARENTS

Name of Father	Year	County	Name of Mother	Year	County
1 Washington Nelson	Dead	Choctaw Roll	Martha Nelson	Dead	Kiamitia Co
2 Noah Foster		non citz	Mittie Foster		non citz

Date of Application for Enrollment. ~~Sept. 16/98~~

Choctaw By Blood Enrollment Cards 1898-1914

RESIDENCE: Chickasaw Nation ~~COUNTY.~~
POST OFFICE: Pauls Valley Ind. Ter.

Choctaw Nation

Choctaw Roll *(Not Including Freedmen)*

CARD NO.
FIELD NO. **186**

Dawes' Roll No.	NAME		Relationship to Person First Named	AGE	SEX	BLOOD	TRIBAL ENROLLMENT Year	County	No.
IW622	1 Jelks, Fred	24		20	M	I.W.		Choctaw residing in Chickasaw District	
373	2 " Julia	20	Wife	16	F	1/16		" "	CCR #2 434
374	3 " Marietta	2	Dau	4mo	F	1/32			
375	4 " Almus T	1	Son	3mo	M	1/32			
	5 ENROLLMENT								
	6 OF NOS. 2 3 and 4 HEREON APPROVED BY THE SECRETARY					No2	1896	Chickasaw Dist	11783
	7 OF INTERIOR DEC 12 1902								
	8 ENROLLMENT								
	9 OF NOS. 1 HEREON APPROVED BY THE SECRETARY					~~No2 on Choctaw roll as Julia Sperling~~ No3 Enrolled May 24, 1900			
	10 OF INTERIOR MAR 26 1904			No4 Born April 30, 1902; enrolled July 31, 1902					
	11								
	12								
	13								
	14								
	15								
	16								
	17								

TRIBAL ENROLLMENT OF PARENTS

	Name of Father	Year	County	Name of Mother	Year	County
1	Robert Jelks		non citizen	Belle Jelks		non citizen
2	H.H. Sperling (I.W.)		Choctaw residing in Chickasaw District	Henrietta Sperling		Choctaw residing in Chickasaw District
3	No1			No2		
4	No1			No2		
5						
6						
7						
8						
9						
10						
11						
12						
13						
14						
15						#1 to 2 inc
16	P.O. Rush Springs I.T. 1/17/03					Date of Application for Enrollment.
17	PO Rush Springs IT 1/19/03					Sept. 16/98

RESIDENCE: Chickasaw Nation ~~COUNTY.~~
POST OFFICE: Pauls Valley Ind. Ter

Choctaw Nation

Choctaw Roll (Not Including Freedmen)

CARD NO.
FIELD NO. 187

Dawes' Roll No.	NAME	Relationship to Person First Named	AGE	SEX	BLOOD	TRIBAL ENROLLMENT Year	County	No.
I.W 211	1 Sperling, Henry H 43	First Named	39	M	I.W.		Choctaw residing in Chickasaw District	C.I. Roll 102
376	2 " Henrietta W 37	Wife	33	F	1/8		" "	CCR #2 434
377	3 " Charles A. 18	Son	14	M	1/16		" "	"
378	4 " Carrie 16	Dau	12	F	1/16		" "	"
379	5 " Gertie 14	"	10	"	1/16		" "	"
380	6 " Clabe[sic] 11	Son	7	M	1/16		" "	"
381	7 " Christina 9	Dau	5	F	1/16		" "	"
382	8 " Nathie Jewell 5	"	14mo	"	1/16			
383	9 " Margret Henrietta 1	Dau	2mo	F	1/16			

No1 was admitted as an intermarried citizen by Dawes Commission Choctaw Case #844: No appeal.
~~No7 admitted by Dawes Comm 1896 #1060~~

ENROLLMENT OF NOS. 2 3 4 5 6 7 8and9 HEREON APPROVED BY THE SECRETARY OF INTERIOR DEC 12 1902

~~No1 1896 Chickasaw Dist 15078 as Henry Sperlin~~
~~No2 1896 " " 11779 " Henrietta W Spring~~

No1 on Choctaw Roll as Henry Sperling
No3 " " " " Charley "
~~No5 " " " " Guthery "~~
~~No7 " " " " Christana "~~

For child of Nos 1&2 see NB (Mar 3-1905) Card #38

TRIBAL ENROLLMENT OF PARENTS

Name of Father	Year	County	Name of Mother	Year	County
1 Charley Sperling		non citizen	Julia Sperling		non citizen
2 Ashley Wright	Dead	" "	Arabella Wright	Dead	Choctaw residing in Chickasaw District
3 No1			No2		
4 No1			No2		
5 No1			No2		
6 No1			No2		
7 No1			No2		
8 No1			No2		
9 No1			No2		

ENROLLMENT OF NOS 1 HEREON APPROVED BY THE SECRETARY OF INTERIOR Sep 12 1903

No3 1896 Chickasaw Dist 11784 as Charlie Sperling
No4 1896 " " 11785 " Carry
~~No5 1896 " " 11786 " Guthery~~
~~No6 1896 " " 11787~~
No7 1896 " " 11788 " Catherine Sperling

For child of No4 see NB (Mar 3rd 1895) #5.
For child of No4 see NB (Apr 26-06) #720
~~" " " 5 " " " " " #794~~

No9 Born Jany 1, 1902: enrolled Feby. 28, 1902
~~No8 " July 19 1897~~

P.O. Rush Springs, I.T.

#1 to 8
Date of Application for Enrollment.
Sept. 16/98

RESIDENCE: Chickasaw Nation ~~COUNTY.~~ **Choctaw Nation** Choctaw Roll (*Not Including Freedmen*) CARD NO.
POST OFFICE: Norman Okl Ter FIELD NO. 188

Dawes' Roll No.		NAME		Relationship to Person First Named	AGE	SEX	BLOOD	TRIBAL ENROLLMENT Year	County	No.
IW623	1	Adkins, John A	26	First Named	22	M	I.W.		Choctaw residing in Chickasaw District	C.I. Roll 4
384	2	" Tobitha	26	Wife	22	F	1/4		" "	CCR #2 23
385	3	" Hugh L	4	Son	2 1/2 mo	M	1/8			
386	4	" Lena	2	Dau	3 1/2 mo	F	1/8			

ENROLLMENT OF NOS. 2,3 and 4 HEREON APPROVED BY THE SECRETARY OF INTERIOR DEC 12 1902

No 1 1896 Chickasaw Dist 14273
No 2 1896 " " 567 as Tobitha M Adkins

ENROLLMENT OF NOS. 1 HEREON APPROVED BY THE SECRETARY OF INTERIOR MAR 26 1904

No1 on Choctaw Roll as John Adkins

No4 Enrolled May 6, 1901.
No3 born July 27, 1898
For children of Nos 1 and 2 see NB (March 3, 1905) #1283

TRIBAL ENROLLMENT OF PARENTS

	Name of Father	Year	County	Name of Mother	Year	County
1	P. Adkins		non citizen	Betty Adkins	Dead	non citizen
2	Wilson Massey		Gaines	Martha Massey	"	Gaines
3	No1			No2		
4	No1			No2		

1 to 3

Date of Application for Enrollment. Sept. 16/98

RESIDENCE: Chickasaw Nation ~~COUNTY.~~ **Choctaw Nation** **Choctaw Roll** *(Not Including Freedmen)* CARD NO.
POST OFFICE: Norman Okl Ty FIELD NO. **189**

Dawes' Roll No.		NAME	Relationship to Person First Named	AGE	SEX	BLOOD	TRIBAL ENROLLMENT Year	County	No.
W212	1	Adkins, Columbus D. 34		30	M	I.W.		Choctaw residing in Chickasaw District	C.I. Roll 23
387	2	" Sarah Jane 37	Wife	27	F	1/4		" "	CCR #2 23
388	3	" Louis Floyd 11	Son	7	M	1/8		" "	"
389	4	" Stella 9	Dau	5	F	1/8		" "	"
390	5	" Wm McKinley 6	Son	1 1/2	M	1/8		" "	"
391	6	" Vivian 3	Dau	6mo	F	1/8			
392	7	" Bettie 1	Dau	2 1/2 mo	F	1/8			
	8	ENROLLMENT							
	9	OF NOS. 2,3,4,5,6 and 7 HEREON				No1	1896	Chickasaw Dist	14274
	10	APPROVED BY THE SECRETARY OF INTERIOR DEC 12 1902				No2	1896	" "	564
	11					No3	1896	" "	565
	12	ENROLLMENT OF NOS. 1 HEREON				No4	1896	" "	566
	13	APPROVED BY THE SECRETARY OF INTERIOR SEP 12 1903				No6 Enrolled May 24, 1900			
	14								
	15								
	16								
	17	For child of Nos 1&2 see NB (Apr 26-06) Card #364							

TRIBAL ENROLLMENT OF PARENTS

	Name of Father	Year	County	Name of Mother	Year	County
1	P. Adkins		non citizen	Betty Adkins	Dead	non citizen
2	John McKinney	Dead	San Bois	Katy McKinney	"	" "
3	No1			No2		
4	No1			No2		
5	No1			No2		
6	No1			No2		
7	No1			No2		
8						
9			No1 on Choctaw Roll as C.D. Adkins			
10			No3 " " " " Lewis F. "			
11			No4 " " " " Estella "			
12		Evidence of birth of No.5 received and filed Feby. 11, 1902				
13			No.7 Born Jany 5, 1902: enrolled March 27, 1902			
14						
15						
16						
17				~~Date of Application~~ for Enrollment.		Sept. 16/98

RESIDENCE: Chickasaw Nation ~~COUNTY.~~ **Choctaw Nation** **Choctaw Roll** *(Not Including Freedmen)* CARD NO.
POST OFFICE: Marietta Ind. Ter. FIELD NO. **190**

Dawes' Roll No.	NAME	Relationship to Person First Named	AGE	SEX	BLOOD	TRIBAL ENROLLMENT Year	County	No.
393	1 Womack, Ida 30		26	F	1/4		Blue	CCR #2 483
394	2 Harris, Willie 12	Dau	8	"	3/8		"	CCR #2 250
	3							
	4 ENROLLMENT							
	5 OF NOS. 1 and 2 HEREON APPROVED BY THE SECRETARY							
	6 OF INTERIOR DEC 12 1902							
	7		No1	1896	Blue	13905 as Ida Womacks		
	8		No2	1896	"	5906		
	9							
	10							
	11							
	12							
	13							
	14							
	15							
	16							
	17							

TRIBAL ENROLLMENT OF PARENTS

Name of Father	Year	County	Name of Mother	Year	County
1 Eli Carter	Dead	non citizen	Mary Carter	Dead	Choctaw Roll
2 Wm Harris	Dead	Choctaw Roll	No1		
3					
4					
5					
6					
7					
8					
9					
10					
11					
12					
13					
14					
15					
16				Date of Application for Enrollment.	Sept. 19/98
17					

RESIDENCE: Chickasaw Nation ~~COUNTY~~.
POST OFFICE: Pauls Valley Ind. Ter.

Choctaw Nation

Choctaw Roll *(Not Including Freedmen)*

CARD NO.
FIELD NO. 191

Dawes' Roll No.	NAME	Relationship to Person First Named	AGE	SEX	BLOOD	TRIBAL ENROLLMENT Year	County	No.
395	1 Ross, Daniel 20	First Named	19	M	1/2		Choctaw residing in Chickasaw District	CCR #2 417
	2							
	3							
	4					1896	Chickasaw Dist	11067
	5							
	6							
	7							
	8							
	9							
	10							
	11							
	12							
	13							
	14							
	15							
	16							
	17							

ENROLLMENT
OF NOS. 1 HEREON
APPROVED BY THE SECRETARY
OF INTERIOR DEC 12 1902

TRIBAL ENROLLMENT OF PARENTS

Name of Father	Year	County	Name of Mother	Year	County
1 Jim L Ross	Dead	Cherokee citizen	Phoebe Ross	Dead	Choctaw residing in Chickasaw District
2					
3					
4					
5					
6					
7					
8					
9					
10					
11					
12					
13					
14					
15					
16					
17					

Date of Application for Enrollment.
~~Sept.~~ Sep 16/98

Choctaw By Blood Enrollment Cards 1898-1914

RESIDENCE: Chickasaw Nation ~~COUNTY.~~ **Choctaw Nation** Choctaw Roll *(Not Including Freedmen)* CARD NO.
POST OFFICE: Norman Okl. Ter. FIELD NO. **192**

Dawes' Roll No.	NAME	Relationship to Person First Named	AGE	SEX	BLOOD	TRIBAL ENROLLMENT Year	County	No.
IW494	Swinney, Louis A 43	First Named	34	M	I.W.		Choctaw residing in Chickasaw District	CCIRoll 102
DEAD	~~" Minerva W~~ 25	~~Wife~~	~~38~~	~~F~~	~~1/16~~		" "	CCR #2 434
14211	" Lola	Dau	3	"	1/32		" "	"
14212	Leeper, Grace Olive	Step dau	14	"	1/32		" "	CCR #2 344
14213	" Myrtle	" "	11	"	1/32		" "	"
14214	" Roy Davis	" son	8	M	1/32		" "	"

ENROLLMENT OF NOS. 3 4 5 and 6 HEREON APPROVED BY THE SECRETARY OF INTERIOR APT 11 1903

ENROLLMENT OF NOS. ~~ 1 ~~ HEREON APPROVED BY THE SECRETARY OF INTERIOR DEC 24 1903

No2 Died Jan. 1899; Proof of Death filed Oct. 18, 1902.

No2 on Choctaw roll as "Sweeney"
No3 " " " " Lula
~~No4 " " " " Grace Leeper~~
~~No6 " " " " Roy "~~

No. 2 HEREON DISMISSED UNDER ORDER OF THE COMMISSION TO THE FIVE CIVILIZED TRIBES OF MARCH 31, 1905.

TRIBAL ENROLLMENT OF PARENTS

Name of Father	Year	County	Name of Mother	Year	County
James Swinney	Dead	non citizen	Mary E Swinney		non citizen
~~Jos. Ward~~	"	" "	~~Elizabeth J Ward~~	~~Dead~~	~~Atoka~~
No1			No2		
W^m P Leeper	Dead	non citizen	No2		
" " "	"	" "	No2		
" " "	"	" "	No2		

No2 1896 Chickasaw Dist 11807 as Minerva W Sweeney
No3 1896 " " 11808 " Lula "
~~No4 1896 " " 8401 " Grace Leeper~~
~~No5 1896 " " 8402~~
No6 1896 " " 8403 " Roy Leeper
No1 1896 " " 15079 " L.A. Sidaney

~~No1 admitted as an intermarried citizen and Nos 2,3,4,5 and 6 as citizens by blood by Dawes Commission in 1896, Choctaw Case #810; no appeal.~~
See additional testimony of No1 taken Oct. 15, 1902

Date of Application for Enrollment.
Sept. 16/98

RESIDENCE: Chickasaw Nation ~~COUNTY.~~
POST OFFICE: Marietta Ind. Ter.

Choctaw Nation

Choctaw Roll *(Not Including Freedmen)*

CARD NO.
FIELD NO. 193

Dawes' Roll No.		NAME		Relationship to Person First Named	AGE	SEX	BLOOD	TRIBAL ENROLLMENT Year	County	No.
14215	1	Askew B. B.	45	First Named	41	M	1/8		Choctaw residing in Chickasaw District	CCR #2 23
IW864	2	" Mamie	(40)	Wife	38	F	I.W.		" "	C.I. Roll 4
14216	3	" Bolden	22	Son	18	M	1/16		" "	CCR #2 23
14217	4	" Shelton	19	"	15	"	1/16		" "	"
14218	5	" Porter	15	"	11	"	1/16		" "	"
14219	6	" Edna	12	Dau	8	F	1/16		" "	"
14220	7	" Willis	10	Son	6	M	1/16		" "	"
14221	8	" Hubert	8	"	4	"	1/16			"
14222	9	" Rual	5	"	1 1/2	"	1/16			
14223	10	" Suepery	1	Dau	3wk	F	1/16			

ENROLLMENT OF NOS. 1,3,4,5,6,7,8,9 10 HEREON APPROVED BY THE SECRETARY OF INTERIOR APR 11 1903

See testimony of №2 Oct 28, 1902.

All except Nos 1 and 9 admitted by Dawes Com Case No 1130 and no appeal taken:

No9- affidavit of mother to be supplied-Received Sept 28/98

~~Marriage certificate to be supplied-Received Dec 18/98~~

No1 Enrolled Sept 24th 1900

No2 admitted as an intermarried citizen in Dawes Com Case #1130 no appeal

Nos 1-4 inclusive admitted by US Indian Agent Feb 8, 1875

TRIBAL ENROLLMENT OF PARENTS

	Name of Father	Year	County	Name of Mother	Year	County
1	Murrell Askew	Dead	Choctaw Roll	Eliza Askew (I.W.)		Choctaw residing in Chickasaw District
2	Dick Alexander	"	non citizen	Eliza Alexander	Dead	non citizen
3	No1			No2		
4	No1			No2		
5	No1			No2		
6	No1			No2		
7	No1			No2		
8	No1			No2		
9	No1			No2		
10	No1			No2		

ENROLLMENT OF NOS. 2 HEREON APPROVED BY THE SECRETARY OF INTERIOR AUG # 1904

See decision of D.M. Wisdom U.S. Indian Agt. filed with Choctaw #3554 Oct. 21, 1902

#1 to 9
Date of Application for Enrollment.
Sept. 19/98

P.O. Oconee, I.T. 1/16/03

RESIDENCE: Chickasaw Nation ~~COUNTY.~~ **Choctaw Nation** **Choctaw Roll** (Not Including Freedmen) CARD NO.
POST OFFICE: Dixie Ind. Ter. FIELD NO. **194**

Dawes' Roll No.		NAME	Relationship to Person First Named	AGE	SEX	BLOOD	TRIBAL ENROLLMENT Year	County	No.
refused	1	~~Lynn, Elzey B.~~	~~Named~~	~~41~~	~~M~~	~~I.W.~~	~~1896~~	~~Choctaw residing in Chickasaw District~~	~~14793~~
396	2	" Ida Belle 42	Wife	38	R	1/16	1893	Kiamitia	#71
397	3	" Wyley Ulysses 14	Son	10	M	1/32	1896	Choctaw residing in Chickasaw District	8385
398	4	" Will Andrew 12	"	8	"	1/32	1896	" "	8386
399	5	" Worlie 10	"	6	"	1/32	1896	" "	8387
400	6	" Laura Belle 8	Dau	4	F	1/32	1896	" "	8388
14499	7	" Durley Elvie 6	"	~~2~~ 3	"	1/32	1896	" "	3677
401	8	" Pearlie Huston 4	Son	5wks	M	1/32			
402	9	" E. E. 3	Son	5mo	M	1/32			
403	10	" Ada Winnie 1	Dau	6wks	F	1/32			

ENROLLMENT OF NOS. 7 HEREON APPROVED BY THE SECRETARY OF INTERIOR May 20 1903

11 No.1 Refused see Decision of May 2, 1903

12 Record and decision refusing No1 forwarded Secty. of Interior, May 2, 1903

14 No.2 identified from Choctaw payroll #4 page 118

15 No.71 as Ida Lynn

ENROLLMENT OF NOS 2 3 4 5 6 8 9and10 HEREON APPROVED BY THE SECRETARY OF INTERIOR Dec 12 1902

TRIBAL ENROLLMENT OF PARENTS

	Name of Father	Year	County	Name of Mother	Year	County
1	~~Jackson Lynn~~	~~dead~~	~~non citizen~~	~~Lucinda Lynn~~	~~dead~~	~~non citizen~~
2	Wiley Johnson	"	" "	Frances Johnson		Choctaw residing in Chickasaw District
3	No1			No2		
4	No1			No2		
5	No1			No2		
6	No1			No2		
7	No1			No2		
8	No1			No2		
9	No1			No2		
10	No1			No2		

Jan 20, 1906 Motion of Chas von Weise for reconsideration of this case as to No1 forwarded Department Feb. 8, 1906. Motion denied.

Dec. 6, 1904 Decision of Commission refusing application of No1 for enrollment as intermarried citizen of Choctaw Nation affirmed by Department (I.T.D. 2196-1904 D.C. 47859-1904)

11 No2 on Choctaw roll as Ida Johnson-Lynn

12 No3 " " " " W. Y. "

~~No4 " " " " Willis "~~

13 ~~No6 " " " " Lorina "~~

14 No7 and 8 affidavit of attending physician to be supplied Received Sept 20/98

15 No9 Enrolled May 24, 1900

~~No10 Born Nov 15, 1901 Enrolled Nov 20, 1901~~

16 ~~No7 on 1896 Choctaw census roll as Durly Elvera~~

Date of Application for Enrollment.

17 P.O. Weaverton I.T. 11/10/02 Date of application for enrollment Sept. 19/98

P.O. Madill I.T. 1/5/05

RESIDENCE: Chickasaw Nation ~~COUNTY.~~
POST OFFICE: Ardmore, Ind. Ter

Choctaw Nation — **Choctaw Roll** (Not Including Freedmen)

CARD NO.
FIELD NO. 195

Dawes' Roll No.		NAME	Relationship to Person First Named	AGE	SEX	BLOOD	TRIBAL ENROLLMENT Year	County	No.
IW495	1	Taylor, Joe N.	First Named	31	M	I.W.		Choctaw residing in Chickasaw District	C.I. Roll 107
14224	2	" Mary H	Wife	29	F	1/8		" "	CCR #2 452
14225	3	" Vera	Dau	10	"	1/16		" "	"
14226	4	" Juanita	"	7	"	1/16		" "	"
14227	5	" Lela	"	4	"	1/16		" "	"
14228	6	" John Davenport	Son	3	M	1/16			
14229	7	" Sur Corine	Dau	1mo	F	1/16			

ENROLLMENT
OF NOS. 2 3 4 5 6 and 7 HEREON
APPROVED BY THE SECRETARY
OF INTERIOR APR 11 1903

No1 1896 Chickasaw Dist 15117 as J.N. Taylor
No2 1896 " " 12525 " Mary "
~~No3 1896 " " 12526 " Vira "~~

All admitted by Dawes Com Case No. 286
~~No2 " " " " as Mary; on Choctaw Roll as Mary~~
No5 " " " " " Sela " " " " Lillie
No6 " " " " " John
No3 on Choctaw roll as Vira
~~No4 " " " " Varnetta~~

TRIBAL ENROLLMENT OF PARENTS

	Name of Father	Year	County	Name of Mother	Year	County
1	N. B. Taylor		non citizen	S.C. Taylor		non citizen
2	John Davenport	Dead	" "	Zuleka Davenport		Choctaw residing in Chickasaw District
3	No1			No2		
4	No1			No2		
5	No1			No2		
6	No1			No2		
7	No1			No2		

ENROLLMENT
OF NOS. ~~ 1 ~~ HEREON
APPROVED BY THE SECRETARY
OF INTERIOR DEC 24 1903

No7 Born October 3, 1901 and
Enrolled October 28, 1901

No4 1896 Chickasaw Dist 12527 as Warnetta Taylor
No5 1896 " " 12528 " Lillie "

#1 to 6 inc
Date of Application for Enrollment.
Sept. 19/98

RESIDENCE: Chickasaw Nation ~~COUNTY~~.
POST OFFICE: Thackerville, Ind Ter

Choctaw Nation — **Choctaw Roll** *(Not Including Freedmen)*

CARD NO.
FIELD NO. **196**

Dawes' Roll No.	NAME	Relationship to Person First Named	AGE	SEX	BLOOD	TRIBAL ENROLLMENT Year	County	No.
404	1 Ritchey Mamie W. 41	First Named	37	F	1/4		Choctaw residing in Chickasaw District	CCR #2 416
405	2 " Vera 18	Dau	14	"	1/8		" "	"
406	3 " Cora 14	"	10	"	1/8		" "	"
407	4 " Jennie 7	"	3	"	1/8		" "	"
IW 169	5 " W. H.	husband	44	M	I.W.	1896	Chick Dist	15001

No1 on Choctaw Roll as Mrs Nannie

ENROLLMENT OF NOS. 1 2 3 and 4 HEREON APPROVED BY THE SECRETARY OF INTERIOR DEC 12 1902

ENROLLMENT OF NOS. ~~ 5 ~~ HEREON APPROVED BY THE SECRETARY OF INTERIOR JUN 13 1903

No1 1896 Chickasaw Dist 11035 as Mrs Nannie Richie
No2 1896 " " 11036 " Vera "
No3 1896 " " 11037 " Cora "
No4 1896 " " 11038 " Jennie "

TRIBAL ENROLLMENT OF PARENTS

Name of Father	Year	County	Name of Mother	Year	County
1 Wm McClary	Dead	non citizen	Minerva Hawkins ^McClary	Dead	Choctaw Roll
2 W.H. Ritchey		" "	No1		
3 " " "		" "	No1		
4 " " "		" "	No1		
5 Sam Ritchey	Dead	" "	Martha Ritchey	Dead	non-citz

~~Nº5 on 1896 Choctaw census roll as W.H. Richey~~
Nº5 Admitted by Dawes Commission in 1896 as an intermarried citizen in Choctaw citizenship case #653 No appeal
Nº5 Transferred from Choctaw card #D.114. See decision of May 1, 1903

17 P.O. Marietta I.T.

Date of Application ~~for Enrollment.~~
Sept. 19/98

RESIDENCE: Chickasaw Nation ~~COUNTY~~.
POST OFFICE: Fox Ind Ter

Choctaw Nation

Choctaw Roll (Not Including Freedmen)

CARD NO.
FIELD NO. 197

Dawes' Roll No.	NAME	Relationship to Person First Named	AGE	SEX	BLOOD	TRIBAL ENROLLMENT Year	County	No.
408	1 Carpenter, Lillie V 35		31	F	1/16		Choctaw residing in Chickasaw District	CCR #2 116
409	2 Powell, Julia A. 20	Dau	16	"	1/32		" "	CCR #2 405
IW 1493	3 Carpenter, Thomas L.	Hus	29	M	I.W.			

ENROLLMENT OF NOS. 1 and 2 HEREON APPROVED BY THE SECRETARY OF INTERIOR DEC 12 1902

ENROLLMENT OF NOS. ~~~ 3 ~~~ HEREON APPROVED BY THE SECRETARY OF INTERIOR NOV 27 1905

No1 1896 Chickasaw Dist 3146 as Lillie V Cochran
No2 1896 " " 10642 " Judy Powell

No2 on Choctaw Roll as Judy Powell

Husband of No1 on Choctaw D434

TRIBAL ENROLLMENT OF PARENTS

Name of Father	Year	County	Name of Mother	Year	County
1 Andrew J Stanton	Dead	Choctaw Roll	Elizabeth Stanton		non citizen
2 Charles Powell	"	" "	No1		
3 T.H. Carpenter		noncitizen	Nora Carpenter		noncitizen

No3 transferred from Choctaw card # #434 October 21, 1905 See decision of October 5, 1905

For child of No2 see NB (Apr 26" 1906) Card No 725

Date of Application for Enrollment. Sept. 19/98

RESIDENCE: Chickasaw Nation ~~COUNTY.~~ **Choctaw Nation** **Choctaw Roll** (Not Including Freedmen) CARD NO.
POST OFFICE: Holder, Ind Ter FIELD NO. **198**

Dawes' Roll No.	NAME	Relationship to Person First Named	AGE	SEX	BLOOD	TRIBAL ENROLLMENT Year	County	No.
14230	1 Askew, Tom V 32	First Named	28	M	1/16		Choctaw residing in Chickasaw District	CCR #2 24
14231	2 " Arbra 5	son	9mo	"	3/64			
14232	3 " Irene 3	dau	1mo	F	3/64			
14233	4 " Dulsa 1	dau	1wk	F	3/64			
15644	5 " Minnie Holder 30	wife	30	F	1/32		Choctaw residing in ~~Chickasaw District~~	CCR #3 25

ENROLLMENT OF NOS. 1 2 3 and 4 HEREON APPROVED BY THE SECRETARY OF INTERIOR Apr. 11 1903

No1 admitted by Dawes Com Case No 1130, and no appeal taken.
No2-affidavit of physician to be supplied - Received Oct 4/98

ENROLLMENT OF NOS. ~ 5 ~ HEREON APPROVED BY THE SECRETARY OF INTERIOR Dec. 2, 1904

~~No1 husband of Minnie H Askew, Choctaw Doubtful Card No D.37~~
No5 on 1893, Pay Roll, Chick Dist, page 25, No. 241
No3 Enrolled Nov. 1/99.

TRIBAL ENROLLMENT OF PARENTS

	Name of Father	Year	County	Name of Mother	Year	County
1	Murrell Askew	Dead	Choctaw Indian	Eliza Askew (IW)		Choctaw residing in ~~Chickasaw District~~
2	No1			Minnie H. Askew		
3	No1			" " "		
4	No1			" " "		
5	George Holder		non-citizen	Bettie Holder	Dead	Choctaw Indian

~~No4 Born Sept 4, 1902: enrolled Sept. 10, 1902.~~
See decision of D.M. Wisdom U.S. Indian Agt filed in Choctaw #3554 Oct 21, 1902
No1 admitted by U.S. Indian Agent Feb. 5, 1895
~~No5 transferred from Choctaw card #D-37 Oct. 31, 1904 See decision of Oct. 15, 1904.~~
~~For child of Nos 1 & 5 see N.B. (Mar 3rd 1905) #70~~

Date of Application for Enrollment.

~~Sept. 19/98~~

P.O. Marietta I.T. 1/22/03

RESIDENCE: Chickasaw Nation ~~COUNTY.~~ **Choctaw Nation** **Choctaw Roll** *(Not Including Freedmen)* CARD NO.
POST OFFICE: Ran, Ind Ter FIELD NO. **199**

Dawes' Roll No.		NAME	Relationship to Person First Named	AGE	SEX	BLOOD	Year	County	No.
14234	1	Starritt, Mattie		33	F	1/8		Choctaw residing in Chickasaw District	CCR #2 433
14235	2	" Steadman	Son	11	M	1/16		" "	"
14236	3	" Clemmy	Dau	10	F	1/16		" "	"
14237	4	" Sidney	Son	4	M	1/16		" "	"
14238	5	" Charles	"	2	"	1/16		" "	"
14239	6	" Thomas B	"	8mo	"	1/16	1896	Chickasaw Dist	11736
IW170	7	" George A	husband	43	M	I.W.			

ENROLLMENT OF NOS. 1 2 3 4 5 and 6 HEREON APPROVED BY THE SECRETARY OF INTERIOR APR 11 1903

No1 admitted by US Indian Agent Feb 8 1895 See decision of D.M. Wisdom U.S. Indian Agt filed with Choctaw #3554 Oct 21, 1902

No1 wife of George A Starritt, Choctaw Doubtful Card No D.38
No3 on Choctaw Roll as Clemie
All admitted by Dawes Com case No 1130, and no appeal taken

ENROLLMENT OF NOS. ~~~ 7 ~~~ HEREON APPROVED BY THE SECRETARY OF INTERIOR JUN 13 1903

Nº7 admitted by Dawes Commission in 1896 as an intermarried citizen, Choctaw citizenship case #1130, no appeal.
Nº7 transferred from Choctaw card #D38 See decision of May 5, 1903.

TRIBAL ENROLLMENT OF PARENTS

	Name of Father	Year	County	Name of Mother	Year	County
1	Murrell Askew	Dead	Choctaw Indian	Eliza Askew (IW)		Choctaw residing in Chickasaw District
2	George A. Starritt		White Man	No1		
3	" " "		" "	No1		
4	" " "		" "	No1 No		
5	" " "		" "	No1		
6	" " "		" "	No1		
7	Anderson Starritt	Dead	non citizen	Nancy Starritt	Dead	non-citizen

~~No1 1896 Chickasaw Dist 11737 as Mrs Mattie Starrett~~
~~No2 1896 " " 11738 " Stidman~~
No3 1896 " " 11741 " Clemon Steward
No4 1896 " " 11742 " Sidney "
~~No5 1896 " " 11743 " Charles "~~

No6 enrolled Dec 1999. Affidavit irregular and returned for corrections. Filed Jany 17, 1900.

Date of Application for Enrollment: Sept. 19/98

Marietta I.T.

RESIDENCE: Blue COUNTY. **Choctaw Nation** Choctaw Roll (Not Including Freedmen) CARD NO.
POST OFFICE: Durant, Ind. Ter. FIELD NO. 200

Dawes' Roll No.		NAME	Relationship to Person First Named	AGE	SEX	BLOOD	TRIBAL ENROLLMENT Year	County	No.
15353	1	Davenport, Frances 23	First Named	19	F	1/16			
15354	2	" John 5	son	14mos	M	1/32			
15355	3	" Clarence G 3	son	4mos	M	1/32			
15356	4	" Arthur 1	son	2wks	M	1/32			
15357	5	" Robert 7	son	7	M	1/32			

ENROLLMENT OF NOS. 1-2-3-4&5 HEREON APPROVED BY THE SECRETARY OF INTERIOR May 9 1904

Take no further action relative to enrollment of Nos 1,2,3 and 4 and 5 Protest of Attys for Choctaw and Chickasaw Nations Jan 23-04

~~Protest over-ruled; See Departmental letter of March 31, 1904.~~

For child of No.1 see N.B.(Apr 26, 1906) Card No 55

Robert H. Davenport infant son of No.1 on Choctaw R 653

P.O. Tishomingo I.T. 2/2/03

~~P.O. Cape, I.T. 7/25/03~~

P.O. Storey I.T. 10/14/03

TRIBAL ENROLLMENT OF PARENTS

	Name of Father	Year	County	Name of Mother	Year	County
1	Jason Matthews	Dead	Choctaw Indian	Josie Matthews	Dead	non citizen
2	Charley Davenport		non citizen	No1		
3	" "			No1		
4	" "		" "	No1		
5	" "		" "	No1		

No.1 admitted by the Dawes Com. case No 1358 as Frances G. Matthews and no appeal taken.

~~No2-affidavit of attending physician to be supplied.~~ Received Sept 26/98.

No.5 born July 10, 1895

No.3 Enrolled May 24, 1900.

No.4 Born Oct. 20, 1901: Enrolled Nov. 7, 1901.

~~Decr 17, '03 Bynam & Apple Attys Tish~~

No. 5 transferred to this card from R 653: March 5, 1904.

No5 was living at time of application of No.1 in 1896; was refused by Com. Dec, 19, 1902 and directed to be enrolled by Dept. Feby 27, 1904.

#1 to 3 Date of Application for Enrollment. Sept. 19/98

RESIDENCE: Blue COUNTY. **Choctaw Nation** **Choctaw Roll** (Not Including Freedmen) CARD NO.
POST OFFICE: Silo, Ind. Ter. FIELD NO. 201

Dawes' Roll No.		NAME	Relationship to Person First Named	AGE	SEX	BLOOD	TRIBAL ENROLLMENT Year	County	No.
15358	1	Davenport, Florence S 27	First Named	23	F	1/16			
15359	2	" Leslie 1	Son	2wk	M	1/32			
15360	3	" Ida Myrtle 7	Dau	7	F	1/32			

ENROLLMENT OF NOS. 1-2-3- HEREON APPROVED BY THE SECRETARY OF INTERIOR May 9 1904

No1 admitted by Dawes Com. Case No 1358 as Florence S. Blanton and no appeal taken. Original Record Set for Decr 4 '03

Protest over-ruled: see letter of Department of March 31, 1904

Take no further action relative to enrollment of Nos 1 2 &3 Protest of Attys for Choctaw & Chickasaw Nations Jany 23.'04

June 19, 1900, Ida Myrtle Davenport daughter of No1 on Choctaw R 654

No2 born Jany 1st 1902: Enrolled Jany 16, 1902

No3 transferred from Choctaw R654 under departmental decision of May 15, 1903

TRIBAL ENROLLMENT OF PARENTS

	Name of Father	Year	County	Name of Mother	Year	County
1	Theodore Blanton	Dead	non citizen	Josie Blanton	Dead	Choctaw Indian
2	Thomas C. Davenport		" "	No1		
3	" "		" "	No1		

See Departmental letter of Oct. 1st 1903 relative to No.3.

No3 was living at time of application of No.1 in 1896: was refused by Com. Dec. 10, 1902: decision reversed by Dept. May 15, 1903 motion for review filed with Dept. by Atty for Nations July 13, 1903: refused by Dept. Feby. 26, 1904.

Decr 17" -03 Bingham & Apple Atty [Illegible]

Protest of Attorneys for Choctaw and Chickasaw Nations as to No3 forwarded Department Feb 13 1904

P.O. Dolberg I.T. 2/3/04

Date of Application for Enrollment. Sept 19/98

RESIDENCE: Chickasaw Nation ~~COUNTY~~.
POST OFFICE: Ran Ind. Ter.

Choctaw Nation — Choctaw Roll (Not Including Freedmen) — CARD NO. FIELD NO. 202

Dawes' Roll No.	NAME		Relationship to Person First Named	AGE	SEX	BLOOD	Tribal Enrollment Year	County	No.
14240	1 Askew, Em	49	First Named	45	M	1/8		Choctaw residing in Chickasaw District	CCR #2 23
14241	2 " Lee	21	son	17	"	1/16		" "	23
14242	3 Wilson, Lizzie	19	dau	15	F	1/16		" "	"
14243	4 Askew, Dora	16	"	12	"	1/16		" "	"
14244	5 " Roscoe	14	son	10	M	1/16		" "	"
14245	6 " Julius	9	"	5	"	1/16		" "	"
14246	7 " Callie	6	dau	2	F	1/16		" "	"
DEAD	8 ~~" Eliza~~		~~mother~~	~~74~~	~~"~~	~~I.W.~~		~~" "~~	C.I. Roll 4
IW 1071	9 Askew, Eliza	46	wife	42	"	I.W.		" "	"
14247	10 " Willie	3	dau	4mo	"	1/16		No8 and 12 Hereon dismissed	
14248	11 Wilson, Reuben Ray	1	grandson	2wks	M	1/32		No2 under order of the Commission	
DEAD	12 ~~Askew, Gertrude~~	1	~~dau~~	~~2wks~~	~~F~~	~~1/16~~		to the Five Civilized Tribes of ~~March~~ 31, 1905.	
14249	13 " Jewell	1	dau of No2	1mo	F	1/32			

14 No 12 died Apr 20,1902; proof of death filed Oct 31, 1902
15 No8 died June 23, 1901; proof of death filed Oct 31, 1902
Child of No3 on NB(Apr 26-06) Card No 312.
16 ~~For child of No2 see N.B.(Mar 3'05) #360~~
17 " " " " " " " " " #361. No13 Born June 12th 1902 Enrolled July 2nd 1902

No.1 Enrolled Nov 1/99

TRIBAL ENROLLMENT OF PARENTS

	Name of Father	Year	County	Name of Mother	Year	County
1	Murrell Askew	dead	Choctaw Roll	Eliza Askew (IW)		Choctaw residing in ~~Chickasaw District~~
2	No1			Elizabeth Mansell Askew		non citizen
3	No1			" " "		" "
4	No1			" " "		" "
5	No1			" " "		" "
6	No1			" " "		" "
7	No1			" " "		" "
8	~~Nick Wright~~	~~Dead~~	~~non citizen~~	~~Missey Wright~~	~~Dead~~	" "
9	Jim Mansell	"	" "	Becky Mansell	"	" "
10	No1			No9		
11	J.W. Wilson		non citizen	No3		
12	~~No1~~			~~Eliza Mansell Askew~~		
13	No2			Mollie Askew		

ENROLLMENT OF NOS. 1,2,3,4,5,6,7,10,11,13 HEREON APPROVED BY THE SECRETARY OF INTERIOR Apr 11, 1903

ENROLLMENT OF NOS. ~~ 9 ~~ HEREON APPROVED BY THE SECRETARY OF INTERIOR NOV 16 1904

All except No8 (mother) admitted by Dawes Com. Case No 1130 and no appeal take

14 No3 is now the wife of J.W. Wilson a non citizen: Evidence of marriage filed July 8, 1901.
15 See decision of D.M. Wisdom US Indian Agt filed with Choctaw #3554 10/21/02
~~No11 Enrolled July 8, 1901 No12 Enrolled Oct. 3, 1901~~
16 ~~Nos 1-4 inclusive admitted by US Indian Agent Feb 8 1890~~
17 PO Marietta I.T. Date of Application for Enrollment Sept. 20/98

1 to 8 Date of Application for Enrollment.

No2 now the Husband of Mollie Askew non-citizen: Evidence of marriage filed July 2"1902 See Choctaw Card"59

RESIDENCE: Chickasaw Nation ~~COUNTY.~~ **Choctaw Nation** **Choctaw Roll** *(Not Including Freedmen)* CARD NO.
POST OFFICE: Ran Ind. Ter. FIELD NO. 203

Dawes' Roll No.	NAME	Relationship to Person First Named	AGE	SEX	BLOOD	TRIBAL ENROLLMENT Year	County	No.
14250	1 Alexander, Eliza 41		37	F	1/8		Choctaw residing in Chickasaw District	~~CCR #2~~ 24
14251	2 " Mattie 17	Dau	13	"	1/16		" "	"
14252	3 " Reder 15	"	11	"	1/16		" "	"
14253	4 " Mamie 7	"	3	"	1/16		" "	"
void	~~5 " Mable 1~~	~~"~~	~~2Mo~~	~~"~~	~~1/16~~			
IW961	6 Alexander, James 39	Hus.	39	M	I.W.			

7 ~~No6 transferred from Choctaw card D #40 August 4, 1904. See decision~~
8 of Commission of July 30, 1903
9 No1 wife of James Alexander Choctaw Card No D.40
10 All admitted by Dawes Com Case No 1130 and no appeal taken.

ENROLLMENT OF NOS. 1 2 3 and 4 HEREON APPROVED BY THE SECRETARY OF INTERIOR Apr 11 1903

ENROLLMENT OF NOS. ~~ 6 ~~ HEREON APPROVED BY THE SECRETARY OF INTERIOR Sep 22 1904

TRIBAL ENROLLMENT OF PARENTS

Name of Father	Year	County	Name of Mother	Year	County
1 Murrell Askew	Dead	Choctaw Roll	Eliza Askew (I.W.)		Choctaw residing in ~~Chickasaw District~~
2 James Alexander		white man	No1		
3 " "		" "	No1		
4 " "		" "	No1		
~~5 " "~~		~~" "~~	~~No1~~		
6 Dick Alexander	Dead	non citizen	Eliza Shelby Alexander	Dead	non citizen

8 No5 Born Jany. 25, 1902: enrolled March 4, 1902
9 See decision of Dew M Wisdom U.S. Indian Agt filed in Choctaw #3554 Oct 21,1902
Nos.1 and [sic] admitted by U.S. Indian Agent Feb. 8, 1895

11 No.5 is not the child of Eliza Alexander hereon, but the child of
12 Eliza Alexander on Choctaw card #3647, to which card
she is transferred Nov. 9, 1902.

Date of Application for Enrollment. #1 to 4 Sept. 20/98

17 P.O. Marietta I.T.

RESIDENCE: Chickasaw Nation ~~COUNTY.~~ **Choctaw Nation** **Choctaw Roll** *(Not Including Freedmen)* CARD NO.

POST OFFICE: Ardmore, Ind. Ter. FIELD NO. **204**

Dawes' Roll No.	NAME	Relationship to Person First Named	AGE	SEX	BLOOD	TRIBAL ENROLLMENT Year	County	No.
15037	1 McLaughlin, George W. 25	First Named	21	M	1/4		Choctaw residing in Chickasaw District	CCR #2 374
DEAD	2 ~~" David W~~ DEAD	~~Bro~~	~~18~~	~~"~~	~~1/4~~		~~" "~~	~~"~~
DEAD	3 ~~" Andrew L.~~ DEAD	~~"~~	~~15~~	~~"~~	~~1/4~~		~~" "~~	~~"~~
15038	4 " Sampson 16	"	12	"	1/4		" "	"
15039	5 " Walter 12	"	8	"	1/4		" "	"
I.W. 1662	6 " Lillie	Wife	23	F	I.W.			

No 2 and 3 hereon dismissed under order of the Commission to the Five Civilized ~~Tribes of March 31, 1905.~~

Nos 1,4 & 5 See decision of Dec. 3' 03

No6 Enrolled by Department 1907

~~For child of Nos 1&6 see NB (Mar 3'05) #497~~

ENROLLMENT OF NOS. ~~~ 6 ~~~ HEREON APPROVED BY THE SECRETARY OF INTERIOR Mar 4-1907

ENROLLMENT OF NOS. -1-4-5- HEREON APPROVED BY THE SECRETARY OF INTERIOR Feb 16 1904

	Year	County	No.
No1	1896	Chickasaw Dist	9478
No2	1896	" "	9479
No3	1896	" "	9480
No4	1896	" "	9482
No5	1896	" "	9481

No2 Died in Feby 1900 Proof of death filed Oct. 31, 1902.

~~No3 Died Dec 19, 1901. Proof of death filed Oct. 31, 1902~~

TRIBAL ENROLLMENT OF PARENTS

	Name of Father	Year	County	Name of Mother	Year	County
1	E.C. McLaughlin		~~Cherokee~~ non citizen	Ellen McLaughlin	Dead	Choctaw residing in Chickasaw District
2	~~" " "~~		~~" "~~	~~" " "~~	~~"~~	~~" "~~
3	~~" " "~~		~~" "~~	~~" " "~~	~~"~~	~~" "~~
4	" " "		" "	" " "	"	" "
5	" " "		" "	" " "	"	" "

No1 on Choctaw Roll as George

No2 " " " " David

~~No3 " " " " Andrew~~

~~No.2 died December 24 1900~~

No.3 died in October, 1898

see testimony of E.C. McLaughlin as to death of Nos 2 and 3

~~Nos 1 to 5 incl. were re-admitted to Cherokee citizenship Nov. 15, 1894.~~

see copy of act filed herewith 5794

E.C. McLaughlin on Choctaw # ~~D720~~ is father of above children.

~~See testimony of No1 and E.C. McLaughlin taken at Ardmore I.T. Oct. 27, 1902:~~

Date of Application for Enrollment Sept 20/98

RESIDENCE: Chickasaw Nation ~~COUNTY~~.
POST OFFICE: Ada, Ind. Ter.

Choctaw Nation

Choctaw Roll (Not Including Freedmen)

CARD NO.
FIELD NO. 205

Dawes' Roll No.		NAME	Relationship to Person First Named	AGE	SEX	BLOOD	TRIBAL ENROLLMENT Year	County	No.
14500	1	Lawrence, J.R. 67	First Named	63	M	1/4		Choctaw residing in Chickasaw District	CCR #2 344
I.W. 865	2	" Dollie (36)	wife	30	F	I.W.			
	3								
	4								
	5								
	6								
	7								
	8								
	9								
	10								
	11								
	12								
	13								
	14								
	15								
	16								
	17								

ENROLLMENT
~~OF NOS. 1 HEREON~~
APPROVED BY THE SECRETARY
OF INTERIOR May 20 1903

ENROLLMENT
OF NOS. 2 HEREON
~~APPROVED BY THE SECRETARY~~
OF INTERIOR Aug 3 1904

No1 on 1893 Blue County Pay-Roll No. 736

~~Evidence of divorce of No.1 from former wife received and filed Nov. 18, 1902~~
Evidence of divorce of No2 from former husband received and filed Nov. 28, 1902

TRIBAL ENROLLMENT OF PARENTS

	Name of Father	Year	County	Name of Mother	Year	County
1	David Lawrence	Dead	non citizen	Mary Lawrence	Dead	Choctaw Roll
2	Bronson	"	" "	Flora Bronson	"	non citizen
3						
4						
5						
6						
7						
8						
9						
10						
11						
12						
13						
14						
15						
16						
17						

Date of Application for Enrollment.
~~Sept. 20/98~~

RESIDENCE: Chickasaw Nation ~~COUNTY.~~ **Choctaw Nation** Choctaw Roll (Not Including Freedmen) CARD NO.
POST OFFICE: Ardmore, Ind. Ter. FIELD NO. 206

Dawes' Roll No.	NAME	Relationship to Person First Named	AGE	SEX	BLOOD	TRIBAL ENROLLMENT Year	County	No.
410	1 Poland, William P. 47	First Named	43	M	1/8		Choctaw residing in Chickasaw District	CCR #2 395
I.W. 213	2 " Emma L 42	Wife	39	F	I.W.		" "	C.I. Roll 86
411	3 " Robert P. 23	Son	19	M	1/16		" "	CCR #2 395
412	4 Cook, Lucy Garland 20	Dau	16	F	1/16		" "	"
413	5 Poland, Raymond G 14	Son	10	M	1/16		" "	"
14501	6 " Dan Grigsby 1	Grandson	3wks	M	1/32			
415	7 Cook, Will Poland 1	Gr.Son	2wks	M	1/32			
	8 ENROLLMENT				No4 on Choctaw roll as Lucy G.			
	9 OF NOS. 1,3,4,5 and 7 HEREON APPROVED BY THE SECRETARY				No5 " " " Raymond F			
	10 OF INTERIOR Dec 12 1902							
	11 ENROLLMENT							
	12 OF NOS. 6 HEREON APPROVED BY THE SECRETARY							
	13 OF INTERIOR May 20 1903							
	14 ENROLLMENT							
	15 OF NOS. 2 HEREON APPROVED BY THE SECRETARY			No				
	16 OF INTERIOR Sep 12 1903							
	17 See testimony of N°s 1 and 2 taken Oct. 31, 1902.							

TRIBAL ENROLLMENT OF PARENTS

Name of Father	Year	County	Name of Mother	Year	County
1 Wm H. Poland	Dead	non citizen	Kizzie Poland	Dead	Choctaw Roll
2 R.C. Garrett	"	" "	Lucy Garrett		non citizen
3 No1			No2		
4 No1			No2		
5 No1			No2		
6 No3			Emer M.G. Poland		white woman
7 Charles H. Cook			N° 4		

8 No1 1896 Tobucksy 10239 as Wm P. Polland
9 No2 1896 " 14928
~~No3 1896 " 10240 as Robt P. Polland~~
10 ~~No4 1896 " 10241 " Lucy G. "~~
11 No5 1896 " 10242 " Raymond F. "
12 No3 is the husband of Emer M.G. Poland on Choctaw Card #5896 Evidence of marriage filed ~~Mar 21, 1901~~
13
14 ~~No6 Enrolled July 17, 1901 Certified copy of marriage of parents filed Sept 15, 1902~~
15 ~~#1 to 5~~
16 Date of Application ~~for Enrollment.~~
17 Sept. 20/98

RESIDENCE: Chickasaw Nation ~~COUNTY.~~
POST OFFICE: Ardmore, Ind. Ter.

Choctaw Nation

Choctaw Roll (Not Including Freedmen)

CARD NO.
FIELD NO. 207

Dawes' Roll No.		NAME	Relationship to Person First Named	AGE	SEX	BLOOD	TRIBAL ENROLLMENT Year	County	No.
415	1	Bonner, Salina Y. 49	First Named	45	F	1/8		Choctaw residing in Chickasaw District	CCR #2 80
416	2	" Frank A. 24	Son	20	M	1/16		" "	CPR #4 125
417	3	" William T. 23	"	19	"	1/16		" "	"

ENROLLMENT OF NOS. 1 2 and 3 HEREON APPROVED BY THE SECRETARY OF INTERIOR DEC 12 1902

No2 on Choctaw Roll as Franklin, Choctaw Pay Roll, No4, Page 125, No 28
No3 " " Pay Roll No4, Page 125, No. 29 as W.T.

No1 1896 Chickasaw Dist 2800 as Selina Y Brown
No2 1896 " " 11030 " Frank E. Bonner
No3 1896 " " 11031 " W.M. "

TRIBAL ENROLLMENT OF PARENTS

	Name of Father	Year	County	Name of Mother	Year	County
1	W.L. Mitchell	Dead	non citizen	Emily Mitchell	Dead	Choctaw Roll
2	Frank A. Bonner	"	" "	No1		
3	" " "	"	" "	No1		

Full name of N°3 is William Mitchell Thomas Bonner-See copy of letter from Eddleman and Graham filed herein Oct. 13, 1902.
N°3 is now the husband of Emma Pearl Folsome on Choctaw card #256 Oct 13, 1902

No 1 admitted by act of Choctaw Council of Nov. 1, 1881

Date of Application for Enrollment. Sept. 20/98

RESIDENCE: Chickasaw Nation ~~COUNTY~~.
POST OFFICE: Daugherty Ind. Ter.

Choctaw Nation

Choctaw Roll *(Not Including Freedmen)*

CARD NO.
FIELD NO. 208

Dawes' Roll No.		NAME		Relationship to Person First Named	AGE	SEX	BLOOD	TRIBAL ENROLLMENT Year	County	No.
14502	1	Mitchell, Jose V.	32	First Named	28	M	1/8		Choctaw residing in Chickasaw District	CCR #0 26
14503	2	" Bernice	2	Dau	2mo	F	1/16			
I.W 1245	3	" Bessie	24	Wife	24	F	I.W.			

ENROLLMENT OF NOS. 1 and 2 HEREON APPROVED BY THE SECRETARY OF INTERIOR MAY 20 1903

ENROLLMENT ~~OF NOS. 3 HEREON~~ APPROVED BY THE SECRETARY OF INTERIOR DEC 30 1904

No1 on 1893 Choctaw Pay-Roll, Chick Dist. No. 365
On Choctaw Census Record No. O, Page 26, No 120

For child of No^s 1 & 3 see N.B. (Apr 26, 06) card #265
Husband of Bessie Mitchell Choctaw Card #D330
No2 Enrolled July 10, 1900.

TRIBAL ENROLLMENT OF PARENTS

	Name of Father	Year	County	Name of Mother	Year	County
1	W. L. Mitchell	Dead	non citizen	Emily Mitchell	Dead	Choctaw Roll
2	No1			Bessie Mitchell		Choctaw D.330
3	Marion Sheffield	dead	non Citz	Margaret Sheffield	dead	non Citz

~~No1 admitted by act of Choctaw Council of Nov. 1, 1881.~~
No3 originally listed for enrollment Aug. 16/99 on Choctaw Card #D-330; transferred to this card Dec. 15, 1904, See decision of Nov. 26, 1904.

No3 P.O. Davis

DEAD(sic)

Date of Application for Enrollment. Sept. 20/98

RESIDENCE: Chickasaw Nation ~~COUNTY~~. **Choctaw Nation** **Choctaw Roll** *(Not Including Freedmen)* CARD NO.
POST OFFICE: Leon, Ind. Ter. FIELD NO. **209**

Dawes' Roll No.		NAME	Relationship to Person First Named	AGE	SEX	BLOOD	TRIBAL ENROLLMENT Year	County	No.
I.W. 866	1	Taliaferro, James R 27		23	M	I.W.			
418	2	" Minnie A 25	Wife	21	F	5/16		Choctaw residing in ~~Chickasaw District~~	CCR #2 252
419	3	" John C. 2	Son	3mo	M	5/32			
420	4	" Gertrude 1	Dau	1mo	F	5/32			

ENROLLMENT OF NOS. 2 3 and 4 HEREON APPROVED BY THE SECRETARY OF INTERIOR DEC 12 1902

ENROLLMENT OF NOS. 1 HEREON APPROVED BY THE SECRETARY OF INTERIOR AUG 3 1904

No2 1896 Atoka 5991 as Minnie A Harkins
No3 Enrolled Oct 6/99
No4 Enrolled June 7, 1901.

For child of Nos 1&2 see NB (March 3, 1905) #1384

TRIBAL ENROLLMENT OF PARENTS

	Name of Father	Year	County	Name of Mother	Year	County
1	Sam Taliaferro		non citizen	Eliza Taliaferro	Dead	non citizen
2	Clay Harkins	Dead	Atoka	Melvina Harkins	"	Atoka
3	No1			No2		
4	No1			No2		

Date of Application for Enrollment.
Sept. 20/98

RESIDENCE: Chickasaw Nation ~~COUNTY.~~ **Choctaw Nation** **Choctaw Roll** (Not Including Freedmen) CARD NO.
POST OFFICE: Overbrook, Ind. Ter. 2/18/05 FIELD NO. **210**

Dawes' Roll No.		NAME	Relationship to Person First Named	AGE	SEX	BLOOD	TRIBAL ENROLLMENT Year	County	No.
421	1	Cross, A.J. 24	First Named	20	M	1/8		Choctaw residing in Chickasaw District	CCR #2 124
IW1494	2	" Rillie[sic] J 22	wife	18	F	I.W.		" "	C.I. Roll 19
422	3	" Cordey Belle 5	dau	1	"	1/16			
423	4	" Geo Washington 2	son	9mo	M	1/16			
424	5	" Ethel Lee 1	dau	1mo	F	1/16			
	6	ENROLLMENT				No1	1896	Chickasaw Dist	3072
	7	OF NOS. 1,3,4 and 5 HEREON APPROVED BY THE SECRETARY				No2	1896	" "	14438
	8	OF INTERIOR Dec 12 1902							
	9								
	10								

No 2 refused see Decision of July 20 '03
Record and decision refusing No2 forwarded Dept July 20, 1903. Aug 5, 1905. Decision of Commission reversed by Department (I.T.D. 5420-1904) D.C. 32285-1905 and No. 2 enrolled by Secretary of Interior Aug. 15, 1905. Notice forwarded applicant and Atty's for Choctaw and Chickasaw Nations.

TRIBAL ENROLLMENT OF PARENTS

	Name of Father	Year	County	Name of Mother	Year	County
1	W.R. Cross		white man	Hannah Cross	dead	Choctaw Roll
2		dead	non citizen		"	non citizen
3	No1			No2		
4	No1			No2		
5	No1			No2		

ENROLLMENT
OF NOS. ~~~ 2 ~~~ HEREON
APPROVED BY THE SECRETARY
OF INTERIOR Nov. 27 1903

No2 on Choctaw roll as R.J. Cross
No3 affidavit of attending physician to be supplied. Received Sept. 22/98
No4 Enrolled May 11, 1902
No. 5 Born April 3, 1902 enrolled May 17, 1902
For child of Nos 1&2 see N.B. (Apr. 26-06) Card No 830

Protest of Attorneys for Choctaw and Chickasaw Nations as to No2 of Jany 23d, 1904, forwarded Secty of Interior Feby 6, 1904

#1 to 3
Date of Application for Enrollment.
Sept. 20/98

P.O. Legal, I.T.

RESIDENCE: Chickasaw Nation ~~COUNTY.~~
POST OFFICE: Overbrook, Ind. Ter.

Choctaw Nation

Choctaw Roll (Not Including Freedmen)

CARD NO.
FIELD NO. 211

Dawes' Roll No.	NAME	Relationship to Person First Named	AGE	SEX	BLOOD	TRIBAL ENROLLMENT Year	County	No.
425	1 Cross, George W. 22	First Named	18	M	1/8		Choctaw residing in Chickasaw District	CCR #2 124
426	2 " Elva Corintha 1	Dau	1mo	F	1/16			
I.W. 1246	3 " Mariah 19	Wife	19	F	I.W.			
	4					1896	Chickasaw Dist	3073

ENROLLMENT OF NOS. 1 and 2 HEREON APPROVED BY THE SECRETARY OF INTERIOR DEC 12 1902

On Choctaw Rolls as J. M. Cross
Also on Choctaw Pay Roll No3, Page 8, No 83

ENROLLMENT OF NOS. ~ 3 ~ HEREON APPROVED BY THE SECRETARY OF INTERIOR DEC 30 1904

No.1 is now the husband of Marie Edwards a noncitizen. Evidence of marriage filed Sept 10, 1901

No.2 Enrolled Sept 24 1901.
No.3 originally enrolled Oct. 30, 1902 on Choctaw card #D-821: transferred to this card Dec. 15, 1904. See decision of Nov. 26, 1904.

TRIBAL ENROLLMENT OF PARENTS

Name of Father	Year	County	Name of Mother	Year	County
1 W.R. Cross		white man	Hannah Cross	Dead	Choctaw Roll
2 No1			Mariah Cross		non citz
3 A.A. Edwards		non citizen	Mary Edwards	dead	non citizen

For child of Nos 1&3 see NB (Apr 26-06) Card #671

#1
Date of Application for Enrollment. Sept. 20/98

RESIDENCE: Chickasaw Nation ~~COUNTY.~~ **Choctaw Nation** **Choctaw Roll** *(Not Including Freedmen)* CARD NO.
POST OFFICE: Davis, Ind. Ter. FIELD NO. **212**

Dawes' Roll No.	NAME	Relationship to Person First Named	AGE	SEX	BLOOD	TRIBAL ENROLLMENT Year	County	No.
dead	~~Agee, W. E.~~	~~Named~~	~~35~~	~~M~~	~~I.W.~~	~~1896~~	~~Choctaw residing in Chickasaw District~~	~~14271~~
15274*	Smith, Anna 28	wife	24	F	1/8	1896	" "	571
15275*	Agee, Florence 14	dau	10	"	1/16	1896	" "	572
15276*	" Obera 12	"	8	"	1/16	1896	" "	573
15277*	" Zora 10	"	6	"	1/16	1896	" "	574
15278*	" Hester Lee 8	"	4	"	1/16	1896	" "	575
15279*	" Pearl 7	"	3	"	1/16	1896	" "	576
dead	~~" William Horner~~	~~son~~	~~6wks~~	~~M~~	~~1/16~~			
15280*	Smith, Napoleon Bonapart	son of No2	2wks	M	1/16			

ENROLLMENT OF NOS. 2-3-4-5-6-7-9 HEREON APPROVED BY THE SECRETARY OF INTERIOR May 9 1904

"Buckholtz Crowd"
No8 was born Aug 1st 1898
No6 was admitted as Lee
~~The above family is supposed to have been enrolled at Ardmore.~~
Admitted by U.S.Court at Ardmore Dec 21, 1897
Court Case 139. (The above notations from
~~Choctaw Card 5226: cancelled April 11th 1900)~~

No4 on Choctaw Roll as Overa
No6 " " " " Hester
No1 " " " " W.C.

Judgment of U.S. Court admitted No 1to7 inclusive and set aside
~~by Decree of Choctaw-Chickasaw Citizenship Dec 17'02~~
now in C.C.C.C. case #951

TRIBAL ENROLLMENT OF PARENTS

Name of Father	Year	County	Name of Mother	Year	County
~~W[m] Agee~~		~~non citizen~~	~~Mary Agee~~	~~dead~~	~~non citizen~~
G.W. Buckholtz		Choctaw residing in Chickasaw District	Julia Orno		" "
No1			No2		
No1			No2		
No1			No2		
No1			No2		
No1			No2		
~~No1~~			~~No2~~		
Robert L Smith		non citizen	No2		

No8 died Nov 8, 1900: proof of death filed Nov. 4, 1902

All except No8 were admitted to Citizenship by the U.S. Court Southern District and Choctaw
Commission given notice that appeal will be taken to U.S. Supreme Court; Dawes No 1407;
~~Court No. 139~~
~~No1 is dead. Evidence of death filed Aug. 29, 1901~~
No2 is now the wife of Robert L. Smith a non citizen. Evidence of marriage filed Aug 29, 1901
No9 Enrolled Aug 23, 1901. Born Aug 11 '01
P.O. Hickory I.T.

Date of Application for Enrollment. Sept. 20/98

Marginal notations:
No 1&8 hereon dismissed under order of the Commission to the Five Civilized Tribes of March 31, 1905.
Proof of marriage between Nos 1&2 on July 31,'87 filed
~~Nos 1to7 inclusive Denied by Dawes Com -96 Case #1407~~
*Nos 2to7 inclusive Admitted by C.C.C.C. March 21,'04 Card #129
For child of No2 see NB (Mar 3rd 1905)

RESIDENCE: Chickasaw Nation ~~COUNTY.~~
POST OFFICE: Ardmore Ind. Ter.

Choctaw Nation

Choctaw Roll *(Not Including Freedmen)*

CARD NO.
FIELD NO. 213

Dawes' Roll No.		NAME	Relationship to Person First Named	AGE	SEX	BLOOD	TRIBAL ENROLLMENT Year	County	No.
I.W. 196	1	Morris, Lawson A 45		48	M	I.W.		Choctaw residing in Chickasaw District	
427	2	" Rhoda Folsom 39	Wife	35	F	1/4		" "	CCR #2 359
14254	3	" Lorin Folsom 17	Son	13	M	1/8		" "	"
14255	4	" Edward P. 15	"	11	"	1/8		" "	"
14256	5	" Walter H 10	"	6	"	1/8		" "	"

ENROLLMENT OF NOS. 2 HEREON APPROVED BY THE SECRETARY OF INTERIOR DEC 12 1902

ENROLLMENT OF NOS. 3 4 and 5 HEREON APPROVED BY THE SECRETARY OF INTERIOR APR 11 1903

No2 1896 Chickasaw Dist 8929
No3 1896 " " 8932 as Loring F Morris
No4 1896 " " 8933 " Edward F "

No2 admitted as an intermarried citizen, and Nos. 3 4 and 5 as citizens by blood by Dawes Commission in 1896: Choctaw Case #1298

ENROLLMENT OF NOS. ~~ 1 ~~ HEREON APPROVED BY THE SECRETARY OF INTERIOR DEC 24 1903

TRIBAL ENROLLMENT OF PARENTS

	Name of Father	Year	County	Name of Mother	Year	County
1	Edward Morris	Dead	non citizen	Mary Morris		non citizen
2	Lorin Folsom		Blue	Melvina Folsom	Dead	Blue
3	No1			No2		
4	No1			No2		
5	No1			No2		

No1 admitted by Dawes Com. Case No 1298 and no appeal taken
Marriage license and certificate on file in office of Dawes Com: Muskogee, I.T.
~~No2 on Choctaw roll as Rhoda Folsom~~
No3 " " " " Lorin F Morris
No4 " " " " Edward T "
No5 " " " " Walter "

P.O. Caddo I.T. 11/17/02

Date of Application for Enrollment. Sept. 20/98

RESIDENCE: Chickasaw Nation ~~COUNTY~~.
POST OFFICE: Orr Ind. Ter.

Choctaw Nation

Choctaw Roll *(Not Including Freedmen)*

CARD NO.
FIELD NO. 214

Dawes' Roll No.	NAME	Relationship to Person First Named	AGE	SEX	BLOOD	TRIBAL ENROLLMENT Year	County	No.
14504	1 Ormsby Lena 24	First Named	20	F	1/8		Blue	CCR #2 17
IW 624	2 Ormsby James C 31	Hus	31	M	IW			
	3					1896	Blue	400

ENROLLMENT OF NOS. 1 HEREON APPROVED BY THE SECRETARY OF INTERIOR MAY 20 1903

ENROLLMENT OF NOS. 2 HEREON APPROVED BY THE SECRETARY OF INTERIOR MAR 26 1904

Lena Ormsby nee Turnbull on Choctaw roll as Lena Armsby
Wife of James C. Ormsby Choctaw card No D.41

No2 transferred from Choctaw card D41 January 25, 1904
See decision of January 7, 1904

TRIBAL ENROLLMENT OF PARENTS

	Name of Father	Year	County	Name of Mother	Year	County
1	Ed. Turnbull	Dead	Choctaw roll	Laura Kelly		Blue
2	Anderson Ormsby		noncitizen	Nancy Ormsby		noncitizen

Date of Application for Enrollment. Sept. 20/98

RESIDENCE: Chickasaw Nation ~~COUNTY~~.
POST OFFICE: Pauls Valley, Ind. Ter.

Choctaw Nation

Choctaw Roll *(Not Including Freedmen)*

CARD NO.
FIELD NO. 215

Dawes' Roll No.	NAME	Relationship to Person First Named	AGE	SEX	BLOOD	TRIBAL ENROLLMENT Year	County	No.
IW1072	1 Moore Jasper N. 48	First Named	44	M	I.W.		Choctaw residing in Chickasaw District	C.I. Roll 72
14257	2 " Maude 14	Dau	10	F	1/16		" "	CCR #2 358

ENROLLMENT
OF NOS. 2 HEREON
APPROVED BY THE SECRETARY
OF INTERIOR APR 11 1903

ENROLLMENT
OF NOS. ~~~~~1~~~~~ HEREON
APPROVED BY THE SECRETARY
OF INTERIOR NOV 16 1904

No1 1896 Chickasaw Dist 14842
No2 1896 " " 8919 as Maud More

TRIBAL ENROLLMENT OF PARENTS

Name of Father	Year	County	Name of Mother	Year	County
1 Matthew Moore	Dead	noncitizen	Rachael Moore	Dead	noncitizen
2 No1			Orilla Moore	"	Choctaw residing in Chickasaw District

No1 admitted as an intermarried citizen and Maude Moore as a citizen by blood by Dawes Commission in 1896, Choctaw Case #1305 no appeal

It is now claimed by the Choctaw representatives that No1 married out Dec 4th 1900

No2 on 1893 Choctaw Pay Roll Chick. Dist. No. 360
For child of No1 see NB (Apr 26 '06) #1149

P.O. Ardmore I.T.

Date of Application for Enrollment. Sept. 28/98

RESIDENCE: Chickasaw Nation ~~COUNTY.~~ **Choctaw Nation** **Choctaw Roll** *(Not Including Freedmen)* CARD NO.
POST OFFICE: Ardmore Ind. Ter. FIELD NO. **216**

Dawes' Roll No.	NAME	Relationship to Person First Named	AGE	SEX	BLOOD	TRIBAL ENROLLMENT Year	County	No.
15951	1 Shelton Daisy 25	First Named	21	F	1/16		Choctaw residing in Chickasaw District	CCR #2 433
15952	2 " Frank 10	Son	6	M	1/32			"
15953	3 " Emma 6	Dau	2	F	1/32		ENROLLMENT OF NOS. 1, 2 and 3 HEREON APPROVED BY THE SECRETARY OF INTERIOR Nov 27 1905	
DEAD	4 ~~" Lidda May~~ DEAD	~~"~~	~~1wk~~	~~"~~	~~1/32~~			
IW 1495	5 Shelton John	Hus	32	M	I.W.			
	6 No.4 hereon dismissed under order							
	7 of the Commission to the Five		No1 wife of John Shelton Choctaw Card D42					
	~~Civilized Tribes of March 31, 1905~~		No2 on Choctaw Roll as Franklin Shelton					
	8 ~~No appeal to C.C.C.C.~~							
	9 "Buckholts Crowd"							

Nos 1,2,3&5 restored to roll by Departmental authority of Jan 19,1909 (Ide 5-51)

11
12 Nos 1,2 and 3 Denied by Dawes Com in 96 Case #1407
~~Admitted by U.S. Court, Ardmore, Dec 21st 1897. Court Case No 139~~
13 ~~Judgement[sic] of U.S. Ct admitting Nos 1,2 and 3 vacated and set aside by decree of~~
14 Choc-Chick Cit Court Dec 17 02

15 No. 1 1896 Chickasaw Dist 11739
16 No. 2 1896 " " 11745 as Franklin Shelton
17 ~~No. 3 1896 " " 11745 " Emory "~~

TRIBAL ENROLLMENT OF PARENTS

Name of Father	Year	County	Name of Mother	Year	County
1 G.W. Buckholts		Choctaw residing in Chickasaw District	Julia Buckholts (I.W.)		~~Choctaw residing in Chickasaw District~~
2 John Selton[sic] (I.W.)			No. 1		ENROLLMENT
3 " "			No. 1		OF NOS. ~5~ HEREON ~~APPROVED BY THE SECRETARY~~
4 ~~" "~~			~~No. 1~~		~~OF INTERIOR Nov 27 1905~~
5 Gilham Shelton	Dead		Catherine Shelton		non citizen
6 These parties are also enrolled on					
7 Choctaw card Cr 269-5224, April 18,1900					
8 ~~Enrollment of Nos. 1,2,3 and 5 cancelled by order of~~			all papers in this case have b[sic]		
~~Department March 4 1907~~			forwarded th[sic] Dept 10/7/08		
9			~~See Dept'al telegram of 10/7/08~~		
10 Nos 1 2 and 3 DISMISSED Aug 30 1904					
~~Sept 14, 1904 Record forwarded Secty of Interior~~					
11 ~~Nos 1,2&3 GRANTED Sep 30 1905~~					
12					
13 No.4 Enrolled Dec 13/98					
14 No.4 Died in December 1898: proof of death filed Nov 22,1902					
~~No.5 denied by Commission in 1896 Choctaw Case #1407 Admitted~~					
15 ~~by U.S. Court Southern District December 21, 1898 # Case #139~~					
16 No5 transferred from Choctaw Card D#42 October 16, 1905 See					Date of Application for Enrollment.
17 decision of September 30, 1905					Sept. 21/98

RESIDENCE: Chickasaw Nation ~~COUNTY.~~ **Choctaw Nation** **Choctaw Roll** *(Not Including Freedmen)* CARD NO.
POST OFFICE: FIELD NO. 217

Dawes' Roll No.	NAME	Relationship to Person First Named	AGE	SEX	BLOOD	TRIBAL ENROLLMENT Year	County	No.
428	1 Callihan, Joseph M 17	First Named	13	M	1/16		Choctaw residing in Chickasaw District	CCR #2 125
429	2 " Daisy Dean 11	Sister	7	F	1/16		" "	"
430	3 " Dienie Day 11	"	7	"	1/16		" "	"
431	4 " Felix G. 9	Bro	5	M	1/16		" "	"
	5							
	6							
	7							
	8							
	9							
	10							
	11							
	12							
	13							
	14							
	15							
	16							
	17							

ENROLLMENT
OF NOS. 1,2,3 and 4 HEREON
APPROVED BY THE SECRETARY
OF INTERIOR DEC 12 1902

No2 on Choctaw roll as Daisy Callihan
No3 " " " " Dosie "
No4 " " " " Felix "

No1 1896 Chickasaw Dist 3115 as Joe Cushman
No2 1896 " " 3116 " Daisy Calihan
No3 1896 " " 3117 " Dosie "
No4 1896 " " 3118 " Felix "

TRIBAL ENROLLMENT OF PARENTS

Name of Father	Year	County	Name of Mother	Year	County
1 F. G. Callihan		non citizen	America Lee Callihan	Dead	Choctaw residing in Chickasaw District
2 " " "		" "	" " "	"	" "
3 " " "		" "	" " "	"	" "
4 " " "		" "	" " "	"	" "
5					
6					
7					
8					
9					
10					
11					
12					
13					
14 No1 P.O.					
15 Dover Brook, I.T. Apr 6 1907					
16 No1 P.O.					~~Date of Application~~ for Enrollment.
17 Roff Okla 3/12/09					Sept. 21/98

RESIDENCE: Chickasaw Nation ~~COUNTY~~.
POST OFFICE: Lone Grove, Ind. Ter.

Choctaw Nation

Choctaw Roll (*Not Including Freedmen*)

CARD NO.
FIELD NO. **218**

Dawes' Roll No.		NAME	Relationship to Person	AGE	SEX	BLOOD	TRIBAL ENROLLMENT Year	County	No.
[Illegible]	1	Johnson, Frances 54	First Named	50	F	1/4		Choctaw residing in Chickasaw District	CCR #2 309
[Illegible]	2	Lynn, Laura 24	Dau	20	"	1/8		" "	"
[Illegible]	3	Lynn, Tamsberry 2	Grand Son	7wks	M	1/16			
[Illegible]	4	" Maggie Tammie 1	Grand Dau	5wks	F	1/16			
[Illegible]	5	" George E.	husband of N°2	27	M	I.W.			
	6								
	7								
	8								
	9								
	10								
	11								
	12								
	13								
	14								
	15								
	16								
	17								

ENROLLMENT
OF NOS. 1,2,3 and 4 HEREON
APPROVED BY THE SECRETARY
OF INTERIOR DEC 12 1902

No1 1896 Chickasaw Dist 7380 as Francis Johnson
No2 1896 " " 7382

ENROLLMENT
OF NOS. ~~~ 5 ~~~ HEREON
APPROVED BY THE SECRETARY
OF INTERIOR JUN 13 1903

No2 is the wife of George E Lynn on Choctaw Card #D422
Marriage license and certificate filed with papers in Choctaw Case #D422
~~See also letter of George E Lynn filed Feby 23, 1901.~~

TRIBAL ENROLLMENT OF PARENTS

	Name of Father	Year	County	Name of Mother	Year	County
1	John Jones	Dead	non citizen	Sophie Jones	Dead	Scullyville
2	Wiley Johnson	"	" "	No1		
3	G. E. Lynn			No2		
4	G E. Lynn		Choctaw Card #D.422	No2		
5	Thos. H. Lynn		non citz	Malinda C Lynn		non-citz
6						
7						
8						
9						
10						
11						
12						
13						
14						
15						
16						
17						

~~No3 Enrolled February 23, 1901~~
No4 Born May 10th 1902 Enrolled June 19th 1902
N°5 Transferred from Choctaw card #D422. See decision of May 5, 1903.

Date of Application for Enrollment. Sept. 21/98

Choctaw By Blood Enrollment Cards 1898-1914

RESIDENCE: Chickasaw Nation ~~COUNTY.~~ **Choctaw Nation** **Choctaw Roll** *(Not Including Freedmen)* CARD NO.
POST OFFICE: Lone Grove, Ind. Ter. FIELD NO. **219**

Dawes' Roll No.		NAME	Relationship to Person First Named	AGE	SEX	BLOOD	TRIBAL ENROLLMENT Year	County	No.
436	1	Leslie, W. J. 34	First Named	30	M	1/8		Choctaw residing in Chickasaw District	CCR #2 344
I.W. 10	2	" Mary 34	Wife	30	F	I.W.		" "	C.I. Roll 66
437	3	" Clifford 13	Dau	9	"	1/16		" "	CCR #2 344
438	4	" Robert E 9	Son	5	M	1/16		" "	"
~~439~~	5	DIED PRIOR TO SEPTEMBER 25, 1902 ~~" Dewey 4~~	~~"~~	~~3mos~~	~~"~~	~~1/16~~			
440	6	" Beatrice 2	Dau	3mos	F	1/16			
	7								
	8								
	9								
	10								
	11								
	12								
	13								
	14								
	15								
	16								
	17								

ENROLLMENT OF NOS. 1,3,4,5 and 6 HEREON APPROVED BY THE SECRETARY OF INTERIOR DEC 12 1902

ENROLLMENT OF NOS. ~~ 2 ~~ HEREON APPROVED BY THE SECRETARY OF INTERIOR JUN 13 1903

~~Married in Gainsville Texas under U.S. Law~~
" under Chickasaw law Sept. 15, 1898
No4 on Choctaw roll as Rosa Lee Leslie
No5 affidavit of physician to be supplied -
~~Received Sept 26/98~~

No.5 died June 17, 1899: Enrollment cancelled by Department Sept 16, 1904

TRIBAL ENROLLMENT OF PARENTS

	Name of Father	Year	County	Name of Mother	Year	County
1	Joe Leslie	Dead	non citizen	Frances Johnson		Choctaw residing in Chickasaw District
2	C. Smith	"	" "	Martha Smith		non citizen
3	No1			No2		
4	No1			No2		
5	~~No1~~			~~No2~~		
6	No1			No2		
7						
8						
9						
10						
11						
12						
13						
14						
15						
16						
17	P.O. Madill, I.T.					

No1 1896 Chickasaw Dist 8404
~~No3 1896 " " 8405 as Clofford Lushie~~
~~No4 1896 " " 8406 " Rosa Lee~~
} Identified also from 1893 pay roll. #3 [illegible] 36, Nos 344-345-346

No6 Enrolled December 3d 1900
~~N°5 Died June 17, 1899; Proof of death filed Nov. 8, 1902.~~
~~For child of Nos 1&2 see N.B. (Mar 3-1905) Card #80~~

Date of Application for Enrollment. Sept. 21/98

RESIDENCE: Chickasaw Nation ~~COUNTY~~. **Choctaw Nation** **Choctaw Roll** (Not Including Freedmen) CARD NO. FIELD NO. 220

POST OFFICE: Lone Grove, Ind. Ter.

Dawes' Roll No.		NAME	Relationship to Person First Named	AGE	SEX	BLOOD	TRIBAL ENROLLMENT Year	County	No.
441	1	Cummings, Minnie Lee 26	First Named	22	F	1/8		Choctaw residing in Chickasaw District	CCR #2 124
442	2	" Vera 9	Dau	5	"	1/16		" "	CCR #2 124
443	3	" Lodeva 6	"	1 1/2	"	1/16			
444	4	" Dawes Bixby 3	Son	6wks	M	1/16			
445	5	" Erner Van 1	Dau	1mo	F	1/16			
I.W. 625	6	" C. S. 33	Hus	33	M	I W			
	7	ENROLLMENT	No1 1896 Chickasaw Dist 3066 as Minnie Cummins						
	8	OF NOS. 1 2 3 4 and 5 HEREON APPROVED BY THE SECRETARY	No2 1896 " " 3067 " Vinie "						
	9	OF INTERIOR DEC 12 1902							
	10	ENROLLMENT							
	11	OF NOS. 6 HEREON APPROVED BY THE SECRETARY							
	12	OF INTERIOR MAR 26 1904							
	13								
	14	No1 wife of C.S. Cummings, Choctaw card No D.43							
	15	No3 affidavit of attending physician to be supplied - Received Sept 23/98							
	16	No4 Enrolled Aug. 4/99							
	17								

TRIBAL ENROLLMENT OF PARENTS

	Name of Father	Year	County	Name of Mother	Year	County
1	Wyley Johnson	Dead	non citizen	Frances Johnson		Choctaw residing in Chickasaw District
2	C.S. Cummings (I.W.)		Choctaw residing in Chickasaw District	No1		
3	" " " "		" "	No1		
4	" " " "		" "	No1		
5	" " " "		" "	No1		
6	Wm Cummings		Non citizen	Nancy Cummings		non citizen
7						
8						
9	No5 born Oct 1, 1901; Enrolled Oct 31, 1901					
10	№1 identified also from 1893 pay roll №3 page 14, №140, as Minnie Cummings					
11						
12						
13						
14	No6 transferred from Choctaw card D43. See decision of January 2, 1904 Jan 19,1904					
15	For child of No1 see NB (Mar 3-05) #584					
16					Date of Application for Enrollment.	#1 to 3
17	P.O. Madill I.T. 3/25/05					Sept. 21/98

RESIDENCE: Chickasaw Nation ~~COUNTY.~~
POST OFFICE: Davis, Ind. Ter.

Choctaw Nation

Choctaw Roll *(Not Including Freedmen)*

CARD NO.
FIELD NO. 221

Dawes' Roll No.	NAME	Relationship to Person First Named	AGE	SEX	BLOOD	TRIBAL ENROLLMENT Year	County	No.
15281	1 Smith, Nellie 18	First Named	14	F	1/16		Choctaw residing in Chickasaw District	CPR #3 5
15282	2 Smith, Martha Virginia	Dau	3wks	F	1/32			

Buckholts Crowd

ENROLLMENT OF NOS. ~ 1 ~ 2 ~ HEREON APPROVED BY THE SECRETARY OF INTERIOR MAY 9 1904

No1 Denied in 96 Case #1407
~~Admitted by U.S. Court Southern District Case No 139~~
~~Affidavit that no appeal has been taken to U.S. Supreme~~
~~Court to be supplied~~

On Choctaw Pay Roll No3 - Page 5, No 50
~~No1 also on 1896 Choctaw Census roll Page #49; No 2005~~
~~as Martha Buckholtz~~
Nº1 is a duplicate of Nº2 on Choctaw card #5225 Entry on 5225 Cancelled
Nº1 is now the wife of C. B. Smith a non citizen Evidence of
~~marriage requested Aug 12, 1902. Received and filed Aug. 21, 1902~~
~~Nº2 Born July 20, 1902; enrolled Aug. 12, 1902.~~
Judgment of U S Ct admitted No1 vacated and set aside by Decree of Choctaw-Chickasaw Citizenship Court Dec 17, 1902
~~Now in C.C.C.C #119T.~~
~~No1 admitted by C.C.C.C. March 21st 04 No2 dismissed for want of jurisdiction~~

TRIBAL ENROLLMENT OF PARENTS

Name of Father	Year	County	Name of Mother	Year	County
1 G.W. Buckholts		Choctaw residing in Chickasaw District	Julia Buckholts		noncitizen
2 C.B. Smith		non-citizen	Nº1		

#1
Date of Application for Enrollment.
Sept. 21/98

RESIDENCE: Chickasaw Nation ~~COUNTY.~~
POST OFFICE: Overbrook, Ind. Ter.

Choctaw Nation — Choctaw Roll (Not Including Freedmen) — CARD NO. FIELD NO. 222

Dawes' Roll No.		NAME		Relationship to Person First Named	AGE	SEX	BLOOD	TRIBAL ENROLLMENT Year	County	No.
446	1	Taylor, Carrol	34	First Named	30	M	1/4		Choctaw residing in Chickasaw District	CCR #2 452
I.W. 1397	2	" Amanda H.	20	Wife	16	F	I.W.			
447	3	" William A.	4	Son	11mo	M	1/8			
448	4	" Pearlie May	2	Dau	2mo	F	1/8			
	5	ENROLLMENT								
	6	OF NOS. 1,3 and 4 HEREON APPROVED BY THE SECRETARY					No1	1896	Chickasaw Dist	12551
	7	OF INTERIOR DEC 12 1902								
	8									
	9	No2 REFUSED See decision of July 20'03								
	10	Record as to No2 forwarded Sec'y of ~~Interior July 20, 1902.~~								
	11	Protest of attorneys for Nations for-								
	12	warded Dept. Feby 6, 1904								
	13			Oct 6/99 There appears to be no evidence as to						
	14			marriage of parents of No1 whose mother was white.						
	15			No3 Enrolled Oct 6/99 ~~No4 Enrolled November 12th 1900~~						
	16									
	17									

TRIBAL ENROLLMENT OF PARENTS

	Name of Father	Year	County	Name of Mother	Year	County
1	Jackson Taylor	Dead	Choctaw Roll	Rebecca Taylor (I.W.)	Dead	Choctaw Roll
2	Oscar Maguire		non citizen	Serilda Maguire		non citizen
3	No1			No2		
4	No1			No2		
5						
6			For child of Nos 1&2 see NB (Apr 26-06) Card #500			
7			Protest of attorneys for Choctaw and Chickasaw Nations as to No2			
8			of July 23d, 1904 forwarded Secty of Interior Feby 6, 1904.			
9						ENROLLMENT
10						~~OF NOS. 2 HEREON~~ APPROVED BY THE SECRETARY
11						OF INTERIOR JUN 12 1905
12			For child of No1 see NB (Mar 3rd 1905) Card #81			
13						
14						
15					Date of Application for Enrollment.	#1&2
16						~~Sept. 21/98~~
17	P.O. Brick I.T. 3/23/05					

RESIDENCE: Chickasaw Nation ~~COUNTY~~.
POST OFFICE: Raysville, Ind. Ter

Choctaw Nation

Choctaw Roll *(Not Including Freedmen)*

CARD NO.
FIELD NO. 223

Dawes' Roll No.	NAME		Relationship to Person First Named	AGE	SEX	BLOOD	TRIBAL ENROLLMENT Year	County	No.
449	1 Jones, C. J.	34		30	M	1/8		Choctaw residing in Chickasaw District	CCR #2 309
I.W. 988	2 " Ella	21	Wife	17	F	I.W.			
450	3 " Gracie V.	5	Dau	1/2	"	1/16			
~~451~~	Died prior to September 25, 1902 ~~4 " Vela May~~	~~1~~	~~Dau~~	~~4mo~~	~~F~~	~~1/16~~			
	5								
	6								
	7								
	8								
	9								
	10								
	11								
	12								
	13								
	14								
	15								
	16								
	17								

ENROLLMENT OF NOS. 1,3 and 4 HEREON APPROVED BY THE SECRETARY OF INTERIOR Dec 12 1902

No.2 Refused. See decision of May 2 '03

No1 1896 Chickasaw Dist 7371 as C.J. James
No4 Enrolled Sept 5, 1901
~~No4 died March 28, 1902; Proof of death filed Nov. 10, 1902~~

ENROLLMENT OF NOS. ~~ 2 ~~ HEREON APPROVED BY THE SECRETARY OF INTERIOR Oct 21, 1904

Record and decision refusing No.2 forwarded Dept. May 2, 1903.

TRIBAL ENROLLMENT OF PARENTS

Name of Father	Year	County	Name of Mother	Year	County
1 Alex Jones	Dead	Choctaw Roll	Skate Jones	Dead	Non citizen
2 Ed Reeves	"	non citizen	Martha Reeves		" "
3 No1			No2		
~~4 No1~~			~~No2~~		
5					
6					
7					
8					
9					
10					
11					
12					
13					
14					
15					#1 to 3 inc
16					**Date of Application for Enrollment.**
17 P.O. Tyler, Ind. Ter.					Sept. 21/98

For child of nos[sic] 1&2 See N.B. (Apr 26-06) Card #616

No4 died March 28-1902: Enrollment cancelled by Department July 8-1904
Aug 29, 1904: Decision of Commission refusing No.2 reversed by Secretary of Interior and enrollment directed (I.T.D. 31882-1904, 6818-1904, 7578-1903)

RESIDENCE: Chickasaw Nation ~~COUNTY.~~
POST OFFICE: Ardmore, Ind. Ter.

Choctaw Nation

Choctaw Roll *(Not Including Freedmen)*

CARD NO.
FIELD NO. **224**

Dawes' Roll No.	NAME	Relationship to Person First Named	AGE	SEX	BLOOD	TRIBAL ENROLLMENT Year	County	No.
15361	1 Lindsey, Nina 35	First Named	31	F	1/16		Dawes Com Case No	25
15362	2 " Quintella 19	dau	15	"	1/32		" " " "	"
15363	3 " Benj B. 17	son	13	M	1/32		" " " "	"
15364	4 " Mattie M 15	dau	11	F	1/32		" " " "	"
~~dead~~	5 ~~" Myrtle I~~	~~"~~	~~9~~	~~"~~	~~1/32~~		~~" " " "~~	~~"~~
15365	6 " Ethel 10	"	6	"	1/32		" " " "	"
15366	7 " Guy 8	son	4	M	1/32		" " " "	"
15367	8 " Eva 4	dau	2mo	F	1/32			
15368	9 " Zoma [or Zorna] 2	dau	3wks	F	1/32			

ENROLLMENT OF NOS. 1-2-3-4-6-7-8-9 HEREON APPROVED BY THE SECRETARY OF INTERIOR May 9 1904

Take no further action relative to enrollment of Nos 1 to 9 inclusive, Protest of Attys for Choctaw and Chickasaw Nations - Jan 23, 1904

Protest overruled: See Departmental Letter of March 31, 1904.

No1 1896 Chickasaw Dist 8394
No2 1896 " " 8395
~~No3 1896 " " 8396~~
~~No4 1896 " " 8397~~
No5 1896 " " 8398
No6 1896 " " 8399 as Estella Lindsey
~~No7 1896 " " 8400~~

~~For child of No.1 see N.B. (Apr 26'06) card #643~~
" " " " 2 " " (Mar 3'05) " #363
" " " " 1 " " " " " #548

TRIBAL ENROLLMENT OF PARENTS

Name of Father	Year	County	Name of Mother	Year	County
1 John Miller	Dead	Choctaw roll	Elizabeth Miller		non citizen
2 S.T. Lindsey		non citizen	No1		
3 " " "		" "	No1		
4 " " "		" "	No1		
~~5 " " "~~		~~" "~~	~~No1~~		
6 " " "		" "	No1		
7 " " "		" "	No1		
8 " " "		" "	No1		
9 " " "		" "	No1		

10 ~~All admitted by Dawes Com (except Eva) no appeal taken as to Nina and the children~~
11 Appeal taken as to husband S.T. Lindsay case No 25
No8 affidavit of attending physician to be supplied: Received Sept. 22/98
12 ~~No5 Died Sept 28, 1898, proof of death filed Nov. 1, 1902~~
13 Husband, Selden T Lindsey, on Choctaw card #5796

~~No5 hereon dismissed under order of~~ the Commission to the Five Civilized Tribes of March 31, 1905

#1 to 8 inc
~~Date of Application~~ for Enrollment.

P.O. Durwood I.T. 5/13/03

No9 Enrolled December 3rd 1900

Sept. 21/98

RESIDENCE: Chickasaw Nation ~~COUNTY.~~ **Choctaw Nation** **Choctaw Roll** *(Not Including Freedmen)* CARD NO.
POST OFFICE: Davis Ind. Ter. FIELD NO. **225**

Dawes' Roll No.	NAME		Relationship to Person First Named	AGE	SEX	BLOOD	TRIBAL ENROLLMENT Year	County	No.
I.W. 989	1 Russell, Perry	54	First Named	50	M	I.W.		Choctaw residing in Chickasaw District	C.I. Roll 96
452	2 " Margaret W	45	wife	41	F	1/16		" "	CCR #2 416
453	3 " John	24	son	20	M	1/32		" "	"
454	4 " Clabon	21	"	17	"	1/32		" "	"
455	5 " William	19	"	15	"	1/32		" "	"
456	6 " Ellen	12	dau	8	F	1/32		" "	"
457	7 " Roda	10	"	6	"	1/32		" "	"
458	8 " Ruthie	7	"	3	"	1/32		" "	"
459	9 " Moses C	5	son	10mo	M	1/32		" "	"
460	10 " Perry Wright	2	son	3m	M	No1 1/32			
461	11 " Matt	1	grandson	3mo	M	No2 1/65			

12 No3 is now the husband of Calistia Russell non citizen. Evidence of marriage filed May 17, 1902 transferred to 7- N.B. 73
No4 on Choctaw Roll as Clabe Russell
No5 " " " " Will "
~~No11 Born Feby 25, 1902, enrolled May 17, 1902~~
No10 Enrolled February 5, 1901
Evidence of birth of No9 received and filed Feby 28, 1902
For child of No3 see N.B. (Mar 3rd 1905) card 73

TRIBAL ENROLLMENT OF PARENTS

	Name of Father	Year	County	Name of Mother	Year	County
1	John Russell	dead	non citizen	Malinda Russell	Dead	non citizen
2	Ashley Wright	"	" "	Arabella Wright	"	Choctaw roll
3	No1			No2		
4	No1			No2		
5	No1			No2		
6	No1			No2		
7	No1			No2		
8	No1			No2		
9	No1			No2		
10	No1			No2		
11	No3			Calistia Russell		non citizen

ENROLLMENT OF NOS. 2,3,4,5,6,7,8,9,10 and 11 HEREON APPROVED BY THE SECRETARY OF INTERIOR Dec. 12, 1902

ENROLLMENT OF NOS. ~~~ 1 ~~~ HEREON APPROVED BY THE SECRETARY OF INTERIOR Oct. 21, 1904

No1 1896 Chickasaw Dist 15003
No2 1896 " " 11052
~~No3 1896 " " 11053~~
No4 1896 " " 11054 as Clabe Russell
No5 1896 " " 11055
No6 1896 " " 11056
~~No7 1896 " " 11057~~
No8 1896 " " 11058

Date of Application for Enrollment.
Sept. 21/98

RESIDENCE: Chickasaw Nation ~~COUNTY.~~ **Choctaw Nation** **Choctaw Roll** (Not Including Freedmen) CARD NO.
POST OFFICE: Davis Ind. Ter. FIELD NO. 226

Dawes' Roll No.	NAME	Relationship to Person First Named	AGE	SEX	BLOOD	TRIBAL ENROLLMENT Year	County	No.
14258	1 Ferguson, Margaret Jane 7	First Named	3	F	1/32		Choctaw residing in Chickasaw District	CCR #0 42
I.W. 1073	2 Ferguson, M. C. 43	Father	43	M	I.W.	1896	Chick Dist.	14551

ENROLLMENT OF NOS. ~~1~~ HEREON APPROVED BY THE SECRETARY OF INTERIOR Apr 11 1903

ENROLLMENT OF NOS. ~~2~~ HEREON APPROVED BY THE SECRETARY OF INTERIOR Nov. 16 1904

Admitted by Dawes Com Case No 459 and no appeal taken
On Choctaw Census Record No. O. Page 42, No 528
Father W.C. Ferguson on Choctaw Card No D 44
~~No.1 also on 1896 Choctaw census roll as Margaret J. Frazier: page 111;~~
No 4582 Chick Dist
No.2 admitted by Com in 1896, case #459; no appeal

TRIBAL ENROLLMENT OF PARENTS

Name of Father	Year	County	Name of Mother	Year	County
1 M.C. Ferguson (IW)		Choctaw residing in ~~Chickasaw District~~	Fannie Ferguson		Choctaw residing in ~~Chickasaw District~~
2 Robert C. Furgeson	Dead	non-citizen	Minerva J. Furgeson		non-citizen

~~No2 transferred from Choctaw Card #D-44 Oct. 31, 1904; See decision of Oct 15, 1904~~
For children of No.2 see N.B. (Apr 26 '06) #1106

See Petition No W 73

Date of Application for Enrollment. Sept. 21/98

RESIDENCE: Chickasaw Nation ~~COUNTY.~~ **Choctaw Nation** Choctaw Roll (Not Including Freedmen) CARD NO.
POST OFFICE: Ryan, Ind. Ter. FIELD NO. 227

Dawes' Roll No.	NAME		Relationship to Person First Named	AGE	SEX	BLOOD	TRIBAL ENROLLMENT Year	County	No.
I.W. 11	1 Benton, Rufus F	41		37	M	I.W.		Choctaw residing in Chickasaw District	C.I. Roll 11
462	2 " Julia	36	Wife	32	F	1/8		" "	CCR #2 82
463	3 " Elmer	9	Son	5	M	1/16		" "	"
464	4 " Osa	4	"	2mos	"	1/16			
465	5 " Effie	16	Step Dau	12	F	1/16		Choctaw residing in Chickasaw District	CCR #2 216
466	6 Gray, Minnie	15	" "	11	"	1/16		" "	"
467	7 " Willie	13	" "	9	"	1/16		" "	"
468	8 Benton, Manda	3	Dau	2mo	"	1/16			
469	9 " Ola May	1	Dau of No.5	3wks	F	1/32			

10 No2 on Choctaw Roll as Julia Gray Benton

ENROLLMENT OF NOS. 2 3 4 5 6 7 8and9 HEREON APPROVED BY THE SECRETARY OF INTERIOR Dec 12 1902

No2 admitted as an intermarried citizen and nos[sic] 3 as a citizen by blood in 1896 Choctaw Case #623; no appeal.
For child of nos1&2 see NB (Mar 3'05) #660

ENROLLMENT OF NOS. ~~ 1 ~~ HEREON APPROVED BY THE SECRETARY OF INTERIOR Jun 13 1903

17 Child of No6 on NB (Apr 26-06) Card #300

TRIBAL ENROLLMENT OF PARENTS

Name of Father	Year	County	Name of Mother	Year	County
1 Wm Benton		non citizen	Elizabeth Benton	Dead	non citizen
2 Wyley Johnson	Dead	" "	Amanda Holloway (Johnson)	"	Choctaw Roll
3 No1			No2		
4 No1			No2		
5 W.C. Gray (IW)	dead	Choctaw Roll	No2		
6 " " "	"	" "	No2		
7 " " "	"	" "	No2		
8 No1			No2		
9 Gilbert M Benton		non citizen	№5		

10 No1 1896 Chickasaw Dist 14362 as R.F. Benton
11 No2 1896 " " 2052 " Julia Gray Benton
12 No3 1896 " " 2053 " Elma "
~~No5 1896 " " 5058~~
13 No6 1896 " " 5059
14 No7 1896 " " 5060

No5 is now the wife of Gilbert M. Benton non-citizen. Evidence of marriage filed Aug. 26, 1902.

15 No8 Enrolled Nov 1/99

#1 to 8 Date of Application for Enrollment. Sept. 21/98

16 №9 Born Aug. 7, 1902; enrolled Aug. 26, 1902

17 See additional testimony of No.1 taken Oct. 15, 1902.

RESIDENCE: Chickasaw Nation ~~COUNTY.~~
POST OFFICE: Eastman Ind. Ter.

Choctaw Nation

Choctaw Roll (*Not Including Freedmen*) CARD NO. FIELD NO. **228**

Dawes' Roll No.	NAME		Relationship to Person First Named	AGE	SEX	BLOOD	TRIBAL ENROLLMENT Year	County	No.
I.W. 214	1 Carroll, James	42	First Named	38	M	I.W.		Choctaw residing in Chickasaw District	CCR #0 58
470	2 " Ida	36	Wife	32	F	Full		" "	CCR #2 124
471	3 " Whit	11	Son	7	M	1/2		" "	"
472	4 " Oliver	7	"	3	"	1/2		" "	"

ENROLLMENT OF NOS. 2, 3 and 4 HEREON APPROVED BY THE SECRETARY OF INTERIOR DEC 12 1902

ENROLLMENT OF NOS. 1 HEREON APPROVED BY THE SECRETARY OF INTERIOR SEP 12 1903

No1 admitted by Dawes Com. Case No 702 and no appeal taken
Marriage license and certificate with the Dawes Com at Muskogee, I.T.
No2 also called Artemesia
No4 on Choctaw roll as Ily
No1 on Choctaw Census Record No.O, Page 58, No15

TRIBAL ENROLLMENT OF PARENTS

	Name of Father	Year	County	Name of Mother	Year	County
1	Abb Carroll		noncitizen	Fannie Carroll	Dead	noncitizen
2	Tom Hayes	Dead	Choctaw Roll	Rhoda Fulsom Hays	"	Choctaw Roll
3	No1			No2		
4	No1			No2		

No2 1896 Chickasaw Dist 3068
No3 1896 " " 3070 as Whitt Carrol
No4 1896 " " 3071 " Ily "

Date of Application for Enrollment.
Sept. 21/98

RESIDENCE: Chickasaw Nation ~~COUNTY~~. **Choctaw Nation** **Choctaw Roll** (Not Including Freedmen) CARD NO.
POST OFFICE: Hewitt, Ind. Ter. FIELD NO. 229

Dawes' Roll No.	NAME	Relationship to Person First Named	AGE	SEX	BLOOD	TRIBAL ENROLLMENT Year	County	No.
473	1 Jones, Vera 19	First Named	15	F	1/8		Choctaw residing in Chickasaw District	CCR #2 151
474	2 " Oma 3	Dau	3mo	"	1/16			
475	3 " Thelma Vivian 1	Dau	3wks	F	1/16			
I.W. 172	4 " Charles P	husband	21	M	I.W.			
	5				No1	1896	Chickasaw Dist	3650

ENROLLMENT OF NOS. 1 2 and 3 HEREON APPROVED BY THE SECRETARY OF INTERIOR DEC 12 1902

ENROLLMENT OF NOS. 4 ~~~ HEREON APPROVED BY THE SECRETARY OF INTERIOR JUN 13 1903

On Choctaw Roll as Vira Dillard

No2 Enrolled Oct. 6/99
~~№3 Born May 21, 1902; enrolled June 7, 1902.~~
№4 Transferred from Choctaw card #D 350 See decision of May 5, 1903.

For child of Nos 1&4 see NB (Apr 26-06) Card #822
" " " " " " " (Mar 3-05) " #446

TRIBAL ENROLLMENT OF PARENTS

	Name of Father	Year	County	Name of Mother	Year	County
1	Hamilton Dillard	Dead	non citizen	Elizabeth Dillard		Choctaw residing in Chickasaw District
2	Charley Jones		" "	No1		
3	" "		" "	№1		
4	John Jones		non-citz	Mattie Jones		non-citz

Date of Application for Enrollment. Sept. 21/98

RESIDENCE: Chickasaw Nation ~~COUNTY.~~
POST OFFICE: Thackerville, Ind. Ter.

Choctaw Nation

Choctaw Roll *(Not Including Freedmen)*

CARD NO.
FIELD NO. **230**

Dawes' Roll No.	NAME	Relationship to Person	AGE	SEX	BLOOD	TRIBAL ENROLLMENT Year	County	No.
~~476~~	DIED PRIOR TO SEPTEMBER 25, 1902 1 ~~Sparks, Zuleika~~ 53	~~First Named~~	~~49~~	~~F~~	~~1/16~~		~~Choctaw residing in Chickasaw District~~	~~CCR #2 151~~
477	2 Taylor, Zuleika 20	Dau	16	"	1/32		" "	"
478	3 Taylor, Johnie Rowena 1	Grand dau	1mo	F	1/64			
IW 1074	4 " Newcomb B 22	Husband of No. 2	22	M	I.W.			
	5 ENROLLMENT OF NOS. 1, 2 and 3 HEREON APPROVED BY THE SECRETARY OF INTERIOR DEC 12 1902							
	8 ENROLLMENT OF NOS. ~~~~ 4 ~~~~ HEREON APPROVED BY THE SECRETARY OF INTERIOR NOV 16 1904							

No1 1896 Chickasaw Dist 3641 as Zuleka Devenport
No2 1896 " " 3642 " " " Jr.
No2 is the wife of Newcomb B Taylor on Choctaw Card #D.615
~~No.3 Enrolled June 14th 1901~~ ~~Feby 8, 1901~~ [sic]

TRIBAL ENROLLMENT OF PARENTS

Name of Father	Year	County	Name of Mother	Year	County
1 ~~David Wall~~	~~Dead~~	~~Choctaw Roll~~	~~Nancy Burks~~	~~Dead~~	~~non citizen~~
2 John Davenport	"	non citizen	No. 1		
3 Newcomb B. Taylor		white-man	No. 2		
4 N.B. Taylor		non-citizen	Susan C. Taylor		non-citizen

No1 Died March 7, 1899; proof of death filed Oct. 13, 1902

No.1 died March 7-1899. Enrollment cancelled.

No.4 transferred from Choctaw card #D-615 Oct 31, 1904: See decision of Oct 15, 1904

For child of Nos 2&4 see NB (March 3 1905) #1411

#1 & 2 inc

~~Date of Application~~ for Enrollment. Sept. 21/98

P.O. Ardmore, I.T. 10/29/02

RESIDENCE: Chickasaw Nation ~~COUNTY.~~
POST OFFICE: Pauls Valley, Ind Ter

Choctaw Nation

Choctaw Roll *(Not Including Freedmen)*

CARD NO.
FIELD NO. **231**

Dawes' Roll No.	NAME	Relationship to Person First Named	AGE	SEX	BLOOD	TRIBAL ENROLLMENT Year	County	No.
I.W. 867	1 Hamm, Thomas I. 33	First Named	29	M	I.W.		Choctaw residing in Chickasaw District	C.I. Roll 47
14505	2 " Ella Camp 25	Wife	21	F	1/16		" "	CCR #2 258
14259	3 Cloud, Bradda 9	Step Dau	5	"	1/32		" "	CCR #2 125
	4 ENROLLMENT							
	5 OF NOS. 3 HEREON APPROVED BY THE SECRETARY							
	6 OF INTERIOR Apr 11 1903							
	7 ENROLLMENT							
	8 OF NOS. 2 HEREON APPROVED BY THE SECRETARY							
	9 OF INTERIOR May 20 1903							
	10 ENROLLMENT							
	11 OF NOS. 1 HEREON APPROVED BY THE SECRETARY							
	12 OF INTERIOR Aug 3 1904							
	13							
	14 See Choctaw Card D #113							
	15							
	16							
	17							

TRIBAL ENROLLMENT OF PARENTS

Name of Father	Year	County	Name of Mother	Year	County
1 Thos. A. Hamm	Dead	non citizen	Mary Hamm		non citizen
2 Brad Camp (I.W.)		Choctaw residing in ~~Chickasaw District~~	Mary Camp		Choctaw residing in Chickasaw District
3 H.D. Cloud		noncitizen	No. 2		

No.1 1896 Chickasaw Dist 14668 as Thomas I Hanner
No.2 1896 " " 6159 " Ella Harson
~~No.3 1896 " " 3095 " Braddie Camp Cloud~~
~~No.3 admitted by Dawes Commission in 1896 as a~~
citizen by blood in Choctaw Case #717; no appeal
No.1 admitted by Dawes Commission in 1896 as an intermarried
citizen: Choctaw Case #1372: No appeal
~~No.2 was until 1894 the wife of H.D. Cloud on~~
Choctaw Card #D 113.

~~Date of Application~~ for Enrollment. Sept. 21/98

RESIDENCE: Chickasaw Nation ~~COUNTY~~.
POST OFFICE: Davis, Ind. Ter.

Choctaw Nation — Choctaw Roll (Not Including Freedmen)

CARD NO.
FIELD NO. 232

Dawes' Roll No.		NAME		Relationship to Person First Named	AGE	SEX	BLOOD	TRIBAL ENROLLMENT Year	County	No.
I.W. 12	1	Moore, William M	26		22	M	I.W.			
479	2	" Alice Camp	22	Wife	18	F	1/16		Choctaw residing in ~~Chickasaw District~~	CCR #2 425
480	3	" Bradford C.	2	Son	1mo	M	1/32			
14506	4	" Will McClain	1	Son	3wks	M	1/32			

ENROLLMENT OF NOS. 2 and 3 HEREON APPROVED BY THE SECRETARY OF INTERIOR Dec 12 1902

No.2 1896 Chickasaw Dist 3100 as Alice Carney

No.3 enrolled November 21st 1900

No4 Born Sept 5, 1902; enrolled Sept 20, 1902

Testimony of №1 as to his status as an intermarried citizen Sept 25, 1902 taken at Pauls Valley, I.T. Oct. 21, 1902

ENROLLMENT OF NOS. ~~ 4 ~~ HEREON APPROVED BY THE SECRETARY OF INTERIOR May 20, 1903

ENROLLMENT ~~OF NOS.~~ ~~ 1 ~~ ~~HEREON~~ APPROVED BY THE SECRETARY OF INTERIOR Jun 13 1903

TRIBAL ENROLLMENT OF PARENTS

	Name of Father	Year	County	Name of Mother	Year	County
1	O.G. Moore		non-citizen	Jane Moore		non citizen
2	Brad Camp (I.W.)		Choctaw residing in ~~Chickasaw District~~	Mary Camp		Choctaw residing in ~~Chickasaw District~~
3	No. 1			No. 2		
4	No. 1			No. 2		

Date of Application for Enrollment. #1 & 2 Sept. 21/98

RESIDENCE: Chickasaw Nation ~~COUNTY.~~
POST OFFICE: Foster, Ind. Ter.

Choctaw Nation

Choctaw Roll (Not Including Freedmen)

CARD NO.
FIELD NO. 233

Dawes' Roll No.	NAME	Relationship to Person First Named	AGE	SEX	BLOOD	TRIBAL ENROLLMENT Year	County	No.
481	1 Gibson, Dixon W. 43	First Named	39	M	Full		Choctaw residing in Chickasaw District	CCR #2 215
482	2 " Dicey 41	wife	37	F	"		" "	CCR #2 216
483	3 " Sammie 17	son	15	M	"		" "	CCR #2 215
484	4 " Lucinda 16	dau	12	F	"		" "	"
485	5 " Amos 14	son	10	M	"		" "	"
486	6 " Charley 10	"	6	"	"		" "	"
487	7 " Annie 7	dau	3	F	"		" "	"
488	8 " Isaac 2	son	9mo	M	"			
	9							
	10							
	11							
	12							
	13							
	14							
	15							
	16							
	17							

ENROLLMENT
OF NOS. 1 2 3 4 5 6 7and 8 HEREON
APPROVED BY THE SECRETARY
OF INTERIOR Dec 12, 1902

TRIBAL ENROLLMENT OF PARENTS

	Name of Father	Year	County	Name of Mother	Year	County
1	Isaac Gibson	Dead	Choctaw Roll	Lucinda Gibson	Dead	Choctaw Roll
2	Brown	"	" "	Jane Brown	"	" "
3	No1			No2		
4	No1			No2		
5	No1			No2		
6	No1			No2		
7	No1			No2		
8	No1			No2		
9						
10	No3 on Choctaw Roll as Sam					
11	No1 1896 Chickasaw Dist 3032					
12	No2 1896 " " 5040 as Dicie Gibson					
	No3 1896 " " 5033 " Sam "					
13	No4 1896 " " 5034					
14	No5 1896 " " 5035					
15	No6 1896 " " 5036 as Charlie Gibson					#1 to 7
	No7 1896 " " 5037					Date of Application for Enrollment.
16	No8 Enrolled May 29, 1901					
17						Sept. 21/98

RESIDENCE: Chickasaw Nation ~~COUNTY.~~ **Choctaw Nation** Choctaw Roll (Not Including Freedmen) CARD NO.
POST OFFICE: Paoli, Ind. Ter. FIELD NO. 234

Dawes' Roll No.	NAME	Relationship to Person First Named	AGE	SEX	BLOOD	TRIBAL ENROLLMENT Year	County	No.
I.W. 1469	1 Sumpter, Jacob D 48	First Named	42	M	I.W.		Choctaw residing in Chickasaw District	C.I. Roll 102
~~Dead~~	2 ~~" Nancy~~	~~Wife~~	~~37~~	~~F~~	~~Full~~		" " No632	CCR FO 49
15645	3 " John 19	Son	15	M	1/2		" " No633	"
15646	4 "Amanda Isabella 14	Dau	10	F	1/2		" " No634	"
15647	5 " Jim Andy 9	Son	7	M	1/2		" " No635	"
15648	6 " Scott Taylor 7	"	4	"	1/2		" " No636	"
15649	7 " Dixon D. 6	"	16mo	"	1/2			

8 No3 Address Private Co K 23 U.S. Infantry Mald any Phil. Id.
9 No2 was sister of No1 on Choc Card
10 No 233 Dec 6/99. No.1 see Dawes Commission record 1896 Case No 1073
11 ~~No2 Dismissed Oct 15 1904~~
12 Additional affidavits relative to birth of
13 No7 and death of No2 filed October 6, 1899
No3 gets mail at Paul's Valley I.T.
14 ~~No4 P.O. Addington I.T. 4/19/07~~
15 ~~No 1,2,3,4,5,6 was denied by Dawes~~
16 Commission in 1896 Choctaw Case
17 #1073; no appeal

Nos 2,3,4 and 5 on 1893 Leased District payment Roll Chick-Dist page 56 No's 526, ~~527, 528, and 529 respectively~~
~~Enrollment of Nos 1,3,4,5,6 and 7 cancelled~~

No1- Granted Jun. 27 1905

Affidavit of attending physician relative to birth ~~of No7 filed Feby 18, 1904 Complete affidavits~~ filed Mch 4/04

Nos 1, 3,4,5,6&7 restored to roll by Departmental authority of January 19, 1909 (File 5-51)

TRIBAL ENROLLMENT OF PARENTS

	Name of Father	Year	County	Name of Mother	Year	County
1	~~E.D. Sumpter~~	~~Dead~~	~~non citizen~~	~~Sumpter~~	~~Dead~~	~~non citizen~~
2	~~Isaac Gibson~~	~~Dead~~	~~Choctaw Roll~~	~~Lucinda Gibson~~	~~"~~	~~Choctaw Roll~~
3	~~No1~~			~~No2~~		
4	No1			No2		
5	~~No1~~			~~No2~~		
6	~~No1~~			~~No2~~		
7	~~No1~~			~~No2~~		

ENROLLMENT OF NOS. 3,4,5,6,7 HEREON APPROVED BY THE SECRETARY OF INTERIOR Dec- 2 1904

ENROLLMENT OF NOS One HEREON APPROVED BY THE SECRETARY OF INTERIOR ~~Aug 22 1905~~

8 ~~No4 on Choctaw Roll as Maude Sumpter~~
~~No5 " " " " James "~~
9 No6 " " " " Scott "
10 No1,2,3,4,5&6 rejected by Dawes Com. Marriage license and certificate on file in office of Dawes Com Muskogee, Ind. Ter.
11 ~~No1 1896 Chickasaw Dist 15080 as Jacob D Sumpter~~
12 No2 1896 " " 11796 " Gipson "
13 No3 1896 Chickasaw Dist 11797
No4 1896 " " 11798 as Maud Sumpter
14 ~~No5 1896 " " 11799 " James "~~
15 No6 1896 " " 11800 " Scott "
16 No2 Died April 1, 1899 proof of death filed Feby 18, 1904
17 P.O. Foster I.T. 11/6/03

~~Date of Application~~ for Enrollment. Sept. 21/98

RESIDENCE: Chickasaw Nation ~~COUNTY.~~ **Choctaw Nation** **Choctaw Roll** (Not Including Freedmen) CARD NO.
POST OFFICE: Healdton, Ind. Ter. FIELD NO. 235

Dawes' Roll No.	NAME	Relationship to Person First Named	AGE	SEX	BLOOD	TRIBAL ENROLLMENT Year	County	No.
489✓	1 Lowery, George L. 43		39	M	1/16		Choctaw residing in Chickasaw District	CCR #2 330
I.W. 215	2 " Rhoda A 32	Wife	35	F	I.W.		" "	C.I. Roll 61
490✓	3 Rexroat, Estelle Belle 20	Dau	16	"	1/32		" "	CCR #2 30
491	4 Gazaway, Cornelia 17	"	13	"	1/32		" "	"
492	5 Lowery, Josephine 15	"	11	"	1/32		" "	"
493	6 " Olive 11	"	7	"	1/32		" "	"
494	7 " Choctaw 9	Son	5	M	1/32		" "	"
495	8 " Coleman 7	"	3	"	1/32		" "	"
496	9 " Renia 4	Dau	3mos	F	1/32		" "	"
497✓	10 Rexroat, Phoebe 1	Grand dau	2mo	F	1/64		" "	"
498	11 Lowery, Goldie Lee 1	Dau	4mo	F	1/64		" "	"
499	12 Gazaway, Marshal Lee 2	Gr Son	3mo	M	1/64		" "	"

For child of No5 see NB (Mar 3-1906) #166 Marriage certificate to be supplied. Received Oct11/98
" " " " 3 " " " " #167
No3 is now the wife of W.R. Rexroat June 25,1900
~~No10 Enrolled June 28, 1901~~
No4 is now the wife of S.C.Gazaway a non-citizen Marriage license & certificate filed this day May 9, 1901.
Full maiden name of No3 was Estella Belle Lowery
See letter of W.T.Rexroat filed July 12, 1901
№12 Born Jany26,1902: enrolled April 22, 1902

TRIBAL ENROLLMENT OF PARENTS

Name of Father	Year	County	Name of Mother	Year	County
1 B.H. Lowery	Dead	non citizen	Lucy Krebbs	Dead	Dan Bois
2 Olliver Pollock	"	" "	E.H. Pollock	"	non citizen
3 No 1			No 2		
4 No 1			No 2		
5 No 1			No 2		
6 No 1			No 2		
7 No 1			No 2		
8 No 1			No 2		
9 No 1			No 2		
10 W.T. Rexroat		non citizen	No 3		
11 No 1			No 2		
12 S.C. Gazaway		non citizen	№ 4		

ENROLLMENT OF NOS. 1,3,4,5,6,7,8,9,10,11 and 12 HEREON APPROVED BY THE SECRETARY OF INTERIOR Dec 12 1902

ENROLLMENT ~~OF NOS. 2 HEREON~~ APPROVED BY THE SECRETARY OF INTERIOR ~~Sept 12 1903~~

No1 1896 Tobucksy 7846
~~No2 1896 " 14755~~
~~No3 1896 Tobucksy 7847 as Estella Lowery~~
No4 1896 " 7848
No5 1896 " 7849
~~No6 1896 " 7852~~
~~No7 1896 " 7850~~
No8 1896 " 7851

No11 Enrolled August 1, 1901
~~No.2 was admitted by Dawes Commission in 1896 as an intermarried citizen Choctaw case 847; no appeal~~

For child of No4 see NB (Apr 26'06) #901
" " " " " " (Mar 3'05) #521

Date of Application for Enrollment. #1 to 9 Sept. 22/98

Choctaw By Blood Enrollment Cards 1898-1914

RESIDENCE: Chickasaw Nation ~~COUNTY.~~
POST OFFICE: Wayne, Ind. Ter.

Choctaw Nation

Choctaw Roll *(Not Including Freedmen)*

CARD NO.
FIELD NO. **236**

Dawes' Roll No.		NAME	Relationship to Person First Named	AGE	SEX	BLOOD	TRIBAL ENROLLMENT Year	County	No.
I.W. 1193	1	McGuire, Emery O 36		32	M	I.W		Blue	C.I. Roll 76
15650	2	" Carrie Whittle 23	Wife	19	F	1/4		"	CCR #2 372
15651	3	" Isie May 5	Dau	7mos	"	1/8		"	"
15652	4	" Emery Willis 3	Son	3mo	M	1/8			
15653	5	" John Lewis 1	Son	2mo	M	1/8			
	6			No1	1896	Blue 14875			
	7			No2	1896	" 13855 as Carrie Whittle			
	8			For child of Nos 1 and 2 see NB (Mar 3, 1905) #472					

Contested by Choctaw Commission, Enrolled on white card sirname MaGuire
Marriage certificate filed and placed on this card Sept 16/98

No4 Enrolled May 24 1900

ENROLLMENT
OF NOS. 1 HEREON
APPROVED BY THE SECRETARY
OF INTERIOR Nov 16 1904

TRIBAL ENROLLMENT OF PARENTS

	Name of Father	Year	County	Name of Mother	Year	County
1	Louis McGuire	Dead	non citizen	Liza E McGuire	Dead	non citizen
2	J.M. Whittle		" "	Sarah Whittle		Blue
3	No 1			No 2		
4	No 1			No 2		
5	No 1			No 2		

ENROLLMENT
OF NOS. 2,3,4 and 5 HEREON
APPROVED BY THE SECRETARY
OF INTERIOR Dec 2 1904

Evidence of birth of No3 received and filed Feby. 11, 1902

No2 denied in 1896 by Dawes Commission
Choctaw Case #941: No appeal. Error

No5 born Nov. 12, 1901: Enrolled Jan. 7, 1902.

#1 to 4
Date of Application for Enrollment.
Sept. 22/98

P.O. Utica I.T. 11/17/02

P.O. Roberta I.T. 3/31/05

RESIDENCE: Chickasaw Nation ~~COUNTY~~. POST OFFICE: Pauls Valley, Ind. Ter.

Choctaw Nation — **Choctaw Roll** *(Not Including Freedmen)* — CARD NO. — FIELD NO. **237**

Dawes' Roll No.		NAME		Relationship to Person First Named	AGE	SEX	BLOOD	TRIBAL ENROLLMENT Year	County	No.
500	1	Whittle, Sarah	49	First Named	45	F	1/2		Blue	~~CCR #2~~ 482
501	2	" Napoleon	25	Son	21	M	1/4		"	"
502	3	" John	21	"	17	"	1/4		"	"
503	4	Carr, Alma	13	Dau	9	F	1/4		"	"
504	5	" Madge L	12	"	8	"	1/4		"	"
505	6	" Susan C	10	"	6	"	1/4		"	"
15040	7	" Arthur	18	Son	14	M	1/4			
	8	ENROLLMENT					No1	1896	Blue	13853
	9	OF NOS. 1 2 3 4 5 and 6 HEREON APPROVED BY THE SECRETARY					No2	1896	"	13854
	10	OF INTERIOR Dec 12 1902					No3	1896	Blue	13856
	11	ENROLLMENT					No4	1896	"	13857
	12	OF NOS. ~~~7~~~ HEREON APPROVED BY THE SECRETARY					No5	1896	"	13858
	13	OF INTERIOR Feb 16 1904					No6	1896	"	13859
	14			For children of No4 see NB (March 3, 1905) #1360						
	15									
	16	Child of No3 on NB (Apr 26-06) Card #297								
	17	" " "4 " " (" " #298								

TRIBAL ENROLLMENT OF PARENTS

	Name of Father	Year	County	Name of Mother	Year	County
1	John Harger	Dead	non citizen	Clara Harger	Dead	Choctaw Roll
2	J. M. Whittle		" "	No. 1		
3	" " "		" "	No. 1		
4	" " "		" "	No. 1		
5	" " "		" "	No. 1		
6	" " "		" "	No. 1		
7	" " "		" "	No. 1		

8 Sarah Whittle and children admitted by act of Choctaw Council, Nov 5/95

9 No4 is now the wife of W.M. Carr, a non-citz July 18, 1902

Taken on colored card Sept 12/98

10 ~~Investigation requested by Choctaw Com and placed on white card Sept 16/98~~

11 No7 Enrolled Sept 21/98 Identification from act of admission Choc Council Nov. 5 1895

12 No. 3 is the husband of Delores Whittle on Choctaw #D306: Notice of divorce Nov 20, 1901

Investigation held, J.M. Whittle stricken off and others placed on this card.

13 ~~No. 4 is now the wife of William M. Carr on Choctaw card #D-766.~~

14 7-5901: July 30, 1902

15 ~~Dec 6/99 - No1 See Dawes Commission~~

16 Record 1896 Case 941

17 P.O. Utica I.T.

Date of Application for Enrollment. Sept. 22/98

RESIDENCE: Chickasaw Nation ~~COUNTY~~. **Choctaw Nation** **Choctaw Roll** *(Not Including Freedmen)* CARD NO.
POST OFFICE: Durwood, Ind. Ter. FIELD NO. 238

Dawes' Roll No.	NAME	Relationship to Person First Named	AGE	SEX	BLOOD	Tribal Enrollment Year	County	No.
15654	1 Mitchell, John Allen 40	Named	36	M	1/8		Choctaw residing in Chickasaw District	CCR #2 358
I.W. 1519	2 " Mattie S. 28	Wife	28	F	I.W.		" "	C I Roll 72
15655	3 " Enna 8	Dau	4	"	1/16		" " No117	CCR #0 27
15656	4 " Allen Yates 7	Son	3	M	1/16		" " No118	"
15657	5 " Willie 6	Dau	2	F	1/16		" " No119	"
	6 ENROLLMENT							
	7 OF NOS. 1,3,4 and 5 HEREON APPROVED BY THE SECRETARY				No1	1896	Chickasaw Dist	8922
	8 OF INTERIOR Dec -2 1904				No2	1896	" "	14846
	9 No 2 Granted Nov 11 1905							
	10 No 2 restored to roll by Departmental authority of January 19 1909 (File 5-51)							
	11 ~~Enrollment of No.2 cancelled by order of Department March 4, 1907~~. Act approved Nov. 1, 1881							
	12							
	13							
	14 No1 with others by name Mitchell and Bonner adopted by Choctaw Council in 1881 or 1882							
	15 ENROLLMENT OF NOS. --- 2 --- HEREON	No3 on Choctaw roll as Ennia						
	16 APPROVED BY THE SECRETARY							
	17 OF INTERIOR Mar 14 1906							

TRIBAL ENROLLMENT OF PARENTS

	Name of Father	Year	County	Name of Mother	Year	County
1	Wm Mitchell	Dead	non citizen	Emily Mitchell	Dead	Choctaw Indian
2	~~Dave Scruggs~~		" "	~~Allie Scruggs~~	"	~~non citizen~~
3	No 1			No 2		
4	No 1			No 2		
5	No 1			No 2		
6						
7	No1 denied by Dawes Commission in 1896: in Choctaw Case Error? Yes.					
8	#1299: no appeal. Note: original application was not made by No.1 but by No.2 on					
9	her own behalf and on behalf of her two children Enna and Allen Yates Mitchell					
	~~Nos 2 3 & 4 denied in '96.~~					
10						
11		No3 Born Sept. 7, 1894, proof of birth filed Oct. 5, 1903				
12		No4 Born Oct. 2, 1895, proof of birth filed Oct. 5, 1903				
		~~No5 Born Oct. 1, 1895, proof of birth filed Oct. 5, 1903~~				
13						
14						
15						
16						Date of Application ~~for Enrollment.~~
17	11/10/02 P.O. Ravia I.T.					Sept. 22/98

RESIDENCE: Chickasaw Nation ~~COUNTY~~.
POST OFFICE: Eli, Ind. Ter.

Choctaw Nation

Choctaw Roll (Not Including Freedmen)

CARD NO.
FIELD NO. 239

Dawes' Roll No.	NAME	Relationship to Person First Named	AGE	SEX	BLOOD	TRIBAL ENROLLMENT Year	County	No.
506	1 Mauldin, Betsie 26	First Named	20	F	1/8		Choctaw residing in Chickasaw District	CCR #2 359
507	2 " Emma E 8	Dau	4	"	1/16		" "	"
508	3 " Minnie M 7	"	3	"	1/16		" "	"
509	4 " Gertie Arizona 1	Dau	3mo	F	1/16			

ENROLLMENT
OF NOS. 1 2 3 and 4 HEREON
APPROVED BY THE SECRETARY
OF INTERIOR DEC 12 1902

No 1 1896 Chickasaw Dist 8930 as Mrs Betsy Manden
No2 1896 " " 8934 " Emna E. "
No3 1896 " " 8935 " Minnie M. "
For child of No.1 see NB (March 3 1905) #803

No1 on Choctaw roll as Mandin
No2&3 " " " Manden
No4 Enrolled Aug 23, 1901

TRIBAL ENROLLMENT OF PARENTS

	Name of Father	Year	County	Name of Mother	Year	County
1	Tom McDaniel	Dead	Choctaw roll	Jackaline Rennie		non citizen
2	Jack Mauldin		non citizen	No1		
3	" "		" "	No1		
4	" "		" "	No1		

#1 to 3

Date of Application for Enrollment. Sept. 22/98

Choctaw By Blood Enrollment Cards 1898-1914

RESIDENCE: Chickasaw Nation ~~COUNTY~~.
POST OFFICE: Wheeler, Ind. Ter.

Choctaw Nation

Choctaw Roll *(Not Including Freedmen)*

CARD NO.
FIELD NO. **240**

Dawes' Roll No.	NAME	Relationship to Person First Named	AGE	SEX	BLOOD	TRIBAL ENROLLMENT Year	County	No.
510	1 Willis, Edward 22	First Named	18	M	1/4		Choctaw residing in Chickasaw District	CCR #2 489
	2							
	3					1896	Chickasaw Dist	14163
	4							
	5							
	6							
	7							
	8							
	9				No			
	10							
	11							
	12							
	13							
	14							
	15							
	16							
	17							

ENROLLMENT
OF NOS. 1 HEREON
APPROVED BY THE SECRETARY
OF INTERIOR DEC 12 1902

TRIBAL ENROLLMENT OF PARENTS

Name of Father	Year	County	Name of Mother	Year	County
1 Abner Willis		Blue	Lou May Willis		noncitizen
2					
3					
4					
5					
6					
7					
8					
9					
10					
11					
12					
13					
14					
15					Date of Application for Enrollment.
16					Sept. 22/98
17					

RESIDENCE: Chickasaw Nation ~~COUNTY.~~
POST OFFICE: Ardmore, Ind. Ter.

Choctaw Nation

Choctaw Roll (Not Including Freedmen)

CARD NO.
FIELD NO. 241

Dawes' Roll No.	NAME	Relationship to Person First Named	AGE	SEX	BLOOD	TRIBAL ENROLLMENT Year	County	No.
15188	1 Buckholts, George W.[51]	First Named	49	M	1/8		Choctaw residing in Chickasaw District	CCR #2 81
I.W. 868	2 " Martha (23)	Wife	25	F	I.W.		" "	
15189	3 " Lillie May 5	Dau	10mo	"	1/16		" "	
DEAD	4 ~~" John William~~	~~Son~~	~~6mo~~	~~M~~	~~1/16~~			
15190	5 " Willie Ann 1	Dau	6wks	F	1/16			
[Illegible] of Atty Sent of Feb 18 04 and letter of Secy of Interior of Feb 24'04 in case of James M Buckholts No 7-1738	6				No1	1896	Chickasaw Dist	2003
	7							
	8 "Buckholts Crowd"							
	9 For child of Nos 1&2 see NB (Apr 26-06) Card #474							
	10 #1 not admitted by Supreme Court in Oct							
	11 1842, when his father Wm Buckholts							
	12 R.T. Jones & John Null alone were ~~admitted~~							
	13	No3 Affidavit of attending physician on file.						
	14							
	15							
	16							
	17							

~~No. 4 HEREON DISMISSED UNDER~~ ORDER OF THE COMMISSION TO THE FIVE CIVILIZED TRIBES OF MARCH 31, 1905.

ENROLLMENT ~~OF NOS. 1-3-5 HEREON~~ APPROVED BY THE SECRETARY OF INTERIOR MAY 9 1904

ENROLLMENT OF NOS. 2 HEREON APPROVED BY THE SECRETARY OF INTERIOR AUG 3 1904

TRIBAL ENROLLMENT OF PARENTS

Name of Father	Year	County	Name of Mother	Year	County
1 Wm Buckholts		Blue	Matilda	Dead	Blue
2 L. M. Casey		non citizen	Betsey Casey		non citizen
3 No1			No2		
4 ~~No1~~			~~No2~~		
5 No1			No2		
6	No2 admitted by Dawes Com Case No 621, and no appeal taken				
7	Marriage papers on file in office of Dawes Com. Muskogee Ind. Ter.				
8 No4 Enrolled May 24 1900					
9 No.5 Born Jany 8, 1902; enrolled Feby 20, 1902					
~~No.4 Died Jan. 20, 1900: Proof of death filed Nov. 3, 1902~~					
10					
11					
12	See testimony of № 2 taken Oct. 30, 1902.				
13					
14	For child of Nos1&2 see NB (Mar 3-1905) Card No 49				
15					
16					
17					Sept. 22/98

Choctaw By Blood Enrollment Cards 1898-1914

RESIDENCE: Chickasaw Nation ~~COUNTY~~.
POST OFFICE: Mansville[sic], Ind. Ter

Choctaw Nation

Choctaw Roll *(Not Including Freedmen)*

CARD NO.
FIELD NO. **242**

Dawes' Roll No.		NAME		Relationship to Person First Named	AGE	SEX	BLOOD	TRIBAL ENROLLMENT		
								Year	County	No.
[IW]216	1	Bogle Henry C.	49	First Named	46	M	I.W.		Choctaw residing in Chickasaw District	CCR #0 30
511	2	" Mary C.	57	Wife	53	F	1/4		" "	CCR #2 81
DEAD	3	~~" David H.~~		~~Son~~	~~20~~	~~M~~	~~1/8~~		" "	"
512	4	" John D.	15	"	11	M	1/8		" "	"

ENROLLMENT OF NOS. 2 and 4 HEREON APPROVED BY THE SECRETARY OF INTERIOR DEC 12 1902

ENROLLMENT OF NOS. 1 HEREON APPROVED BY THE SECRETARY OF INTERIOR SEP 12 1903

No2 1896 Chickasaw Dist 2004 as Mary C Boyle
No3 1896 " " 2007 " David H Bogle
No4 1896 " " 2008 " Jno D. "

No1 on Choctaw Census Record No. O, Page 30, No 30, Intermarried Division

No3 transferred to Choctaw Card 3369 at Durant I.T. 8/14/99

TRIBAL ENROLLMENT OF PARENTS

	Name of Father	Year	County	Name of Mother	Year	County
1	J. Hile Bogle	Dead	non citizen	Elsie Bogle	Dead	non citizen
2	David Lawrence	"	" "	Mary Fisher Lawrence	"	Choctaw roll
3	~~No1~~			~~No2~~		
4	No1			No2		
17	P.O. Cheek, I.T.					

Date of Application for Enrollment Sept. 22/98

Choctaw By Blood Enrollment Cards 1898-1914

RESIDENCE: Chickasaw Nation ~~COUNTY.~~
POST OFFICE: Mansville[sic], Ind. Ter.

Choctaw Nation

Choctaw Roll *(Not Including Freedmen)*

CARD NO.
FIELD NO. 243

Dawes' Roll No.		NAME	Relationship to Person First Named	AGE	SEX	BLOOD	TRIBAL ENROLLMENT Year	County	No.
513	1	Lynn, Elsie L. 21	First Named	17	F	1/8		Choctaw residing in Chickasaw District	CCR #2
514	2	" Lena B. 4	dau	10mo	"	1/16			
~~515~~ DIED PRIOR TO SEPTEMBER 25, 1902	3	~~" Gladice 2~~	~~dau~~	~~2mo~~	~~F~~	~~1/16~~			
516	4	" Mary Cordelia 1	Dau	2mo	F	1/16			
I.W. 173	5	" J. Y.	husband	24	M	I.W.			
	6				No1	1896 Chickasaw Dist 2006 as Elsia Bough			

ENROLLMENT OF NOS. 1 2 3 and 4 HEREON APPROVED BY THE SECRETARY OF INTERIOR DEC 12 1902

ENROLLMENT OF NOS. 5 ~~~~~~ HEREON APPROVED BY THE SECRETARY OF INTERIOR JUN 13 1903

TRIBAL ENROLLMENT OF PARENTS

	Name of Father	Year	County	Name of Mother	Year	County
1	Henry C. Bogle (IW)		Choctaw residing in Chickasaw District	Mary C Bogle		Choctaw residing in Chickasaw District
2	Jno. Y. Lynn		white man	No1		
3	~~" " "~~		~~" "~~	~~No1~~		
4	" " "		" "	No1		
5	J. H. Lynn		non-citizen	Emma Lynn		non-citizen

On Choctaw roll as Elsie Bogle
Wife of J. Y. Lynn, Choctaw Card 16 D.45 Evidence of marriage filed therein
No2 Enrolled Sep 6/99
~~No3 Enrolled November 21st 1900~~
~~№4 Born April 28, 1902; enrolled June 13, 1902~~
№3 Died Nov 3, 1901; Proof of death filed Nov 3, 1902
№5 Transferred from Choctaw card #D.45. See decision of May 5, 1903.
No3 died Nov 3-1901. Enrollment cancelled
For child of No.1 see NB (Mar 3'05) #486

P.O. Oakland IT 3/20/05

Date of Application for Enrollment.
Sept. 22/98

Choctaw By Blood Enrollment Cards 1898-1914

RESIDENCE: Chickasaw Nation ~~COUNTY~~.
POST OFFICE: Raysville, Ind. Ter.

Choctaw Nation — **Choctaw Roll** (Not Including Freedmen) — CARD NO. — FIELD NO. **244**

Dawes' Roll No.	NAME	Relationship to Person First Named	AGE	SEX	BLOOD	TRIBAL ENROLLMENT Year	County	No.
517	1 Stowers, Laura 31	First Named	27	F	3/8		Choctaw residing in Chickasaw District	CCR #2 433
518	2 " Richard Henry 15	Son	11	M	3/16		" "	"
519	3 " Lou 13	dau	9	F	3/16		" "	"
520	4 " Cordelia 11	"	7	"	3/16	1893	" "	#510
521	5 " Melvina 10	"	6	"	3/16		" "	CCR #2 433
522	6 " Mattie 8	"	4	"	3/16		" "	"
523	7 " Amos Henry 5	Son	14mo	M	3/16			
~~524~~	8 ~~" Laura F~~	~~dau~~	~~4mo~~	~~F~~	~~3/16~~			
14507	9 " David Sidney 3	Son	2yrs	M	3/16			
525	10 " John Rally 2	"	1mo	M	3/16			

11 No2 on Choctaw roll as Dick Stowers

12 No7 affidavit of physician to be supplied. Received Sept 26/98

ENROLLMENT OF NOS. 1,2,3,4,5,6,7,8 and 10 HEREON APPROVED BY THE SECRETARY OF INTERIOR DEC 12 1902

13 No8 Enrollment cancelled under Departmental instructions of November 14, 1902 (D.C. 32033-1903)

14 ~~No9 Proof of birth received and filed Sept. 15, 1902~~

15 No4 identified from 1893 pay roll Chic Dist page 54 #510

16 Child of No2 on NB(Ap 26-06) Card #299

17 " " "1 " " (Mar 3'05) " #534

TRIBAL ENROLLMENT OF PARENTS

Name of Father	Year	County	Name of Mother	Year	County
1 Lucas Wilson	Dead	Cherokee citz	Mary C Bogle		Choctaw residing in Chickasaw District
2 Monroe Stowers		non citizen	No1		
3 " "		" "	No1		
4 " "		" "	No1		
5 " "		" "	No1		
6 " "		" "	No1		
7 " "		" "	No1		
~~8 " "~~		~~" "~~	~~No1~~		
9 " "		" "	No1		
10 " "		" "	No1		

11 No1 1896 Chickasaw Dist 11746 as Mrs Laura Stormer

12 No2 1896 " " 11747 " Dick "

No3 1896 " " 11748 " Lou "

13 ~~No5 1896 " " 11749 " Malvina "~~

14 No6 1896 " " 11750 " Mattie "

ENROLLMENT OF NOS. 9 HEREON APPROVED BY THE SECRETARY OF INTERIOR MAY 20 1903

15 No8 Enrolled Oct 6/99

16 No9 Enrolled May 8 1901. See letter on file in case.

17 P.O. Tyler I.T. No10 Enrolled May 8, 1901.

Date of Application for Enrollment. Sept. 22/98

RESIDENCE: Chickasaw Nation ~~COUNTY~~. **Choctaw Nation** **Choctaw Roll** *(Not Including Freedmen)* CARD NO.
POST OFFICE: Elk, Ind Ter. FIELD NO. **245**

Dawes' Roll No.	NAME	Relationship to Person First Named	AGE	SEX	BLOOD	TRIBAL ENROLLMENT Year	County	No.
526	1 McDaniels, Jennette 59	First Named	55	M	1/8		Choctaw residing in Chickasaw District	CCR #2 374
I.W. 217	2 " Mary Jane 53	Wife	48	F	I.W.		" "	C.I. Roll 77
527	3 " Tenny 14	Dau	14	"	1/16		" "	CCR #2 374
528	4 McDaniels James 5	Son	11	M	1/16		" "	"

ENROLLMENT OF NOS. 1, 3 and 4 HEREON APPROVED BY THE SECRETARY OF INTERIOR Dec 12 1902

ENROLLMENT OF NOS. 2 HEREON APPROVED BY THE SECRETARY OF INTERIOR Sep 12, 1903

No2 on Choctaw roll as Dollie
Affidavit of Judge S.E. Lewis as to marriage ~~relationship to be supplied.~~
Affidavit of Mrs. J.L. Roney received Oct 21/98

TRIBAL ENROLLMENT OF PARENTS

Name of Father	Year	County	Name of Mother	Year	County
1 Geo. McDaniels	Dead	non citizen	Betsey McDaniels	Dead	Wade
2 John Weeks	"	" "		"	non citizen
3 No1			No2		
4 No1			No2		

No1 1896 Chickasaw Dist 9483 as Junnett McDaniel
No2 1896 " " 14882 " Dolie "
No3 1896 " " 9493 " Tinnie "
~~No4 1896 " " 9494 " James "~~
~~No3 is now the wife of Charles Dill a non-citizen. Evidence of marriage filed Nov. 3, 1902~~
See affidavit of S.E. Lewis filed July 1, 1903

Date of Application for Enrollment. Sept 22/98

RESIDENCE: Chickasaw Nation ~~COUNTY.~~ **Choctaw Nation** **Choctaw Roll** *(Not Including Freedmen)* CARD NO.
POST OFFICE: Elk Ind Ter FIELD NO. **246**

Dawes' Roll No.	NAME		Relationship to Person First Named	AGE	SEX	BLOOD	TRIBAL ENROLLMENT Year	County	No.
529	1 Shults, Effie	23	First Named	17	F	1/16		Choctaw residing in Chickasaw District	CCR #0 30
530	2 " Jennette	5	Dau	6mo	"	1/32			

ENROLLMENT
OF NOS. 1 and 2 HEREON
APPROVED BY THE SECRETARY
OF INTERIOR DEC 12 1902

No1 on 1893 pay roll #3 page 44 No 425 as Effie McDaniels
No1 on Choctaw Census Record No C, Page 30, No 185
No2 affidavit as to birth of[sic] to be supplied - Received Sept 22/98.

TRIBAL ENROLLMENT OF PARENTS

Name of Father	Year	County	Name of Mother	Year	County
1 Jennette McDaniels		Choctaw residing in Chickasaw District	Mary J McDaniels (IW)		Choctaw residing in Chickasaw District
2 Wade Shults		noncitizen	No1		

Date of Application for Enrollment.
Sept. 22/98

RESIDENCE: Chickasaw Nation ~~COUNTY.~~ **Choctaw Nation** **Choctaw Roll** *(Not Including Freedmen)* CARD NO.
POST OFFICE: Atlee, Ind. Ter. FIELD NO. 247

Dawes' Roll No.	NAME	Relationship to Person First Named	AGE	SEX	BLOOD	TRIBAL ENROLLMENT Year	County	No.
14508	1 Whitner, Lizzie 27	First Named	23	F	1/4		Choctaw residing in Chickasaw District	CPR #3 3
14509	2 " Annie 3	Dau	7mo	"	1/8			
14510	3 " James Henry 1	Son	1mo	M	1/8			
	4							
	5							
	6							
	7							
	8							
	9							
	10							
	11							
	12							
	13							
	14							
	15							
	16							
	17							

ENROLLMENT OF NOS. 1, 2 and 3 HEREON APPROVED BY THE SECRETARY OF INTERIOR May 20 1903

No 1 on Choctaw Pay Roll, No3, Page 3, No 31 as Lizzie Alfred
No2 Enrolled Nov. 1/99

No3 Born April 30, 1902: enrolled June 14, 1902.
For child of No.2 see NB (Mar. 31, 1905) #664

TRIBAL ENROLLMENT OF PARENTS

Name of Father	Year	County	Name of Mother	Year	County
1 Jonathan Stidham	Dead	non citizen	Mary Stidham	Dead	Choctaw Roll
2 A. J. Whitner		" "	No1		
3 " " "		" "	No1		
4					
5					
6					
7					
8					
9					
10					
11					
12					
13					
14					
15					
16				#1	
17 P.O. is now at Orr, I.T.			Date of Application for Enrollment.		Sept. 22/98

RESIDENCE: Chickasaw Nation ~~COUNTY.~~
POST OFFICE: Atlee, Ind. Ter.

Choctaw Nation

Choctaw Roll (*Not Including Freedmen*)

CARD NO.
FIELD NO. 248

Dawes' Roll No.		NAME	Relationship to Person First Named	AGE	SEX	BLOOD	TRIBAL ENROLLMENT Year	County	No.
531	1	Stidham, Zachariah 23	First Named	19	M	1/4	1893	Choctaw residing in Chickasaw District No561	CPR #3 3
532	2	" Marion 21	Bro	17	"	1/4	"	" " No562	"
533	3	Wright, Sarah 19	Sister	15	F	1/4	"	" " No563	"
DEAD	4	~~Stidham, Druscilla~~ DEAD	~~"~~	~~13~~	~~"~~	~~1/4~~	~~"~~	~~" "~~ No564	~~"~~
534	5	" Lillie P 14	"	10	"	1/4	"	" " No565	"
I.W. 1278	6	" Laura 18	Wife	25	F	I.W.			
535	7	" Ada 4	Dau	1/2	F	1/8			
536	8	" Jonathan S 2	Son	6mo	M	1/8			

ENROLLMENT OF NOS. 1,2,3,5,7and 8 HEREON APPROVED BY THE SECRETARY OF INTERIOR Dec 12 1902

No6 refused. See decision of July 31'03

Decision of Commission of July 31, 1903, refusing No.6 reversed and Commission directed by Secty of Interior to enroll her as an intermarried Choctaw (I.T.D.2220-1904) Dec 7 1904

No4 died Sept 20 1901: Evidence of death rec'd Dec 9 1901

No3 now the wife of J.H.Wright non-citizen: Evidence of marriage filed July 15th 1902

~~No2 is found on C.P.R. page 59 as Z. Marion Stidham.~~

For child of No3 see N.B.(Apr 26-06) card #831

~~" " " " 1 " " (Mar 3 '05) " #537~~

" " " No1 " " " " " #1065

No4 hereon dismissed under order of the Commission to the Five Civilized Tribes of March 31, 1905

TRIBAL ENROLLMENT OF PARENTS

	Name of Father	Year	County	Name of Mother	Year	County
1	Jonathan Stidham	Dead	non citizen	Mary Stidham	Dead	Choctaw roll
2	" "	"	" "	" "	"	" "
3	" "	"	" "	" "	"	" "
4	~~" "~~	~~"~~	~~" "~~	~~" "~~	~~"~~	~~" "~~
5	" "	"	" "	" "	"	" "
6	Lou Griscoll		non citizen			
7	No1			~~No2~~ No6		
8	No1			No6		

For child of No.3 see N.B.(March 3, 1905)#1230

ENROLLMENT OF NOS. 6 HEREON APPROVED BY THE SECRETARY OF INTERIOR Mar 14 1905

No1 husband of Laura Stidham white woman

~~No6 and 7 Enrolled Sept 12 1899.~~

~~See if original license is on file with the Commission~~

Put on card with husband, Zack Chandler.

The name of Zack Chandler in above notation should be Zack Stidham see memorandum on file with papers in this case. Record and decision of Commission refusing No.6 forwarded Secty of Interior July 31, 1903

No.8 Enrolled Aug 27, 1902.

#1 to 5

Date of Application for Enrollment.

Sept. 22/98

RESIDENCE: Chickasaw Nation ~~COUNTY~~.
POST OFFICE: Ardmore, Ind. Ter.

Choctaw Nation **Choctaw Roll** *(Not Including Freedmen)*

CARD NO.
FIELD NO. 249

Dawes' Roll No.	NAME	Relationship to Person First Named	AGE	SEX	BLOOD	TRIBAL ENROLLMENT Year	County	No.
537	1 Fulsome, David M^c 22	First Named	18	M	1/2		Choctaw residing in Chickasaw District	CCR #2 187
	2							
	3 ENROLLMENT							
	4 OF NOS. 1 HEREON APPROVED BY THE SECRETARY			1896 Blue 4383 as David Mc Folsum				
	5 OF INTERIOR DEC 12 1902							
	6							
	7							
	8							
	9							
	10							
	11							
	12							
	13							
	14							
	15							
	16							
	17							

TRIBAL ENROLLMENT OF PARENTS

Name of Father	Year	County	Name of Mother	Year	County
1 Dave Fulsome	Dead	Choctaw Roll	Pamelia[sic] A Pierce	Dead	Choctaw Roll
2					
3					
4					
5					
6					
7					
8					
9					
10					
11					
12					
13					
14					
15					
16					
17 Caddo, I.T.			~~Date of Application~~ for Enrollment.		Sept. 22/98

RESIDENCE: Chickasaw Nation ~~COUNTY~~.
POST OFFICE: Ardmore, Ind. Ter.

Choctaw Nation

Choctaw Roll *(Not Including Freedmen)*

CARD NO.
FIELD NO. 250

Dawes' Roll No.		NAME	Relationship to Person First Named	AGE	SEX	BLOOD	TRIBAL ENROLLMENT Year	County	No.
DP 1/28/07	1	~~Owen, Oliver P~~	~~Named~~	~~70~~	~~M~~	~~I.W.~~			
	2								
	3								
	4								
	5								
	6								
	7								
	8								
	9								
	10								
	11								
	12								
	13								
	14								
	15								
	16								
	17								

DISMISSED
FEB 4- 1907

Divorced from Choctaw wife.
Admitted by Dawes Com. Case No 246, no appeal taken
Certified copy of marriage license and certificate on
~~file with Dawes Com. at Muskogee Ind. Ter.~~

TRIBAL ENROLLMENT OF PARENTS

	Name of Father	Year	County	Name of Mother	Year	County
1	~~I.P. Owen~~	~~Dead~~	~~noncitizen~~	~~Elizabeth Owen~~	~~Dead~~	~~non citizen~~
2						
3						
4						
5						
6						
7						
8						
9						
10						
11						
12						
13						
14						
15						
16						Date of Application for Enrollment.
17						Sept. 22/98

RESIDENCE: Chickasaw Nation ~~COUNTY~~.
POST OFFICE: Dougherty, Ind. Ter.

Choctaw Nation

Choctaw Roll (Not Including Freedmen)

CARD NO.
FIELD NO. 251

Dawes' Roll No.		NAME		Relationship to Person First Named	AGE	SEX	BLOOD	TRIBAL ENROLLMENT Year	County	No.
I.W. 218	1	Frost, Severe W.	38		34	M	I.W.		Choctaw residing in Chickasaw District	C.I. Roll 33
538	2	" Belle	29	Wife	25	F	1/8		" "	CCR #2 194
539	3	" Ruth	3	Dau	1mo	"	1/16			

ENROLLMENT OF NOS. 2 and 3 HEREON APPROVED BY THE SECRETARY OF INTERIOR Dec 12 1902

No 1 1896 Chickasaw Dist 14548
No 2 1896 " " 4578 as Belle Forrest.

ENROLLMENT ~~OF NOS. 1 HEREON~~ APPROVED BY THE SECRETARY OF INTERIOR Sep 12 1903

No 2 on Choctaw Roll Belle Forest.
No 3 Enrolled Oct 6/99.

TRIBAL ENROLLMENT OF PARENTS

	Name of Father	Year	County	Name of Mother	Year	County
1	Matthew Frost	Dead	non citizen	Nancy J. Frost	Dead	non citizen
2	D. B. Cotten[sic]	"	" "	Susan Cotten	"	Choctaw Roll
3	No 1			No 2		
17	P.O. Mill Creek I.T.					

Date of Application for Enrollment. Sept. 22/98

RESIDENCE: Chickasaw Nation ~~COUNTY.~~
POST OFFICE: Leon, Ind. Ter.

Choctaw Nation

Choctaw Roll (Not Including Freedmen)

CARD NO.
FIELD NO. 252

Dawes' Roll No.		NAME	Relationship to Person First Named	AGE	SEX	BLOOD	TRIBAL ENROLLMENT Year	County	No.
15554	1	Thompson, Robert E L [3]	First Named	27	M	1/8		Choctaw residing in Chickasaw Dist A	CCR #2 452
IW 1279	2	" Clara May [32]	Wife	48	F	I.W.		" A	C.I. Roll 107
IW 1956	3	Johnson, Lydia M [49]	Mother	45	F	I.W.		A	

ENROLLMENT OF NOS. ~~~ 1 ~~~ HEREON APPROVED BY THE SECRETARY OF INTERIOR Aug 20 1904

ENROLLMENT OF NOS. ~~~ 3 ~~~ HEREON APPROVED BY THE SECRETARY OF INTERIOR Aug 20 1904

ENROLLMENT OF NOS. 2 HEREON APPROVED BY THE SECRETARY OF INTERIOR Mar 14 1905

No1 1896 Chickasaw Dist 12534 as Robt E Thompson
No2 1896 " " 15118 " Clara "
No2 admitted as an intermarried citizen by C.C.C.C. Nov 29 '04
Both admitted by Dawes Com Case No 1052, and judgement[sic] sustained S.D.#107
Marriage certificate on file in office of Dawes Com Muskogee Ind Ter
No1 in penitentiary at Leavenworth, Kas

№3 Judgement[sic] of U.S. Court admitting No3 vacated and set aside by Decree of C.C.C.C. Dec. 17-19/02

See Petition No E14

TRIBAL ENROLLMENT OF PARENTS

	Name of Father	Year	County	Name of Mother	Year	County
1	Thomas Thompson	Dead	Choctaw Roll	Lydia Thompson		non citizen
2	E. Briggemeyer		non citizen	Emma Briggemeyer		" "
3	Starlon Evans	Dead	non citizen	Evans	Dead	" "

Judgement[sic] of U.S. Ct. admitting Nos 1 and 2 vacated and set aside by decree of Choctaw and Chickasaw Citizenship Ct Dec 17 '02
Now in C.C.C.C. Case #104T
~~No.1 admitted as a citizen by blood by C.C.C.C. Case 104T June 23 '04~~
No.3 transferred from 7-5210
No.3 admitted by U.S. Court Ardmore Dec 21, 1897 Court Case #107
No.3 denied in 1896 Case #1052
~~No.3 admitted as a citizen by inter-marriage by C.C.C.C. Case #104T June 12 1904~~

Date of Application for Enrollment. Sept. 22/98

RESIDENCE: Chickasaw Nation ~~COUNTY.~~
POST OFFICE: Simon, Ind. Ter.

Choctaw Nation

Choctaw Roll *(Not Including Freedmen)*

CARD NO.
FIELD NO. 253

Dawes' Roll No.		NAME	Relationship to Person First Named	AGE	SEX	BLOOD	TRIBAL ENROLLMENT Year	County	No.
540	1	Tucker, William 37	First Named	33	M	1/16		Choctaw residing in Chickasaw District	CCR #2 452
I.W. 1280	2	" Janie 31	Wife	27	F	I.W.		" "	
541	3	" Georgia Ethel 9	Dau	5	"	1/32		" "	CCR #2 452
542	4	" Pearl 7	"	3	"	1/32		" "	"
543	5	" Charles Edward 4	Son	8wks	M	1/32			
✓544	6	DIED PRIOR TO SEPTEMBER 25, 1902 ~~" Lula Bell 2~~	~~Dau~~	~~1mo~~	~~F~~	~~1/32~~			
545	7	" Joell Shelton 1	Son	1mo	M	1/32			
	8	ENROLLMENT							
	9	OF NOS. 1,3,4,5,6 and 7 HEREON APPROVED BY THE SECRETARY							
	10	OF INTERIOR Dec 12 1902							
	11	No3 on Choctaw roll as Georgie.							
	12	No.6 died March 22, 1901. Enrollment cancelled by Department July 8, 1904.							
	13	For child of Nos 1&2 see NB(Mar 3'05) #986							
	14	No 5 Enrolled Nov. 26/98.							
	15	No2 admitted by Dawes Com Case No 287 as Janie Tucker and no appeal taken.							
	16	Marriage certificate on file in office of Dawes Com. Muskogee Ind. Ter.							
	17								

TRIBAL ENROLLMENT OF PARENTS

	Name of Father	Year	County	Name of Mother	Year	County
1	Shelton Tucker	Dead	non citizen	Elizabeth Tucker	Dead	Choctaw Roll
2	Joel Hodges		" "	Eliza Hodges	"	non citizen
3	No 1			No 2		
4	No 1			No 2		
5	No 1			No 2		
6	~~No 1~~			~~No 2~~		
7	No 1			No 2		
8	No1 1896 Chickasaw Dist 12566					
9	No3 1896 " " 12567 as Georgia Tucker					
10	No4 1896 " " 12568					
11	No6 Enrolled Oct. 16th 1900.					
12	№7 Born March 1, 1902; enrolled April 15, 1902					
13	~~№6 Died March 22, 1901; proof of death filed Oct 31, 1902~~					
14				ENROLLMENT		
15				OF NOS. 2 HEREON APPROVED BY THE SECRETARY		#1 to 5
16				OF INTERIOR Mar 14 1905		~~Date of Application for Enrollment.~~
17	Lone Grove I.T.					Sept. 23/98

RESIDENCE: Chickasaw Nation ~~COUNTY.~~ **Choctaw Nation** **Choctaw Roll** (*Not Including Freedmen*) CARD NO.
POST OFFICE: Ardmore, Ind. Ter FIELD NO. **254**

Dawes' Roll No.		NAME	Relationship to Person First Named	AGE	SEX	BLOOD	TRIBAL ENROLLMENT Year	County	No.
Void	1	Conner Edna	Named	18	F	1/16		Choctaw residing in Chickasaw District	

Wife of W.R. Watkins Jr, Chickasaw roll Card No 537

Name found on Chickasaw roll, Pickens County, Page 13, transferred to Choctaw roll by Dawes Com

On Chickasaw roll as Etna Watkins

N^os[sic] See Chickasaw Card No. 537
Nº1 is now wife of S.R. Conner-non-citizen, proof marriage filed Oct. 25, 1902

CANCELLED

Transferred to Chickasaw Card No 1658 Jan. 2?, 1903

TRIBAL ENROLLMENT OF PARENTS

	Name of Father	Year	County	Name of Mother	Year	County
1	Albert Shelton	Dead	non-citizen	Ada B. Shelton now Conner		Choctaw residing in Chickasaw District

Date of Application for Enrollment.
Sept. 23/98

RESIDENCE: Chickasaw Nation ~~COUNTY~~. **Choctaw Nation** **Choctaw Roll** (Not Including Freedmen) CARD NO.
POST OFFICE: Berwyn, Ind. Ter. FIELD NO. 255

Dawes' Roll No.	NAME	Relationship to Person First Named	AGE	SEX	BLOOD	TRIBAL ENROLLMENT Year	County	No.
VOID.	1 ~~Morris, W. H.~~	First Named	~~55~~	~~M~~	~~I.W.~~			
VOID.	2 ~~" Elizabeth~~	~~wife~~	~~50~~	~~F~~	~~1/8~~			
VOID.	3 ~~" Joseph Daniel~~	~~son~~	~~24~~	~~M~~	~~1/16~~			
VOID.	4 ~~" Catherine~~	~~dau~~	~~12~~	~~F~~	~~1/16~~			
VOID.	5 ~~" Lilla~~	~~"~~	~~9~~	~~"~~	~~1/16~~			
VOID.	6 ~~" Lena~~	~~"~~	~~5~~	~~"~~	~~1/16~~			

No1 married in 1864 to Choctaw woman. On Chickasaw roll, Pickens County, Page 77
Nos 2-3-4-5 and 6 on Chickasaw roll, Pickens County, Page 20
No2 " " " " " as Lizzie
No3 " " " " " as Joseph
No4 " " " " as Kittie

CANCELLED

Transferred to Chickasaw Card No 1644 Nov. 17, 1902

TRIBAL ENROLLMENT OF PARENTS

	Name of Father	Year	County	Name of Mother	Year	County
1	~~Jonathan Morris~~	~~Dead~~	~~non citizen~~	~~Mary Morris~~	~~Dead~~	~~non citizen~~
2	~~Joseph D Harris~~	~~"~~	~~Chickasaw Roll~~	~~Catherine Nail Harris~~	~~"~~	~~Choctaw Roll~~
3	~~No 1~~			~~No 2~~		
4	~~No 1~~			~~No 2~~		
5	~~No 1~~			~~No 2~~		
6	~~No 1~~			~~No 2~~		
17	Roff, I.T. 11/16/02					Date of Application for Enrollment. Sept. 23/98

RESIDENCE: Chickasaw Nation ~~COUNTY~~. **Choctaw Nation** **Choctaw Roll** (Not Including Freedmen) CARD NO.
POST OFFICE: FIELD NO. 256

Dawes' Roll No.	NAME	Relationship to Person First Named	AGE	SEX	BLOOD	Tribal Enrollment Year	County	No.
546	1 Folsome I. W. 56		50	M	1/2		Choctaw residing in Chickasaw District	CCR #2 194
I.W. 219	2 " Lula Belle 40	wife	37	F	I.W.		" "	C.I. Roll 33
547	3 " Emma Pearl 20	dau	16	"	1/4		" "	CCR #2 194
548	4 " Wirt Telle 7	son	3	M	1/4		" "	"
14511	5 Bonner, Wellington Folsom 1	Gr Son	3wks	M	1/8			

ENROLLMENT OF NOS. ~~1 3 and 4~~ HEREON APPROVED BY THE SECRETARY OF INTERIOR DEC 12 1902

ENROLLMENT OF NOS. 5 HEREON ~~APPROVED BY THE SECRETARY~~ OF INTERIOR MAY 20 1903

ENROLLMENT OF NOS. 2 HEREON APPROVED BY THE SECRETARY OF INTERIOR SEP 12 1903

No1 1896 Chickasaw Dist 4568 as I.W. Fulsom
No2 1896 " " 14550 " Lula B Fulsom
No3 1896 " " 4569 " Pearl E. Fulsom
~~No4 1896 " " 4570 " West Telle~~

TRIBAL ENROLLMENT OF PARENTS

Name of Father	Year	County	Name of Mother	Year	County
1 Israel Folsome	Dead	Choctaw Roll	Louvisa Folsome	Dead	Choctaw Roll
2 W.W. Russell	"	non citizen	Louisa Russell		non citizen
3 No 1			No 2		
4 No 1			No 2		
5 W.T. Bonner		Choctaw Card #207	No 3		

~~Marriage certificate on file in office of Dawes Com. Muskogee I.T. Case No 472.~~
No2 admitted by Dawes Com. Case No 472, and no appeal taken.
No2 on Choctaw roll as Lula B. Folsome
~~No3 " " " " Pearl E. "~~

~~№3 is now the wife of William T. Bonner on Choctaw card #207. Evidence of~~ marriage requested Oct. 13, 1902

№5 Born Sept. 23, 1902, enrolled Oct. 13, 1902.

Date of Application for Enrollment. #1 to 4 Sept. 23/98

RESIDENCE: Chickasaw Nation ~~COUNTY.~~ **Choctaw Nation** **Choctaw Roll** *(Not Including Freedmen)* CARD NO.
POST OFFICE: Ardmore, Ind. Ter. FIELD NO. **257**

Dawes' Roll No.		NAME	Relationship to Person First Named	AGE	SEX	BLOOD	TRIBAL ENROLLMENT Year	County	No.
14585	1	Cotten, David Oscar [34]	First Named	30	M	1/16		Choctaw residing in Chickasaw District	CCR #2 124
I.W. 869	2	" Cora J. [30]	Wife	25	F	I.W.		" "	C.I. Roll 19
14260	3	" Hester [8]	Son	4	M	1/32		" "	CCR #2 124
DEAD	4	~~" White~~	~~"~~	~~2~~	~~"~~	~~1/32~~		~~" "~~	~~"~~
DEAD	5	~~" Otto~~	~~"~~	~~8mos~~	~~"~~	~~1/32~~	name stricken from original judgment by order of U.S. Court		
14586	6	" Fay [1]	Dau	1mo	F	1/32			
14587	7	" Maude [3]	Dau	2mo	F	1/32			

ENROLLMENT OF NOS. 3 HEREON APPROVED BY THE SECRETARY OF INTERIOR Apr 11 1903

ENROLLMENT OF NOS. 1. 6 and 7 HEREON APPROVED BY THE SECRETARY OF INTERIOR May 20 1903

ENROLLMENT OF NOS. 2 HEREON APPROVED BY THE SECRETARY OF INTERIOR Aug 3 1904

No.1 1896 Chickasaw Dist 3075 as Mrs D.O. Cotten
No.2 1896 " " 1440 " Cora "
No.3 1896 " " 3076
~~No.4 1896 " " 3077~~

Dec 8, 1903 Protest of Attys for Nations filed
Jan 4 1904 Decision of Commission as to No2 together with protest, forwarded Department

№6 Born Jany 29, 1902; enrolled Feby 21, 1902

No2 admitted as a citizen by intermarriage of Choctaw Nation Nov. 28 '04 Case 1037

TRIBAL ENROLLMENT OF PARENTS

	Name of Father	Year	County	Name of Mother	Year	County
1	David B. Cotten	Dead	non citizen	Susan L Cotten	Dead	Choctaw Roll
2	B. Ne Smith		" "	Elizabeth J Ne Smith	"	non citizen
3	No 1			No 2		
4	~~No 1~~			~~No 2~~		
5	~~No 1~~			~~No 2~~		
6	No 1			No 2		
7	No 1			No 2		

No1 on Choctaw Roll as D.O. Cotten
No2 " " " " Cora "
No5 affidavit of attending physician to be supplied. Received Sept 23/98
~~No7 born November 24 1899; transferred to this card May 24, 1902~~
All except David Oscar & Otto admitted by Dawes Com Case No 700 and no appeal taken
Maude Cotten born Nov. 24/99, on Card No D-546

June 3, 1904: Decision of Commission enrolling No.2 approved by Secretary of Interior.

For child of nos[sic] 1&2 see NB (Mar 3'05) #731

Date of Application for Enrollment. #1 to 5 inc Sept 23/98

No[s] 1and3 also admitted by C.C.C.C. Case #103T June 30'04 Proof of death of 4&5 requested 8/10/05

RESIDENCE: Chickasaw Nation ~~COUNTY.~~ **Choctaw Nation** Choctaw Roll (*Not Including Freedmen*) CARD NO.
POST OFFICE: Simon, Ind. Ter. FIELD NO. 258

	NAME	Relationship to Person First Named	AGE	SEX	BLOOD	TRIBAL ENROLLMENT Year	County	No.
1	Flint, Delilah J 84	First Named	80	F	1/8		Choctaw residing in Chickasaw District	CCR #2 195
2								
3	ENROLLMENT OF NOS. 1 HEREON APPROVED BY THE SECRETARY OF INTERIOR DEC 12 1902							
4								
5								
6								
7	1896 Chickasaw Dist 4588 as Deliah Flint							
8								
9								
10								
11								
12								
13								
14								
15								
16								
17								

TRIBAL ENROLLMENT OF PARENTS

	Name of Father	Year	County	Name of Mother	Year	County
1	Joel Nail	Dead	Choctaw Roll	Lousanna Nail	Dead	Int. Choctaw
2						
3						
4						
5						
6						
7						
8						
9						
10						
11						
12						
13						
14						
15						
16						**Date of Application for Enrollment.**
17						Sept. 23/98

RESIDENCE: Chickasaw Nation ~~COUNTY~~. **Choctaw Nation** **Choctaw Roll** *(Not Including Freedmen)* CARD NO.
POST OFFICE: Ardmore, Ind. Ter. FIELD NO. 259

Dawes' Roll No.	NAME	Relationship to Person First Named	AGE	SEX	BLOOD	TRIBAL ENROLLMENT Year	County	No.
Void	1 ~~Brown, Charles A~~		~~41~~	~~M~~	~~1/4~~			
Void	2 ~~" Josephine~~	~~wife~~	~~39~~	~~F~~	~~I.W.~~			
Void	3 ~~" Nathaniel~~	~~son~~	~~18~~	~~M~~	~~1/8~~			
Void	4 ~~Lindsey Ethel~~	~~dau~~	~~16~~	~~F~~	~~1/8~~			
Void	5 ~~Elmore Lorena~~	~~"~~	~~14~~	~~"~~	~~1/8~~			
Void	6 ~~Brown Martin E~~	~~son~~	~~10~~	~~M~~	~~1/8~~			
Void	7 ~~" Martha J~~	~~dau~~	~~5~~	~~F~~	~~1/8~~			
Void	8 ~~" Joe E~~	~~son~~	~~5mos~~	~~M~~	~~1/8~~			
Void	9 ~~Elmore Floyd Lee~~	~~G.Son~~	~~1mo~~	~~M~~	~~1/16~~			
Void	10 ~~Lindsey, Gracie~~	~~G.Dau~~	~~4wks~~	~~F~~	~~1/16~~			
Void	11 ~~Brown, Bessie A~~	~~Dau~~	~~8mo~~	~~F~~	~~1/8~~			

All except Josephine on Chickasaw roll Pickens County Page 25 transferred to Choctaw roll
~~No2 " " " " " 78 " " " "~~
No4 on Chickasaw roll as Etta
No5 " " " " Rena
Marriage certificate destroyed. Affidavit of some outside party as to their having lived ~~together and been recognized as man and wife to be supplied. Received Sept 23/98~~
No5 is now the wife of Geo M Elmore a noncitizen Evidence of marriage filed Sept 21, 1901

CANCELLED

Transferred to Chickasaw Card No 1659 Jan 29th '03

TRIBAL ENROLLMENT OF PARENTS

Name of Father	Year	County	Name of Mother	Year	County
1 ~~Joshua Brown~~	~~Dead~~	~~Chickasaw Roll~~	~~Nancy Curtis Brown~~	~~Dead~~	~~Choctaw Roll~~
2 ~~Jim Kemp~~	~~"~~	~~non citizen~~		~~"~~	~~non citizen~~
3 ~~No 1~~			~~No 2~~		
4 ~~No 1~~			~~No 2~~		
5 ~~No 1~~			~~No 2~~		
6 ~~No 1~~			~~No 2~~		
7 ~~No 1~~			~~No 2~~		
8 ~~No 1~~			~~No 2~~		
9 ~~Geo. M. Elmore~~		~~non citizen~~	~~No 5~~		
10 ~~[No information given]~~					
11 ~~[No information given]~~					

12 Father of Nº11 is Nº1. Mother of Nº11 is Nº2
13 Nº11 Born Dec 23, 1901-enrolled July 31, 1902 No.9 Enrolled Sept 21, 1901
14
15 ~~No4 is now the wife of B.H. Lindsey a noncitizen. Evidence of marriage filed Sept 27, 1901~~
16 Parents of No.10: Mother No.4 Father B.H. Lindsey a non-citz
17 No.10 born Dec. 2, 1901 : Enrolled Dec. 27, 1901.

Date of Application for Enrollment. Sept 23/98

RESIDENCE: Chickasaw Nation ~~COUNTY.~~ **Choctaw Nation** Choctaw Roll *(Not Including Freedmen)* CARD NO.
POST OFFICE: Graham, Ind. Ter. FIELD NO. **260**

Dawes' Roll No.		NAME		Relationship to Person First Named	AGE	SEX	BLOOD	TRIBAL ENROLLMENT Year	County	No.
550	1	Airington, Jackson	49	First Named	45	M	1/4	1896	Choctaw residing in Chickasaw District	551
I.W. 1075	2	" Elmina	39	wife	35	F	I.W.		" "	CCR #0 254
551	3	" Mary Elizabeth	10	dau	6	"	1/8	1896	" "	544
552	4	" Rosa Valentine	8	"	4	"	1/8	1896	" "	545
553	5	" Lilly Ann	5	"	10mo	"	1/8		" "	
554	6	" Andrew Jackson	22	Son	18	M	1/8	1896	" "	540
555	7	" Arthur Garvin	20	"	16	"	1/8	1896	" "	541
556	8	" John L.	17	"	13	"	1/8	1896	" "	542
557	9	" Jesse	3	"	3½ mo	"	1/8			
558	10	" Charlie Jackson	1	"	5mo	M	1/8			
	11									
	12									
	13									
	14									
	15									
	16									
	17									

ENROLLMENT OF NOS. 1,3,4,5,6,7,8,9 and 10 HEREON APPROVED BY THE SECRETARY OF INTERIOR Dec 12 1902

ENROLLMENT OF NOS. ~~ 2 ~~ HEREON APPROVED BY THE SECRETARY OF INTERIOR Nov 16 1904

TRIBAL ENROLLMENT OF PARENTS

	Name of Father	Year	County	Name of Mother	Year	County
1	Drew Airington	Dead	non citizen	Nancy Airington	Dead	Choctaw Roll
2	Sebe Owens	"	" "	Elizabeth Owens		non citizen
3	No 1			No 2		
4	No 1			No 2		
5	No 1			No 2		
6	No 1			Sarah Airington	Dead	non citizen
7	No 1			" "	"	" "
8	No 1			" "	"	" "
9	No 1			No 2		
10	№ 1			№ 2		

11 No2 on Choctaw Roll as E. Endslow Airington
12 No3 " " " " Mary "
13 No4 " " " " Rosie "
No6 " " " " Andrew "
14 No7 " " " " John "
15 No1 " " " " Jackson "
16 No9 Enrolled Jany 17, 1900
17 №10 Born Nov. 18, 1901; enrolled April 11, 1902

For child of No6 see NB (Mar 3-1905) #25
" " " No7 " " " " #505
" children" Nos1&2 " " " " #626

Date of Application for Enrollment. #1 to 8 Sept. 23/98

RESIDENCE: Chickasaw Nation ~~COUNTY.~~
POST OFFICE: Purcell, Ind. Ter.

Choctaw Nation

Choctaw Roll *(Not Including Freedmen)*

CARD NO.
FIELD NO. 261

Dawes' Roll No.		NAME		Relationship to Person First Named	AGE	SEX	BLOOD	TRIBAL ENROLLMENT Year	County	No.
14263	1	Taylor, Lucy	32	First Named	28	F	1/2			
14264	2	" Henry	15	son	11	M	1/4			
14265	3	" Ella	13	dau	9	F	1/4			
14266	4	" George	11	son	7	M	1/4			
14267	5	" Lilly	9	dau	5	F	1/4			
14268	6	" Frances	7	"	3	"	1/4			
	7									
	8	ENROLLMENT								
	9	OF NOS. 1 2 3 4 5 and 6 HEREON APPROVED BY THE SECRETARY								
	10	OF INTERIOR APR 11 1903								
	11	All admitted by Dawes Com. Case No 282, and no appeal taken.								
	12									
	13									
	14									
	15									
	16									
	17									

TRIBAL ENROLLMENT OF PARENTS

	Name of Father	Year	County	Name of Mother	Year	County
1	Joe Murray		Choctaw Freedman	Ella Murray	dead	Choctaw Indian
2	Henry Taylor		noncitizen	No 1		
3	" "		" "	No 1		
4	" "		" "	No 1		
5	" "		" "	No 1		
6	" "		" "	No 1		
7						
8						
9						
10						
11						
12						
13						
14						
15						
16						Date of Application for Enrollment.
17				Date of application for enrollment		Sept 23/98

RESIDENCE: Chickasaw Nation ~~COUNTY.~~
POST OFFICE:

Choctaw Nation

Choctaw Roll *(Not Including Freedmen)*

CARD NO.
FIELD NO. **262**

Dawes' Roll No.		NAME	Relationship to Person First Named	AGE	SEX	BLOOD	TRIBAL ENROLLMENT Year	County	No.
559	1	Airington, Monroe 27	First Named	23	M	1/8		Choctaw residing in Chickasaw District	CCR #2 6
I.W. 1076	2	" Minnie 21	Wife	17	F	I.W.			
560	3	" Luther 2	Son	11mo	M	1/16			
	4								
	5					No 1	1896	Tobucksy	137
	6								
	7								
	8								
	9								
	10								
	11								
	12								
	13								
	14								
	15								
	16								
	17								

ENROLLMENT
OF NOS. 1 and 3 HEREON
APPROVED BY THE SECRETARY
OF INTERIOR DEC 12 1902

ENROLLMENT
OF NOS. ~~2~~ HEREON
APPROVED BY THE SECRETARY
OF INTERIOR NOV 16 1904

No3 Enrolled June 29, 1901
For child of Nos 1and2 see N.B. (Apr. 26-06) No 537
" " " " " " " (Mar 3-05) No 11

TRIBAL ENROLLMENT OF PARENTS

	Name of Father	Year	County	Name of Mother	Year	County
1	Jackson Airington		Choctaw residing in ~~Chickasaw District~~	Sarah Airington	Dead	non citizen
2	Jim Callon	Dead	non citizen	Ada Callon		" "
3	No 1			No 2		
4						
5						
6						
7						
8						
9						
10						
11						
12						
13						
14						
15						
16						Date of Application for Enrollment.
17	P.O. Graham I.T. June 29, 1901					Sept 23/98

RESIDENCE: Chickasaw Nation ~~COUNTY.~~
POST OFFICE: Ardmore, Ind. Ter.

Choctaw Nation **Choctaw Roll** (Not Including Freedmen)

CARD NO.
FIELD NO. 263

Dawes' Roll No.	NAME	Relationship to Person First Named	AGE	SEX	BLOOD	TRIBAL ENROLLMENT Year	County	No.
561	1 Cotten, Pink 25	First Named	21	M	1/16		Choctaw residing in Chickasaw District	CCR #2 124
I.W. 1077	2 " Haidee 32	Wife	28	F	I.W.			
562	3 " Pinkie 1	Dau	1wk	F	1/32			

ENROLLMENT OF NOS. 1 and 3 HEREON APPROVED BY THE SECRETARY OF INTERIOR DEC 12 1902

No1 1896 Chickasaw Dist 3078 as Pink Cotton.

ENROLLMENT OF NOS. 2 HEREON APPROVED BY THE SECRETARY OF INTERIOR NOV 16 1904

No1 brother of E.W. Cotten, Choctaw Card No. D.46.
No2 sister of Minnie B Cotten " " " D.46.

TRIBAL ENROLLMENT OF PARENTS

Name of Father	Year	County	Name of Mother	Year	County
1 David B Cotten	Dead	non citizen	Susan L Cotten	Dead	Choctaw Roll
2 N. NeSmith		" "	Elizabeth J NeSmith	"	non citizen
3 No 1			No 2		

No3 born Jany 9th, 1902: Enrolled Jany 16th, 1902

For child of Nos 1 and 2 see NB (Mar 3-1905) #478

#1&2
Date of Application for Enrollment. Sept. 23/98

P.O. Hickory I.T.

RESIDENCE: Chickasaw Nation ~~COUNTY.~~ **Choctaw Nation** Choctaw Roll (Not Including Freedmen) CARD NO.
POST OFFICE: Simon, Ind. Ter. FIELD NO. 264

Dawes' Roll No.	NAME	Relationship to Person First Named	AGE	SEX	BLOOD	TRIBAL ENROLLMENT Year	County	No.
I.W. 547	1 Beard, William F. 53	First Named	50	M	I.W.		Choctaw residing in Chickasaw District	C.I. Roll 11
14512	2 " Mary Jane 64	Wife	60	F	1/16		" " No1026	CCR #0 108
	3							
	4							
	5							
	6							
	7							
	8							
	9							
	10							
	11	No1 1896 Chickasaw Dist 14361 as W.F. Beard						
	12	No2 on 1893 Kiamitia County 1893 pay roll No 87 page 119						
	13							
	14							
	15							
	16							
	17							

ENROLLMENT OF NOS. 2 HEREON APPROVED BY THE SECRETARY OF INTERIOR MAY 20 1903

ENROLLMENT OF NOS. ~~ 1 ~~ HEREON APPROVED BY THE SECRETARY OF INTERIOR FEB -8 1904

TRIBAL ENROLLMENT OF PARENTS

Name of Father	Year	County	Name of Mother	Year	County
1 Daniel Beard	Dead	noncitizen	Olivia Beard	Dead	noncitizen
2 G.W. Harkins	"	Choctaw roll	Salina Harkins	"	Choctaw Roll
3					
4					
5					
6					
7					
8					
9					
10					
11					
12					
13					
14					
15					
16					
17 P.O. Ardmore I.T.				Date of Application for Enrollment.	Sept. 23/98

No1 admitted by Dawes Com Case No. 606, and no appeal taken
Marriage license and certificate on file in office of Dawes Com. at Muskogee, Ind. Ter

RESIDENCE: Chickasaw Nation ~~COUNTY.~~ POST OFFICE: Ardmore, Ind. Ter.

Choctaw Nation — Choctaw Roll (*Not Including Freedmen*) CARD NO. FIELD NO. 265

Dawes' Roll No.		NAME	Relationship to Person First Named	AGE	SEX	BLOOD	TRIBAL ENROLLMENT Year	County	No.
I.W. 870	1	Walcott, Arthur 33	First Named	30	M	I.W.		Choctaw residing in Chickasaw District	C.I. Roll 118
14269	2	" Lutie Mary 30	wife	26	F	1/32		" "	CCR #2 ~~489~~
14270	3	" Helen Haley 7	dau	3	"	1/64		" "	"
DEAD	4	~~" Jessie Olive~~	~~"~~	~~5mo~~	~~"~~	~~1/64~~		~~" "~~	~~"~~
14271	5	" Marjorie N. 2	dau	3mo	F	1/64			
	6								
	7	ENROLLMENT OF NOS. 2, 3 and 5 HEREON APPROVED BY THE SECRETARY OF INTERIOR APR 11 1903							
	10	ENROLLMENT OF NOS. 1 HEREON APPROVED BY THE SECRETARY OF INTERIOR AUG 3 1904				No2 on Choctaw Roll as Lutie H. Walcott			
	11					No3 " " " " Helen H "			
	12					~~No4 " " " " Jessie "~~			
	15	No. 4 HEREON DISMISSED UNDER ORDER OF THE COMMISSION TO THE FIVE CIVILIZED TRIBES OF MARCH 31, 1905							

TRIBAL ENROLLMENT OF PARENTS

	Name of Father	Year	County	Name of Mother	Year	County
1	~~Jas. D. Walcott~~	~~Dead~~	~~noncitizen~~	~~Martha N. Walcott~~		~~noncitizen~~
2	D.M. Haley (I.W.)		Tobucksy	Helen Haley		Tobucksy
3	No 1			No 2		
4	No 1			No 2		
5	No 1			No 2		

No1 1896 Chickasaw Dist 15194
No2 1896 " " 14181 as Leutie H. Welcot
No3 1896 " " 14182 " Helen H Welcot
~~No.5 Enrolled Aug 6th 1900.~~

No1 admitted as an intermarried citizen, and Nos 2 and 3 as citizens by blood by Dawes Commission: Choctaw Case #539, No appeal

No.4 died June 24, 1899; Proof of death filed Dec. 23, 1902.
For child of Nos 1 and 2 see NB (March 3, 1905) #1225

#1 to 4 inc
Date of Application for Enrollment Sept. 23/98

RESIDENCE: Chickasaw Nation ~~COUNTY.~~
POST OFFICE: Washita, Ind. Ter

Choctaw Nation

Choctaw Roll (Not Including Freedmen)

CARD NO.
FIELD NO. **266**

Dawes' Roll No.	NAME		Relationship to Person First Named	AGE	SEX	BLOOD	TRIBAL ENROLLMENT Year	County	No.
I.W. 548	1 Wolf, Matt	52	First Named	47	M	I.W.		Choctaw residing in Chickasaw District	C.I. Roll 118
563	2 " Ellen	51	wife	47	F	1/16		" "	CCR #2 489
See 4648	3 ~~" Mettie[sic]~~		~~dau~~	~~19~~	~~"~~	~~1/32~~		~~" "~~	~~"~~
564	4 " Amelia	21	"	17	"	1/32		" "	"
565	5 " Fannie	17	"	14	"	1/32		" "	"
566	6 " Kochantubbi	16	Son	12	M	1/32		" "	"
567	7 " Matt	12	"	9	"	1/32		" "	"
	8								
	9								
	10								
	11								
	12								
	13								
	14								
	15								
	16								
	17								

ENROLLMENT
OF NOS. 2,4,5,6 and 7 HEREON
APPROVED BY THE SECRETARY
OF INTERIOR DEC 12 1902

ENROLLMENT
OF NOS. ~~~1~~~ HEREON
APPROVED BY THE SECRETARY
OF INTERIOR FEB -8 1904

No3 on Choctaw roll as Nettie Wolf.
No5 " " " " Lena "
No7 " " " " Mattie "

No 3 put on card 4648 with husband.

No 2 said to be 1/8 blood.

TRIBAL ENROLLMENT OF PARENTS

	Name of Father	Year	County	Name of Mother	Year	County
1	Thos H Wolf	Dead	non citizen	Elizabeth Wolf	Dead	non citizen
2	Calvin Howell	"	" "	Rhoda Howell		" "
3	~~No 1~~			~~No 2~~		
4	No 1			No 2		
5	No 1			No 2		
6	No 1			No 2		
7	No 1			No 2		
8						
9						
10						
11						
12						
13						
14						
15						
16						
17	P.O. Davis I.T. 10/22/02					

No1 1896 Chickasaw Dist 15195
No2 1896 " " 14157
No3 1896 " " 14158 as Nettie Wolf.
~~No4 1896 " " 14159~~
No5 1896 " " 14160 as Lena Wolf.
No6 1896 " " 14161
No7 1896 " " 14162 as Mattie Wolf.

Date of Application for Enrollment. Sept. 23/98

RESIDENCE: Chickasaw Nation ~~COUNTY.~~
POST OFFICE: Ardmore, Ind. Ter.

Choctaw Nation

Choctaw Roll *(Not Including Freedmen)*

CARD NO.
FIELD NO. 267

Dawes' Roll No.	NAME	Relationship to Person First Named	AGE	SEX	BLOOD	TRIBAL ENROLLMENT Year	County	No.
	1 ~~Boyd, John Thomas~~	~~First Named~~	~~24~~	~~M~~	~~1/8~~		Choctaw residing in ~~Chickasaw District~~	~~CCR #2 80~~
	2 ~~" Louis Hill~~	~~Bro~~	~~17~~	~~"~~	~~1/8~~		~~"~~	~~"~~
	3							
	4				No 1	1896	Chickasaw Dist	2001
	5				No 2	1896	" "	2002
	6							
	7							
	8							
	9							
	10							
	11							
	12							
	13							
	14							
	15							
	16							
	17							

No 1 on Choctaw roll as J.T. Boyd.
No 2 " " " " Lewis H "
Nos 1 and 2 Admitted by U.S. Court at Ardmore, Nov 15 1897
~~Case No 113~~

CANCELLED

Duplicate of Nos (2) & (3) on Choctaw Card #5141

TRIBAL ENROLLMENT OF PARENTS

	Name of Father	Year	County	Name of Mother	Year	County
1	~~John T. Boyd~~		~~non citizen~~	~~Annie S. Boyd~~	~~Dead~~	Choctaw residing in ~~Chickasaw District~~
2	~~" " "~~		~~" "~~	~~" " "~~	~~"~~	~~" "~~
3						
4						
5						
6						
7						
8						
9						
10						

7/16/02 Nos 1&2 are same as Nos 2 and 3 on card 5141. Mother of Nos 1&2 with mother of Nos 1,2,3 & 4 on card 2515. No 1 on card R334 and No 2 on card 2514. Mother of No1 on card ~~R.291 and Mother of Nos 1 2 & 3 on card R.306 were[sic] admitted to citizenship in Choctaw Nation by Act of Choctaw Council, Approved April 8, 1891 found on page 320 of Durants~~ Digest of Choctaw laws. See Nos 2514, 2515, R-291, R 306 & R 334. See file containing copies of 1896 papers in Jas T. Boyd case.

Chickasha I.T.

Date of Application for Enrollment. Sept. 23/98

RESIDENCE: Chickasaw Nation ~~COUNTY.~~ **Choctaw Nation** **Choctaw Roll** (Not Including Freedmen) CARD NO.
POST OFFICE: Keller, Ind. Ter FIELD NO. 268

Dawes' Roll No.	NAME	Relationship to Person First Named	AGE	SEX	BLOOD	TRIBAL ENROLLMENT Year	County	No.
568	1 Dillard, Hamilton 40	First Named	36	M	1/4	1896	Choctaw residing in Chickasaw District	3638
I.W. 497	2 " Victoria 35	Wife	31	F	IW	1896	" "	14487
569	3 " Lee Hamilton 18	son	14	M	1/8	1896	" "	3644
570	4 " Joseph Carpenter 17	"	13	"	1/8	1896	" "	3645
571	5 " William Guy 14	"	10	"	1/8	1896	" "	3646
572	6 " Minnie Victoria 12	Dau	8	F	1/8	1896	" "	3647
573	7 " Bula Mamie 9	"	5	"	1/8	1896	" "	3648
574	8 " Cubby Fowler 7	son	3	M	1/8	1896	" "	3649
575	9 " Floyd 5	"	1	"	1/8			
576	10 " Vella 3	Dau	5mos	F	1/8			
577	11 " Douglas H 1	son	3wks	M	1/8			
14513	12 " Walter 1	Gr Son	7wks	M	1/16			

ENROLLMENT OF NOS. 1,3,4,5,6,7,8,9,10 and 11 HEREON APPROVED BY THE SECRETARY OF INTERIOR Dec 24 1903

13 No.10 enrolled Oct 6/99
14 No11 enrolled June 22, 1901
15 No.3 is now husband of Alpha Vituria Dillard on Choctaw card #D 780 Aug 29,1902 - ~~Transferred to 7-5868~~
16 No.12 born July 27, 1902 Enrolled Sept 11, 1902
17 No9 affidavit of attending physician to be supplied, rec'd Nov. 4, '98

TRIBAL ENROLLMENT OF PARENTS

Name of Father	Year	County	Name of Mother	Year	County
1 M. Dillard	Dead	non citizen	Elizabeth Dillard		Choctaw residing in Chickasaw District
2 P. M. Buckner		" "	Emily Buckner	Dead	non-citizen
3 No. 1			No. 2		
4 No. 1			No. 2		
5 No. 1			No. 2		
6 No. 1			No. 2		
7 No. 1			No. 2		
8 No. 1			No. 2		
9 No. 1			No. 2		
10 No. 1			No. 2		
11 No. 1			No. 2		
12 No. 3			Alpha Vituria Dillard		intermarried

ENROLLMENT OF NOS. ~~ 2 ~~ HEREON APPROVED BY THE SECRETARY OF INTERIOR Dec 24 1903

ENROLLMENT OF NOS. 12 HEREON APPROVED BY THE SECRETARY OF INTERIOR May 20 1903

13 No1 also on 1896 roll Page 385 No 1448 as J.H. Dillard Atoka Co.
14 No3 on Choctaw roll as Lee Dillard
~~No4 " " " " Joseph "~~
15 No5 " " " " Guy "
16 No6 " " " " Minnie "
~~No7 " " " " Mary "~~
17 No8 " " " " Cubby "

For child of No3 see N.B.(Apr 26'06) No 797
" " " Nos1&2 " " (Mar 3' 05) " 1024

Date of Application for Enrollment. Sept. 23/98
1 to 9 inc

RESIDENCE: Chickasaw Nation ~~COUNTY~~.
POST OFFICE: Marietta, Ind. Ter.

Choctaw Nation

Choctaw Roll (Not Including Freedmen)

CARD NO.
FIELD NO. 269

Dawes' Roll No.		NAME		Relationship to Person First Named	AGE	SEX	BLOOD	TRIBAL ENROLLMENT Year	County	No.
I.W.549	1	Arbuckle, Jeff	40	First Named	36	M	I.W.		Choctaw residing in Chickasaw District	C.I. Roll 4
14514	2	" , Carrie	38	wife	34	F	1/2		" "	CCR #2 22
14515	3	" , Winnie	12 ✓	dau	8	"	1/4		" "	"
14516	4	" , Leatier	10 ✓	"	6	"	1/4		" "	"
14517	5	" , Juanita	8 ✓	"	4	"	1/4		" "	"
14518	6	" , Fulsom	7 ✓	son	3	M	1/4		" "	"
14519	7	" , Tessie	5	dau	10mo	F	1/4			
14520	8	" , Verdy	3	dau	3mo	F	1/4			
	9									
	10						No.1	1896	Chickasaw Dist	14269
	11						No.2	1896	" "	536

ENROLLMENT OF NOS. 2,3,4,5,6,7&8 HEREON APPROVED BY THE SECRETARY OF INTERIOR May 20 1903

12 Marriage license and certificate on file in office of Dawes Com. Muskogee, Ind. Ter.
13 No.6 on Choctaw roll as Folsom Arbuckle.

14 No.3 1896 Chickasaw Dist. 546
15 No.4 1896 " " " 547 as Letta Arbuckle
16 No.5 1896 " " " 548 " Warnetta "
~~No.6 1896 " " " 549 " Folsom "~~

TRIBAL ENROLLMENT OF PARENTS

	Name of Father	Year	County	Name of Mother	Year	County
1	Hugh Arbuckle	Dead	non citizen	M.F. Arbuckle		non citizens[sic]
2	Wm Martin	"	" "	Jincy Beans	Dead	Choctaw Roll
3	No 1			No 2		
4	No 1			No 2		
5	No 1			No 2		
6	No 1			No 2		
7	No 1			No 2		
8	No 1			No 2		

ENROLLMENT OF NOS. ~~~ 1 ~~~ HEREON APPROVED BY THE SECRETARY OF INTERIOR Feb -8- 1904

10 No.1 admitted by Dawes Com Case No. 497 under name of Jefferson, and no appeal taken
11 No.5 " " " " " " 497 " " Wanetia, " " " "
~~No.6 " " " " " " 497 " " Folsom, " " " "~~
12 ~~No.8 Enrolled May 24, 1900.~~

14 For child of Nos.1&2 see N.B. (Mar 3rd 1905) card No. 74

Date of Application for Enrollment.

17 P.O. Grantham, I.T. Sept. 23/98

P.O. Madill, I.T. 3/23/04

RESIDENCE: Chickasaw Nation ~~COUNTY.~~ **Choctaw Nation** Choctaw Roll (Not Including Freedmen) CARD NO.
POST OFFICE: Marietta Ind Ter FIELD NO. 270

Dawes' Roll No.		NAME		Relationship to Person First Named	AGE	SEX	BLOOD	TRIBAL ENROLLMENT Year	County	No.
578	1	Bourne, Maud	19	First Named	15	F	1/4		Choctaw residing in Chickasaw District	CCR #2 80
579	2	" Annie	17	Sister	13	"	1/4		" "	"
580	3	" Hattie	15	"	11	"	1/4		" "	"

ENROLLMENT OF NOS. 1, 2 and 3 HEREON APPROVED BY THE SECRETARY OF INTERIOR DEC 12 1902

No1 1896 Chickasaw Dist 1997 as Maud Burnie
No2 1896 " " 1999 " Annie "
No3 1896 " " 1998 " Hattie "

TRIBAL ENROLLMENT OF PARENTS

	Name of Father	Year	County	Name of Mother	Year	County
1	Henry Bourne	Dead	non citizen	Carrie Arbuckle		Choctaw residing in Chickasaw District
2	" "	"	" "	" "		" "
3	" "	"	" "	" "		" "

Mother Carrie Arbuckle, on Choctaw roll, Card No 269.

Date of Application for Enrollment. Sept 23/98

Choctaw By Blood Enrollment Cards 1898-1914

RESIDENCE: Chickasaw Nation ~~County~~ **Choctaw Nation** **Choctaw Roll** *(Not Including Freedmen)* CARD NO.
POST OFFICE: Kingston, Ind. Ter. FIELD NO. **271**

Dawes' Roll No.		NAME	Relationship to Person First Named	AGE	SEX	BLOOD	TRIBAL ENROLLMENT Year	County	No.
VOID.	1	~~Bounds, Young Walker~~	~~Named~~	~~21~~	~~M~~	~~1/16~~		~~Choctaw residing in Chickasaw District~~	~~CCR #2 82~~
VOID.	2	~~" , James~~	~~Bro~~	~~20~~	~~"~~	~~1/16~~		~~" "~~	~~"~~
	3								
	4					No1	1896	Chickasaw Dist	2038
	5					No2	1896	" "	2016
	6								
	7								
	8		No 1 on Choctaw roll as Y.W. Bounds						
	9		No 2 " " " J.H. " , Jr.						
	10								
	11								
	12								
	13	Oct 25/99 Above parties also							
	14	appear on Court Card No C.179							
	15	No1 on 1896 roll as Y.W. Bonds							
	16	No2 on 2896 roll as James Bond							
	17								

CANCELLED

TRIBAL ENROLLMENT OF PARENTS

	Name of Father	Year	County	Name of Mother	Year	County
1	~~J.H. Bounds (I.W.)~~		~~Choctaw residing in Chickasaw District~~	~~Joanna Bounds~~	~~Dead~~	~~Choctaw residing in Chickasaw District~~
2	~~" " "~~		~~" "~~	~~" "~~	~~"~~	~~" "~~
3						
4						
5						
6						
7						
8						
9						
10						
11						
12	~~Oct 25/99 These parties were also~~					
13	admitted by U.S. Court, Southern Dist. December 21, 1897,					
14	Case 155, No1 as Young Walker Bounds, No2 as James					
15	Bounds Jr.					Date of Application for Enrollment. Sept. 23/98
16	~~These parties were also admitted by Dawes Com.~~ case No 863. No1 as Young Walker Bounds. No2 as James					
17	Bounds.					

Choctaw By Blood Enrollment Cards 1898-1914

RESIDENCE: Chickasaw Nation ~~COUNTY.~~
POST OFFICE: Ardmore, Ind Ter

Choctaw Nation

Choctaw Roll (Not Including Freedmen) CARD NO. FIELD NO. 272

Dawes' Roll No.	NAME	Relationship to Person First Named	AGE	SEX	BLOOD	TRIBAL ENROLLMENT Year	County	No.
15169	1 Hyden, Frank S. 33	First Named	29	M	1/8		Choctaw residing in Chickasaw District	CCR #2 258
IW 1601	2 " Georgia 28	wife	24	F	I.W		"	C.I. Roll 47
15634	3 " Maude 10	dau	6	"	1/16		"	CCR #2 258
16102	4 " Eva Marguerite 6	"	2	"	1/16			
15170	5 " Ahalahona 4	"	6mos	"	1/16			

ENROLLMENT OF NOS. ~~~4~~~ HEREON APPROVED BY THE SECRETARY OF INTERIOR MAR 4 1907

No4 on Choctaw Roll as Emmie Hyden

ENROLLMENT OF NOS. ~~~2~~~ HEREON APPROVED BY THE SECRETARY OF INTERIOR FEB 12 1907

Enrollment of No2 cancelled by order of Department of March 4, 1907

No2 restored to roll by Departmental authority of August 9 1909 (File 5-51)

ENROLLMENT OF NOS. 1 and 5 HEREON APPROVED BY THE SECRETARY OF INTERIOR MAR 26 1904

ENROLLMENT OF NOS. ~~ 3 ~~ HEREON APPROVED BY THE SECRETARY OF INTERIOR OCT 21 1904

No2 denied by CCCC as "Georgie Hyden or Georgia Hyden" DENIED CITIZENSHIP BY THE CHOCTAW AND
" 3 " " " " "Eva Margaret " " CHICKASAW CITIZENSHIP COURT Nov 28'04

TRIBAL ENROLLMENT OF PARENTS

Name of Father	Year	County	Name of Mother	Year	County
1 Whit W Hyden		Choctaw residing in Chickasaw District	Martha E Hyden (I.W.)		Choctaw residing in Chickasaw District
2 L.F. Bowman		non citizen	Margaret Bowman		non citizen
3 No 1			No 2		
4 No 1			No 2	No	
5 No 1			No 2		

Nov 17, 1906 Dept affirmed decision of Com'r of Oct 1/06 granting enrollment of Nos. 2 & 4
Nov. 30, 1906, Parties herein notified

Nos1&3 admitted by act of Choctaw Council, approved Oct.31,1895, No1 as Frank Hyden
No1 1896 Chickasaw Dist 6146 as Frank Hyden
No2 1896 " " 14666 " Georgie "
No3 1896 " " 6154 " Maud "
~~No4 1896 " " 6155 " Emmie "~~
No5 Affidavit of attending physician filed Born March 7 1898

Judgement[sic] of U.S. Ct admitting Nos 2and 4 vacated and set aside by Decree of Choctaw and Chickasaw Citizenship Court Dec 17 '02

#4 GRANTED OCT 1 1906

Oct 21 1906 Record forwarded Dept.

Nos 2&4 were admitted by U.S. Court at Ardmore I.T.
November 15, 1897 Court Case #141
Nos (2) and (4) denied by Dawes Com Case #1344

Date of Application for Enrollment. 9/24/98

Choctaw By Blood Enrollment Cards 1898-1914

RESIDENCE: Chickasaw Nation ~~COUNTY.~~
POST OFFICE: Ardmore, Ind. Ter.

Choctaw Nation — **Choctaw Roll** *(Not Including Freedmen)* — CARD NO. — FIELD NO. 273

Dawes' Roll No.	NAME	Relationship to Person First Named	AGE	SEX	BLOOD	TRIBAL ENROLLMENT Year	County	No.
I.W. 1671	1 Turner, Katie 46	First Named	42	F	I.W.			
15369	2 " Martin Franklin 12	Son	8	M	1/16			
15370	3 " Myrtle L. 10	dau	6	F	1/16			
15371	4 Percer, Walter 19	nephew in law	15	M	1/16			
15372	5 " Wiley 15	" "	11	"	1/16			
15373	6 " Ludenna 13	niece in law	9	F	1/16			

ENROLLMENT OF NOS. One HEREON APPROVED BY THE SECRETARY OF INTERIOR Mar 4- 1907

ENROLLMENT OF NOS. 2-3-4-5-6 HEREON APPROVED BY THE SECRETARY OF INTERIOR May 9 1904

~~All admitted by Dawes Com. Case No. 295 and no appeal taken as to these applicants~~
No.1 wife of John Franklin Turner, Choctaw Card ~~No.D.49~~ 5206
Marriage certificate on file with Dawes Com Muskogee, Ind. Ter.
~~Nos2 and 3 restored to roll by Departmental authority of June 9,~~ 1907 (File 5-51)
No.6 admitted by Dawes Com as Ludrany Percer.

Mch 4-07 Dept reversed decision of Com'r of Jan 21-07 and directed enrollment of #1 as intermarried citizen
Notify Cruce Cruce & Bleakmore of Ardmore as to No. 1
~~H.A. Ledbetter, Ardmore, I.T. as to No.1~~

~~Nos 2 and 3 Canceled[sic] by order of Department of March 4, 1907 (I.T.D. 7936-1907)~~

TRIBAL ENROLLMENT OF PARENTS

	Name of Father	Year	County	Name of Mother	Year	County
1	Martin Ritz		non citizen	Lorana Ritz		non citizen
2	~~John Franklin Turner~~			~~No 1~~		
3	~~" " "~~			~~No 1~~		
4	Jim Percer	Dead	non citizen	Susie Percer	dead	Choctaw Roll
5	" "	"	" "	" "	"	" "
6	" "	"	" "	" "	"	" "

Take no further action relative to enrollment of Nos 1 to 6 incl.
Protest of Attys for Choctaw and Chickasaw Nations for 2304
Protest overruled see Departmental letter of March 31-1904

*See affidavits of No.1 Hattie Fields and W.J. Brown as to ~~inability of No.1 to appear in person before the Commission and~~ as to abandonment of No.1 by her husband filed Nov. 17, 1902

*REFUSED. Jan. 21, 1907

Record Forwarded Department Jan 21 1907
~~Cruce Cruce & Bleakmore Attys See letter #38792-04~~

Date of Application for Enrollment. Sept. 24/98

[On back of card]
~~Feb 25, 1909 Department requests report a to Nos 2 and 3 hereon~~
March 12, 1909 Report to Department
March 25, 1909 Department refers for report letter of W.S. Fields
May 4 1909 Report to Department
~~June 9 1909 Department holds case is analogous to Goldsby case and~~ directs restoration of these applicants to the roll

Over

RESIDENCE: Chickasaw Nation ~~COUNTY~~.
POST OFFICE: Minco, Ind. Ter.

Choctaw Nation

Choctaw Roll *(Not Including Freedmen)*

CARD NO.
FIELD NO. **274**

Dawes' Roll No.	NAME	Relationship to Person First Named	AGE	SEX	BLOOD	TRIBAL ENROLLMENT Year	County	No.
I.W. 871	1 Wright, James E. [49]	First Named	45	M	I.W.		Choctaw residing in Chickasaw District	C.I. Roll 118
581	2 " Abbie [34]	wife	30	F	1/4		" "	CCR #2 488
~~582~~	~~3 Bench, Josiah~~ [23]	~~Bro in law~~	~~19~~	~~M~~	~~1/4~~		" "	CCR #2 82
583	4 " Nancy [21]	Sister in law	17	F	1/4		" "	"
584	5 Curry, Clara [17]	" "	13	"	1/4		" "	"
585	6 Bench, Clay [13]	Bro " "	9	M	1/4		" "	"
586	7 " Edna May [4]	niece " "	5mo	F	1/8			
~~587~~	~~8 " Henry~~ ✓ DIED PRIOR TO SEPTEMBER 25, 1902	~~nephew " "~~	~~2mo~~	~~M~~	~~1/8~~			
588	9 Curry, Howard F. ✓	son of No. 5	1mo	M	1/8			

DIED PRIOR TO SEPTEMBER 25, 1902

ENROLLMENT OF NOS. 2,3,4,5,6,7,8and 9 HEREON APPROVED BY THE SECRETARY OF INTERIOR Dec 12 1902

No.5 is now the wife of Burnett Curry, non-citizen; evidence of marriage filed May 23, 1902.
No.9 Born April 15, 1902: enrolled May 23, 1902.

No7-affidavit of attending physician to be supplied. Received Oct 17/98

Evidence of marriage between No 1 and 2 ~~filed July 29, 1903~~

Copy of divorce proceedings between N°1 and his former wife filed July 29, 1903.

For child of No4 see NB (Mar 3-1905) Card #10
" No5 " " " " " #988

TRIBAL ENROLLMENT OF PARENTS

Name of Father	Year	County	Name of Mother	Year	County
1 James Wright	Dead	non citizen	Annie Wright		non citizen
2 Christopher Bench	"	Choctaw Roll	Nancy Bench	Dead	Choctaw Roll
~~3 " "~~	~~"~~	~~" "~~	~~" "~~	~~"~~	~~" "~~
4 " "	"	" "	" "	"	" "
5 " "	"	" "	" "	"	" "
6 " "	"	" "	" "	"	" "
7 (Illegitimate)			No. 4		
~~8 (Illegitimate)~~			~~No 5~~		
9 Burnette Curry		non citizen	No. 5		

No.1 1896 Chickasaw Dist 15202
No.2 1896 " " 14144
No.3 1896 " " 2040 as Josiah Birch
~~No.4 1896 " " 2041 " Maney "~~
No.5 1896 " " 2042 " Carrie "
No.6 1896 " " 2043 " Clay "
No.3 Died August 4, 1901: Proof of Death filed Oct 18-1902
~~No.8 Enrolled June 5, 1900.~~
See testimony of No.1 taken Oct. 15, 1902
P.O. New Castle, I.T.

ENROLLMENT OF NOS. 1 HEREON APPROVED BY THE SECRETARY OF INTERIOR Aug 3 1904

Date of Application for Enrollment. Sept. 24/98

No8 died May 1900. Enrollment cancelled by Department Dec. 24, 1904

RESIDENCE: Chickasaw Nation ~~COUNTY.~~
POST OFFICE: Pauls Valley, Ind. Ter.

Choctaw Nation

Choctaw Roll *(Not Including Freedmen)*

CARD NO.
FIELD NO. 275

Dawes' Roll No.	NAME	Relationship to Person First Named	AGE	SEX	BLOOD	TRIBAL ENROLLMENT Year	County	No.
I.W. 1078	1 Goodson, Nettie 27		23	F	I.W.		Choctaw residing in Chickasaw District	C.I. Roll 39
	2							
	3							
	4							
	5							
	6							
	7							
	8							
	9							
	10							
	11							
	12							
	13							
	14							
	15							
	16							
	17							

ENROLLMENT OF NOS. ~~~ 1 ~~~ HEREON APPROVED BY THE SECRETARY OF INTERIOR Nov. 16 1904

Affidavit of minister who married her to J.J. Goodson, to be supplied
Received Oct 21/98
Abandoned by her husband
~~No. 1 is the wife of John J. Goodson on Choctaw Card #3~~
For child of No.1 see N.B. (Apr. 26 '06) #1127.
Correct given name of No 1 is Nettie
O.W. Patchell, Pauls Valley, I.T. Atty for applicant
~~Evidence of divorce between No.1 and her husband John J. Goodson, filed July 6, 1903.~~

TRIBAL ENROLLMENT OF PARENTS

Name of Father	Year	County	Name of Mother	Year	County
1 J.D. Yoder		non-citizen	M.J. Yoder		non citizen
2					
3					
4					
5					
6					
7					
8					
9					
10					
11					
12					
13					
14					Date of Application ~~for Enrollment.~~
15					Sept. 24/98
16					
17 Whitebead, I.T.					

RESIDENCE: Chickasaw Nation ~~COUNTY.~~ **Choctaw Nation** **Choctaw Roll** *(Not Including Freedmen)* CARD NO.
POST OFFICE: Ryan, Ind. Ter. FIELD NO. 276

Dawes' Roll No.	NAME	Relationship to Person First Named	AGE	SEX	BLOOD	TRIBAL ENROLLMENT Year	County	No.
I.W. 550	1 Campbell, W.H.L. 36	First Named	33	M	I.W.			
	2							
	3							
	4							
	5							
	6							
	7							
	8							
	9							
	10							
	11							
	12							
	13							
	14							
	15							
	16							
	17							

ENROLLMENT
OF NOS. ~~~~ 1 ~~~~ HEREON
APPROVED BY THE SECRETARY
OF INTERIOR FEB -8 1904

~~Original marriage license and certificate on file in office of Dawes Com. at~~
Muskogee Ind. Ter.

~~Widower of Elizabeth Campbell nee Bonner (Choctaw)~~

TRIBAL ENROLLMENT OF PARENTS

	Name of Father	Year	County	Name of Mother	Year	County
1	R. T. Campbell	Dead	non citizen	Mary Campbell		non citizen
2						
3						
4						
5						
6						
7						
8						
9						
10						
11						
12						
13						
14						
15						
16						
17	P.O. Ada, I.T.			Date of Application for Enrollment.		Sept. 24/98

RESIDENCE: Chickasaw Nation ~~COUNTY~~.
POST OFFICE: Hewitt, Ind. Ter.

Choctaw Nation

Choctaw Roll (Not Including Freedmen)

CARD NO.
FIELD NO. 277

Dawes' Roll No.	NAME	Relationship to Person First Named	AGE	SEX	BLOOD	TRIBAL ENROLLMENT Year	County	No.
589	1 Stidham, Jesse 30	First Named	26	M	1/8		Choctaw residing in Chickasaw District	CCR #2 434
I.W. 872	2 " Nannie (28)	wife	24	F	I.W.		" "	C.I. Roll 102
590	3 " Walter Marion 8	son	4	M	1/16		" "	CCR #2 434
591	4 " Jessie May 5	dau	1	F	1/16			
592	5 " Nettie Anna Bell 3	dau	3mo	F	1/16			
	6							
	7 ENROLLMENT OF NOS. 1,3,4 and 5 HEREON APPROVED BY THE SECRETARY OF INTERIOR Dec 12, 1902		No.1 on Choctaw Roll as Jesse Staytham					
	8		No.2 " " " Nannie Statham					
	9		No.3 " " " Walter Staytham					
	10							
	11 ENROLLMENT OF NOS. 2 HEREON APPROVED BY THE SECRETARY OF INTERIOR Aug 3 1904				No.1	1896	Chickasaw Dist	11781
	12				No.2	1896	" "	15081
	13				No.3	1896	" "	11782
	14							
	15							
	16							
	17							

TRIBAL ENROLLMENT OF PARENTS

Name of Father	Year	County	Name of Mother	Year	County
1 Henry Stidham	Dead	non citizen	Marie J. Stidham		Choctaw residing in Chickasaw District
2 Frank Tucker		" "	Farina Tucker	Dead	non citizen
3 No. 1			No.2		
4 No. 1			No.2		
5 No. 1			No.2		
6					
7					
8 No.5 Enrolled June 23rd 1900					
9 For evidence of birth of No.4 see affidavit of attending					
physician dated Sept. 21, 1898.					
10 ~~For child of Nos. 1&2 see N.B. (March 3, 1905) #1027~~					
11					
12					
13					
14					
15				#1 to 4 inc	
16				Date of Application for Enrollment.	
17 Blanco, I.T.					Sept. 24/98

P.O. Alma I.T 1/10/04 P.O. Alma Ok 2/19/08

RESIDENCE: Chickasaw Nation ~~COUNTY.~~
POST OFFICE: Hewett, Ind. Ter

Choctaw Nation

Choctaw Roll (Not Including Freedmen)

CARD NO.
FIELD NO. 278

Dawes' Roll No.		NAME	Relationship to Person First Named	AGE	SEX	BLOOD	TRIBAL ENROLLMENT Year	County	No.
593	1	Dillard, Joseph George 46	First Named	42	M	1/16		Choctaw residing in Chickasaw District	CCR #2 151
I.W. 551	2	" Sarah Ellen 46	wife	41	F	I.W.		" "	C.I. Roll 25
594	3	" Jesse 12	son	8	M	1/32		" "	CCR #2 151
595	4	" Julius C. 5	"	2	"	1/32			
596	5	" Ed. Russell 3	"	1/2	"	1/32			
	6	ENROLLMENT							
	7	OF NOS. 1,3,4 and 5 HEREON APPROVED BY THE SECRETARY							
	8	OF INTERIOR Dec 12 1902		No 2 on Choctaw Roll as S.E. Dillard					
	9			No 4 " " " " J.C. "					
	10	ENROLLMENT							
	11	OF NOS. ~~~ 2 ~~~ HEREON APPROVED BY THE SECRETARY							
	12	OF INTERIOR Feb 8 1904							
	13			No.1 1896 Chickasaw Dist 3654 as George Dillard					
	14			No.2 1896 " " 14488 " S.E. [sic]					
	15			~~No.3 1896 " " 3656~~					
	16								
	17								

TRIBAL ENROLLMENT OF PARENTS

	Name of Father	Year	County	Name of Mother	Year	County
1	Ham. Dillard (I.W.)	Dead	Choctaw Roll	Elizabeth L. Dillard		Choctaw residing in Chickasaw District
2	John Elliott		non citizen	Docelia Elliott		non citizen
3	No 1			No 2		
4	No 1			No 2		
5	No 1			No 2		

~~No.5 Enrolled Oct 6/99.~~
Evidence of birth of No.4 filed Feby 1st,1902.
Certified copy of divorce proceedings between No.2 and her former husband filed Feby 3, 1903.

#1 to 4
Date of Application for Enrollment.
Sept. 24/98

Spencerville, I.T.

Choctaw By Blood Enrollment Cards 1898-1914

RESIDENCE: Chickasaw Nation ~~COUNTY.~~
POST OFFICE: Ardmore, Ind. Ter.

Choctaw Nation

Choctaw Roll
(Not Including Freedmen)

CARD NO.
FIELD NO. 279

Dawes' Roll No.		NAME	Relationship to Person First Named	AGE	SEX	BLOOD	TRIBAL ENROLLMENT Year	County	No.
VOID.	1	~~Colbert, Walter~~		~~33~~	~~M~~	~~1/8~~			
VOID.	2	~~" Czarina M~~	~~Dau~~	~~14mo~~	~~F~~	~~1/16~~			
VOID.	3	~~" Walter Cevera~~	~~Son~~	~~9days~~	~~M~~	~~1/16~~			

On Chickasaw Roll Pickens County, Page 16 transferred to Choctaw Roll
[Illegible] Com.
Husband of Henrietta C Colbert, Chickasaw roll, Card No. 613

No2 was born July 20, 1897 and enrolled on Chickasaw card #613 Sept. 24, 1898
transferred to this card Feby 4, 1902
No3 was born Sept 15, 1898 and enrolled on Chickasaw card #613 Sept. 24, 1898
~~transferred to this card Feby 4, 1902~~
(No. 2 also on 1897 Chickasaw roll, page 93 as Czarina Colbert.)
Evidence of marriage between Nº1 and Henrietta C. Juzan filed Feby 27, 1902

CANCELLED

TRIBAL ENROLLMENT OF PARENTS

	Name of Father	Year	County	Name of Mother	Year	County
1	~~Jim Colbert~~	~~Dead~~	~~Chickasaw Roll~~	~~A.M. Colbert~~		~~Chickasaw Roll~~
2	~~No 1~~			~~Henrietta C. Colbert~~	~~1897~~	~~Intermarried Chickasaw roll~~
3	~~No 1~~			~~" " "~~	~~"~~	~~" "~~

Date of Application for Enrollment.
Sept. 24/98

RESIDENCE: Chickasaw Nation ~~COUNTY~~. **Choctaw Nation** **Choctaw Roll** (Not Including Freedmen) CARD NO.
POST OFFICE: Ardmore, Ind. Ter. FIELD NO. 280

Dawes' Roll No.		NAME	Relationship to Person First Named	AGE	SEX	BLOOD	TRIBAL ENROLLMENT Year	County	No.
597	1	McKinney, Charley 32	First Named	30	M	1/8		Choctaw residing in Chickasaw District	CCR #2 366
I.W. 552	2	" Cleo 23	wife	20	F	I.W.		" "	C.I. Roll 74
598	3	" Ruby May 6	dau	2	"	1/16			
599	4	" Chester Cecil 4	Son	4days	M	1/16			
600	5	" Bessie Jewell 3	Dau	3mo	F	1/16			

ENROLLMENT OF NOS. 1 3 4 and 5 HEREON APPROVED BY THE SECRETARY OF INTERIOR DEC 12 1902

ENROLLMENT OF NOS. ~~~~ 2 ~~~~ HEREON APPROVED BY THE SECRETARY OF INTERIOR FEB -8 1904

No2 on Choctaw roll as Leo McKinney

No1 1896 Wade 9229 as Charlie McKinney
No2 1896 " 14869 " Leo [sic]

No4 Enrolled Nov 26/98
No5 Enrolled June 23rd 1900

For child of Nos 1&2, see N.B. (Apr. 26/06) Card #275.

TRIBAL ENROLLMENT OF PARENTS

	Name of Father	Year	County	Name of Mother	Year	County
1	Morris McKinney	Dead	Choctaw Roll	Sio Tucker McKinney	Dead	noncitizen
2	George Abner		noncitizen	Vic Abner		" "
3	No 1			No 2		
4	No 1			No 2		
5	No 1			No 2		
17	Provence I.T.			For Nos. 1,2 &3		Sept. 24/98

Date of Application for Enrollment.

Sept. 24/98

RESIDENCE: Chickasaw Nation ~~COUNTY.~~ **Choctaw Nation** **Choctaw Roll** *(Not Including Freedmen)* CARD NO.
POST OFFICE: Tishomingo, Ind. Ter. FIELD NO. 281

Dawes' Roll No.		NAME	Relationship to Person First Named	AGE	SEX	BLOOD	TRIBAL ENROLLMENT Year	County	No.
VOID.	1	~~Harris, R.M~~	~~Named~~	~~48~~	~~M~~	~~1/8~~			
VOID.	2	~~" Jennie~~	~~wife~~	~~29~~	~~F~~	~~3/8~~			
VOID.	3	~~" Dixie~~	~~dau~~	~~5~~	~~"~~	~~1/4~~			
VOID.	4	~~" Halley~~	~~"~~	~~3~~	~~"~~	~~"~~			
VOID.	5	~~" Robert Maxwell~~	~~son~~	~~3w~~	~~M~~	~~1/4~~			
	6								
	7								
	8								
	9								
	10								
	11								
	12								
	13								
	14								
	15								
	16								
	17								

All on Chickasaw roll, Tishomingo County, Page 38, transferred to Choctaw roll by Dawes Commission.

No5 Enrolled January 19 1901

No1 is father of children on Chickasaw card #617

CANCELLED

Transferred to Chickasaw Card No [illegible]

TRIBAL ENROLLMENT OF PARENTS

	Name of Father	Year	County	Name of Mother	Year	County
1	~~Joe D. Harris~~	~~Dead~~	~~Chickasaw Roll~~	~~Catherine Nail Harris~~	~~Dead~~	~~Choctaw Roll~~
2	~~Wyatt~~	~~"~~	~~non citizen~~		~~"~~	~~" "~~
3	~~No 1~~			~~No 2~~		
4	~~No 1~~			~~No 2~~		
5	~~No 1~~			~~No 2~~		
6						
7						
8						
9						
10						
11						
12						
13						
14						
15						
16						
17						

Date of Application for Enrollment.
Sept 26/98

RESIDENCE: Chickasaw Nation ~~COUNTY.~~ **Choctaw Nation** Choctaw Roll (*Not Including Freedmen*) CARD NO.
POST OFFICE: ~~Palma~~ Palmer, Ind. Ter. FIELD NO. 282

Dawes' Roll No.	NAME	Relationship to Person First Named	AGE	SEX	BLOOD	TRIBAL ENROLLMENT Year	County	No.
DEAD	1 ~~McClung, L. M.~~	~~Named~~	~~53~~	~~M~~	~~I.W.~~		~~Choctaw residing in Chickasaw District~~	~~C.I. Roll 78~~
601	2 " Emma 52	wife	48	F	1/8		" "	CCR #2 375
602	3 McClung, George 25	son	21	M	1/16		" "	"
603	4 " Eddie 18	"	14	"	1/16		" "	"
604	5 " Arto 11	dau	7	F	1/16		" "	"
	6				No 1 married in 1868			
	7 ENROLLMENT OF NOS. 2,3,4 and 5 HEREON APPROVED BY THE SECRETARY OF INTERIOR Dec 12 1902							
	8							
	9							
	10 No. 1 hereon dismissed under order of the Commission to the Five Civilized Tribes of March 31, 1905.							
	11							
	12							
	13							
	14							
	15							
	16							
	17							

TRIBAL ENROLLMENT OF PARENTS

Name of Father	Year	County	Name of Mother	Year	County
1 ~~Josiah McClung~~	~~Dead~~	~~non citizen~~	~~Elizabeth McClung~~	~~Dead~~	~~non-citizen~~
2 John Goins	"	" "	Amanda Goins	"	Choctaw Roll
3 No. 1			No. 2		
4 No. 1			No. 2		
5 No. 1			No. 2		
6					
7	No.2	1896 Chickasaw Dist 9498			
8	No.3	1896 " " 9500			
9	No.4	1896 " " 9502 as Eddy McClung.			
	~~No.5~~	~~1896 " " 9503 " Aito "~~			
10	No.1	admitted as an intermarried citizen by Dawes			
11	Commission: Choctaw Case #1259: No appeal				
12	No.1	died Jan'y 12, 1901: Proof of death filed Oct. 28, 1902			
	~~No.2~~	~~is now named Carmichael~~			
13					
14					
15					
16				Date of Application for Enrollment.	Sept. 26/98
17					

RESIDENCE: San Bois COUNTY. **Choctaw Nation** Choctaw Roll (Not Including Freedmen) CARD NO.
POST OFFICE: Garland, Ind. Ter. FIELD NO. 283

Dawes' Roll No.		NAME	Relationship to Person First Named	AGE	SEX	BLOOD	TRIBAL ENROLLMENT Year	County	No.
605	1	Folsom, Charles 22	First Named	18	M	3/8		San Bois	CCR #2 164
606	2	" Andreth 1	Son	6wk	M	3/16			
I.W. 1551	3	" Mary G.	Wife	21	F	I.W.			

ENROLLMENT OF NOS. 1 and 2 HEREON APPROVED BY THE SECRETARY OF INTERIOR Dec 12 1902

No. 1 1896 Sans Bois 3870 as Chas. Folsom

ENROLLMENT OF NOS. ~~~~ 3 ~~~~ HEREON APPROVED BY THE SECRETARY OF INTERIOR Aug 2 1906

~~No 1 is the husband of Mary G. Folsom a non citizen~~
Marriage certificate filed Nov. 26, 1901

No.2 born Oct 4, 1901: Enrolled Nov 26, 1901

TRIBAL ENROLLMENT OF PARENTS

	Name of Father	Year	County	Name of Mother	Year	County
1	Arnold Folsom		~~Chickasaw residing in Choctaw N 1st Dist~~	Louvinia Folsom	Dead	Choctaw roll
2	No. 1			Mary G. Folsom		non citz.
3	John Cox		non citizen	Prudence Cox		non citizen

No.3 placed hereon under order of Commissioner to Five Civilized Tribes of February 26,1906 holding that application was made for her enrollment within the time provided by the Act of Congress approved July 1, 1902

No. 3 GRANTED Apr 16 1906

~~Date of Application~~ for Enrollment. Sept. 20/98

RESIDENCE: Chickasaw Nation ~~COUNTY.~~ **Choctaw Nation** **Choctaw Roll** *(Not Including Freedmen)* CARD NO.
POST OFFICE: Oakland, Ind. Ter. FIELD NO. **284**

Dawes' Roll No.	NAME	Relationship to Person First Named	AGE	SEX	BLOOD	TRIBAL ENROLLMENT Year	County	No.
15191	Null, John 56	First Named	52	M	1/8		Choctaw residing in Chickasaw District	CCR #2 385
I.W. 873	" Elizabeth ~~52~~ 49	wife	45	F	I.W.		" "	C.I. Roll 82
15192	" Fannie 21	dau	17	"	1/16		" "	CCR #2 385
15193	" Robert Henry 17	son	13	M	1/16		" "	"
15194	" Bessie 15	dau	11	F	1/16		" "	"
15195	" Leota 14	"	10	"	1/16		" "	"

See opinion of Atty Genl of Feb 18 04 and letter of Secy of Interior of Feb 26 '04 in case of James M Buckholts et al 7-5738

John Null, father of No1 admitted by Choctaw Council by no other member of his family mentioned. No1 never admitted. Dec 6/99

No2 on Choctaw roll as Elizabeth Neile, admitted by Dawes Com. Case No 1148 and no appeal taken. Marriage certificate on file in office of Dawes Com Muskogee Ind Ter

No4 on Choctaw roll as Robert
~~No6 " " " " Lattie~~

TRIBAL ENROLLMENT OF PARENTS

Name of Father	Year	County	Name of Mother	Year	County
John Null	Dead	non citizen	Sarah Null	Dead	Choctaw Roll
Carter Hamilton	"	" "	Mary E. Hamilton	"	non citizen
No 1			No 2		
No 1			No 2		
No 1			No 2		
No 1			No 2		

~~No2 1896 14907 as Elizabeth H Neile~~
No3 1896 Chickasaw District 9888
No4 1896 " " 9889 as Robert Null
~~No5 1896 " " 9890~~
~~No6 1896 " " 9891 " Lottie Null~~
No1 also on 1896 roll as John Will Page 223, No 8898, Chick Dist.
For child of No.4 see N.B. (Apr 26, 1906) Card No 49.

ENROLLMENT OF NOS. 2 HEREON APPROVED BY THE SECRETARY OF INTERIOR AUG 3 1904

ENROLLMENT OF NOS. 1-3-4-5-6 HEREON APPROVED BY THE SECRETARY OF INTERIOR MAY 9 1904

P.O. Grantham I.T.

Date of Application for Enrollment. Sept. 20/98

Choctaw By Blood Enrollment Cards 1898-1914

RESIDENCE: Chickasaw Nation ~~COUNTY.~~
POST OFFICE: Oakland, Ind Ter

Choctaw Nation

Choctaw Roll *(Not Including Freedmen)*

CARD NO.
FIELD NO. **285**

Dawes' Roll No.	NAME	Relationship to Person First Named	AGE	SEX	BLOOD	TRIBAL ENROLLMENT Year	County	No.
I.W. 962	1 Taliaferro, William N 44	First Named	40	M	I.W.		Choctaw residing in Chickasaw District	C.I. Roll 107
15196	2 " Mary Estella 30	wife	26	F	1/16		" "	CCR #2 452
15197	3 " Eliza Mabel 12	dau	8	"	1/32		" "	"
15198	4 " John Ambrose 10	son	6	M	1/32		" "	"
15199	5 " Janie Madison 9	dau	5	F	1/32		" "	"
15200	6 " Henry Buford 7	son	3	M	1/32		" "	"
15201	7 " Robert Dorsey 1	son	1mo	M	1/32			

See opinion of Atty Genl of Feb 18'04 and letter of Secy of Interior of Feb 24'04 in case of James M Buckholts et al 7-5738

No 1 See Decision of July 19'04

ENROLLMENT OF NOS. 2-3-4-5-6-7 HEREON APPROVED BY THE SECRETARY OF INTERIOR MAY 9 1904

No2 is grand-daughter of John Null who was admitted by Supreme Court Choctaw Nation Oct 1872

TRIBAL ENROLLMENT OF PARENTS

	Name of Father	Year	County	Name of Mother	Year	County
1	T.D. Taliaferro		non citizen	Eliza Taliaferro	Dead	non citizen
2	John Null (I.W.)		Choctaw residing in Chickasaw District	Elizabeth Null		Choctaw residing in Chickasaw District
3	No 1			No 2		
4	No 1			No 2		
5	No 1			No 2		
6	No 1			No 2		
7	No 1			No 2		

ENROLLMENT OF NOS. ~~ 1 ~~ HEREON APPROVED BY THE SECRETARY OF INTERIOR SEP 22 1904

No1 on Choctaw Roll as William W. - 1896 Chickasaw Dist No 15116
No2 " " " Esther N. 1896 " " " 12516
No3 " " " Mabel 1896 " " " 12517
~~No4 " " " John 1896 " " " 12518~~
No5 " " " Janie A. 1896 " " " 12519
No6 " " " Henry B. 1896 " " " 12520

No7 born Oct 24, 1901; Enrolled Nov. 19, 1901
No1 admitted as an intermarried citizen and Nos 5 and 6 as citizens by blood by Dawes Commission Choctaw Case #280. No appeal.
~~No1 also admitted as an intermarried citizen in 1896 case #283~~

Madill, I.T.

Date of Application for Enrollment. Sept. 26/98

RESIDENCE: Chickasaw Nation ~~COUNTY.~~ **Choctaw Nation** **Choctaw Roll** *(Not Including Freedmen)* CARD NO.
POST OFFICE: Tishomingo Ind. Ter FIELD NO. 286

Dawes' Roll No.	NAME	Relationship to Person First Named	AGE	SEX	BLOOD	TRIBAL ENROLLMENT Year	County	No.
Void	1 ~~Kemp, Elizabeth Minerva~~	~~Named~~	~~35~~	~~F~~	~~1/4~~			
Void	2 ~~" Theodocia Abagail~~	~~Dau~~	~~19~~	~~"~~	~~1/8~~			
Void	3 ~~" Eli Clem~~	~~Son~~	~~12~~	~~M~~	~~1/8~~			
Void	4 ~~" James Earl~~	~~"~~	~~10~~	~~"~~	~~1/8~~			
Void	5 ~~" Frances Elizabeth~~	~~Dau~~	~~8~~	~~F~~	~~1/8~~			
Void	6 ~~" Mary Montressa~~	~~"~~	~~5~~	~~"~~	~~1/8~~			
Void	7 ~~" Raymond Herrell~~	~~Son~~	~~2~~	~~M~~	~~1/8~~			
Void	8 ~~" Joel L.~~	~~"~~	~~9mo~~	~~"~~	~~1/8~~			

Nos 1,2,3 and 4 on Chickasaw Roll Tishomingo Co Page 34 transferred to Choctaw Roll by Dawes Com.
Nos 5,6 and 6 " " " " " " 33 " " " " " "

CANCELLED

Transferred to Chickasaw Card #1660
Jan. 30, 1903

TRIBAL ENROLLMENT OF PARENTS

	Name of Father	Year	County	Name of Mother	Year	County
1	~~Morgan Perry~~	~~Dead~~	~~Chickasaw Roll~~	~~Isabel Perry~~	~~Dead~~	~~Choctaw Roll~~
2	~~Joel Carr Kemp~~		~~Chick residing in Tishomingo County~~	~~No 1~~		
3	~~" " "~~		~~"~~ ~~"~~	~~No 1~~		
4	~~" " "~~		~~"~~ ~~"~~	~~No 1~~		
5	~~" " "~~		~~"~~ ~~"~~	~~No 1~~		
6	~~" " "~~		~~"~~ ~~"~~	~~No 1~~		
7	~~" " "~~		~~"~~ ~~"~~	~~No 1~~		
8	~~" " "~~		~~"~~ ~~"~~	~~No 1~~		

No1 on Chickasaw Roll as E.M. Kemp
No2 " " " " Theo Docien
~~No3 " " " " Eli C~~
~~No4 " " " " James E.~~
No5 " " " " Frances E.
No6 " " " " Mary M
~~No7 " " " " Raymond H~~

No8 Enrolled Dec 14/99

Date of Application for Enrollment Sept. 26/98

RESIDENCE: Skullyville COUNTY. POST OFFICE: Burgevin Ind. Ter.

Choctaw Nation — Choctaw Roll (*Not Including Freedmen*) CARD NO. FIELD NO. 287

Dawes' Roll No.	NAME	Relationship to Person First Named	AGE	SEX	BLOOD	TRIBAL ENROLLMENT Year	County	No.
607	1 McDaniel, Ed 48	First Named	44	M	1/4		Skullyville	CCR #2 361
	2							
	3 ENROLLMENT OF NOS. 1 HEREON APPROVED BY THE SECRETARY OF INTERIOR DEC 12 1902					1896	Skullyville	9034
	4							
	5							
	6							
	7							
	8							
	9							
	10							
	11							
	12							
	13							
	14							
	15							
	16							
	17							

Husband of Mary McDaniel Chickasaw roll Card No. 638

See Choc [illegible] #5394

TRIBAL ENROLLMENT OF PARENTS

	Name of Father	Year	County	Name of Mother	Year	County
1	George McDaniel	Dead	non citizen	Betsy McDaniel	Dead	Choctaw Roll
2						
3						
4						
5						
6						
7						
8						
9						
10						
11						
12						
13						
14						
15						
16						Date of Application for Enrollment.
17						Sept. 26/98

P.O. Address is now Cowlington Ind. Ter. Feby 9/1901

RESIDENCE: San Bois COUNTY. **Choctaw Nation** Choctaw Roll (Not Including Freedmen) CARD NO.
POST OFFICE: Garland, Ind. Ter. FIELD NO. 288

Dawes' Roll No.		NAME		Relationship to Person First Named	AGE	SEX	BLOOD	TRIBAL ENROLLMENT Year	County	No.
608	1	Folsom, Charlotte	28	First Named	24	F	1/2		San Bois	CCR #2 164
609	2	" Blanche	7	Dau	21/2	"	1/4		" "	"
610	3	" Bertha	5	"	8mos	"	1/4			
611	4	" Edwin Lee	3	Son	5mo	M	1/4			
612	5	" Ervin Moore	2	Son	1mo	M	1/4			

ENROLLMENT
OF NOS. 1 2 3 4 and 5 HEREON
APPROVED BY THE SECRETARY
OF INTERIOR DEC 12 1902

No1 wife of Frank Folsom Chickasaw roll Card No 641
No3 - affidavit of attending physician to be supplied. Received Oct 11/98

TRIBAL ENROLLMENT OF PARENTS

	Name of Father	Year	County	Name of Mother	Year	County
1	Jim Garland	Dead	Choctaw Roll	Melviney Garland	Dead	Choctaw roll
2	Frank Folsom		Chick residing in Choctaw N. 1st Dist	No 1		
3	" "		" " "	No 1		
4	" "		" " "	No 1		
5	" "		" " "	No 1		

No1 1896 Sans Bois 3858 as Charlotte Folsum
No2 1896 " " 3859 " Blanche "
No4 Enrolled May 24, 1900
No5 Enrolled March 6th, 1901
For child of No. 1 see NB (March 3, 1905) #841

#1 to 3
Date of Application for Enrollment. Sept. 26/98

Choctaw By Blood Enrollment Cards 1898-1914

RESIDENCE: San Bois COUNTY. **Choctaw Nation** Choctaw Roll (Not Including Freedmen) CARD NO.
POST OFFICE: San Bois, Ind. Ter. FIELD NO. 289

Dawes' Roll No.	NAME		Relationship to Person First Named	AGE	SEX	BLOOD	TRIBAL ENROLLMENT Year	County	No.
613	1 Cooper, Israel	48	First Named	44	M	Full		San Bois	CCR #2 84
614	2 " Lorinda	17	dau	13	F	"		" "	CCR #2 84
615	3 " Edmund	14	son	10	M	"		" "	"
616	4 " Sam	12	"	8	"	"		" "	"

ENROLLMENT OF NOS. 1 2 3 and 4 HEREON APPROVED BY THE SECRETARY OF INTERIOR DEC 12 1902

No1 Husband of Becky Cooper Chickasaw Roll Card No. 644.

TRIBAL ENROLLMENT OF PARENTS

Name of Father	Year	County	Name of Mother	Year	County
1 Wm Cooper	Dead	Choctaw roll	Susan Cooper	Dead	Choctaw Roll
2 No 1			Sally Cooper	"	" "
3 No 1			" "	"	" "
4 No 1			" "	"	" "

No1 1896 Sans Bois 2074
No2 1896 " " 2077 as Lourinda Cooper
~~No3 1896 " " 2078~~
No4 1896 " " 2079 as Samuel Cooper.
For child of No.2 see NB (Apr 26, 1906) Card No.57.

P.O Kinta I.T. 1/13/08

Date of Application for Enrollment. Sept. 26/98

RESIDENCE: San Bois COUNTY. **Choctaw Nation** Choctaw Roll (*Not Including Freedmen*) CARD NO.
POST OFFICE: Garland, Ind. Ter. FIELD NO. **290**

Dawes' Roll No.		NAME	Relationship to Person First Named	AGE	SEX	BLOOD	TRIBAL ENROLLMENT Year	County	No.
617	1	Folsom, William Lee 33	First Named	29	M	1/2		San Bois	CCR #2 165
I.W. 553	2	" Sallie 30	wife	25	F	I.W.		" "	C.I. Roll 28
618	3	" McKee 11	son	7	M	1/4		" "	CCR #2 165
619	4	" Ora 14	dau	10	F	1/4		" "	"
620	5	" Velda 9	"	5	"	1/4		" "	"
	6								
	7								
	8								
	9								
	10								
	11								
	12								
	13								
	14								
	15								
	16								
	17								

ENROLLMENT OF NOS. 1,3,4 and 5 HEREON APPROVED BY THE SECRETARY OF INTERIOR Dec 12 1902

No.1 on Choctaw roll as Will Folsom
No.2 marriage certificate to be supplied

ENROLLMENT OF NOS. ~~~ 2 ~~~ HEREON APPROVED BY THE SECRETARY OF INTERIOR Feb 8 1904

TRIBAL ENROLLMENT OF PARENTS

	Name of Father	Year	County	Name of Mother	Year	County
1	Arnold Folsom		Chick residing in Choctaw N. 1st Dist	Lovena Folsom	Dead	Choctaw Roll
2	Tom Gibson	Dead	non-citizen	Prudence Gibson		non citizen
3	No 1			No 2		
4	No 1			No 2		
5	No 1			No 2		
6						
7						
8						
9						
10						
11						
12						
13						
14						
15						
16						
17						

No1 1896 Sans Bois 3886 as Will Folsom
No2 1896 " " 14508
No3 1896 " " 3888 as McKee Folsum
No4 1896 " " 3887 " Ora "
No5 1896 " " 3889 " Velda "

Date of Application for Enrollment. Sept. 26/98

RESIDENCE: Jack Fork COUNTY.
POST OFFICE: Stringtown, Ind. Ter

Choctaw Nation

Choctaw Roll *(Not Including Freedmen)*

CARD NO.
FIELD NO. **291**

Dawes' Roll No.		NAME		Relationship to Person First Named	AGE	SEX	BLOOD	TRIBAL ENROLLMENT Year	County	No.
621	1	Bond, Lizzie	29	First Named	25	F	3/4		Jack Fork	CCR #2 76
622	2	" Alice	5	Dau	6mos	"	3/4		" "	"
623	3	" Alphaeus	2	Son	6w	M	3/4			
	4	" Clarence								
	5						No.1	1896	Jacks Fork	1880

ENROLLMENT OF NOS. 1,2 and 3 HEREON APPROVED BY THE SECRETARY OF INTERIOR Dec 12, 1902

No.1 wife of Henry J. Bond Chickasaw Roll, Card No. 647
No.3 Enrolled, January 29, 1901.

Evidence of birth of No.2 received and filed Feby 13, 1902

For child of No.1 see NB (Mar 3'05) card #191

TRIBAL ENROLLMENT OF PARENTS

	Name of Father	Year	County	Name of Mother	Year	County
1	Graham Anderson	Dead	Choctaw Roll		Dead	Choctaw Roll
2	Henry J. Bond		Chick residing in Choctaw N. 3rd Dist	No 1		
3	" " "			No 1		
4	" " "					

#1 & 2

Date of Application for Enrollment. Sept. 26/98

RESIDENCE: Chickasaw Nation ~~COUNTY.~~
POST OFFICE: Linn Ind. Ter.

Choctaw Nation

Choctaw Roll *(Not Including Freedmen)*

CARD NO.
FIELD NO. **292**

Dawes' Roll No.	NAME	Relationship to Person First Named	AGE	SEX	BLOOD	TRIBAL ENROLLMENT Year	County	No.
624	1 Moore, Jesse L. 48	First Named	44	M	1/16		Choctaw residing in Chickasaw Dist	CCR #2 358
I.W. 1281	2 " Frances Emma 41	wife	37	F	I.W.		" "	C.I. Roll 72
625	3 " Rosie Jessie 10	Dau	6	"	1/32		" "	CCR #2 358
626	4 " Joseph Hillary 9	Son	5	M	1/32		" "	"
627	5 " Ivy 4	dau	5mos	F	1/32			
628	6 " Sylvia 3	"	1mo	"	1/32			
629	7 " Samual[sic] 1	son	2wk	M	1/32			

8 No.2 refused by Decision of the Commissioner Oct. 10 1903. Record forwarded to the Department Oct 10'03

ENROLLMENT OF NOS. 1,3,4,5,6 and 7 HEREON APPROVED BY THE SECRETARY OF INTERIOR Dec 12, 1902

Jan. 14, 1905 Decision of Commission of Oct 10, 1903 refusing No.2 reversed by Department (I.T.D. 11854, 12884-1904) D.C #3034-1905.

TRIBAL ENROLLMENT OF PARENTS

	Name of Father	Year	County	Name of Mother	Year	County
1	J. G. Moore	Dead	Choctaw Roll	Mary Moore	Dead	non citizen
2	Hillary Jones	"	non citizen	Mary E. Jones		" "
3	No. 1			No.2		
4	No. 1			No.2		
5	No. 1			No.2		
6	No. 1			No.2		
7	No. 1			No.2		

No.2 on Choctaw Roll as F.E.J. Moore
No.3 " " " " Rosie J "
No.4 " " " " Joseph "
No.5 affidavit of attending physician to be supplied Received Oct 4/98

ENROLLMENT OF NOS. 2 HEREON APPROVED BY THE SECRETARY OF INTERIOR Mar 14 1905

~~No 1 1896 Chickasaw Dist 8902~~ ~~No.7 born Dec. 11, 1901: Enrolled Dec. 21st 1901~~
No.2 1896 " " 14843
No.3 1896 " " 8910
~~No.4 1896 " " 8911~~
~~No.6 enrolled Nov 1/99~~
For child of No.1 see NB (Apr 26'06) Card No 215.
P.O. Linn I.T.

#1 to 5
~~Date of Application~~ for Enrollment.
Sept. 26/98

Choctaw By Blood Enrollment Cards 1898-1914

RESIDENCE: Chickasaw Nation ~~COUNTY~~. **Choctaw Nation** **Choctaw Roll** *(Not Including Freedmen)* CARD NO.
POST OFFICE: ~~Lynn~~ Ind. Ter. FIELD NO. 293

Dawes' Roll No.	Linn NAME	Relationship to Person First Named	AGE	SEX	BLOOD	TRIBAL ENROLLMENT Year	County	No.
14521	1 Walker, Sophia E. 41	First Named	37	F	1/16		Choctaw residing in Chickasaw District	CCR #2 489
14522	2 Stockman, Emely Elizabeth 17	Dau	13	"	1/32		" "	CCR #2 433
14523	3 " Jesse L 15	Son	11	M	1/32		" "	"
14524	4 " Joseph Venzel 12	"	8	"	1/32		" "	"
14525	5 Walker, Jane 8	Dau	4	F	1/32		" "	CCR #2 489
14526	6 " Thomas 4	Son	1	M	1/32			
14527	7 " Benjaman 2	Son	3mo	M	1/32			
	8							
	9 ENROLLMENT				No1	1896	Chickasaw Dist	14177
	10 OF NOS. 1,2,3,4,5,6 and 7 HEREON APPROVED BY THE SECRETARY				No2	1896	" "	11731
	11 OF INTERIOR MAY 20 1903				No3	1896	" "	11732
	12				No4	1896	" "	11733
	13				No5	1896	" "	14178
	14				No 6 Enrolled Nov 1/99			
	15							
	16							
	17							

TRIBAL ENROLLMENT OF PARENTS

Name of Father	Year	County	Name of Mother	Year	County
1 Joseph G. Moore	Dead	Choctaw Roll	Mary E Moore	Dead	non citizen
2 Louis Stockman	"	non citizen	No 1		
3 " "	"	" "	No 1		
4 " "	"	" "	No 1		
5 James Walker		" "	No 1		
6 " "		" "	No 1		
7 " "		" "	No 1		
8					
9	No1 on	Choctaw Roll as	Sophia M Walker		
10	No2 "	" " "	Emely Stockman		
11	No3 "	" " "	Jesse "		
12	~~No4~~ "	" " "	~~Joseph~~ "		
13	No5 "	" " "	Jeanie Walker		
14			No 5 admitted by Dawes Commission		
15			in 1896, Choctaw Case #531.		No appeal.
16		No.7 Enrolled May 8, 1901.			#1 to 5 inc
17					Date of Application for Enrollment. Sept. 27/98

RESIDENCE: Chickasaw Nation ~~COUNTY.~~
POST OFFICE: ~~Lynn~~ Linn, Ind. Ter.

Choctaw Nation

Choctaw Roll (Not Including Freedmen)

CARD NO.
FIELD NO. **294**

Dawes' Roll No.		NAME	Relationship to Person First Named	AGE	SEX	BLOOD	TRIBAL ENROLLMENT Year	County	No.
630	1	Moore, William H 45	First Named	39	M	1/16	1896	Choctaw residing in Chickasaw District	8903
I.W. 1079	2	" Hattie 33	Wife	29	F	I.W.	1896	" "	14844
631	3	" Mary Cordelia 15	Dau	11	"	1/32	1896	" "	8906
632	4	" Martha Ann 14	"	10	"	1/32	1896	" "	8907
633	5	" Janie Lizzie 12	"	8	"	1/32	1896	" "	8908
634	6	" Onie Hester 9	"	5	"	1/32	1896	" "	8909
635	7	" William Lyles 5	Son	1 1/3	M	1/32			
636	8	" Olley Robert 3	Son	3mo	M	1/32			
637	9	" Ira Tabitha 1	Dau	2wks	F	1/32			

ENROLLMENT OF NOS. 1,3,4,5,6,7,8 and 9 HEREON APPROVED BY THE SECRETARY OF INTERIOR Dec 12 1902

No.2 on Choctaw roll as Hettie Moore
No.3 " " " " Mary C. Moore
~~No.4 " " " " A. Martha "~~
~~No.5 " " " " Jannie S. "~~
No.6 " " " " Annie H. "

For child of No.3 see NB (Apr 26-06) No 570

ENROLLMENT OF NOS. ~~~2~~~ HEREON APPROVED BY THE SECRETARY OF INTERIOR Nov 16 1904

TRIBAL ENROLLMENT OF PARENTS

	Name of Father	Year	County	Name of Mother	Year	County
1	Joseph G. Moore	Dead	Choctaw Roll	Mary E. Moore	Dead	non-citizen
2	Oliver Van Deventer	"	non-citizen	Mary Van Deventer	"	" "
3	No 1			No 2		
4	No 1			No 2		
5	No 1			No 2		
6	No 1			No 2		
7	No 1			No 2		
8	No 1			No 2		
9	No 1			No 2		

Marriage certificate or copy to be supplied. Received Oct.12/98.

No.7 affidavit of attending phyaician to be supplied. Received Oct. 12/98.
No.1 on Choctaw roll as Wm Moore
~~No.8 enrolled May 24, 1900.~~
~~Nº9 Born April 11, 1902: enrolled April 24, 1902~~

#1 to 7

P.O. Tishomingo I.T. 3/25/05

Date of Application for Enrollment. Sept. 21/98

For child of Nos 1&2 see NB (Mar. 3rd 1905) Card #82.

RESIDENCE: Chickasaw Nation ~~COUNTY~~. **Choctaw Nation** **Choctaw Roll** (Not Including Freedmen) CARD NO.
POST OFFICE: Sulphur, Ind. Ter. FIELD NO. 295

Dawes' Roll No.		NAME		Relationship to Person First Named	AGE	SEX	BLOOD	TRIBAL ENROLLMENT Year	County	No.
15202	1	Jones, Perry	34	First Named	30	M	1/32		Choctaw residing in Chickasaw Nation	CCR #2 309
I.W. 1080	2	" Martha E	30	wife	26	F	I.W.	1896	Chick Dist	14951
15203	3	" Benjamin	12	son	8	M	1/64		Choctaw residing in Chickasaw District	CCR #2 309
15204	4	" Florence	11	dau	7	F	1/64		" "	"
15205	5	" Forbes	9	son	5	M	1/64		" "	"
15206	6	" Everett	7	"	3	"	1/64		" "	"
15207	7	" Lele	4	dau	3wks	F	1/64			
15208	8	" Ethel	1	dau	1wk	F	1/64			
	9	See opinion of Atty. Genl of Feb.18'04 and letter of Secy of								
	10	Interior of Feb 24'04 in case of James M Buckholts et al 7-5738								
	11					No.1	1896	Chickasaw Dist 7390 as Terry Jones		
	12						No.2	1896	Blue	14701
	13						No.3	1896	Chickasaw Dist	7391
	14						No.4	1896	" "	7392
	15	ENROLLMENT					No.5	1896	" "	7393
	16	OF NOS. ~~~2~~~ HEREON APPROVED BY THE SECRETARY					No.6	1896	" "	7394
	17	OF INTERIOR Nov 16 1904								

TRIBAL ENROLLMENT OF PARENTS

	Name of Father	Year	County	Name of Mother	Year	County
1	R.T. Jones		non citizen	Deraney Jones		Blue
2	Jim Hinchey	Dead	" "	Adeline Hinchey	Dead	non-citizen
3	No 1			No 2		
4	No 1			No 2		
5	No 1			No 2		
6	No 1			No 2		
7	No 1			No 2		
8	No 1			No 2		

9 No.1 Son of R.T. Jones admitted by Supreme Court Choctaw Nation Oct '72.
10 No.8 born Dec. 1, 1901: Enrolled Dec. 12, 1901
See testimony of No.1 taken October 20, 1902.
11 For child of Nos 1&2 see NB (Mar 3'05) #479
12 No2 admitted by Dawes Com Case No 1044 as Mrs Mattie Jones and no appeal taken
13 No.6 on Choctaw roll as Earnest Jones
14 No.2 on 1896 Roll as Mattie Perry
15 No.7 born August 17, 1898. See affidavit of attending physician dated Sept 24, 1898 on file
16 with papers in this case.
17 P.O. Palmer I.T.

ENROLLMENT OF NOS. 1-3-4-5-6-7-8 HEREON APPROVED BY THE SECRETARY OF INTERIOR May 9 1904

Date of Application for Enrollment. Sept. 27/98

RESIDENCE: Chickasaw Nation ~~COUNTY.~~
POST OFFICE: ~~Lynn~~, Ind. Ter.

Choctaw Nation

Choctaw Roll (Not Including Freedmen)

CARD NO.
FIELD NO. 296

Dawes' Roll No.	Linn NAME	Relationship to Person First Named	AGE	SEX	BLOOD	TRIBAL ENROLLMENT Year	County	No.
638	1 Spicer, Julia Ann Margaret 26	First Named	22	F	3/8		Choctaw residing in Chickasaw Dist	CCR #2 433
639	2 " Nancy Belle 8	Dau	4	"	3/16		" "	"
640	3 " Harmon Carter 5	Son	1	M	3/16			
641	4 " Joseph C. 3	"	1mo	"	3/16			

ENROLLMENT OF NOS. 1,2,3 and 4 HEREON APPROVED BY THE SECRETARY OF INTERIOR Dec 12 1902

No.1 1896 Chickasaw Dist 11734 as Margaret A. Spicer
No.2 1896 " " 11735 " Nancy B. "

TRIBAL ENROLLMENT OF PARENTS

Name of Father	Year	County	Name of Mother	Year	County
1 Wesley Anderson		non citizen	Patsey Taylor		Kiamisha[sic]
2 W.M. Spicer		" "	No.1		
3 " " "		" "	No.1		
4 " " "		" "	No.1		

No. 1 on Choctaw Roll as Mrs Margaret A. Spicer
No. 3 affidavit of attending physician to be supplied. Received Oct 4/98.
No. 4 Enrolled Nov. 1/99
~~No. 2 admitted as a citizen by blood by Dawes Commission: Choctaw Case #821: No appeal~~

#1 to 3
~~Date of Application~~ for Enrollment. Sept. 23/98

RESIDENCE: Atoka COUNTY. **Choctaw Nation** Choctaw Roll (*Not Including Freedmen*) CARD NO.
POST OFFICE: Coalgate, Ind. Ter. 1906 FIELD NO. 297

Dawes' Roll No.		NAME		Relationship to Person First Named	AGE	SEX	BLOOD	TRIBAL ENROLLMENT Year	County	No.
642	1	James, Silas	60	First Named	56	M	1/2		Atoka	CCR #2 306
I.W. 554	2	" Mary	24	Wife	19	F	I.W.		"	C.I. Roll 53
643	3	" Onina	5	Dau	6mo	"	1/4			
644	4	" Silas Jackson	2	Son	4mo	M	1/4			
	5									
	6	ENROLLMENT					No. 1	1896	Atoka	7310
	7	OF NOS. 1,3 and 4 HEREON APPROVED BY THE SECRETARY					No. 2	1896	"	14707
	8	OF INTERIOR Dec 12 1902								
	9	For child of Nos 1 and 2 see NB (April 26, 1906) No. 527								
	10	ENROLLMENT								
	11	OF NOS. ~~~ 2 ~~~ HEREON APPROVED BY THE SECRETARY								
	12	OF INTERIOR Feb 8 - 1904								
	13									
	14									
	15									
	16									
	17									

TRIBAL ENROLLMENT OF PARENTS

	Name of Father	Year	County	Name of Mother	Year	County
1	Robinson James	Dead	Chickasaw Roll	Mary James	Dead	Choctaw Roll
2	Jim Gower	"	non citizen	Sally Gower		non citizen
3	No. 1			No. 2		
4	No. 1			No. 2		
5						
6						

7 Marriage certificate and license on file in office of Dawes Com. Muskogee, Ind. Ter. ~~in Case No. 1023~~
8 ~~No.2 admitted by Dawes Com. Case No. 1023, and no appeal taken.~~
9 No.3 affidavit of physician to be supplied. Received Jan 4/99.
10 No.4 Enrolled June 11, 1900.
~~Daniel James, son of No.1 on Chickasaw card #671.~~
11 ~~For child of Nos 1&2 see NB (March 3-1905) No. 16~~
12
13
14
15
16
17 ~~P.O. Talihina, I.T. 4/20/04~~ Date of Application for Enrollment. Sept. 27/98

RESIDENCE: Chickasaw Nation ~~COUNTY.~~
POST OFFICE: Nebo, Ind. Ter.

Choctaw Nation

Choctaw Roll (Not Including Freedmen)

CARD NO.
FIELD NO. 298

Dawes' Roll No.	NAME	Relationship to Person First Named	AGE	SEX	BLOOD	TRIBAL ENROLLMENT Year	County	No.
DEAD	~~James, Eastman~~	~~Named~~	~~50~~	~~M~~	~~Full~~			
Void	~~" George Newton~~	~~Son~~	~~4~~	~~"~~	~~1/2~~			
Void	~~" Sallie Ann~~	~~Dau~~	~~2~~	~~F~~	~~1/2~~			
Void	~~" Malsy~~	~~"~~	~~5mo~~	~~"~~	~~1/2~~			

No 1 on 1893 Chickasaw Pay Roll, No 1, Page 93, as No 165[illegible] Husband of Lyddy Ann James Choctaw Card No D52

No 2 admitted as a Chickasaw by Dawes Com. Case No. 51, and no appeal taken.

~~No 3 affidavit of attending physician to be supplied. Affidavit of midwife substituted Sept 27/98~~

All Transferred to Choctaw roll, by Dawes Com, Sept 27/98

Oct 6/99 As to death of No1 see affidavit attached

CANCELLED

#1 died prior to Ratification of Choctaw-Chickasaw agreement Sept 25, 1902

TRIBAL ENROLLMENT OF PARENTS

Name of Father	Year	County	Name of Mother	Year	County
~~George James~~	~~Dead~~	~~Choctaw roll~~	~~Biccy James~~	~~Dead~~	~~Choctaw roll~~
~~No 1~~			~~Lyddy Ann James (I.W.)~~		~~Choctaw residing in Chickasaw Dist~~
~~No 1~~			~~" " "~~		~~" "~~
~~No 1~~			~~" " "~~		~~" "~~

See original paper in Chickasaw Case No #[sic]51. No 1 was denied by docket entry as an inter-married Chickasaw and original application stated as follows, "Eastman James being a [illegible] denied Chickasaw citizenship. No 2 was admitted by docket entry as a Chickasaw by blood, but notation on original application reads "all Choctaws".

See Choctaw card D.52
See Chickasaw card D.10

Date of Application for Enrollment.
Sept. 27/98

No4 enrolled Oct 6/99

RESIDENCE: Chickasaw Nation ~~COUNTY~~.
POST OFFICE: Hickory, Ind. Ter.

Choctaw Nation

Choctaw Roll *(Not Including Freedmen)*

CARD NO.
FIELD NO. 299

Dawes' Roll No.		NAME	Relationship to Person First Named	AGE	SEX	BLOOD	TRIBAL ENROLLMENT Year	County	No.
VOID.	1	~~Kay, Fred~~		~~8~~	~~M~~	~~1/2~~			
	2								
	3								
	4								
	5	On Chickasaw roll as Fred Key, Tishomingo Co, Page 29 transferred to Choctaw Roll							
	6	ward of and lives with Newton Galloway Frazier Chickasaw roll Card No 690							
	7								
	8								
	9								
	10								
	11								
	12								
	13								
	14								
	15								
	16								
	17								

CANCELLED

Transferred to Chickasaw Card [illegible]

TRIBAL ENROLLMENT OF PARENTS

	Name of Father	Year	County	Name of Mother	Year	County
1	~~Charley Kay~~	~~Dead~~	~~non citizen~~	~~Minnie Kay~~	~~Dead~~	~~Choctaw Roll~~
2						
3						
4						
5						
6						
7						
8						
9						
10						
11						
12						
13						
14						
15						
16						
17						

Date of Application for Enrollment. Sept. 27/98

Choctaw By Blood Enrollment Cards 1898-1914

RESIDENCE: Jack Fork COUNTY. **Choctaw Nation** Choctaw Roll (Not Including Freedmen) CARD NO.
POST OFFICE: Stringtown FIELD NO. 300

Dawes' Roll No.	NAME	Relationship to Person First Named	AGE	SEX	BLOOD	TRIBAL ENROLLMENT Year	County	No.
DEAD	1 ~~Moore, Tennessee~~[sic] DEAD	~~First Named~~	~~24~~	~~F~~	~~Full~~		~~Jack Fork~~	CCR #2 ~~357~~
645	2 Holson, John B. 10	Son	6	M	"	1896	" "	6126
646	3 Moore, Preston 2	Son	7W	M	1/2	(No 1) 1896	Jacks Fork	8862

ENROLLMENT OF NOS. 2 and 3 HEREON APPROVED BY THE SECRETARY OF INTERIOR DEC 12 1902

Wife of Christopher D Moore Chickasaw Roll Card No 706
No 2 on 1896 roll as Jno B Holson
~~No 3 Enrolled January 29 1901~~
No 2 Enrolled Aug 28/99

No. 1 HEREON DISMISSED UNDER ORDER OF THE COMMISSION TO THE FIVE ~~CIVILIZED TRIBES OF MARCH 31, 1905.~~

TRIBAL ENROLLMENT OF PARENTS

Name of Father	Year	County	Name of Mother	Year	County
1 ~~Stephen Holsen~~	~~Dead~~	~~Choctaw Roll~~	~~Liza Holsen~~		~~Jack Fork~~
2 Messiah Calvin	"	Jacks Fork	No 1		
3 Christopher D Moore			No 1		

№1 Died Feby. 12, 1901: proof of death filed April 19, 1902.
C. D. Moore has legally adopted #2. Certified copy of papers in the matter ~~filed May 25, 1903.~~

Date of Application for Enrollment. Sept. 28/98

www.ingramcontent.com/pod-product-compliance
Lightning Source LLC
Chambersburg PA
CBHW030235030426
42336CB00009B/111

* 9 7 8 1 6 4 9 6 8 0 0 1 3 *